OXFORD WORLD'S CLASSICS

SELECTED PHILOSOPHICAL WRITINGS

ST THOMAS AQUINAS (1225–74), a Dominican friar, was the greatest of the Western European medieval philosopher-theologians, and a leading figure in the thirteenth-century resurgence in Aristotelian studies. Many of the issues he discusses are still alive today: Is there order in the world, and does that reveal the transcendent presence of a God? Have we words to talk about him? Is he active even in chance events and freely willed action? How can mind and body in human beings be one? What role do theories of virtue and natural law play in ethics? His discussions have exerted the single greatest influence on the Catholic theological tradition after the Bible itself, and as philosophical work stand comparison with those of Plato and Aristotle, Kant and Hegel.

TIMOTHY MCDERMOTT has taught philosophy, theology, and computer science in Oxford and Cambridge, in London, Hobart, and Cape Town, and is at present a visiting professor at the Aquinas Center of Theology, Emory University, Atlanta.

OXFORD WORLD'S CLASSICS

For over 100 years Oxford World's Classics have brought readers closer to the world's great literature. Now with over 700 titles—from the 4,000-year-old myths of Mesopotamia to the twentieth century's greatest novels—the series makes available lesser-known as well as celebrated writing.

The pocket-sized hardbacks of the early years contained introductions by Virginia Woolf, T. S. Eliot, Graham Greene, and other literary figures which enriched the experience of reading. Today the series is recognized for its fine scholarship and reliability in texts that span world literature, drama and poetry, religion, philosophy and politics. Each edition includes perceptive commentary and essential background information to meet the changing needs of readers.

OXFORD WORLD'S CLASSICS

THOMAS AQUINAS

Selected Philosophical Writings

Selected and translated with an Introduction and Notes by
TIMOTHY McDERMOTT

OXFORD
UNIVERSITY PRESS

Great Clarendon Street, Oxford OX2 6DP

Oxford University Press is a department of the University of Oxford. It furthers the University's objective of excellence in research, scholarship, and education by publishing worldwide in

Oxford New York

Athens Auckland Bangkok Bogotá Buenos Aires Calcutta Cape Town Chennai Dar es Salaam Delhi Florence Hong Kong Istanbul Karachi Kuala Lumpur Madrid Melbourne Mexico City Mumbai Nairobi Paris São Paulo Singapore Taipei Tokyo Toronto Warsaw

with associated companies in Berlin Ibadan

Oxford is a registered trade mark of Oxford University Press in the UK and in certain other countries

Published in the United States by Oxford University Press Inc., New York

First published as a World's Classics paperback 1993
Reissued as an Oxford World's Classics paperback 1998
Reissued 2008

British Library Cataloguing in Publication Data

Data available

Library of Congress Cataloging in Publication Data

Thomas, Aquinas, Saint, 1225?–1274.
[Selections. English. 1993]
Selected philosophical writings / Thomas Aquinas ; selected and translated by Timothy McDermott.
p. cm.—(Oxford world's classics)
Translated from the Latin.
Includes bibliographical references and index.
1. Philosophy—Early works to 1800. 2. Theology—Early works to 1800. I. McDermott, Timothy S. II. Title. III. Series.
B765.T51 1993 189'.4—dc20 92–45583

ISBN 978–0–19–954027–3

19

Printed and bound in Great Britain by
Clays Ltd, Elcograf S.p.A.

Contents

Introduction

THE passages collected in this book offer as comprehensive an account as space allows of the philosophy of St Thomas Aquinas—hereafter called simply Thomas: in Anthony Kenny's opinion 'one of the dozen greatest philosophers of the western world'.[1] Both enemies and friends have at times dissented from this view on the grounds that Thomas was first and foremost a Christian theologian. Bertrand Russell accused him of a lack of philosophical spirit: 'The finding of arguments for a conclusion given in advance is not philosophy, but special pleading.'[2] But much of philosophy consists in trying to discover some good reasons for our normal human beliefs and ways of proceeding, and Russell himself—as Kenny pointed out—'took three hundred and sixty dense pages to offer a proof that 1 + 1 = 2'![3] Thomas, it is true, is not so much interested in the bases of arithmetic as in the bases for belief in God, and—as a Christian theologian—interested too in defending his Christian faith against unbelievers. But he thought that, as a consequence, one of his greatest tasks was to distinguish between beliefs that were philosophically provable ('discoverable by natural reason', as he puts it), assertions of faith which, though unproven, were philosophically sound in the sense of not disprovable, and beliefs demonstrably false.

Natural reason cannot discover the Trinity of persons in God; it learns about God from his causing of creatures, and knows only what characterizes him as the source of everything that exists. This was the starting-point we adopted earlier when discussing God... Indeed, trying to prove the Trinity by reason would injure the faith... and make it a laughing-stock to unbelievers, who would think our belief relied on such unconvincing arguments. The only

[1] Anthony Kenny (ed.), *Aquinas: A Collection of Critical Essays* (London, 1969), 1.

[2] Bertrand Russell, *History of Western Philosophy* (New York, 1945), 463.

[3] Kenny (ed.), *Aquinas*, 2.

way of proving matters of faith is to quote authorities to those who accept them; to those who don't, we must be content to show [by natural reason] that what the faith teaches is not impossible ...[4]

So Thomas felt called on to be a philosopher—to know what is provable by philosophical argument and what is not. And it was precisely for that reason that he played such a large part in the thirteenth-century renewal in philosophy, and especially in that century's re-evaluation and reassimilation of the philosophy of Aristotle.

For Thomas lived at a propitious time, in the full maturity of Europe's medieval Renaissance. Europe had spent centuries recovering from two enormous traumas: the fifth-century fall of the western Roman Empire to barbarian tribes, and the eighth-century fall of the Mediterranean Sea to Islam. By slow degrees society had regained a certain political stability and economic prosperity; and in the process learning too had expanded and prospered. In the century before Thomas the pace of that expansion quickened noticeably: in the contemplative monastic schools, nourished on the biblical text and long centuries of inherited Christian wisdom, inhabited by people committed to lifelong religious service in common, but also in newer shorter-term groupings of professional scholars, gatherings of masters and students engaged in specialist academic study of Christian and non-Christian texts alike; and from these—at the end of the twelfth century—the early universities of Bologna, Paris, and Oxford took shape. In this new cultural milieu the treasures of ancient logic and mathematics, of philosophy and law, of medicine and science were avidly sought after and assimilated and brought into living contact with the divine teaching in the Scriptures; and in the process Christendom had to learn to converse, not only with the ancient thinkers of Greece and Rome, but with the contemporary thinkers of Judaism and Islam.

Into this world in 1225 Thomas was born at Roccasecca,

[4] This and subsequent quotations from Thomas are from *St Thomas Aquinas, Summa Theologiae: A Concise Translation*, ed. Timothy McDermott (London, 1989). This quotation comes from p. 71 (1a.32.1).

near Aquino, the youngest son of an impoverished landowner of Lombard extraction and a woman with Norman blood in her veins. His father was vassal to Frederick II, king of Sicily, Holy Roman Emperor—a sort of Renaissance prince before his time—always in friction, often engaged in outright war with the papacy; and the family demesne was sandwiched between the lands of the emperor to the south and the papal territories to the north. From the age of 5 Thomas was brought up in the school of the Benedictine monastery of Monte Cassino, amid a life of manual labour, prayer, scriptural reading, and meditation, and possibly he was intended to spend the rest of his life there, perhaps to become abbot of the place. But the fighting between Frederick and the Pope brought the emperor's troops into the monastery in 1239, and the 14-year-old was sent on to the University of Naples. Here the course of his life totally changed.

The University of Naples had been founded by Frederick for the secular education of his court functionaries, and at the time of Thomas's arrival it was the only university teaching Aristotle's works of natural philosophy. Aristotle's logic was already familiar in the schools; the Roman senator Boethius had translated many of those works into Latin as early as the sixth century, though not all were in circulation. But in the twelfth century more and more of his works were translated, occasionally through the intermediary of Arabic translations, but most often directly from the Greek. Together with these translations came translations of the great works of Arabic culture: among them the works of Ibn Sīnā (980–1037), the Aristotelian commentaries of Ibn Rushd (1126–98), and the work of the Jewish scholar Moses Maimonides (1135–1204). To this world of human learning Thomas, as a young student of arts, was introduced by his Naples teachers, Peter of Ireland and Martin of Denmark. But he also met there a new religious order, one very different in its orientation from the monastic order of St Benedict that had formed his first years. This was the newly founded mendicant Order of Preachers, dispersed twenty years earlier throughout Europe by their founder, St Dominic, from an original community in the south of France. They were not as the

Benedictines were, men of the land, communally rich, aristocrats, and representatives of the established order. They were rather men of the new towns, begging friars, 'not very respectable', as Brian Davies[5] puts it: *going out two by two to preach in town after town, taking nothing for their journey but a staff: no bread, no wallet, no money in their belts, wearing sandals and only one tunic.*[6] To train themselves for this task the friars were sent to study at the universities of the day, and at Naples Thomas made acquaintance not only with the philosophy of Aristotle, but with the religious spirit of the Dominicans. In 1244, at the age of 19 or 20, Thomas applied to join them; and after a two-year struggle with his family—during which, it would seem, he was forcibly imprisoned—the family gave in. From now on Thomas was to live his life in the universities and schools of the new thirteenth-century society, deeply involved in the confluence and reconciliation of Aristotelian learning and Christian teaching.

After a novitiate spent in Paris, he went on to study in Cologne under Albert the Great for the four years 1248–52. In the latter year he returned to Paris as a 'bachelor' commenting firstly on the Scriptures, and then on the theological textbook of the time, the *Sentences* of Peter Lombard; and there he started the copious writing which was to occupy him for the next twenty years. He was licensed as a 'master' in 1256, and at the age of 32 occupied one of the Paris chairs in theology. At this time the ban on public and private study of Aristotle's non-logical and non-ethical works in the arts faculty of the university, imposed in 1215 and periodically renewed, was being relaxed; so that the arts faculty had begun to transform itself from a grammar school, so to speak, to a philosophy faculty. In any case, by an irony of history, the ban had never been imposed on the theology faculty, and Albert the Great, among others, had led the way in Aristotelian studies. So Thomas's acquaintance with the Greek philosopher was growing apace.

After three years Thomas was moved from Paris to the

[5] Brian Davies, *The Thought of Thomas Aquinas* (Oxford, 1992), 3.
[6] Cf. Mark 6: 6–13.

papal court at Orvieto, then after a further six years to Rome, and finally, with the court, to Viterbo. Here perhaps he met the Dominican translator William of Moerbeke, just starting on a great series of retranslations of Aristotle's works from the Greek. To what extent Thomas's influence contributed to these translations being made we cannot tell; certainly he took advantage of their appearance to begin an enormous work of commentary on them, designed to purify the Latin understanding of Aristotle, and to some extent to offset the influence of Ibn Rushd's commentaries.

In 1269 he was recalled to Paris where hostility had developed between secular and religious masters, and there he engaged more than once in controversy with the Averroistic interpreters of Aristotle. Three years later he was back again in Italy founding a study-house at Naples, the city he had left to join the Dominicans twenty-eight years before. There, in 1273, he suddenly ceased all writing and teaching, and by March 1274 he was dead at the relatively early age of 49 or 50. He left behind him a mass of writings: commentaries on Aristotle, on scripture, and on other important authors, records of hundreds of disputations (public debates) on theological and philosophical subjects, small and large works on questions of the day, and several comprehensive textbooks of theology. These writings stretch to over eight and a half million words[7]—an average of some 1,190 words a day every day for twenty years. From such an immense output this World's Classics volume can select less than 2 per cent for translation: a mere 150,000 words!

What principles then have guided the selection and translation? Thirty-eight fairly lengthy passages have been chosen from a wide range of Thomas's works for their relevance to what nowadays is called 'philosophy of religion', though such a description of Thomas's work is something of an anachronism. The passages are lengthy because serious reading cannot thrive on snippets. The passages must provide a medium of thought to which we can acclimatize, enough depth to dive into and swim around in; snippets are sprinkles

[7] Computer-generated figures in the *Index Thomisticus* show 8,767,854 words in 118 works, 18 of which (comprising 81,277 words) are inauthentic or doubtful.

which evaporate on contact. And the passages have been newly translated, with the aim of making sense of them to people who are not historians, and whose idiom of understanding is modern rather than medieval. Subject to the absolute requirement of faithfulness to Thomas's philosophical meaning, I have, by preferring contemporary turns of phrase to more traditional translations, tried to enable a thoughtful communication with Thomas.

The thirty-eight passages have been arranged in six parts, which, read in order, form a comprehensive introduction to Thomas's 'philosophy of religion' (perpetuating for the moment the anachronism). Part I, for example, concentrates on Thomas's own views of philosophy and theology. It contains a single passage, the longest in the collection, extracted from a commentary on a work of the sixth-century Christian Boethius already mentioned. In it Thomas explains what characterizes Aristotelian science—the deduction of truths about some subject-matter from premisses defining that subject-matter—and sketches out the broad branches into which Aristotelian science divides. He distinguishes natural philosophy from mathematics, and metaphysics from both, defining their limits clearly and describing their different styles. He identifies metaphysics as the science that includes whatever natural reason has to say about God, and distinguishes this 'natural' theology from the 'revealed' theology based on scripture with which he has so often been accused of confusing it. It would have been possible to find the same teaching in the early pages of St Thomas's *Summa Theologiae*, but not in anything like the detail presented here. And in any case, it has been deliberate policy to choose the passages in this selection from a wide range of Thomas's writings and not just from the pages of the *Summa Theologiae*. Some passages, of course, do come from that work—a World's Classics volume could hardly ignore the main classic St Thomas wrote. But the majority of the passages are lengthier treatments of their topics, drawn from other writings at other periods, to illustrate the range and continuity of Thomas's work, and the way his different writings can illuminate and comment on each other.

And here, while talking of the first passage in this collection, seems to be the place to say a few words about Thomas's style and the style of medieval philosophical writing in general, lest the word 'writing' should lead to a sort of misunderstanding. Books, we must remember, were not common currency in the Middle Ages; there was no printed word, and students had far less access to the written than to the spoken word. Behind all Thomas's works then, in varying degree, stands the culture of the *lectio*, a word meaning at one and the same time reading and lecture. For lectures were normally exercises in reading a text in common, the lecturer alone, perhaps, having an actual copy of the text before him. As a result a certain structure of lecture became traditional, and we see it reflected in the works of philosophy and theology committed to writing at this time. Passage 1 is a good example: the way it illustrates medieval style and structure was indeed another reason for choosing it to head this selection.

For Passage 1 is itself the reading (or *lectio*) of another author's text: a short work of Boethius called the *De Trinitate*: our passage joins in Thomas's reading of it at chapter 2 of Boethius' text. As he reads it, the lecturer gives us a minute dissection of the text's structure showing how its parts relate one to the next, and then, taking part after part, he quotes and, if necessary, expands it so that we see how the structure works in practice, and includes explanatory comment on any odd words or difficult turns of thought as they occur. In all probability some questions of special interest arise in the course of this *exposition*. If so they can be dealt with in one of two ways: either they can form the subject of a *digression* in which the commentator signals his intention to depart from close textual exposition by saying 'But we ought to note that...' or some similar phrase, or they can form the subject of a *disputation* or debate structured in the formal way everyone was familiar with—for disputation was the second sort of oral exercise in which medieval universities engaged.

Disputations were regular occurrences during the university terms, some on prepared subjects, some on subjects proposed extempore by the audience. In general they began with questions from the floor designed to throw doubt on the thesis the master had indicated he would uphold. These questions from the floor would be answered, there and then, in the presence of the master, by a bachelor deputed to the task—it was a searching exercise for him too. After a certain amount of time—maybe, on the following day—the master would deliver a summing-up in which he would be required to give a definitive defence of his thesis, taking into account the whole range of objections that had been brought against it. This summing-up would consist of an argument in depth for the thesis, to which would be appended definitive explanations of how his argument answers the objections with which the disputation started. Later still, at more leisure, the master might be able to edit such disputations for publication, and it is thought that the works of Thomas known as *quaestiones disputatae* (disputed questions) are such edited accounts of actual disputations. In these edited accounts the disputations are collected into groups—and later editors called the groups 'questions' and the individual disputations 'articles', so that a particular disputation might be referred to in the literature by some such title as *Quaestiones Disputatae de Veritate*, question 10, article 6. Several of the texts below are drawn from *quaestiones disputatae* in this way (and are always indicated as such), and the reader must read them as public debates. They always start with arguments casting doubt on the thesis the master might be expected to uphold. These are arguments actually thrown up from the floor during the disputation, and are not therefore in general the view of the master (of Thomas in the case of our passages) and cannot be quoted as such. Nor, and this is less often noticed, are they merely arbitrarily arranged, one after the other. Frequently they are themselves structured, betraying a to-and-fro that went on between the floor participants and the bachelor respondent. Thus sometimes, after an argument from the floor, will occur the words 'But it was said by the respondent...', and then 'But against that...' and there will follow a buttressing argument not now addressed immediately to disproving the thesis but to disproving whatever extra remark the respondent had made. Such arguments upon arguments can go on at several levels of remove from the main argument. So it will be seen that the linear numbering of these arguments in the editions and in my translation (but not in the manuscripts) can sometimes be misleading, and I have tried to counter this by occasionally indenting arguments that are, so to speak, parasitic on remarks of the respondent.[8] After all these arguments *against* the expected thesis come arguments in its favour. Don't be confused by the introductory phrase 'But against that...'; these are not arguments against the thesis but defences of it, attempts to rebut the doubts being raised from the floor, often by means of quoted authorities. At least, this is how the debate usually goes, though sometimes the master may decide that neither the doubts nor their rebuttals are to be upheld, and sum up in favour of some new position. In the written texts this summing-up by the master comes next, heralded by the phrase 'In reply'. In the disputations as we have them, this summing-up constitutes the body of the disputation, and contains the mature reflections of the text's author. After it come his mature replies to all the objections that began the debate (this time numbered in the manuscripts); and occasionally there follow, as I have said, replies to the arguments in favour as well. Such is the bare-bones structure of an edited *quaestio disputata*, but one can't be rigid about it. The key to interpretation is always to be flexibly aware that behind the text lies a living debate, and that variations in structure may unexpectedly occur. One very good example of this is the *quaestio disputata* on God's Omnipotence included in Passage 26 (the last article); the structure, though clearly based on what we have just been saying, is so *sui generis* that it would take longer for me to describe it here than it would for the student to turn up the page and examine it for herself.

This structure of the living *quaestio disputata* was so familiar that it was imitated in expositions of text where no living disputation took place. To return, for example, to the

[8] e.g. Passages 9, 17, 21, 33 (Article 8).

exposition of Boethius' text from the *De Trinitate* which we have taken as our prime example: here the major questions arising during exposition of the text are not the subjects of digressions in the exposition but are held back to the end and then treated in imaginary debates or disputations which can be of some complexity. In general the structure is as described above: objections to a thesis, contrary arguments in favour, a summing-up 'in reply', and numbered answers to the objections. This structure is seen complete in the Boethius text in Part I (with the exception that I have sometimes omitted an objection and its answer that seemed less interesting, in order to keep the size of the whole volume within limits); it is a structure which also underlies the passages taken from Thomas's commentary on Peter Lombard's *Sentences*,[9] but there I have always omitted Peter Lombard's text, together with Thomas's textual analysis and exposition, including only the parts that imitate *quaestiones disputatae*. And in the *Sentences* the grouping of questions is considerably more complex than the usual gathering of articles into 'questions'; there we have queries (*quaestiunculae*) within articles within questions within distinctions. By the time Thomas came to write his *Summa Theologiae*, he had decided not to write a commentary on some author's text, but to raise the questions he wanted to raise in the order he wanted to raise them. Nevertheless, the structure he adopts is that of sets of disputed questions, though each article in a set is very much simplified in its microstructure. The simplification he adopts generally (but not always—see Passages 22 and 36) limits the objections to three and the arguments in favour to one, and he keeps the summing-up (or body of the article) to a modest length by multiplying articles rather than by dealing with too many points within each one.

Thomas's commentaries on the text of Aristotle do not contain *quaestiones disputatae*. The structure of the *lectio* is there (text, analysis, and exposition), but it is not followed by disputed questions; questions of special interest suggested by the text are dealt with by digressions within the exposi-

[9] Passages 24 and 34.

tory comment. For this reason I have included only a few examples of this type of writing, for I wanted to give the reader passages in which he could reliably ascribe the thought to Thomas himself rather than to Aristotle expounded by St Thomas. However, Passage 5 from the commentary on the *Physics* and Passage 11 from the commentary on the *De Memoria et Reminiscentia* characteristically juxtapose exposition of Aristotle's text (in which embedded italicized text is quoted from Aristotle) with Thomas's digression (where no italicized text occurs). Passage 30 from the commentary on the *De Interpretatione* (known to Thomas as the *Perihermeneias*) is pure digression of Thomas, extracted from its context in an exposition of Aristotle's text. Many of the other short works included in Parts II and III can be thought of on the model of such 'digressions', designed to deal with some special point of interest: how elements are present within compounds, for example (Passage 8); though works like those on the principles of nature (Passage 4) or on being and essence (Passage 6) should perhaps rather be thought of as summary notes for students, collecting together and reconciling passages from several parts of Aristotle or similar authorities.

Part I of this World's Classics volume, then, contains one long passage from an early work, chosen because it introduces the student to science, philosophy, and theology as Thomas understood them, and also because it illustrates the general style and structure of his writings.

Part II—Passages 2–6—is also introductory, dealing not so much with the structure of our thought as with the very general ways in which Thomas (following Aristotle) sees structure in things. Passage 2 starts with very general notions or ways of regarding things—as existent beings, as true, as good—notions not synonymous, but interconvertible in the sense that whatever is is good and is true. The problem is to preserve their interconvertibility without yielding to synonymity. Passage 3 deals with Aristotle's most basic division of being according to Thomas—that between existing potentially and existing actually; Passage 4 (a complete small work, or *opusculum*) treats of the so-called four Aristotelian causes: matter, form, agent, and goal; and Passage 5 with the Aristotelian categories, laying special emphasis on the categories of action and passion and the Aristotelian thesis that action exists not in the agent but in the patient—a thesis of great importance in Thomas's later analysis of the relationship between agent God and patient universe. Finally, Passage 6 is another complete *opusculum*: the fine early work in which—with many references to the Arabic scholars Ibn Sīnā and Ibn Rushd—Thomas discusses the Aristotelian concept of *ousia*, here called essence, and explains among other things his thesis that in God and only in God is essence identical with existence.

Part III—Passages 7–19—is still concerned with the Aristotelian philosophical account of the world we live in, but not now in general terms. What concerns us here is the variety of beings to which the general descriptions of Part II apply: a variety stretching from inanimate matter through the lower forms of life to the life of human beings. Passage 7 is a short introduction to this 'ladder of being'; Passage 8 (another complete *opusculum*) gives us a quick view of Thomas's physics and chemistry, based on the four elements of earth, air, fire, and water; Passages 9 and 10 distinguish levels of life in general, relating them to the abilities or powers that develop as life becomes more complex; Passages 11–17 deal with particular levels and abilities of life—with the senses, with mind, with the emotions, and with free will. Finally, Passages 18–19 deal with the thesis that being human in some way transcends the material order. Here we get Thomas's account of Aristotle's thesis that mind is the form of the human body, so treated as to provide us with a point of insertion for his whole theology of human beings derived from the Judaeo-Christian scriptures. It is for this reason that Passage 19 from a commentary on scripture is included. It illustrates how philosophy and theology interact in Thomas: for here he says that an Aristotelian such as himself—to whom the soul is only *part* of man, and exists by nature in a body—would find the Platonic doctrine of the immortality of the soul hard to believe were it not shored up by the Christian doctrine of the resurrection of the body.

From here on the parts and their passages turn explicitly to God, drawing out of Aristotle implications that Aristotle would not have known to be there, but which, nevertheless, in Thomas's opinion, are matters of human learning and fall short of revealed theology. They therefore constitute points of insertion for revealed theology into Aristotelian philosophy of the sort already remarked on in relation to the soul; we shall have a word to say about such 'points of insertion' later.

Part IV—Passages 20–6—is concerned with a philosophical view of God derived by way of reflection on the world, but not explicitly treating of God's relationship to that world. Thus Passage 20 discusses how to prove God's existence, Passage 21 (a deeply thought-out passage) explains the thesis that God *is* his existence, Passage 22 deals with God's transcendence of time, Passages 23–4 with his transcendence of language, and Passages 25 and 26 with his transcendent knowledge and power.

The final two parts go on to explore the world's relation to God, divided in the way Thomas always divided his treatment of this subject: into passages dealing with God as the world's beginning and with God as the world's end. Passages 27–33 (Part V) deal with God as creator, architect, designer, and manager of the world: in short with God as doer of the world—the one whose doing the world's being is. For his doing is not something we can identify over and above the world's being, it is the world's being as done. From this profound conception spring Thomas's accounts of God's agency in regard to chance and free will, and in regard to evil, and the notion that he is not at work in the world side by side with nature but as the cause of nature's own natural activity. The final passage of Part V is a sort of test-bed for the whole part: one must see why Thomas says *both* that God is at work in all nature and *also* that there is no commingling of creating with natural activity, in order to understand what Thomas has done to Aristotle, how he inserts theology into philosophy, the way in which he conceives creation (actively considered) as totally transcending and outside of the universe—indeed it is God himself—and yet (passively considered) as the universe itself existing in its relation to that transcendent act.

Part VI deals with God as the end of things. It too is a point of insertion: of Christian views of what life is about into Aristotelian ethics. Passage 34 explains in what sense God and in what sense happiness is the goal of human living; Passage 35 is a profound analysis of the morality of human actions; Passage 36 introduces the notion of virtue and Passage 37 that of law. And finally Passage 38 reminds us that for Thomas all that we have seen is but preparation. Although he thinks we should try and understand the world philosophically as a first stage, nevertheless he wants more: he wants to expand such human views of God and the world so as to accommodate specifically Christian notions of God's self-revelation through Christ and the religion of Israel. And in the final passage of this selection, we see him trying to articulate the very heart of Christian living—God as love, and the love of God—in ways that might appeal to an Aristotelian philosopher.

And this brings us back to the relation of philosophy to theology in Thomas and the anachronism of calling him a 'philosopher of religion'. The relation of philosophy to theology in Thomas seems to me to be very subtle and quite often misunderstood. To clarify it let me take a particular example of his building on Aristotelian philosophy, and identify four *layers* in the process. And what example could be more appropriate than Thomas's 'philosophy of religion' in a strict sense: his philosophical reflections on the nature of religion, and the way he uses them when building up his theology of Christ and Christianity?

The first layer is Thomas's recapitulation of the basic Aristotelian philosophy from which the process must start: in this case Aristotle's account of virtue in the *Nicomachean Ethics*. Passage 36 in this collection—Thomas's account of virtue in the *Summa Theologiae*—is such a recapitulation. There Thomas expounds the general Aristotelian notion of virtue as a disposition perfecting some ability of ours, and sketches the special claim moral or social or political virtues have to the title of virtue: dispositions which perfect our abilities to will and desire in certain crucial areas of moral life, especially in the area of our dealings with others.

All moral virtues concerned with activity as such [rather than with the passions] can be grouped generally under justice, concerned with whatever is owed to others. But there are many different sorts of debt: to equals, to superiors, to inferiors; and owed by contract, by promise or in gratitude. So diverse virtues exist: religion for repaying God, loyalty to family and country, gratitude to benefactors, and so on. Only one of these special virtues is justice in the strict sense: concerned with debts strictly repayable by a measure of equivalence.[10]

But this passage already begins to develop Aristotle's account, not just to recapitulate it. The hints that Aristotle gives of sorts of justice to those who are not our equals are elaborated so as to provide a place for Thomas's own interests: in particular for a sort of justice to God, called here religion. In turning his Aristotelian eye on religion and its obligations, Thomas starts to draw on data available to him in scripture and the life of the Church. Nevertheless in this second layer of development, superimposed on recapitulation, he is still elaborating a *philosophy* of religion. He uses the Scriptures and the Church not to teach him something lying above and beyond the reach of his reason, but simply to provide him with data about natural religion and the way humankind elaborates its natural social and moral relation to God. He uses it as we today would use the mass of anthropological data now available from all shapes and sizes of religions around the world.

Natural reason tells us that because of the inadequacies we perceive in ourselves we need to subject ourselves to some superior source of help and direction; and whatever that source might be, everybody calls it *God*. Our natural way of expressing such things is by using sensible signs, since we derive our knowledge from the senses. So natural reason leads us to offer sensible things to God as a sign of the subjection and honour we owe him, rather as we offer things to our temporal masters in recognition of their authority. This is what we call *sacrifice*, so offering sacrifice is an act of natural justice. The

[10] *Aquinas*, ed. McDermott, 238 (1a2ae.60.3).

particular sacrifices offered are determined by human or divine institution, and for that reason differ from people to people.[11]

Notice here the careful repetitions of the word 'natural'. Notice also the way room is made for a diversity in human natural religion by the recognition of its symbolic nature. To show God honour in symbolic rites is natural to all humankind; but what particular form the symbolic rites take will depend, and depend as of right, on the culture and law of various societies. This view that human laws and cultures have a right to build in their own ways on what is a law to us by our nature is further explored in Passage 37 of this collection. Thomas takes an attitude to natural religious worship that differs considerably from a more traditional view of non-Christian religions as devil-worship.

Having made this advance on Aristotle's philosophy of virtue, by developing within it a concept of natural religion, Thomas is now in a position to add a third layer: linking now not only to scripture as anthropological source-book, but also to what faith tells him scripture is saying. This, as Passage 1 says, is where Thomas thinks he steps across from philosophy to revealed theology. The particular crossing-point, the insertion point for theology within philosophy in this matter of religion, has already been hinted at: when Thomas talked of the particular sacrifices differing peoples offer as determined not by a law of nature but by human *or divine* institution.[12] That has made room for him to regard a particular human culture as divinely chosen, a particular human law to be adopted, so to speak, as God's human law.

Since man is also related to God . . . by external actions in which he confesses himself God's servant—ritual acts of worship—the Old Law also contained ritual or ceremonial injunctions regulating God's worship. The injunctions of the law that is in us by nature are general and require particular specification. Such specifications made by human law form part . . . of positively enacted law, and in a similar way the specifications made by God's law remain distinct

[11] *Aquinas*, ed. McDermott, 405 (2a2ae.85.1).

[12] Thomas is developing hints occurring in a somewhat confused form in Aristotle's *Nicomachean Ethics*, book 5, ch. 7.

from the moral injunctions of the law that is in us by nature. Thus the worship of God is virtuous behaviour commanded by a moral injunction, but the specifications put on this command—that God must be worshipped with such and such sacrifices and gifts—are ritual injunctions. Pseudo-Dionysius says God can't be revealed to men except through sense-images; so the scriptures express him not only verbally in figures of speech, but also symbolically to the eye in prescribed rituals.[13]

This quotation shows the serene way in which Thomas reconciles his philosophical and theological vision. He can see in the religion of Israel one particular example of the nature of human beings, of their social life, of their natural propensity to worship, of their need to specify in particular symbolic ways their open natural relation to their creator, and yet at the same time recognize it as the vehicle of a special revelation of God taking us beyond and above the natural world to look into the face of God himself. His last sentence above points to an analogy with language: the religion of Israel is at one and the same time an example of the languages men devise in order to address and express their gods, and God's exploiting of that example to speak about himself. Thomas's view of the interaction between such human ritual language and its divine message is quite sophisticated. Take, for example, this analysis of the symbolism of Old Testament religion:

There was no natural reason for the Old Law observances, e.g. for refusing to make garments of wool and linen. The reason was symbolic... However, just as Old Testament history has a literal sense besides the figurative sense in which its happenings symbolize Christ, so too the ritual injunctions of the Old Law have literal [symbolic] reasons as well as figurative [symbolic] reasons. The literal reasons explain the ritual injunctions in terms of what the divine worship meant at that time. The figurative reasons relate rather to Christ and the church to come. So, just as to understand metaphorical turns of phrase in scripture as metaphors is to grasp their literal sense (since that's what the words were used to mean), so the literal significance of Old Law rituals is to be found in the symbolic reason for instituting them at the time, namely, to

[13] *Aquinas*, ed. McDermott, 297 (1a2ae.99.3).

commemorate some deed of divine favour. The literal significance of the Passover is that it symbolized the liberation of the Jews from Egypt, and of circumcision that it symbolized God's pact with Abraham.[14]

The nuanced way in which the same phenomena show both a natural and a revealed face to Thomas—the symbolic is both humanly literal and divinely figurative—is typical of the openness of his theological account of God's grace to his philosophical account of the world's nature. He exhibits a calm determination to do justice to every facet of what he observes; it enables him to engage with the thoughts of various traditions in his own time, and makes him alive and readable today in our pluralist society. For him nature is a tool of grace, used to do something beyond its own powers, but only because it does have its own powers to contribute: if nature had no 'edge' of its own, grace could not do anything with it. The Christian sacraments, for instance, are not simply, as for some other medieval theologians, mysterious 'medicines' that act merely by God's will; but the way they work can be articulated, and involves seeing what the Christian sacraments are in nature, ritual religious performances akin to those of natural religion but now become tools of God.

You can't unite men in a religion unless they share visible symbols or sacraments keeping them together [Augustine, *Contra Faustum*, 19.11] . . . Since the sacred realities signified by the sacraments are spiritual things that only mind can grasp, the sacraments must signify them with things our senses can perceive, just as the scriptures express them with analogies drawn from the perceptible world . . . But sacraments are used both in man's worship of God and in God's sanctification of men, and since this latter lies in God's power, man cannot decide what should be used for the purpose: that is for God to determine . . . Just as the Holy Spirit decided the symbols this or that passage of scripture would use to signify spiritual things, so God determined what things should act as signs in this or that sacrament. For whether a thing makes us holy or not depends not on its natural power, but on God's decision. In the period when men

[14] *Aquinas*, ed. McDermott, 301 (1a2ae.102.1–2).

relied on the law that is in them by nature, interior instinct alone prompted them to worship God and choose what signs to use in worship. Later, men had to be given a law from above: partly because the law in their nature had become obscured by sins, and partly to make more explicit that it was the grace of Christ which was to make the whole race of mankind holy.[15]

The intricate interlayering of philosophy and theology is, I hope, becoming clearer. Thomas is not just interested in recapitulating Aristotle; he wants, at a second level, to develop him philosophically in ways which will illuminate how the natural world could be invaded by God's revelation. At a third level he then wants to develop his theology of that revelation in such a way that it shows the natural world still operative within the revealed world. But the full intricacy of the relation becomes clear only when we recognize a fourth and final interlayering of philosophy and theology in Thomas: one that we can also discern at work in the last quotation. Thomas believes that the whole symbolic 'substance' of religion as described in his philosophy becomes in Christianity a 'tool' of God's self-gift to man. Now the words *substance* and *tool* here are words taken from Thomas's philosophical armoury, but used to express the very essence of what is happening in the Christian sacraments, something that can only be 'seen' by faith, something that can only be the subject of a revealed theology. This is the final layer in an intricate use of philosophy by Thomas: the use of terms developed and understood in a philosophical context to express the very theological message that transcends philosophy. Words like *substance* and *tool* developed in a philosophical context have to be taken up again and re-evaluated within a wholly theological vision. Within that vision things are focused as playing parts analogical with the parts played by substances and tools in the natural world. Words with their roots in philosophy must be allowed to bear new and richer flowers within the world of theology. This last layer of philosophy-within-theology—I am contrasting it with the third layer, in which theology was rather inserted within

[15] Ibid. 547–9 (3a.61.1; 60.4–5).

philosophy—has, I believe, led to many grievous misunderstandings of Thomas: the idea, for example, that in the doctrine of the Eucharist, transubstantiation is saying something that we can reconstruct from an understanding of what substance and accident meant to Aristotle. But that is not so. Rather each word of such a philosophy-within-theology account has to be born again, so to speak, within the theological reflection, has to be generated anew by the role it plays in a wholly theological context; only then can it play its part in what is primarily theological explanation, just as mathematical symbols have to be generated by physical facts before they can become of any explanatory use in physics (though that too is often overlooked). The sacraments 'cause' grace for Thomas, it is true, but by a causality which, to nature's eye, is a mere 'symbolizing', and which only by the power of God revealed in Christ becomes a 'causing'—as Thomas says, a causing by symbolizing. 'For whether a thing makes us holy or not depends not on its natural power, but on God's decision.' And in the same way, Christ is present as 'substance' in the Eucharist by a mode of substantial presence new to philosophy, which can see here only the merely symbolic: a mode of presence not by some curious supernatural metaphysical mechanism construed on the model of a physical mechanism and lying behind or alongside the symbolic core of the rite, but by God's power operating through Calvary in those ritual human actions and natural significances of things, the obedience of a hearing world to God's voice in Christ asserting meaning: 'This is my body'.

I have been giving an example of how Thomas, by recognizing a sharp difference between philosophy—man's learning—and theology—God's teaching, enables himself to layer the two intricately together in his writing. It is this intricate layering, I believe, rather than any *confusion* between philosophy and theology, that has caused much misunderstanding of Thomas. Much ink has been spilt on the question of whether he is a theologian or a philosopher; I think it is like discussing whether somebody is a cyclist or a pedestrian! Most people have both skills, and use whichever is the more appropriate in the context.

A final remark about the passages: they date from different periods of Thomas's teaching life. But because we cannot date precisely many of the works, and because Thomas did not change his opinions drastically throughout his life (though there are some rare cases of importance, like his rethinking of Christ's human knowledge), I have contented myself with the following chronological sketch of Thomas's life and works:[16]

Year	Age	Events and Main Works	Passages
1225		Birth	
1231–9	5	Monte Cassino	
1239–44	15	Student at Naples University Joined Dominicans	
1244	20	Imprisoned by his family	
1245–8		Novice in Paris?	
1248–52	25	Student in Cologne	
1252–6		Bachelor in Paris	4, 6
	30	Commentary on the *Sentences*	24, 34
1256–9		Master (i.e. professor) in Paris	
		Quaestiones Disputatae de Veritate	2, 14
		In Boethii de Trinitate	1
1259–64	35	Lecturer at papal curia, Orvieto	
		Summa contra Gentiles	7, 13, 16, 25, 29, 31
1265–7	40	Rome	
		Quaestiones Disputatae de Potentia	3, 21, 26–8, 33
		Summa Theologiae, part 1	12, 20, 22–3
1268–9		Viterbo	
		Quaestio Disputata de Spiritualibus Creaturis	9
1269–72	45	Recalled to Paris	
		Quaestio Disputata de Anima	10, 11, 18

[16] For further details see J. A. Weisheipl, *Friar Thomas d'Aquino: His Life, Thought and Works* (Oxford, 1974; with corrections: Washington, DC, 1983).

Year	Age	Events and Main Works	Passages
		Quaestiones Disputatae de Virtutibus	19, 30, 38
		Quaestiones Disputatae de Malo	5, 17, 32
		Summa Theologiae, part 2	15, 35–7
1272–4		Return to Naples	
		Summa Theologiae, part 3	
1274		Death	

Note on Sources and Text

THE Leonine commission's critical text has been used when available. Otherwise, a preliminary note to the first passage drawn from the work in question mentions the text consulted. In many cases, however, I have been allowed to make use of Leonine texts in preparation, and for this I express my thanks to the Leonine editors, and especially to Père Louis Bataillon, OP. I have ventured to disagree with even the Leonine text at one or two points explained in the notes.

In all cases square brackets denote editorial additions to the text. References have been dealt with in the following way. All that remains of the references Thomas makes in his text is the name of the author referred to; further details are deferred to the endnote. There details that are Thomas's own are not enclosed in square brackets; what is added in square brackets is editorial addition. One exception: in the case of references to Aristotle's works, Aristotle's name always occurs in the text, even when Thomas omitted it.

Select Bibliography

Other Translations and Collections

An Aquinas Reader, ed. Mary T. Clark (New York, 1972).
The Philosophy of Thomas Aquinas, ed. Christopher Martin (London, 1988).
The Pocket Aquinas, ed. Vernon J. Bourke (New York, 1960).
St Thomas Aquinas, Summa Theologiae, 60 vols., ed. Thomas Gilby (London, 1963).
St Thomas Aquinas, Summa Theologiae: A Concise Translation, ed. Timothy McDermott (London, 1989).

Life

CHESTERTON, G. K., *St Thomas Aquinas* (London, 1933).
FOSTER, Kenelm (ed.), *The Life of St Thomas Aquinas* [documents] (London, 1959).
WEISHEIPL, J. A., *Friar Thomas d'Aquino: His Life, Thought and Works* (Oxford, 1974; with corrections: Washington, DC, 1983).

Thought and Work

BURRELL, David, *Aquinas, God and Action* (London, 1979).
CHENU, M.-D., *Toward Understanding St Thomas* (Chicago, 1964).
COPLESTON, F. C., *Aquinas* (Harmondsworth, 1955).
DAVIES, Brian, *The Thought of Thomas Aquinas* (Oxford, 1992).
GILSON, Étienne, *The Christian Philosophy of St Thomas Aquinas* (London, 1971).
KENNY, Anthony (ed.), *Aquinas: A Collection of Critical Essays* (London, 1969).
KENNY, Anthony, *Aquinas on Mind* (London, 1993).
PIEPER, Josef, *Guide to Thomas Aquinas* (Notre Dame, Ind., 1987).

Other Background Material

WILLIAM WALLACE, A., 'Aristotle in the Middle Ages', in Joseph R. Strayer (ed.), *Dictionary of the Middle Ages* (New York, 1982). Further bibliography can be found in Ralph McInerny, 'Aquinas, St Thomas', in this dictionary.
VAN STEENBERGHEN, F., *Aristotle in the West: The Origins of Latin Aristotelianism* trans. L. Johnson (Louvain, 1955).

Kenny, A., Kretzmann, N., and Pinborg, J. (eds.), *The Cambridge History of Later Medieval Philosophy* (Cambridge, 1982).
Benson, R. L. and Constable G. (eds.), *Renaissance and Renewal in the Twelfth Century* (Oxford, 1985).

SELECTED PHILOSOPHICAL WRITINGS

Part I

Structures of Thought

Passage 1

On Natural Science, Mathematics, and Metaphysics

Source: Thomas's commentary on chapter 2 of Boethius' *De Trinitate* (incorporating questions 5 and 6). Text from the critical edition of Thomas's original manuscript: *Expositio super Librum Boethii de Trinitate*, ed. B. Decker, 2nd edn. (Leiden, 1959), with some corrections from the future Leonine editor, published in *Bulletin Thomiste*, 11.54, pp. 41–4.

Date: Between 1255 and 1259, first stay in Paris, aged 30–4.

Type of passage: Textual commentary with appended disputed questions (see Introduction).

How to read: The initial section (in italics) is Boethius' text; the second section Thomas's textual commentary into which are woven Boethius' actual words, picked out in italics; the third section collects together questions raised by Boethius' text, each having the structure of a disputed question (see Introduction). Each disputed question consists of four sections (here headed in bold): first, the **It seems...** marshalling many arguments that cast doubt on what Boethius says (the translation omits some of these arguments); second, the **But against that**, which rather more briefly collects authorities in support of Boethius' point; third, the **In reply**, which is Thomas's extensive argument meant to decide the point; and fourth, the **Hence**, which answers the opening arguments of the question in order. In one case—Question 6, Article 1—the structure is more complex: three doubts are cast in the one article (I have labelled them **Queries**) and the three doubts are first raised by way of a thrice-repeated **It seems** and **But against that**, and then answered by a thrice-repeated **In reply** and **Hence**.

[Boethius' text, Chapter 2]

Come then, let us enter into each matter, discussing[1] it so it can be grasped and understood, for it seems well said that educated people try for such certainty as the matter itself allows.

For since theoretical science divides into three—

> *natural science, changing, non-abstract, unseparated: which considers bodily forms as forms-in-matter, forms that cannot exist separated from bodies that are changing—like falling earth or rising fire—so that what changes is the form-in-matter;*
>
> *mathematics, changeless, non-abstract: which conceives bodily forms apart from matter and thus from change, though those forms exist in matter and so cannot be separated from matter and change;*
>
> *theology, changeless, abstract, and inseparable:*[2] *for God's being lacks both matter and change—*

in natural science we make use of reason, in mathematics discipline, in divine science intellect, not relying on imagination but rather scrutinizing Form itself [true form and no image, Existence itself from which all existence exists].

[Thomas's explanation of the text]

Having already set out Catholic belief in the unity of a three-person God and given the ground for that belief, Boethius now wants to start investigating these matters; but, guided by Aristotle's opinion[3] that before starting a science we must investigate the ways of that science, he proceeds in two steps, first showing the proper way to investigate divine matters, and then, at *true form and no image*, pursuing his investigation in that way. In the first step he first says why we must know the way to investigate, and then, at *For since theoretical science divides*, shows the way best suited to the present investigation.

So he says: *Come*—exhorting us—*then*, given that Catholics believe in the unity of a three-person God on the ground of undifferentiation, *let us enter into each matter*, that is, delve within, into the innermost principles of things, penetrating to the truth that lies veiled as it were and hidden; and do this in the proper way, which is why he adds: *discuss-*

ing each so it can be grasped and understood, that is, in such a way that it can be grasped and understood. He uses these two verbs since the way things are discussed must suit both the things and ourselves: the things if they are to be understood, ourselves if we are to grasp them. For example, the divine, of its nature, can be known only by intellect: so those who try to grasp it using imagination won't *understand* it since the thing itself isn't understandable that way; whereas those who try to see it in itself with the sort of certainty and comprehensiveness with which we comprehend what our senses experience or mathematics can prove, won't get a *grasp* of it that way, since, however much[4] it itself is open to such understanding, our understandings are not up to it.

That there is a proper way of conducting each investigation he proves by citing the beginning of Aristotle's *Ethics*, continuing: *for it seems well said*, namely, by Aristotle, *that educated people try for such certainty as the matter itself allows*, that is, as the way of approach suited to the matter allows. For not all matters allow the same certainty and clarity of demonstration. Aristotle's actual words[5] are: 'It is the mark of an educated person to require as much certainty in a particular domain as the nature of the matter allows.'

Next, when he says: *For since theoretical science divides into three*, he begins to distinguish the way this investigation should be conducted from ways used by other sciences. And because the way must suit the subject-matter under consideration he first classifies the sciences by subject-matter, and then, at *in natural science*, describes the way each should be conducted. The classification proceeds in three steps: first he points out the subject-matter of natural science; then, at *mathematics*, that of mathematics; and finally, at *theology*, that of divine science.

So, given that it seems well said that we should try for such certainty as the matter itself allows, he says: *For since theoretical science*, that is to say, philosophy, as distinct from ethics, which is practical and concerned with action, *divides into three*, each branch needs to be conducted in a way suited to its subject-matter. The three branches referred to are physical or natural science, mathematics, and theology or divine science. Since, to repeat, there are these three: *natural science*—one of them—is *changing, non-abstract*, that is, considers things which change, un-abstracted from matter; and this he proves by example as seen in the text. But his phrase *what changes is the form-in-matter* needs interpretation: either it means that what changes as such is the thing itself, composed of matter under this form, or that what gives rise to the change is the form itself, existing in the matter; so that considering bodies as material or as changing amounts to the same thing.

Next he explains mathematics' subject-matter: *mathematics* is *changeless*, that is, doesn't consider change and changing things (in this regard differing from natural science), *non-abstract*, that is, concerned with forms that never exist in abstraction from matter (in this regard agreeing with natural science). How this can be he explains: *which*, namely, mathematics, *conceives bodily forms apart from matter and thus from change* (for as Aristotle proves,[6] wherever there is change there is matter corresponding to the change); so that the mathematician's way of looking at forms is free from matter and change, *though those forms*, namely, the forms mathematics looks at, *exist in matter and so cannot be separated*—in their existence—*from matter and change*. So they can be separated from matter conceptually but not in actual fact.

Next he points out divine science's subject-matter: *theology*, that is, the third branch of theoretical science, called also divine science or metaphysics or first philosophy, is *changeless*, in this regard agreeing with mathematics and differing from natural science, *abstract*, that is, from matter, *and inseparable*, in these two regards differing from mathematics. For the divine actually exists abstracted from matter and change whereas mathematical objects exist unabstracted; mathematical objects, however, are separable conceptually whereas the divine is inseparable since only what is joined can be separated.[7] So the divine is not conceptually separable from matter but is actually abstracted from matter: the exact opposite of the mathematical case. For proof he refers to *God's being*, the principal subject-matter of divine science from which its name derives.

Next, when he says *in natural science* he points out the ways in which each branch of science should be conducted: firstly, summarizing the ways suited to each branch (and this part of our explanation we will leave to the disputation that follows), and secondly, expanding the last way which is the one proper to the present investigation. Here he first clears away an obstacle, saying: ***not relying on imagination***, that is, not using imagination to judge the way divine matters are; and then, secondly, he points out the proper way: ***but rather scrutinizing Form itself*** without matter and without change, the Form whose conditions he treats later when he actually enters on his proposed investigation.

[Questions raised by Thomas in connection with the text]
Here two questions need debate:

the branches into which the text divides theoretical science; and

the different methods of approach ascribed to those branches.

[Question 5] The first question **[the branches into which the text divides theoretical science]** divides into four:

Is the division of theoretical science into natural, mathematical, and divine science acceptable?

Is natural philosophy concerned with changing material things?

Does mathematics see the material things it is concerned with in an unchanging and immaterial way?

Is divine science concerned with immaterial unchanging things?

[Article 1] The first question **[Is the division of theoretical science into natural, mathematical, and divine science acceptable?]** we approach as follows:

The division of theoretical science into these branches seems unacceptable:

For [1] the branches of theoretical science are meant to dispose and perfect our mind's ability to see and understand things. But Aristotle[8] says our mind's capability of science—its theoretical part—is perfected by the three dispositions of wisdom, science, and understanding. These then should be the three branches of theoretical science and not those proposed in the text.

Moreover, [2] Augustine[9] says logic, the science of reason, is a branch of theoretical or contemplative science. A classification which makes no mention of logic is therefore defective.

Moreover, [3] people usually divide philosophy into the seven liberal arts, which include no natural or divine science, but only logic and mathematics. So natural and divine science should not be counted as branches of theoretical science.

Moreover, [4] of all sciences medicine seems the most practical, yet it has a theoretical as well as a practical part. For the same reason then every other practical science has its theoretical part, and mention should have been made in the classification of ethics or moral science—though practical—because of its theoretical part.

Moreover, [5] medical science, and certain other mechanical [= non-liberal] arts like agriculture, metallurgy, etc., are parts of natural science. Since these are practical sciences it seems natural science can't be classed simply as theoretical.

Moreover, [6] a whole shouldn't be classified alongside its parts. Now divine science seems to be a whole with natural science and mathematics as parts, since its subject-matter includes theirs. For, as first philosophy, its subject-matter is being, and that, as Aristotle makes clear,[10] includes changing substances—the subject-matter of natural science—and quantity—the subject-matter of mathematics. So divine science shouldn't be classified alongside natural science and mathematics . . .

Moreover, [9] sciences presupposed to others should rank before them. Now all other sciences presuppose divine science, submitting their first principles to its judgements. Divine science then should head the list of sciences.

Moreover, [10] mathematics is learnt before natural science, because, as Aristotle points out,[11] even children can learn it easily, whereas natural science demands advanced study.

And so in olden days, we are told, the sciences were learnt in this order: logic, mathematics, natural science, ethics, and finally divine science. Mathematics then should be listed before natural science, and the classification given here seems defective.

But against that:

[1] That this is an acceptable classification we have on Aristotle's authority:[12] *So theoretical philosophy has three branches: mathematics, natural science, and theology.*

Moreover, [2] the three modes of scientific thought mentioned by Aristotle in the *Physics*[13] seem also to be these three.

Moreover, [3] Ptolemy[14] too uses this classification.

In reply:

Speculative or theoretical, as distinct from operative or practical, understanding is characterized by attention to truth for its own sake, rather than as the means to some other activity. Aristotle[15] calls this a distinction of goal, 'the goal of theoretical understanding being truth but of practical understanding action'.[16] Now since subject-matter must match goal, the subject-matter of practical sciences has to be things we can make or do, which we can be seeking to know for activity's sake, so to say. The subject-matter of theoretical sciences, on the other hand, has to be things not made by us, which we can't be seeking to know for activity's sake; and differences between things of this sort will differentiate theoretical sciences.

But we must remember that when abilities and dispositions are differentiated by the objects they bear on, not any and every difference in object is relevant, but only differences that affect the way objects are objects. Whether an object of our senses is animal or plant is irrelevant to its ability to be sensed, and so we don't differentiate the senses by such a difference, but rather by the difference between colour and sound. We must differentiate speculative sciences then by differences relevant to objects of speculation precisely as such.

Now to be an object of our ability to speculate a thing must suit both our basic ability to understand and that further disposition to know things with certainty which perfects our understanding with science. The ability to understand, being itself non-material, requires its objects to be non-material; and the disposition to science requires its objects to be necessary—since we can know with certainty only what must be so.[17] What must be so is, as such, unchanging, since what changes, as such, can be or not be—exist or not exist in the unqualified sense, or be or not be the way it is.[18] Any objects of speculation or theoretical science, then, must, as such, position themselves in relation to matter and change, and according to their degrees of distance from matter and change such objects will determine different theoretical sciences.

Some objects of our speculation, then, depend on matter for their existence, unable to exist except in matter. But a distinction is possible. Some depend on matter not only for existence but also for understanding: since 'perceptible matter' is included in their definition they can't be understood without that perceptible matter. Thus flesh and bone are included in the definition of human being. Such things are studied by **physics,** or **natural science.** Other things depend on matter for existence but not for understanding, since 'perceptible matter' is not included in their definition: things like lines and numbers. And such things are studied by **mathematics.** Then there are other objects of speculation which don't depend for their existence on matter and are able to exist out of matter, either never existing in matter, like God and the angels, or sometimes existing in matter but sometimes not, like substance, qualities, potentiality and actuality, the one and the many, etc. All such things are studied by **theology**—science of the divine—so-called because God is its prime object of study. But it is also called **metaphysics**—'after-physics'—because we learn it after physics, only able to reach what can't be sensed through what can. And again it is called **first philosophy,** since all other sciences come after it in the sense of deriving their first principles from it. But because nothing can depend on matter for understanding and not for existence—understanding being as such immaterial—no fourth division of philosophy exists beside the ones mentioned.

Hence:

to 1: In the *Ethics*[19] Aristotle is inquiring about mental dispositions as virtues [or strengths], called that because of their perfecting activity: *a virtue renders its possessor and his activity good.*[20] So he distinguishes these virtues according to their different ways of perfecting and strengthening. The way our speculating mind is strengthened by understanding—disposing us to recognize the self-evident truths which serve as first premisses of our thought—differs from the way we know conclusions deducible from those principles, whether the deduction be from low-level causes, as in science, or from the highest-level ones, as in wisdom. But when we are distinguishing sciences as dispositions we must distinguish them with reference to their objects or subject-matters. And that is the way the three branches of theoretical science are distinguished here and by Aristotle.[21]

to 2: As Aristotle makes clear,[22] theoretical science concerns itself with anything we seek to know for its own sake. But what logic deals with is not sought for its own sake, but as a support to the other sciences. So logic is not classified as a major branch of theoretical science, but as something that serves philosophy, providing it with tools of speculation: the syllogisms and definitions we need in the theoretical sciences. That is why Boethius[23] calls it not so much a science as a scientific instrument.

to 3: The seven liberal arts don't cover all theoretical philosophy, but according to Hugh of St Victor[24] other sciences were left out and these seven collected together because they constitute the first steps in learning philosophy, and so are themselves divided into the three-ways (the *trivium*) and the four-ways (the *quadrivium*), *pathways by which an alert spirit can enter philosophy's secret places*. This agrees with Aristotle's opinion[25] that before tackling science one must learn its methods, on which Ibn Rushd commented that logic, since it teaches the method of every science, must be learnt before all other sciences (hence the *trivium*); and since Aristotle[26] also said that children can learn mathematics but haven't enough experience for natural science, we can deduce that mathematics should follow on logic (hence the *quadrivium*). By these then, as by pathways, we prepare our spirit for the other philosophical disciplines. Alternatively, these sciences are singled out as *arts*, because they yield products as well as knowledge—direct products of reason, such as grammatical constructions, syllogisms, speeches, enumerations, measurements, melodies, and computed courses of stars. Other sciences either yield no products but only knowledge (e.g. natural science, divine science) and so are not called arts at all, since art according to Aristotle[27] is productive reason; or yield bodily products (e.g. medicine, metallurgy, etc.) and so are not called liberal [i.e. free-man] arts, since their activities belong to the body, the servant part of a human being. And though ethics too aims at activity, it aims as Aristotle[28] says not at knowing but at acting virtuously; so ethics isn't called an art either, since in such activity virtue substitutes for art. And that is why the ancients defined virtue as *the art of living rightly and well*, as we read in Augustine.[29]

to 4: Ibn Sīnā[30] points out that the distinction between theoretical and practical means something different in philosophy, in the arts, and in medicine. In philosophy and the arts the distinction arises from a distinction of goal, the theoretical seeking only knowledge of truth whereas the practical has activity in mind. But philosophy as a whole makes the distinction in a different way from the arts. For philosophy has regard to the goal of all human life, happiness—as Augustine[31] says, quoting Varro, *what other reason is there for doing philosophy but to be happy*—and so, since philosophers according to Aristotle[32] distinguish two kinds of happy life, one contemplative and the other active, they divide philosophy into two, calling ethics practical and natural science and logic theoretical. But when the arts are divided into theoretical and practical arts we have regard to goals special to each, calling agriculture practical but dialectic theoretical. As for medicine, its division into theoretical and practical doesn't arise from any distinction of goal, for in that respect all medicine is practical, aimed at activity. But the division depends on how closely matters dealt with in medicine relate to that activity; practical medicine teaches healing techniques—what drugs should be prescribed for what disease, for example—while theoretical medicine teaches the deeper principles governing such techniques—the existence of three kinds of 'spirit'[33] and umpteen kinds of fever. So calling one part of a practical science theoretical doesn't mean it must be a branch of theoretical science.

to 5: There are two ways in which one science can include another: as a part, with a subject-matter which is part of its own (as botany is part of natural science because plants are one group of naturally existing bodies), or as a subordinate, the lower-level science knowing only what is the case and needing the higher-level science to supply the 'why' (as harmony is subordinate to arithmetic). Medicine then is not a part of natural science: its subject-matter is not part of natural science's in the same sense in which it is medicine's, for although the body to be healed is a natural body, it is studied by medicine as healable by artifice, not as healable by nature. Because, however, even in healing by artifice, artifice is at nature's service aiding nature's powers of healing, we must examine natural properties if we are to supply the 'why' of the healing by artifice. So medicine is a subordinate of natural science, just as metallurgy and agriculture are. That leaves natural science and all its parts theoretical, even if some sciences subordinate to it are practical.

to 6: Although the subject-matters of all other sciences are included under being, the subject-matter of metaphysics, it doesn't follow that these other sciences are parts of metaphysics. For each of them considers its part of being in a special way distinct from the way metaphysics considers being, so that properly speaking its subject-matter is not part of metaphysics' subject-matter: it is not included under being in the same respect in which being is studied by metaphysics, the respect which makes metaphysics itself a special science that can be classified alongside others. What *can* be called parts of metaphysics in the sense suggested are its treatments of potentiality, actuality, oneness, etc., all of which are considered in the same way as metaphysics considers being . . .

to 9: Although divine science is the first of all sciences, our natural approach to it is through the others. As Ibn Sīnā says[34] in order of learning it comes after the natural sciences, which teach many things this science makes use of, such as the generation and decomposition of substances, change, and the like. For the same reason it is learnt after mathematics, for it learns about immaterial substances through numbering and ranking the celestial spheres, and that needs astronomy, which in turn needs all mathematics. And other sciences like music and ethics this science needs if it is to be done well.

This doesn't involve circularity—this science presupposing the conclusions of sciences to which it itself is providing premisses—because a science like natural science doesn't prove what it hands on to first philosophy by premisses derived from first philosophy, but by other self-evident premisses; and in the same way the first philosopher doesn't prove the premisses he hands down to natural science by premisses drawn from it, but by other self-evident premisses. So there is no circular definition here.

Moreover, the effects which we sense and on which natural science's demonstrations are based start better known to us, but once they have led us to knowledge of their first causes those causes show us the 'why' of the effects which previously showed us the fact of the causes. So natural science has something to offer divine science, yet has its starting-points illuminated by divine science. And this is why Boethius puts divine science in last place, as last known by us.

to 10: Natural science is learnt after mathematics because its generalizations require experience and time, but the objects of its study, because they can be sensed, are naturally better known than mathematical objects abstracted from perceived matter.

[Article 2] The second question [**Is natural philosophy concerned with changing, material things?**] we approach as follows:

It seems natural science is not concerned with changing, material things:

For [1] matter makes things individual. But, as Porphyry[35] tells us Plato believed, science is concerned with the general, never with individuals. So natural science is not concerned with material things.

Moreover, [2] science is something in the mind, and the mind knows by abstracting from matter and material conditions. So you can't have a science of things unabstracted from matter.

Moreover, [3] according to Aristotle[36] natural science is concerned with the ultimate cause of movement, an ultimate cause which is altogether free from matter. So natural science is not exclusively concerned with material things.

Moreover, [4] science studies what must be so. Now Aristotle[37] proves that everything changing, as such, can be or not be so. Of the changing then there can be no science, and thus no natural science.

Moreover, [5] it is not the general that changes: doctors cure particular men, not man in general, as Aristotle says.[38] Science, however, studies the general case. So natural science can't be about what changes.

Moreover, [6] natural science reaches conclusions about certain unchanging things like the soul[39] and the [stationary] earth;[40] moreover, as Aristotle[41] proves, [when natural things change their forms] the forms as such don't come into and go out of existence, so change only in a derived sense. Not everything, then, that natural science concerns itself with is changing.

Moreover, [7] all creatures are changeable and only God, as Augustine[42] says, unchanging. So if natural science were about changing things it would be about everything, which is clearly false.

But against that:

[1] natural science studies natural things, things with an interior tendency to move and change. But, as Aristotle[43] says, wherever there is change there must be material to change. So natural science is concerned with material, changing things.

Moreover, [2] some theoretical science must treat material, changing things; otherwise philosophy, our knowledge of being, would come to us incomplete. But no other science treats such things, neither mathematics nor metaphysics. So it must be natural science.

Moreover, [3] Aristotle leaves us in no doubt about it.[44]

In reply:

It was the difficulty of this question that forced Plato into postulating his *Ideas*. Since, as Aristotle[45] tells us, he accepted Cratylus' and Heraclitus' opinion that nothing we sense stays steady, and thought that there could therefore be no sure or scientific knowledge of such things, he postulated certain substances outside the realm of sense which we can know with certainty and define. His mistake lay in confusing what is true of something as such with what is true of it in a derived sense. This fallacy of the derived sense traps many people, even the cleverest, as Aristotle[46] says. For within anything we sense, as Aristotle[47] has proved, we must distinguish the composite thing itself—the whole which comes into and goes out of existence as such—from the form or rule it is exemplifying—which does not come into and go out of existence as such, but only in a derived sense. *For it is not house as such that is built, but particular houses.* Now things can be considered in abstraction from what does not belong to them as such, so that, considered as such, rules and forms are not what change, though they give form to things that change. So, Aristotle goes on to say, we can have sciences and definitions of them, and, as he proves, in order to have science of what we sense we don't need to know substances outside the realm of sense.

Now these rules that the sciences of things consider are

considered in abstraction from change, and therefore in abstraction from everything that accompanies change in changing things. Since all change is measured by time, and since no other type of change would exist unless there first was change of place, things, in order to change, must exist in a here and a now. And to do that changing things must be this and that individual by reason of matter having these or those particular dimensions. So the rules which give us scientific knowledge of changing things must be considered in abstraction from this or that particular matter and from anything consequent on matter's particularity; though not in abstraction from the general notion of matter, since the very notion of a rule or form is that of something giving shape to matter. Thus the rule or form of being human, expressed in a definition and providing us with the base for a science, abstracts from these bones and this flesh, but not from bones and flesh as such. And because the individual's rule or form includes this or that matter whereas the general's includes only matter in general, as Aristotle[48] says, the type of abstraction we are talking of is not said to abstract form from matter as such, but to abstract the general from the particular.

Rules and forms so abstracted can be thought of in two ways: firstly, in themselves, abstracted from change and from this or that matter, and this mode of existence they have only in our minds; and secondly, as rules determining things which are themselves material and changing, starting-points therefore for understanding those things, since all things are known through their forms. So this is how natural science, by way of unchanging rules abstracted from this and that matter, gives us knowledge of the changing material things that exist outside the mind.

Hence:

to 1: Only matter having these or those particular dimensions makes things individual, and even natural science abstracts from matter so considered.

to 2: The form of a thing that mind understands is its whatness: as Aristotle[49] puts it, the mind's object is the *what*. But what a composite thing is in general—a human being, for example, or an animal—involves matter in general, though not any particular matter, as Aristotle says.[50] So our minds in natural science abstract from this or that matter and any conditions consequent on thisness or thatness but not from matter in general, even if natural scientists consider such matter only as something formed. So even natural scientists are concerned primarily with form rather than with matter.

to 3: Natural science doesn't concern itself with the ultimate cause of movement as if that were part of its subject-matter, but as a limit towards which natural science is led. Now limits don't share the nature of what they limit but relate to it in some way, just as the end-points of lines are not lines but relate to them; and in the same way the ultimate cause of all movement differs in nature from natural things yet relates to them, inasmuch as they move under its influence. So that is the respect under which natural science is concerned with it: not in its own nature but as movement's cause.

to 4: A science is about things in two different senses: first and foremost it is about general rules basic to it as that science, but, secondly, it turns back, so to speak, to the things that obey those rules, and uses our bodily powers to apply the rules to particular things that exemplify them. For to the scientist his rule is both an object of knowledge and a means of knowledge. By means of my general rule about what constitutes a human being, I can make judgements about this or that human being. Now general rules don't change, so in that respect all science studies what must be so. But the things exemplifying the rules sometimes must be how they are unchangingly, and sometimes can be or not be and change; so it is in this respect that we talk of sciences of changing things that can be or not be.

to 5: Though the general doesn't change, it expresses a rule about things that do.

to 6: Though souls and other natural forms may be unchanging in themselves, they are involved in change incidentally. Moreover, as perfections of changing things they fall under natural science. And though the earth as a whole is stationary, that is only true by chance because it already occupies its natural place and is kept there by the same forces that would otherwise move it there; as indeed its parts move to their proper places when away from them. So the earth is subject-matter for natural science, both as a stationary whole and as having parts that move.

to 7: The vulnerability to change common to all creatures is not some natural tendency to change, but a dependence on God, without whom, if left to themselves, they would lose hold on existence. That dependence, however, is a subject for metaphysics rather than natural science. And though spiritual creatures can also change by choosing this or that, such change is a subject for divine rather than natural science.

[Article 3] The third question [**Does mathematics see the material things it is concerned with in an unchanging and immaterial way?**] we approach as follows:

It seems mathematics does not see things that exist in matter in an immaterial way:

For [1] since truth consists in a correspondence of mind to things it must be false to see things other than as they are. So if mathematics sees things that exist in matter immaterially, it will be false, and thus, since science is always of truths, no science.

Moreover, [2] Aristotle[51] says a science, in studying its subject-matter, must study every part of its subject-matter. But matter is a part of anything existing in matter. So a science can't study things existing in matter without studying matter.

Moreover, [3] straight lines constitute a single species. Now mathematics when considering straight lines counts them, talking of three-sided and four-sided figures. So it treats lines as many individuals of one species. But what distinguishes individuals of a common species is their matter, as we saw earlier.[52] So mathematicians consider matter.

Moreover, [4] no science that abstracted altogether from matter could argue from material causes. But certain proofs in mathematics appeal to causes which can only be material, as when something about a whole is proved from its parts, for, as Aristotle[53] says, parts are the material of wholes. Thus he[54] calls the proof that the angle in a semicircle is a right-angle because each part of it is a semi-right-angle a proof by material causes. So mathematics can't abstract from matter altogether.

Moreover, [5] movement can't exist outside of matter. But mathematicians must consider movement, since movements are measured across space intervals, so that the same rules and science are involved in measuring movement as in measuring space, which is mathematics' business. Mathematics then can't altogether refrain from considering matter.

Moreover, [6] astronomy, and the sciences of moving spheres, of weights, and of music, are all parts of mathematics, and in all of them we consider change and changing things. So mathematics is not entirely abstracted from matter and change.

Moreover, [7] natural science's whole concern is with matter and change. But certain of natural science's conclusions are also conclusions of mathematics, as that the earth is round and at the centre of the universe. So mathematics can't altogether abstract from matter. If you say, it abstracts only from perceived matter, then on the contrary: Perceived matter seems to mean this or that particular matter, since the senses perceive things in their particularity. But all sciences abstract from that, so mathematics shouldn't be called any more abstract than the other sciences...

But against that:

[1] Aristotle says the opposite.[55]

Moreover, [2] there are things existing in matter into the definition of which matter doesn't enter, as, for example, concavity, which contrasts with snubness in this regard. Now philosophy has to consider everything that exists. So some part of philosophy must consider such things, and in the absence of any other it must be mathematics.

Moreover, [3] what the mind grasps first can be thought without whatever comes along later. Now mathematical objects are prior to things in matter and change, which, as Aristotle points out,[56] add something to mathematical objects. So mathematics can consider things without considering matter and change.

In reply:

For clarity on this point we need to consider how our minds abstract. Now we know that Aristotle[57] distinguishes two ways of exercising understanding: so-called *simple intuition*, knowing what something is; and *making connections and disconnections*, forming affirmative or negative propositions. This doubleness in our activity answers to a doubleness in things: for on the one hand a thing has its nature—that which gives what we are understanding a place in the hierarchy of being, whether it be something whole and complete in itself or a part or a supervening attribute of such a whole; and on the other hand it has its existence—that which in composite things results from the components coming together, but in non-composite things accompanies the non-composite nature as such.

Now, because truth of understanding is a matter of conforming to how things are, clearly this second way of understanding cannot with truth abstract what in fact is joined, because such abstraction would be saying a disjunction really existed in the thing. Thus, were I to abstract being human from whiteness by saying 'The human being is not white', I would be saying such a disjunction existed in fact; so that if in fact the human being *was* white my understanding of the situation would be false. This second way of understanding then can abstract with truth only what is disjoined in fact, as when we say 'The human being is not a donkey'.

However, our first way of understanding can abstract what is not in fact disjoined: not in all cases, but in some. For since, as Aristotle[58] says, it is what gives things actuality that makes them understandable, we understand a thing's nature—what it *is*—either as itself actuality (e.g. non-composite substances and forms as such), or through what gives it actuality (as composite substances through their forms), or through something mimicking that role (so that we understand unformed matter as an *ability* to be formed, and empty space as *lack* of an occupant). In every case we know the nature by what gives it definition. So when what gives definition to a nature and lets us understand it relates to and depends on some other factor, clearly we can't understand that nature without that other factor. Sometimes the nature and factor are joined—either as part to whole (thus feet can't be understood outside of animals, since what makes feet feet depends on what makes animals animals), or as form to the material it shapes (whether that shaping constitutes some whole, or merely adds a supervening attribute like snubness, which can't be understood outside of noses); but sometimes the factor is in some separate thing (as with fatherhood, which can't be understood without sonship, though the two relationships belong in different things). If, however, what gives definition to a nature does not depend on some factor, we can abstract it from this factor, understanding one without the other, and this we can do whether they be disjoined in fact (human being and rabbit), or joined as part to whole (letters can be understood separately from their syllable and animals without their feet, but not vice versa), or joined as form to material or as supervening attribute to underlying subject (whiteness can be understood separately from being human, and vice versa).

So we have two ways of making distinctions corresponding to our two ways of understanding things: when making connections and disconnections we distinguish *A* from *B* by understanding it to exist outside of *B*, but when understanding what things are we distinguish *A* from *B* by understanding what *A* is without having to understand *B* at all, whether *B* exists joined to *A* or separate from it. So only the first way of distinguishing things can properly be called 'disjunction'; the second is rightly called 'abstraction', though only if the two things understood apart from one another are in reality joined (understanding animals without understanding stones is not called 'abstracting' animality from stoneness).

So now, since only what is in reality joined can properly speaking be abstracted, we have two sorts of abstraction corresponding to the two sorts of joining just mentioned (part and whole, form and material), in one of which we abstract form from material, and in the other a whole from its parts.

The forms some material takes on can be abstracted from it only if they can be defined independently of it, not if their definition depends on the material. Now every supervening property of a substance is a form that substance takes on, depending on the substance for its definition; so such forms can't be separated from the substance. Nevertheless, such properties supervene on the substance in an order: first comes its muchness [its bulk quantity], then its suchness [its qualities], and then the changes it is susceptible to. As a result substances—the material—can be understood as having muchness before they are understood as having the perceptible qualities which make them into *perceptible* material. Quantity, therefore, does not depend for its definition on material-as-perceptible but only on material-as-thinkable: namely, substance without its supervening properties, which is something only thought can comprehend, and to which our senses cannot penetrate. Mathematics is the science of objects abstracted in this way, and considers only quantity in things and whatever accompanies quantity: shapes and the like.

Wholes too cannot be abstracted from every sort of part. For wholes depend for their definition on certain parts: namely, when being this whole consists precisely in having these components (as syllables need letters, for example, and compounds elements). Such component parts are called specifying or constitutive parts, and a whole cannot be understood without them since they form part of its definition. But some parts merely supervene on the whole as such: the two semicircles in a circle, for instance, for how you divide a circle into such parts—equal or unequal, two or more—is irrelevant to its circularity. This contrasts with a triangle, where the three lines don't supervene but constitute the triangle a triangle. In the same way it is constitutive of human beings that they have reasoning souls and bodies composed of all four elements, and we can't understand human being without such parts: they define being human, as specifying or constitutive parts. But fingers, feet, hands, and the like supervene on what we understand being human to be: they do not define being human, and human beings can be understood without them. Whether it has feet or not, whatever is composed of a reasoning soul and a body chemically combining elements in just the way needed to take on a reasoning soul as its form is a human being. Parts that don't define the whole, but are rather defined by it, we call *material parts*, and all parts in their here-and-now particularity—this soul, that body, this bone, and so on—are related to human being in this way. Such parts are parts essential to Socrates or Plato but not to human being as human being. So from such parts we can abstract the idea of human being, and that is how universals are abstracted from particulars.

The mind then abstracts in two ways. One corresponds to the way form is joined to material or supervening property to underlying subject, and abstracts [mathematical] forms from perceptible material. The other corresponds to the way whole is joined to part, and abstracts universals from particulars, abstracting some nature as a whole in its own definiteness abstracted from all non-constitutive, supervening parts.

We don't find the opposite abstractions of parts from wholes or material from its form. For parts are either material parts into whose definition the whole enters, and then they can't be mentally abstracted from the whole; or constitutive parts which can exist outside of their whole, as lines can outside triangles, letters outside syllables, and elements outside compounds, and when things can exist apart we don't use abstraction but disjunction. In the same way we don't talk of abstracting a form from its material if the form gives the material its substance, for such a form and its corresponding material are mutually dependent: they can't be understood without each other since they are the actualizing and the potentiality of one and the same thing. Rather we are talking of the supervening form of quantity or shape. Now material-as-perceptible can't be mentally abstracted from such a form, since we can't understand something having perceptible qualities unless we first understand it to have quantity, can't understand colour except in a surface; nor can we think of something as subject to change without thinking of it as extended. Substance itself, however, material-as-thinkable, can *exist* without extension; so that to think it without quantity is rather a sort of disjunction than an abstraction.

So we can use our minds to make distinctions in three ways. Firstly, by making connections and disconnections, and this is properly called *disjunction* and characterizes divine science or metaphysics. Secondly, when articulating what things are, by abstracting form from material-as-perceptible, and this is characteristic of mathematics. And thirdly, when doing the same thing, by abstracting a universal from particulars, and this is common to all sciences, even physics, since all sciences lay aside what is irrelevant and attend only to what is essential. It is because certain people didn't understand how different the last two are from the first that they fell into error, adopting the Pythagorean and Platonist opinion that mathematical objects and universals were things outside the realm of sense.

Hence:

to 1: When he abstracts a mathematician doesn't see things other than as they are. For he doesn't think lines exist apart from matter-as-perceptible, but only considers lines and their attributes without considering their perceptible material. His mind hasn't ceased to correspond with things, because even in things a line's nature doesn't depend on what makes material perceptible, but rather the reverse. Obviously then, to quote Aristotle,[59] *to abstract is not to lie.*

to 2: The word *material* is used not only of things of which matter is a part, but also of things existing in matter, and it is in this sense that the lines we perceive are called material. Now that doesn't prevent lines being understood without matter, for matter-as-perceptible is not part of lines, but a subject in which they exist; and this is the case with surfaces and solid bodies too. For mathematicians don't think of solid bodies as substances, composed of matter and form, but as three-dimensional objects in the genus of quantity, related to the body that exists as a substance with physical matter as a part of it, as a supervening property to its subject.

to 3: The material in things can't numerically differentiate them unless it itself is first divided into many parts which, by all taking on the same form, become many individuals of the same species. But material can't be so divided unless quantitative extension is presupposed in it, and without that all substances would stay indivisible. So the basic reason for individuality within a common species is quantitative extension. Quantitative extension is capable of this because it includes positioning—that is, order of part outside part—as its defining characteristic. As a result, even when quantitative extension is abstracted from its perceived matter by the mind, we can still imagine numerically different individuals of one species in it, as, for example, several equilateral triangles or several straight lines of the same length.

to 4: Mathematics abstracts from matter-as-perceptible but not from all matter. The quantitative parts from which we argue as from material causes are not matter-as-perceptible but parts of matter-as-thought, and that mathematics does consider, as Aristotle points out.[60]

to 5: Movement isn't of its own nature a quantity, but derives its quantitativeness from elsewhere when we divide movements up by spatial intervals or by division in the things which move. So movement is not part of the subject-matter of mathematics, but mathematical principles apply to it. And so by applying quantitative principles to movement a natural scientist can treat multiplicity and continuity of movement, as Aristotle shows.[61] And sciences intermediate between mathematics and natural science can measure movement, as in the science of moving spheres and astronomy.

to 6: The simple and its attributes exist, transformed, within the complex (for example, the characteristic qualities and movements of the elements are found within compounds), but what is proper to the complex is not found within the simple. As a result the more abstract a science is and the more concerned with the simple, the more its principles can be applied in other sciences. So mathematical principles apply to natural things, but not vice versa: it is natural science that adds to mathematics, as Aristotle[62] says, and not the reverse. That is why there are three levels of science about natural and mathematical objects: the purely natural sciences concerned with properties of natural things as such: e.g. natural science, agriculture, etc.; the purely mathematical sciences concerned with quantities as such: e.g. geometry with extension and arithmetic with number; and intermediate sciences, applying mathematical principles to natural things: music, astronomy, etc. Because such sciences treat nature as a sort of material underlying a mathematical form, they are nearer to mathematics than natural science: music, for example, considers sounds as numerical ratios rather than sounds, and other sciences do likewise. As a result they prove conclusions about natural things starting from mathematical ideas. Such sciences then share with natural science its study of perceptible matter, but share with mathematics its abstractness.

to 7: These intermediate sciences we are discussing consider the same material as natural science but not the same form. So nothing stops them proving the same conclusions, but not with the same arguments, except in so far as sciences interpenetrate and sometimes use each other's methods. Thus natural science proves the earth round by the way heavy objects move [towards a centre] whilst astronomy proves it by considering [the round shape of] lunar eclipses . . .

[**Article 4**] The fourth question [**Is divine science concerned with immaterial, unchanging things?**] we approach as follows:

It doesn't seem divine science is concerned with things separated off from matter and change:

For [1] divine science seems to be concerned above all with God. But, as Paul in Romans 1 [20] says, God we can come to know only through such effects of his as we can see, because they exist in changing matter. So divine science cannot abstract from matter and change . . .

Moreover, [5] divine science—as we are calling the third branch of theoretical science—is identical with metaphysics, the subject-matter of which is being, and principally being-a-substance, as Aristotle makes clear.[63] But neither being nor substance abstracts from matter, for then no being could contain matter. So divine science does not abstract from matter.

Moreover, [6] Aristotle[64] says a science when considering its subject-matter must consider every part and property of that subject-matter. So since the subject-matter of divine science is being, as we have just said, it must consider anything that is in being. Now there is a sense in which matter and change are in being. So metaphysics must consider them, and divine science cannot abstract from them.

Moreover, [7] Ibn Rushd, commenting on Aristotle's *Physics*,[65] tells us that divine science appeals in its proofs to three kinds of cause: agents, forms, and goals. But, as Aristotle[66] has remarked, you can't think agents or goals without thinking change, and mathematics, in its proofs, appeals to neither kind of cause precisely because it studies unchanging objects. So divine science doesn't abstract from change.

Moreover, [8] theology has things to say about the creation of heaven and earth, and human action, and many other things that involve matter and change. So theology, it seems, doesn't abstract from matter and change.

But against that:

[1] Aristotle[67] says *first philosophy is concerned with things separable* (i.e. from matter) *and unchanging*, and in the same place says first philosophy is divine science. So divine science abstracts from matter and change.

Moreover, [2] the noblest science must deal with the noblest beings. If then divine science is the noblest science, and immaterial, unchanging beings are the noblest beings, divine science must be about them.

Moreover, [3] Aristotle[68] says divine science deals with

ultimate principles and causes. Now these are immaterial and unchanging; so that's what divine science must be about.

In reply:

To be clear on this point consider what science can claim divine status. We know that every science must treat the beginnings of its subject-matter, since, as Aristotle[69] makes clear, a science is incomplete unless it knows its own beginnings.

Now there are two sorts of beginnings. Some are things complete in their own right, yet originating other things: the heavenly bodies, for example, somehow originate bodies here below, and elements start off compounds. These then science considers in both roles: as beginnings, and as things in themselves; and so they are studied not only in the science concerned with the things they originate, but also in a separate science devoted to them themselves. Thus a special branch of natural science is devoted to heavenly bodies over and above the branch that deals with bodies here below, and a special branch deals with elements over and above that dealing with compounds. But other sorts of beginning are not things complete in their own right, but simply the starting-off points for other things, in the way unity starts number off, and points lines, and form and matter the bodies of physics: and such beginnings are treated only in the sciences of the things they start off.

Now just as in any particular genus of being there are beginnings common to everything[70] in that genus, so also all beings, because they have being in common, have common beginnings that are the beginnings of all being. Ibn Sīnā[71] says beginnings can be common in two senses: predicably common, in the way what I call *form* is common to all forms, being predicated of each; and causally common, in the way the one sun originates all life. Now there are beginnings common to all being not only in the first sense—which Aristotle[72] calls common to all beings by proportion or analogy—but also in the second sense—since all things take their beginning from a certain fixed number of things, the beginnings of all supervening properties leading back to the beginnings of substances, and the beginnings of perishable substances leading back to imperishable substances, and so on up the rungs of a ladder till we are led back to certain beginnings of all beings. And because, as Aristotle[73] says, that which begins all being must itself exist the most, such beginnings must themselves be the most perfect and hence the most actual beings, with no or very little potentiality, since, according to Aristotle,[74] actual being is prior to and more potent than potential being. They must therefore lack matter, which is a potential to be, and lack change, which is the actualizing of something's potential to be. And such things are divine, since, as Aristotle[75] says, *if there anywhere exists something divine it must surely be in such a nature*, namely, immaterial and unchanging.

These divine things then, because they are at the beginning of all beings and yet are complete things in their own right, we can study in two ways: as the common beginnings of all being, and as things themselves. But because ultimate beginnings, though in themselves most knowable, are present to our minds *like the light of the sun to owls' eyes*, as Aristotle[76] says, our natural light of reason can penetrate to them only by way of their effects: and this, as Romans 1 [20] shows, is the way philosophers penetrated to them: *The unseen things of God have been clearly seen by understanding the things he has made*. So philosophers treat divine things only as the universal beginnings of things, in that teaching which lays down whatever is common to all beings, having as its subject-matter being as such; and that is the science they call divine science.

But there is another way of knowing such things, not as their effects reveal them, but as they themselves reveal themselves. And this is the way described by St Paul in 1 Corinthians 2 [11]: *No one knows the things of God save the spirit of God. We however have received a spirit not of this world but from God, that we may know*; and *God has revealed it to us by his spirit*. And in this way divine things are treated not simply as the beginnings of other things, but as they subsist in themselves.

So there exist two theologies or divine sciences: in one divine things are not the subject-matter of the science but beginnings of the subject-matter, and this theology philosophers pursue and also call metaphysics; in the other divine things are considered for themselves as subject-matter of the science, and this theology is the one taught us in holy scripture. Both are about things existing outside matter and change, but in two different ways corresponding to two different senses in which something can exist outside matter and change. In one sense things so exist outside that by definition they cannot exist inside matter and change, and this is the sense in which God and the angels are said to exist outside matter and change; in the other sense things by definition need not exist in matter and change, can exist outside them, but sometimes exist within them, and this is the sense in which being and substance and potentiality and actuality exist outside matter and change, not depending on matter and change for their existence as mathematical objects do, which can exist only within matter although they can be understood abstracted from matter-as-perceptible. Philosophical theology takes as its subject-matter things outside in this second sense, and treats things outside in the first sense as beginnings of its subject-matter. But the theology of sacred scripture takes as its subject-matter things outside in the first sense, though it treats too of certain changing things existing within matter in so far as the revelation of divine things requires it.

Hence:

to 1: Whatever science uses only to illustrate something else is not as such the subject-matter of the science but something extraneous. This is the way natural science uses mathematical ideas, and there is no reason why divine science shouldn't include certain material and changing things in the same way...

to 5: Being and substance are said to be outside matter and change, not because they are defined to be outside matter and change (as donkeys are defined to be without reason), but because they are not defined to be inside matter and change, even if sometimes they are (as being animal abstracts from reason even though one type of animal is rational).

to 6: A metaphysician considers even individual beings, not as exemplifying this or that type of being, but as sharing what all beings have in common; and that is the way he considers even matter and change.

to 7: To act and be acted on entities must exist in fact, not just in thought. Now the abstract entities mathematicians think about exist only in thought, so that such entities, mathematically considered, can neither initiate movements nor end them. As a result mathematics doesn't appeal in its proofs to either agents or goals. But the objects divine science thinks about exist separate [from matter] in very fact, able to initiate movements and end them; so there is nothing to stop it using agent and final causality in its proofs.

to 8: Just as faith, which disposes us to accept theology's initial premisses, has as object ultimate Truth, though the articles of faith also include other things relating to creatures which touch on ultimate Truth in some way, so theology's principal subject-matter is God, though it touches a great deal on creatures as the effects of God or as relating to him in various other ways.

[Question 6] The next question for debate concerns the different methods of procedure ascribed to the theoretical sciences, and it raises four points:

Must natural science use reason in its procedures, mathematics discipline, and divine science intellect?
In divine matters should we abandon imagination altogether?
Are our minds able to scrutinize the divine form itself?
Can they do this by way of some theoretical science?

[Article 1] The first question [Must natural science use reason in its procedures, mathematics discipline, and divine science intellect?] we approach as follows:

[Query 1] It doesn't seem that natural science must use reason in its procedures:

For [1] logic is distinct from natural philosophy, and using reason is logic's characteristic. So it would be inappropriate to ascribe it to natural science.

Moreover, [2] in Aristotle's *Physics* logical arguments are often distinguished from physical or natural arguments. So using reason or logic is not characteristic of natural science.

Moreover, [3] we shouldn't characterize one science by what is common to all. Now all sciences reason: from effects to causes or from causes to effects or from symptoms. So that shouldn't characterize natural science.

Moreover, [4] Aristotle[77] distinguishes what is scientifically true from what is reasonable. Since natural philosophy is scientific we shouldn't characterize it as using reason.

But against that:

[1] We read[78] that reason concerns itself with bodily nature, and that is the main subject-matter of natural science. So it seems right to say it uses reason.

Moreover, [2] Boethius[79] says *reason, by addressing the universal, comprehends what is sense-perceptible and imaginable without using sense-perception or imagination.* Now comprehending the perceptible and imaginable is the work of natural science. So the use of reason is appropriate to it.

Further, [Query 2] it seems inappropriate to say mathematics uses discipline in its procedures:[80]

For [1] discipline seems to mean scientific learning, and that happens in every branch of philosophy, since philosophy proceeds by proof. So all branches of philosophy use discipline, and it shouldn't characterize mathematics.

Moreover, [2] disciplined learning seems easiest when things are most certain. Now the subject-matter of natural science seems more certain than that of mathematics, since we can perceive it with our senses, the source of all our knowledge. So disciplined learning is more appropriate to natural science than mathematics . . .

But against that:

[1] To use discipline is to proceed by sure and proven steps. Now as Ptolemy[81] says, *Only mathematics, if you examine*

matters closely, builds up in its students sure and stable beliefs by means of irrefutable proofs. So use of discipline is most characteristic of mathematics.

Moreover, [2] Aristotle in several places in his books calls the mathematical sciences disciplines.

Further, [Query 3] using intellect in its procedures doesn't seem appropriate to divine science:

For [1] according to Aristotle[82] intellect understands premisses and science knows conclusions. Now not everything in divine science is premiss, but some of it conclusion. So it is not appropriate to say divine science uses intellect.

Moreover, [2] you cannot use intellect on things which transcend all intellectual understanding. Now pseudo-Dionysius[83] and Aristotle[84] both say that divine things transcend intellectual understanding. So they cannot be approached with intellect...

Moreover, [4] theology concerns itself principally with matters of faith, and intellectual understanding is faith's goal, as a textual variant of Isaiah says: 'unless you believe you will not understand'. So intellectual understanding of the divine is a characteristic of theology's goal rather than of its procedures.

But against that:

[1] We read[85] that *with intellect we know created spirits and with intelligence God himself*. But these are the principal subject-matter of divine science, so that use of intellect seems characteristic of that science.

Moreover, [2] the approach of a science should be fitted to its subject-matter. Now things divine are things intellectually understandable of their very nature. The appropriate approach for divine science is thus to use intellect.

In reply to Query 1 [Must natural science use reason in its procedures?]:

A procedure of science can be said to use reason in three senses.

Firstly, because of its starting-point. A proof that bases itself on notions reason has elaborated—logical concepts like 'genus' and 'species' and 'opposite' and suchlike—uses logic or reason in the sense of using logic's teachings, propositions derived from logic, in another science. Such an approach cannot suitably characterize any particular science, which is at fault when it overlooks what is peculiar about its subject-matter. It is only proper and suitable in logic and metaphysics, which are both general sciences, having a sort of shared subject-matter.

In another sense, a procedure can be said to use reason because of its ultimate destination. All reasoned enquiry reaches its ultimate destination when it so understands its starting-point that it can see the truth of its conclusions broken down in that starting-point. A procedure that reaches this destination is called not simply a reasonable proof but a demonstrative [or apodeictic] one. But sometimes reasoned enquiry fails to reach that destination, and comes to a stop when the enquiry is still at a crossroads; that happens when our reasoning is only 'probable', sufficient to ground opinions or belief but not scientific knowledge. Such a procedure we call a reasonable proof rather than a demonstrative one. And any science can use reason in this way, since proofs of a truth's probability prepare the way for proofs of its necessity. It is yet another way of using logic within the demonstrative sciences, not now logic's teachings but its methods.

In both the senses above reason means the science of reason, for as Ibn Rushd[86] points out they are ways we employ logic, the science of reason, in the demonstrative sciences. But there is a third sense of using reason in which reason means our native ability to reason: namely, using reason's characteristic way of knowing things, and such use of reason is characteristic of natural science. For the approach of natural science uses reason's characteristic way of proceeding in two respects. Firstly, just as reason starts from things our senses see, most knowable to us, and comes to know things our intellects see, most knowable in their own natures, so natural science, as Aristotle[87] makes clear, starts from what is more knowable to us and less knowable in its own nature, using proofs from symptoms and effects. Secondly, reason characteristically argues from one thing to another, and this is especially typical of natural science, in which we derive knowledge of one thing from knowledge of something external to it—knowledge of effects, for example, from knowledge of their cause—and do not simply argue from one idea of a thing to another idea of the same thing—as when we conclude something about human beings from their being animals. In the mathematical sciences we argue from the definitions of things, proving conclusions by appeal to formal principles, never deriving truths about something by appeal to something external to it but by appeal to its own definition; for even when we prove truths about circles by considering triangles (or vice versa) this is because we find the triangle potentially present in the circle (or vice versa). In natural science, however, there occur proofs from external causes which prove truths about one thing by appeal to another altogether external to it. So this characteristic of reason is especially typical of natural science, and makes natural science more suited to the human mind than any other. Natural science then is said to use reason not because it is the only science to do so, but because that approach is most characteristic of natural science.

Hence:

to 1: This argument understands *using reason* in the first sense, in which it is characteristic of logic and metaphysics but not of natural science.

to 2: This argument understands *using reason* in the second sense.

to 3: All sciences reason from one idea to another, but not all reason from one thing to another thing; that is characteristic of natural science and is the sense in which it is said to *use reason*, as we have said.

to 4: At that point Aristotle is identifying the reasonable with opinion, understanding using reason in the second sense above. In the same place he says that about things to be done, the subject-matter of ethics, we can only have reasonable opinions, because of their indeterminate nature. So from all that has been said we can gather that in its first sense using reason characterizes logic, in its second ethics, and in its third natural science.

In reply to Query 2 [Must mathematics use discipline in its procedures?]:

Mathematics is said to use discipline in its procedures not because it is the only science to do so, but because the approach is most characteristic of mathematics. Since learning means acquiring scientific knowledge from another, a disciplined learning procedure must lead to science, that is, to knowledge which is certain, and this is especially the case in mathematics. For mathematics lies half-way between natural and divine science and is more certain than either.

It is more certain than natural science because it abstracts from matter and change whereas natural science must deal with both. Because it must deal with matter natural scientific knowledge depends on a lot of things: on matter itself, on the forms matter takes on, on the dispositions previously in the matter, and on the properties that result when matter takes on a form. But when knowledge depends on a lot of considerations it is more difficult to acquire: Aristotle[88] says that the *more abstract* sciences are the more certain, *arithmetic, for example, more than geometry*. Again, because natural science must deal with things in change that behave irregularly, its knowledge is shakier, often predicting what is likely to happen but occasionally happens otherwise. And this is also why the more involved science becomes in individual cases—as in practical sciences like medicine and metallurgy and ethics—the less certain it becomes: partly because of the many more things such sciences have to consider if they are not to make mistakes, and partly because those things behave so irregularly.

Mathematical procedure is also more certain than that of divine science, because divine science's subject-matter is further away from what we can sense, where our knowledge starts: whether that subject-matter be immaterial substances about which we are insufficiently informed by what our senses tell us, or those attributes all beings have in common which are the most general of attributes and so the furthest removed from the particulars we sense. Mathematical entities like figures, lines, and numbers are things we sense and can imagine, and so the human mind, dependent on images, grasps those entities more easily and certainly than it can immaterial intelligences or even notions like substance or actuality and potentiality, etc.

Clearly then mathematics is easier and more certain than either natural or divine science, and much more so than other practical sciences; and for this reason it above all is said to use discipline in its procedures. And this was what Ptolemy[89] was saying: *The other two branches of theoretical science generate opinions rather than scientific notions: theology because of its hidden and mysterious subject-matter, physics because its matter is unstable and unclear. Only mathematics builds up in its students sure and stable beliefs by means of irrefutable proofs.*

Hence:

to 1: As we have said, all branches of science use discipline, but none as easily and certainly as mathematics.

to 2: Natural objects are the sort we can perceive with our senses, but because of their fluidity we can't be sure of them unless we are actually perceiving them. But of mathematical objects we can, since they don't change and yet exist in perceptible matter, and so can be both perceived and imagined . . .

In reply to Query 3 [Must divine science use intellect in its procedures?]:

Just as we say natural science's procedures use reason, because that science above all conforms to reason's way of acting, so we say divine science's procedures use intellect, because that science above all conforms to intellect's way of acting. Reason differs from intellect like the many from the one: or as Boethius[90] says: *the relation of reason to intellect is like that of time to eternity or a circle to its centre.* For the characteristic of reason is to explore many matters and simplify them into a single idea. Thus pseudo-Dionysius[91] says *our minds are rational and fall short of the angels when they wander round exploring truths everywhere, though they match the angels in a sense when they turn the many into one.* Intellect, on the other hand, starts with a single simple truth and in considering that finds it knows a whole multitude of other things, as God by understanding his own being knows everything else. Thus pseudo-Dionysius in the same place says *angelic minds are intelligences, because they understand all they can understand of the divine with one and the same idea.* Clearly then reason when analysing ends in intelligence, simplifying many things into a single truth, and when synthesizing and discovering begins from intelligence, where many things are comprehended in one.

So that consideration above all is intellectual, which concludes all human reasoning. Now the whole of reason's analysis pursued throughout the sciences concludes with the considerations of divine science. For sometimes as we have already said reason argues from one thing to another thing really distinct from it, as when things are proved by appealing to their causes or their external effects: synthesizing when we move from cause to effect, analysing in a sense when we move from effects to cause, since causes are simpler and more constant and stably lasting than their effects. And the ultimate conclusion of such analysis in this life is arrival at the simplest supreme causes which are immaterial substances. Sometimes, however, reason argues from one idea of a thing to another, as when we argue causes within the thing: synthesizing when we move from the more general to the more detailed,[92] analysing when we move the other way, since the more general is simpler. Now what is most general is what is common to all beings; and so the ultimate conclusion of such analysis in this life is consideration of being as such and everything consequent on it. But these things—immaterial substances and what is common to all being—are the subject-matter of divine science, as we have said. So its considerations are the most intellectual.

It is also for this reason that divine science provides the starting-points for every other science, rational considerations having their beginning in intellectual ones; and as a result this science is called *first philosophy*. Nevertheless, because rational considerations have their end in intellectual ones, divine science is learnt after physics and the other sciences; and as a result it is called *metaphysics*—beyond physics—because analysis leads us to it after physics.

Hence:

to 1: We don't say divine science uses intellect as if it didn't reason from premisses to conclusions, but because its reasoning comes closest to intellectual insight, and its conclusions to premisses.

to 2: God exceeds the comprehension of all created intellects, but not of uncreated intellect, since he by intellect comprehends himself. But, as regards knowing what he is, he transcends every intellect in this life, though not as regards knowing that he is. And the happiness of the next life consists in also knowing what he is, seeing his very being. However, divine science is not only about God, but about other things that, as regards knowing what they are, do not transcend the human intellect even in this life...

to 4: Even knowledge through faith is above all a matter of intellect. For we don't acquire the things we believe by reasoned investigation, but hold to them by a simple consent of intellect. We say we don't understand them because our intellect hasn't full knowledge of them; that is precisely our promised reward.

[Article 2] The second question **[In divine matters should we abandon imagination altogether?]** we approach as follows:

It seems that in divine matters we ought to have recourse to imagination:

For **[1]** divine science has never been more ably communicated than in holy scripture. But scripture relies on imagination in divine matters, describing the divine to us in symbols our senses can grasp. In divine matters then we must have recourse to imagination.

Moreover, [2] only intellect can grasp the divine, which is why we said that in divine science we must use intellect. But, as Aristotle[93] says, *the intellect can't operate without images*. In divine matters then we must have recourse to imagination.

Moreover, [3] the divine is chiefly revealed through divine illumination. But, as pseudo-Dionysius[94] says, *the divine light can shine on us from above only if it is shrouded in a variety of sacred veils*; and by *sacred veils* he means sense-imagery. In divine matters then we must have recourse to imagination.

Moreover, [4] in dealing with what our senses perceive we must use imagination. But we acquire our knowledge of the divine by way of effects perceived by our senses: as St Paul says in Romans 1 [20], *The unseen things of God have been clearly seen by understanding the things he has made*. In divine matters then we must have have recourse to imagination.

Moreover, [5] knowledge must be regulated mostly by the starting-point of that knowledge: in the domain of nature, for example, by the senses where our knowing starts. But our intellectual knowledge starts from imagination, since, as Aristotle[95] says, *images are to our mind as colours to sight*. In divine matters then we must have recourse to imagination.

Moreover, [6] since mind uses no bodily organ, injury to bodily organs only prevents mental activity in so far as it is has recourse to images. But injury to a bodily organ, namely, the brain, prevents the mind thinking about the divine. So the mind when thinking about the divine is having recourse to imagination.

But against that:

[1] Pseudo-Dionysius[96] tells Timothy: *Timothy, my friend, to see mysteries you must leave the senses behind*. But imagination is restricted to what can be sensed, since, as Aristotle[97] says, it is *a change brought about in us by activity of the senses*. So, since it is thinking about the divine that most involves us in mystery, such thinking should not have recourse to imagination.

Moreover, [2] in any scientific thinking we should avoid what will lead us into mistakes. But, as Augustine[98] says, the first mistake in divine matters is trying to apply to the divine what we know to be true of bodily things. Since then imagination is concerned only with the bodily, it would seem that in divine matters we ought not to have recourse to imagination.

Moreover, [3] lesser abilities can't trespass on the speciality of greater abilities, as Boethius[99] explains. But we are told[100] that knowledge of the divine and the spiritual is the characteristic of intellect and intelligence. The same authority says that imagination ranks lower than intelligence and intellect, so it would seem that in divine and spiritual matters we ought not to have recourse to imagination.

In reply:

All knowing has a beginning and an end: it begins by taking in information and it ends with the judgement in which it fulfils itself as knowledge. All our knowing begins from sense-perception: what informs the senses informs the imagination—*a movement*, Aristotle says, *brought about by the senses*—and in us goes on to inform understanding, since what our mind tries to understand is [the world of] our images, as Aristotle[101] explains. However, where our knowing ends up is not always the same: sometimes it returns to sense, sometimes to imagination, and sometimes remains in the mind alone.

For when a thing's characteristics and attributes as perceived by our senses adequately express its nature, then our mental judgement of its nature must conform to our sense-perceptions. Everything in nature defined to contain perceptible matter is of this sort, so that natural science's knowing must end up in the senses, making judgements about natural things according to our sense-perceptions of them, as Aristotle[102] explains. In nature to neglect sense-experience is to fall into error, where by nature we mean the domain of things containing perceptible matter and subject to change both in fact and in the way we think of them.

But there are other things which we don't judge according to our sense-perceptions, because, though they exist in perceptible matter in reality, they are nevertheless defined abstracting from their perceptible matter; and judgements about anything are most cogent when they accord with how they are defined. But because such things are not defined abstracting from matter in every respect but only from matter as perceptible, and because, when we think away their perceptible qualities, something remains that can be imagined, our judgements of such things must accord with how we imagine them. Such are the objects of mathematics; so in mathematics knowing ends up not in the senses but in imagination, yielding judgements which transcend the information taken in from the senses. This is why judgements about mathematical lines differ on occasion from judgements about lines perceived by the senses: as, for example, that a straight line touches a sphere at a single point, something which Aristotle[103] points out is true of straight lines in the abstract but not of straight lines in matter.

There are yet other things which transcend not only the domain of sense but that of imagination as well, namely, things that don't depend on matter at all, either in reality or in our way of thinking about them, the knowing of which ends up in judgements conforming neither to imagination nor to sense-perception. Of course, we come to know such things by way of information that our senses and imagination provide, but we submit it to causal argument, deducing from effects causes that incommensurately surpass them, or to processes of transcendence and denial, abstracting from our ideas of such things anything that sense or imagination could take in. These are the ways put forward by pseudo-Dionysius[104] for coming to know the divine from what we sense. Knowledge of the divine, then, can begin with sense and imagination but cannot end there, as it would if we judged the divine to be like the things sense and imagination take in.

Now to have recourse to something is to end up with it. So in divine science we must have recourse neither to sense nor to imagination, in mathematics to imagination but not to sense, but in natural science even to sense. Hence those who want to proceed in the same way in all three branches of theoretical science make a big mistake.

Hence:

to 1: Holy scripture presents the divine to us in symbols our senses can grasp, not as a place for our mind to rest in, but as a place it can start climbing from, to immaterial things. For that reason, as pseudo-Dionysius[105] says, it presents the divine under even the vilest of symbols, to minimize the chances of our staying attached to them.

to 2: In our present state our intellect can't operate without images to start from, but that doesn't mean our knowing must always end up in images, in the sense of judging what we understand to be like what we imagine.

to 3: The authority quoted from pseudo-Dionysius describes how our knowing begins, not how it ends.

[to 4:][106] From the effects perceived by our senses we come to our knowledge of the divine in the three ways already mentioned, but this does not force us to make judgements about the divine modelled on how the effects themselves are perceived to be.

to 5:[107] This argument is valid only when the starting-point of our knowledge is adequate to lead us to what we seek to know, as sense-perception is in the domain of nature but not in divine matters, as we have said.

to 6:[108] Images are starting-points of our knowing not as starting off our mental activity and then passing away, but as staying there, underlying our mental activity, just as the starting-points of a proof must remain active throughout the deductive process. For images are the objects of our thinking, in which the mind sees what it is looking at either perfectly represented or negated. So when we are prevented from imagining we must needs be prevented from mentally knowing anything, even the divine. For obviously we can't understand God to cause bodies or surpass all bodies or lack bodiliness if we can't imagine bodies. However, this doesn't conform our judgement of the divine to our imagination. So, though in our present life images are necessary if we are to consider divine matters, we must never in such matters have recourse to our imagination.

[Article 3] The third question [**Are our minds able to scrutinize the divine form itself?**] we approach as follows:

It doesn't seem we can scrutinize the divine form itself, at least in this life:

For . . . [2] the divine form is the very substance of God. And since no one can see the very substance of God in this life, no one can scrutinize the divine form itself.

Moreover, [3] to scrutinize the form of a thing is to know it in some way. But pseudo-Dionysius[109] says that our mind can best be united with God when it knows absolutely nothing of him. So we cannot scrutinize the divine form.

Moreover, [4] as we have said, all our knowledge begins in the senses. But the things we perceive with the senses cannot adequately reveal to us the form of the divine, nor indeed that of any other immaterial substance. So we can't scrutinize the divine form itself.

But against that:

[1] St Paul in Romans 1 [20] says that *the unseen things of God, his eternal power, and his godhead have been clearly seen from the creation of the world*, i.e. by man, *by understanding the things he has made*. But God's form is precisely his godhead. So the very form of God can be known by our understanding in some manner.

Moreover, [2] the gloss[110]—quoting Gregory—says: *Unless a man somehow saw it*, namely, the truth of God, *he couldn't feel he didn't see it*. But we feel we can't perfectly see the divine substance. So somehow we must see it.

Moreover, [3] pseudo-Dionysius[111] tells us that *the human spirit learns to expand through what it can see to heights outside this world*, which are nothing else than the immaterial forms themselves. So in some way we can know immaterial forms.

In reply:

There are two ways of knowing: knowing *that* and knowing *what*. We know *what* something is when we understand the essence of it—what makes it what it is—either directly, or [indirectly] by way of something that sufficiently displays what it essentially is. Now during this life our understanding can't directly take in what makes God God or what makes immaterial substances like angels angels, since what we understand directly are images: *images are to understanding as colours are to sight*, Aristotle[112] says. So we can directly conceive what something is when our senses grasp it, but not when only the mind can grasp it. That is why pseudo-Dionysius[113] says *we lack ability directly to contemplate the invisible*. However, the natures of certain invisible things—what they are—are perfectly expressed in the natures of things sensed *as known*, and so, indirectly, we *can* know what such things are. Thus because we know what it is to be human and what it is to be animal the relationship between the two becomes clear enough for us to know what a genus is and what a species. But the natures of things sensed cannot sufficiently express what God is or what immaterial beings are, since these beings are not in the same natural genus; indeed words like 'what' have hardly the same meaning used of things we can see and things we can't. That is why pseudo-Dionysius[114] calls analogies for immaterial substances drawn from objects we sense *unlike likenesses that mean one thing here and another thing there*. So analogy from substances we sense can't lead us to know immaterial ones sufficiently well; and neither can causal argument, since any effects such substances produce here below fall short of their causes' full potential and so cannot reveal to us their essential nature.

During this life then we have no way of knowing what these immaterial substances are, either by natural knowledge or by revelation, since, as pseudo-Dionysius[115] says, *the ray of divine revelation reaches us in our mode*. Revelation raises us to know things we otherwise wouldn't, but we don't know them in any other way than through what we sense—

as pseudo-Dionysius[116] says: *the divine ray can only enlighten us when veiled around with many sacred veils*—and through what we sense we can never reach an adequate knowledge of what immaterial substances are. So we are left not knowing what such immaterial forms are, knowing only *that* they are, whether we know this by natural reason's arguments from created effects or by revelation's use of analogies drawn from what we sense.

However, we should note that to know *that* something exists implies some knowledge of what it is, if not perfect knowledge then at least the kind of vague knowledge Aristotle[117] says we have of what we want to define before we formulate its definition. If you know human beings exist and want to define them you must at least know how the phrase *human being* is used. And how could you do this unless you had some concept of what you know to exist even though you don't yet know how to define it: a concept composed of certain generic features of human beings, not yet specific enough, and of some of their surface properties. For knowledge of definitions, like proofs, must base itself on some prior knowledge. So knowing *that* God or any other immaterial substance exists implies some vague knowledge of *what* they are.

But now this can't be knowledge of generic features that aren't yet specific enough, since God belongs to no genus, not having what Ibn Sīnā[118] says is requisite for membership of a genus, namely, a *what one is* added on to one's existence. And though other created immaterial substances *are* in genera and share the same broad logical genus of substance with substances we sense, yet they are no more in the same natural genus than heavenly bodies are with earthly bodies: the perishable and the imperishable, as Aristotle[119] says, belong to different genera. For logicians consider concepts as such, and they can be applied now to material and perishable things, now to immaterial and imperishable ones; but the natural and divine scientists consider natures as they exist in things, and so where different modes of existence imply different modes of potentiality and actuality they talk of different genera. Furthermore, God has no extrinsic properties, as we shall see later, and if other immaterial substances do we don't know them.

So our vague knowledge of immaterial substances can't be based on generic features and surface properties. In such substances generic knowledge is replaced by knowledge through denials, as when we know them to be without matter, without bodies, without shape, etc. The more such denials we make, the less vague our knowledge is, for subsequent denials make preceding ones more determinate and precise, just as specific differentiations make the broad genus more precise. It is the same way in which we differentiate heavenly bodies from earthly bodies, mostly by denials, affirming, for example, that they are neither light nor heavy, hot nor cold. Again, in the substances we are talking about, knowing surface properties is replaced by knowing their relationships to the substances we sense, relationships of cause to effect, or of transcendence.

So then, we know *that* immaterial forms exist, but instead of knowing *what* they are we know them through *denial, causality, and uplifting*, as pseudo-Dionysius[120] puts it. And this is how Boethius understands *scrutinizing the divine form itself*: not as knowing what God is, but as denying all images.

And this answers all the opposing arguments: the first group which had in mind perfect knowledge of what God is, and those against which had in mind the imperfect knowledge we have just described.

[**Article 4**] The fourth question [**Can they do this (i.e. scrutinize the divine form) by way of some theoretical science?**] we approach as follows:

It seems we can come to scrutinize the divine form through some theoretical science:

For . . . [2] there is a theoretical science which studies immaterial substances, namely, divine science. But a science that studies a substance must scrutinize its form, since we know things through their forms and all proof, as Aristotle[121] says, must start from *what a thing is*. So we can scrutinize immaterial forms by theoretical sciences.

Moreover, [3] the ultimate happiness of human beings, as philosophy sees it, consists in knowing the immaterial substances. For since happiness is whatever activity most fulfils us, it ought, as Aristotle[122] suggests, to be concerned with the most perfect objects of intellect. Now the happiness of which philosophers talk is an activity deriving from wisdom, since wisdom is the crowning strength and virtue of our most perfect ability, intellect, and that sort of activity is happiness, as Aristotle[123] says. So immaterial substances are understood by wisdom. But wisdom is a branch of speculative science, as we see from Aristotle.[124] So we can understand immaterial substances by way of theoretical sciences...

Moreover, [5] everything with a natural goal has built in to it beforehand the ability to attain that goal, and an inclination to pursue it; for natural movements start from within. But human beings have the knowing of immaterial substances as their natural goal, as both philosophers and saints declare. So they have built in to them by nature the beginnings of that knowledge. But everything we can come to know by naturally known principles falls under some theoretical science. So the knowledge of immaterial substances falls under some theoretical science.

But against that:

[1] Ibn Rushd[125] says that *to accept this position would imply either that theoretical sciences are not yet perfect since sciences which can understand immaterial substances have not yet been discovered (and this is the alternative if we don't yet understand those substances because of ignorance of some principles), or (if we can't discover such sciences because of some defect in our nature) the implication would be that people who could invent such sciences would be human beings in some quite different sense from ourselves. The first of these alternatives is improbable and the second impossible.* So it cannot be through a theoretical science that we understand such substances.

Moreover, [2] the theoretical sciences investigate definitions in which the essences of things are understood by dividing up some genus according to differentiating characteristics, and by inquiring into the causes and attributes of things which make a great contribution to knowledge of what the things are. But in the case of immaterial substances we can't know such things, because, as we have said already, they don't belong to the same natural genus as anything we know through the senses; and either, like God, they haven't a cause, or, like angels, their cause is most unclear to us, and their attributes are unknown to us too. So there can't be any theoretical science by way of which we might come to understand immaterial substances . . .

Moreover, [3] in the theoretical sciences we know the essences of things through definitions, where a definition is a phrase made up of a genus and differentiating characteristics. But the essences of immaterial substances are non-composite, and no composition enters in to what they are, as Aristotle and Ibn Rushd[126] make clear. So we cannot know such substances by way of theoretical sciences.

In reply:

In the theoretical sciences we always base ourselves on something already known, whether we are proving propositions or discovering definitions. For just as we draw knowledge of a conclusion from propositions previously known, so we come to know a thing's species through concepts of its genus and differentiation and causes. But we can't go on in this way for ever: that would spell the death of all science, its proofs, and its definitions, since *you can't bridge the infinite*. So all the considerations of theoretical sciences lead back to certain starting-points that human beings don't have to learn or discover, for then we would have to go on for ever, but have natural knowledge of. These starting-points are the self-evident premisses of proofs to which all proofs lead back, such as that *wholes are greater than their parts*, and the primary mental conceptions on which all the definitions in such sciences rely, such as being and oneness and so on.

But this shows that theoretical science can know nothing,

either by proof or by definition, unless it is reachable through these things we know naturally. But what human beings know naturally is what the natural light of our agent intellect makes clear to us, and the only way it can do that is by illuminating our images and making them actually understandable. For that is our agent intellect's function, according to Aristotle.[127] Now images are derived from the senses, so that, as Aristotle[128] explains, our knowledge of the starting-points referred to begins in our senses and our memory. As a result such starting-points cannot lead us outside what we can know from things our senses comprehend.

Now we have already shown that what immaterial substances are cannot be known through what we sense, though that such substances exist and have certain features can be known from what we sense. So no theoretical science can lead us to know what immaterial substances are, though theoretical science can prove they exist and show us their intellectuality and imperishability and so on. This also was Ibn Rushd's[129] opinion, though Ibn Bajjah had said the opposite, thinking that what the substances we sense are could adequately express what immaterial substances were. But, as Ibn Rushd[130] says, this is clearly false, for the word *what* means something almost completely different in the two cases.

Hence: . . .

to 2: Some things we know in themselves, and theoretical science throws light on such things by using their definitions to demonstrate their properties, as in all the sciences which show the 'why' of things. But some things we know not in themselves, but only by way of their effects. And if indeed an effect matches up to its cause, what that effect is can act as a starting-point to prove the cause exists and to enquire into what it is, from which we can then demonstrate its properties as before. But if an effect doesn't match up to its cause, then the effect can serve as a starting-point for proving that the cause exists and has certain features, but what the cause is will always remain unknown; and this is what happens with immaterial substances.

to 3: The happiness of human beings is twofold. There is an imperfect happiness in this life of which Aristotle is speaking, consisting in the contemplation of immaterial substances to which wisdom disposes us, an imperfect contemplation such as is possible in this life, which does not know what such substances are. The other happiness is the perfect happiness of the next life, when we will see the very substance of God himself and the other immaterial substances. But what brings that happiness won't be any theoretical science, but the light of glory . . .

to 5: There are built in to us beginnings which enable us to prepare for the perfect knowledge of immaterial substances, but don't enable us to attain it. For though human beings are inclined to their ultimate goal by nature, because of the goal's eminence they cannot reach it by nature, but only by God's grace.

Part II
Structures of Things in General

Passage 2
Being, Unity, Goodness, Truth

Source: Thomas's public disputations on Truth, 1.1–3, 21.1. Text from *Quaestiones Disputatae de Veritate* (*Opera Omnia*, Leonine edn., vol. xxii).
Date: 1257–8, first stay in Paris, aged 32–3.
Type of passage and how to read: Disputed question (see Introduction).

[Question 1] The subject for debate is **Truth.**

[Article 1] And in the first place we are asked: **What is truth?**

Being true it seems is just the same as existing:

For [1] Augustine[1] says *the true is what is*, but what is is what exists. Being true then is just the same as existing.

But it was said [by the respondent] that though they refer to the same thing they don't have the same meaning.

Against that: [2] what something means is expressed in its definition; now Augustine settled on *what is* as a definition of the true, after rejecting several other definitions. If then what is true and what exists are both definable as *what is*, they seem to have the same meaning...

Moreover, [6] things that aren't the same must differ in some way. But there is no way what is true differs from what exists: not in substance because what exists is in substance true, and not by added differentiations for then there would have to be some genus both share. So they are just the same.

Again, [7] if they weren't just the same, being true would have to add some further condition to existing; but being true is broader than existing, not narrower. Aristotle[2] shows this when he says we define truth as *saying what is is and what is not is not*, thus including in the true both what is and what isn't. Being true then adds no new condition to existing, and it seems the two are precisely the same.

But against that:

[1] useless repetition is tautologically trivial. So if being true and existing were the same, saying that what exists is true would be tautologically trivial, which it isn't. So they are not the same.

Again, [2] existing and being good are interchangeable, but being true and being good aren't: for example, that someone has unmarried sex may be true but not good. So being true isn't interchangeable with existing either, and they are not the same.

Moreover, [3] Boethius[3] says that in any creature *that it is differs from what is*. Now by things being true we mean *that* they are. So, in creatures, being true differs from *what* is. But what is is what exists; so in creatures being true differs from existing . . .

In reply:

In defining what things are, just as in proving things, we must be led back eventually to intellectually self-evident starting-points; otherwise both processes would go on for ever, spelling death to all science and all knowledge. Now Ibn Sīnā[4] says our first mental conception—the most known as it were to which analysis of all our conceptions leads us—is what exists. Consequently, every other mental conception adds something to what exists. But to what exists you can't add anything from outside as it were, in the way specifying differentiations are added to a genus, or supervening properties to a substance, since any sort of nature already is by its nature something that exists (and this is how Aristotle proves[5] that what exists names no genus). So adding something to what exists means expressing some way in which what exists exists not expressed in the word *existing*, and there are two ways in which this can happen.

Firstly, the way expressed can be a *special* way of existing. For existing can have different levels which correspond to different ways of existing and define different categories of thing. Thus, a substance is not some sort of generic existent differentiated by adding a certain nature, but the word *substance* expresses a certain special way of existing—namely, existing on its own; and other genuses likewise.

Secondly, the way expressed can be a *general* way attaching to everything that exists, either in itself or as related to another. In the first case the way can express something positive or something negative. The only non-relative positive thing found in every existent is its nature, which determines what we say exists, and as having a nature we call anything that exists a *thing*; for Ibn Sīnā[6] distinguishes being and thing by saying that being derives from the act of existing but the word thing expresses a being's whatness or essence. The non-relative negation that attaches to every existent thing is its non-dividedness, expressed in the word *one*, for to be one is to exist undivided [as an individual].[7]

Again if we take the second case, in which a way of existing attaches to each existent thing as related to another, there are two possibilities. One possibility is that the way of existing attaches to an existent thing as divided off from others, and that is expressed by the word *something*, in Latin *aliquid*, which is short for *aliud quid*, a some-or-other thing (so that just as things existing undivided in themselves are called one, so as existing divided off from others they are called something-or-other). The second possibility arises because of the ways one existent thing can agree with another, and depends on finding something with which everything can agree. Such is the [human] soul, which Aristotle[8] says *is in a way all things*. Human souls can both know and desire, and to express the way in which what exists is agreeable to desire we call it *good* (for as Aristotle[9] says *everything desires the good*), and to express the way in which what exists is agreeable to mind we call it *true*.

Now all knowledge is achieved by way of some assimilation of the knower to the thing known, an assimilation which causes the knowledge: thus sight is aware of colour because it suffers modification by the kind of the colour. So the first way in which what exists relates to mind understanding it is by harmonizing with it—a harmonizing we call the matching of understanding and thing—and it is in this matching that the formal notion of truth is achieved. So this is what being true adds to existing, namely, the conformity or match of thing and understanding, from which knowledge of the thing follows, as we have said. So that the existence of things precedes their being true, but knowledge follows on as a certain effect of their being true.

This allows us to define truth or being true in three ways. Firstly, by referring to that which precedes the *notion* of truth but provides being true with its basis: and this is the way Augustine[10] defined *the true* as *what is*; Ibn Sīnā,[11] *the truth of a thing* as *the possession of the existence established for it*; and someone else, *being true* as *the undividedness of existence and what is*. In a second way we define it by referring to that in which the notion of the true is formally achieved: and in this way *truth* was defined by Isaac[12] as *the matching of thing and understanding*; and by Anselm[13] as *rightness that only the mind perceives*—rightness here expressing a sort of matching; and Aristotle[14] said that we define the true as *saying what is is and what is not is not*. In yet a third way we define being true by referring to the effect that follows on from it: and in this way Hilary[15] defined *the true* as *revealing and making clear what exists*; and Augustine,[16] *truth* first as *that which shows what exists* and again[17] as *that which we judge lesser things by*.

Hence:

to 1: This definition of Augustine's defines truth by referring to its basis in things rather than to the matching of thing to understanding in which the notion of truth is realized. Or one might answer that when Augustine says *the true is what is* the word *is* here is not to be taken to mean the act of existing, but to be a sign of the mind constructing and asserting a proposition: so that it means *something is true* *when it is*, i.e. when we say of something that is that it is. So that Augustine's definition comes down to Aristotle's one previously quoted. And this gives us the answer to 2...

to 6: Being true differs in meaning from existing because there is something in its definition which is not in the definition of existing; but there is nothing in the definition of existing which isn't in the definition of being true. So they are distinguished neither in substance nor by any opposing differentiations.

to 7: Being true isn't broader than existing: for in a certain sense existing also applies to non-existents when non-existence is apprehended by mind. Thus Aristotle[18] says that there is a sense in which absence or lack of being can be said to exist, and Ibn Sīnā[19] too says you can't form a proposition about anything unless it exists, since what you are forming the proposition about must exist in mind. Clearly then whatever is true exists in a sense.

As to the arguments against that:

to 1: Saying that what exists is true is not tautologically trivial; not because the words *true* and *existent* refer to different things, but because one of them expresses something that the other doesn't.

to 2: Although having unmarried sex is an evil, yet as existing it can agree with an understanding of it, and in that way realize the notion of being true; so that being true is neither narrower nor broader than existing.

to 3: Saying *that it is differs from what is* distinguishes the act of existing from what is able to exist. Now the word *existent* derives from the act of existing, not from what is able to exist; so the argument is invalid...

[Article 2] And in the second place we are asked: **Is truth primarily something in the mind or something in things?**

And it seems In things:

For **[1]** being true, we said, is interchangeable with existing. Now things first exist in themselves and then in mind. So the same must hold of their being true...

Moreover, [3] whatever exists in something is determined by it. If then truth exists primarily in mind, our judgements of truth will be determined by how mind sees things and we will resurrect the mistake of those earliest philosophers who said that every opinion is true and contradictories can be true together, all of which is absurd . . .

But against that:

[1] We have Aristotle:[20] *Truth and falsehood are in the mind, not in things.*

Moreover, [2] *truth is a matching of thing and mind*; but such matching can only exist in the mind. So truth too can only exist in mind.

In reply:

When a word has a hierarchy of applications, what it first applies to is not necessarily the cause of everything else to which it applies, but is something in which the word's meaning is first realized to the full. Thus, *healthy* applies first to animals, for there the full meaning of health is first realized, even though medicine is called *healthy* as causing that health. So, since *being true* has a hierarchy of applications, what it first applies to is the thing in which the meaning of truth is first fully realized. Now the full realization of any change or activity occurs at its end. And the activity of knowing ends up in the mind—for the known must be taken into the knower in the knower's mode—whereas the activity of desiring ends up in things. That is why Aristotle[21] says our mental activities describe a sort of circle: something existing externally moves our mind, as existing in our mind it moves our desire, and our desire moves to attain whatever started the movement; and because as we said, *good* expresses the way everything that exists relates to desire and *true* the way it relates to mind, Aristotle[22] says that *good and bad are in things but truth and falsehood in the mind.* Things, however, are called true only in so far as they match up to mind, so that truth exists first in mind and only later in things.

But now note that things relate in one way to practical understanding [that directs behaviour] and in another to theoretical understanding [that pursues truth]. Practical understanding causes things and is the measure of what it makes; but theoretical understanding acquires knowledge from things, being changed by them in a certain sense, so that things are the measure of it. So clearly the things of nature, from which our mind draw its science, are the measure of the human mind, as Aristotle[23] says, but are themselves measured by God's mind, in which everything exists in the way a craftsman's handiwork exists in a craftsman's mind. God's mind then measures but is not itself measured, things in nature measure and are measured, and human minds are measured and measure not the things of nature but only things artificially made. The things of nature then exist between God's mind and ours and can be called *true* by matching either. What matches God's mind is called true in the sense of fulfilling what God's mind has laid down, as we see in the definitions of Anselm[24] and Augustine[25] and in the one quoted from Ibn Sīnā:[26] *the truth of a thing is the possession of the existence established for it*. What matches [human] minds is called true if it is intrinsically likely to cause true judgements, in contrast to things we call deceiving because, as Aristotle[27] says, they *are designed to seem something other than they are*. Since a thing's relationship to God's mind precedes its relationship to human minds, its truth in the first sense precedes its truth in the second; so, if human minds did not exist, things would still be called true in relation to God's mind, but if we were to think away both minds leaving things by themselves—an impossibility—truth would no longer mean anything.

Hence:

to 1: The foregoing shows that what is true is first true understanding and then the thing that matches it. In both senses what is true is interchangeable with what exists, but differently. When said of things what is true is interchangeable with what exists as subject and predicate: for everything that exists matches God's understanding, and is able to match human understanding to itself, and vice versa. But when said of understanding what is true is interchangeable with what exists outside the mind not as subject and predicate, but as condition and consequence, in that to every true understanding there must correspond something that exists, and vice versa . . .

to 3: The attributes of something are determined by it only when caused by it: light in the air, for example, because it is caused by the external sun, follows the sun's movements rather than those of air. In the same way truth in the mind, because caused by things, isn't determined by how the mind sees things but by how things are: for *statements*—and the understanding they embody—*are called true or false inasmuch as things are or are not so* . . .

[Article 3] And in the third place we are asked: **Does truth exist only in a mind making propositional connections and disconnections?**

And it seems not:

[1] For the true is what exists, seen as related to mind. But mind first relates to things when it conceives definitions articulating what things are. So truth is first found in minds doing this.

Moreover, [2] being true is a matching of things and understanding. But understanding matches things just as much when understanding what things are as when making propositional connections and disconnections. So truth doesn't exist only in minds making connections and disconnections.

But against that:

[1] Aristotle[28] says that *truth and falsehood exist not in things but in mind; and where simple understanding of what things are is concerned, not even in mind.*

Moreover, [2] he says,[29] *understanding simples occurs where there is no truth and falsehood.*

In reply:

Just as it is first understanding that is true and then things, so also it is first understanding as making connections and disconnections and then understanding as articulating what things are. For the meaning of true consists in a matching of thing and understanding, and matching presupposes diversity, not identity. So the notion of truth is first found in understanding when understanding first starts to have something of its own which the external thing doesn't have, yet which corresponds to the thing and can be expected to match it. Now when articulating what things are, understanding possesses only a likeness of the external thing, just as the senses do when they take in the appearance of what they sense. But when understanding starts to make judgements about the thing it has taken in, then those are the understanding's own judgements not found in the thing outside, yet called true judgements in so far as they match what is outside. Now understanding makes judgements about the thing it takes in when it says something about how it is or is not, and that we call understanding making connections and disconnections. Thus Aristotle also says[30] that *connections and disconnections are in mind, not in things*. So that is why truth is found first in understanding making connections and disconnections.

But as a consequence, in minds articulating definitions of what things are we find truth in a secondary sense. Thus definitions are called true or false because of some true or false connection [they imply]; the application of a definition to something it doesn't define, the definition of a circle, say, to a triangle; or putting together parts of a definition that can't be connected: defining something as a *non-sensing animal*, for example, where the implied connection—that some animal is non-sensing—is false. Definitions then can only be called true or false by reference to some connection, just as things can only be called true by reference to mind.

Clearly then being true applies first to the connections and disconnections made in understanding, secondarily to definitions of things that imply true or false connections, thirdly to things as matching God's understanding or able to match human understanding, and fourthly to human beings choosing truth, or giving a true or false impression of themselves or others by what they say or do. And words can be called true in just the same senses as the understandings they express.

Hence:

to 1: Although mind starts by articulating what things are, that doesn't give mind anything of its own to match against things; so truth in the strict sense isn't found there. And that gives us the answer **to 2**...

[**Question 21**] The subject for debate is **Goodness.**

[**Article 1**] And in the first place we are asked: **Does being good add anything to existing?**

And it seems it does:

[1] for things exist by nature, but creatures aren't good by nature but by participating [God's goodness]. So being good adds something real to existing...

Moreover, [4] as one can gather from pseudo-Dionysius,[31] good radiates itself and existence. So what makes a thing good is what makes it radiate. Now radiating is a kind of activity, and substances act by way of powers; so things are called good because of something added to their substance. Being good then adds something real to existing...

Moreover, [10] relationships are differentiated in kind by the term they relate to. Now being good relates to a determinate term, namely, that of goal; so being good is a particular kind of relationship. But any particular kind of existing adds something real to existing in general; so being good adds something real to existing.

Moreover, [11] being good and existing are interchangeable in the way being a human being and having a sense of the ridiculous are. Now despite the interchangeability, a sense of the ridiculous still adds something real to a human being, a property characteristic of human beings but supervening on what defines them. So being good adds something real to existing.

But against that:

[1] Augustine[32] says that *we exist because God is good, and because we exist we are good.* So it seems being good doesn't add anything to existing.

Moreover, [2] whenever one thing adds to another, really or notionally, one can be understood without the other. But you can't understand things existing without being good. So being good doesn't add anything to existing, really or notionally. To prove the link-proposition: though God can make more things than human beings can understand, he can't make something exist without it being good, because its very deriving from a good is good, as Boethius points out in *De Hebdomadibus*. And if he can't make it, neither can we understand it.

In reply:

One thing can be added to another in three ways.

Firstly, what is added can be extraneous to what it's added to, as white adds to body by being something extraneous to what body is.

In a second way, what is added can narrow or further delimit what it's added to, as being human adds to being animal, not because anything in humans is entirely extraneous to animal nature (for that would mean human beings aren't totally animals but only have an animal part), but because the notion of being human narrows down that of being animal, containing explicitly and actually things that the notion of animal contains only implicitly and as it were potentially (for being human involves a life of reason, whereas being animal involves life without saying explicitly whether that is a life of reason or not). And this narrowing of notion which being human adds to being animal has a basis in reality.

In a third way, what is added is entirely notional, in the sense that the notion of one includes something that isn't in the notion of the other, but of a conceptual rather than real nature, whether it narrows the notion it is added to or not. For being blind adds something—namely, blindness—to being human, but blindness exists not as a real entity but as an entity conceived by reason as a way of apprehending a lack. Being blind said of humans narrows what it's added to, since not all humans are blind, but said of moles it adds without narrowing.

Now in the first sense of *add* nothing can add to existing in general though one can add to particular forms of existing; for nothing in nature is extraneous to what constitutes existing in general though things can be extraneous to this or that existent thing. But in the second sense we can add to existing, since existing can be narrowed into ten genuses or categories, in each of which something is added to existing: not, it is true, any property or differentiation extraneous to what existing is, but a determinate way of existing with a basis in real existence. Being good, however, doesn't add to existing in this way since being good is divided among the ten genuses in the same way as existing, as Aristotle[33] shows.

So being good either adds nothing to existing or adds something entirely notional, for adding something real would narrow existing into some special genus. But because, as Ibn Sīnā says, existing is the first notion mind conceives, all other words must either be synonymous with existing (which can't be said of being good, since it is not tautologically trivial to call what exists good) or at least add something notional. So because being good doesn't narrow existing it must add to it something entirely notional.

But only two kinds of entirely notional additions are possible: negations or relations; for all positive non-relative notions signify things existing in nature. So then, to existing as first conceived by mind, being one adds an entirely notional negative (for being one means existing undivided), whilst being true and being good mean something positive and so all they can add is some entirely notional relationship. Now, according to Aristotle,[34] a purely notional relationship is one relating *A* to *B* when *A* does not depend on *B* but *B* on *A*,[35] for relation as such is a sort of dependence. We see this in the cases of knowing and known, sensing and sensed, for knowing depends on the known and not vice versa; so the relationship of knowing to known is real, but the relationship of known to knowing entirely notional, the known being said to have that relationship, according to Aristotle, not because it itself relates but because the other relates to it. And the same happens wherever there is a situation of measure and measured or perfecting and perfected. So what being true and being a good must add to existing is some relation of perfecting.

Now there are two things to consider in anything that exists: the nature that defines it, and the fact that it exists as something defined by that nature. So anything that exists can perfect in two ways. Firstly, it can perfect by way of its defining nature, and that is the way it perfects mind, for it doesn't enter mind with the existence it has in nature and yet mind takes in how it is defined. And this is the way of perfecting which being true adds to existing: being true, as Aristotle[36] says, is in the mind and everything existing can be called true in so far as it matches or is matchable to mind; and this is why when truth is correctly defined the definition includes a reference to mind. But there is another way in which what exists can perfect something, not merely by way of its defining nature but even with the real existence it has in nature, and this is the way a good perfects; for good is in things, as Aristotle[37] says. But in so far as the existence of one being perfects and fulfils another it relates to what it perfects as a goal; and this is why when good is correctly defined the definition includes some reference to its role as goal: thus Aristotle[38] says that *good is well defined by those who say it is what everything desires*. So first and foremost then a good is something that perfects something else by being its goal, though secondarily we call goods things that lead to a goal—namely, useful goods—and things that are natural consequences of a goal; just as we call healthy not only what possesses health but also what produces or preserves or gives an indication of our health.

Hence:

to 1: Because existing is something non-relative whereas being good adds the relationship of being a goal, a thing's own nature standing alone unrelated to anything else is enough ground for calling it existent, but not enough for calling it good. For just as in other types of cause the relationship of secondary cause depends on that of a primary cause which depends on nothing further, so with goals: secondary goals derive their relationship of goal from some ultimate goal which has that relationship of itself. This is why God's own nature, everything's ultimate goal, is sufficient ground for calling him good; but creatures' natures need to participate in God's relationship of goal before they can be called good. And to that extent we can say, in one way of talking, that creatures are not good by nature but by participation, thinking of the nature itself as notionally different from the relationship to God which gives it its character of goal and to whom it is ordered as to a goal. But in another way of talking we can say creatures are good by nature, inasmuch as their nature can't exist without this relation to God's goodness: Boethius' point in his *De Hebdomadibus*...

to 4: Although literally *radiating* seems to imply activity by an agent cause, broadly understood it implies any causal relationship, just as words like influencing, making, etc. do. So when we say good of its nature radiates, we shouldn't understand this to mean it acts like an agent but rather plays the role of goal, a sort of radiating that doesn't need any intermediate added powers. Being good implies radiating like a goal rather than agent activity because agents as such don't impose standards of perfection on things but simply initiate them, and also because agents radiate to effects merely a likeness of form, whereas goals radiate to things achievement of their whole existence; and that is what the notion of being good consists in...

to 10: Although being good refers to a particular kind of relationship, namely, that of goal, the relationship in question can attach to anything that exists, and doesn't posit any further reality in what exists. So the argument doesn't follow.

to 11: Although having a sense of the ridiculous is interchangeable with being a human being, it still adds something extraneous to human beings, in the sense of something not included in their definition. But nothing can add to existing in this way as we have said.

As to the arguments against that:

to 1: We concede that being good adds nothing real to existing.

to 2: But the second argument argues that it adds nothing notional either, so to this we say: understanding one thing without another has two senses. Firstly, it could mean understanding the statement that one exists without the other, and in this sense if mind can understand one without another God can make it exist that way: but existing can't be understood without being good in this sense (mind can't understand something to have existence yet not be good). But the second sense of understanding one thing without another is that of understanding a definition, in which one thing is understood without reference to another, in the way we understand animality without having to understand humanity and the other species; and this is the way existing can be understood without being good. But it doesn't follow that God can make things exist without being good, since making precisely brings the things into existence.

Passage 3
Actual and Potential Being

Source: Thomas's public disputations on the Power of God, 1.1. Text from *Quaestiones Disputatae de Potentia*, Marietti edn. (Turin, 1953), with corrections from the Leonine text in preparation.

Date: 1265–7, in Italy, aged 40.

Type of passage and how to read: Sections extracted from the summing-up (*corpus*) of a disputed question and from an answer to an objection (see Introduction).

Notes on translation: Power, potential, potency all translate *potentia*, which I often translate elsewhere as ability, since it derives from the verb *posse*, to be able. Act, actual, actuality translate *actus*; action, active, activity translate *actio*—both words deriving from the verb *agere*, to do.

. . . A thing's power or potential is its openness to some act or actuality, either the primary act of having form, or the secondary act of action. The way we commonly understand the word *act* suggests that originally it meant action—it is well-nigh universally understood in that way—and was later adopted to mean form, because a thing's form of existence determines its activity and goal. So things can have a double potential: an active potential of the act of activity (the original meaning of words like *potency* and *power*), and a passive potential of the primary act of form (a derived and secondary meaning of the words).

To be acted on things must have passive potential, and to act they must have the primary act of form. (The word *act*, as we said, though it first meant being active, has come to mean this primary actuality of having form.) So God, who is pure and primary act, must of all things be the most active spreading his likeness abroad, and so must of all things be the most powerful or actively potential source of activity.

... **to 10:** There can be something real corresponding to notions in our mind mediately or immediately: immediately when what mind conceives is the form of something existing outside the mind, of a human being, say, or a stone; mediately when the very act of understanding produces something which the mind reflects on, so that something real corresponds to what the mind is reflecting on only mediately, that is, by way of mind's own understanding of what is real. For example, our mind understands human beings, horses, and many other species all to have the nature of animal, and reflecting on that understands animal to be a genus. Now nothing real outside corresponds immediately to the notion of genus, but to the understanding which gave rise to the notion there does correspond some reality.

The case of the relationship of source which the notion of [God's] power adds to that of [God's] substance is similar: something real corresponds to it, but mediately, not immediately: for our mind understands creatures to have a relationship of dependence on their creator, and for that very reason—since it can't understand a relationship going one way without also understanding it going back the other way—it understands God to have a relationship of source; and this corresponds to reality, but only mediately since it arises from our way of understanding things.

Passage 4
Matter, Form, Agent, and Goal

Source: On the Principles of Nature (complete). Text from *De Principiis Naturae* (*Opera Omnia*, Leonine edn., vol. xliii).

Date: Probably from early days in Paris, 1250s, aged about 25.

Type of passage and how to read: A sort of student's vade-mecum, an introduction to causality, heavily dependent on Ibn Rushd's interpretation of Aristotle's teaching in *Physics*, 1 and 2.

[Matter]

[1] Some things are, while some things can be, but aren't. We say that what can be exists *potentially*, and what already is exists *actually*. But existence has two senses. The essential existence of things as substances—a human being being a human being, for instance—is existing (period!); but non-essential existence—a human being being white, for instance—is existing in a certain respect.

In both senses things can exist potentially: sperm and menstruae are potentially a human being, and human beings are potentially white. And we can call whatever exists potentially *matter* or *material*—whether its potentiality is to exist as a substance (sperm to be a human being), or to exist in some non-essential respect (human being to be white); though there is this difference: we call material with potential to exist as substance *material from which*, but material with potential to exist non-essentially *material in which*. Putting this another way, only what has the potential to exist as a substance is properly called *matter* or *material*, and what has the potential of existing in some non-essential way is called, strictly speaking, a *subject*. An indication that *subject* means what has the potential of existing in some non-essential way is that we talk of a subject's non-essential properties as inhering in it, but not of its essential form as inhering in it. Matter and subject differ in this way: of itself a subject exists completely, needing nothing more in order to exist (human beings don't depend for existence on being white); but matter exists incompletely of itself, needing something more in order to exist. So, strictly speaking, form gives matter its existence, whereas non-essential properties are given existence by their subject. But sometimes we use these words interchangeably: matter for subject, and subject for matter.

[Form]

Now just as anything potential can be called *material*, so anything that gives existence, be the existence essential or non-essential, can be called *form*: whiteness makes a potentially white human being actually white, and the soul makes sperm—potentially a human being—into an actual human being. Because forms make things actual, forms are called *actualizations* or *acts*: substantial form makes something actually exist as a substance, and non-essential forms make it actually exist in various non-essential modes.

And since the change that introduces a form is called *being generated*, there are two senses of being generated corresponding to the two senses of form: being generated (period!), corresponding to substantial form, and being generated in a certain respect, corresponding to non-essential forms. Introduction of substantial form we call coming to be (period!); but introduction of a non-essential form we call coming to be such-and-such, not coming to be (period!): when a human being turns white we don't talk of it coming to be or being made (period!), but coming to be or being made white. And to these two senses of being generated correspond two senses of decomposition: one strict, the other in a certain respect. Being generated and decomposing in the strict sense apply only in the genus of substance, but in the qualified sense they apply also in other genuses of being.

And because being generated moves from not existing to existing (decomposing moving in the opposite direction from existing to not existing), generation starts not from any sort of not existing but from a not existing which is potential of existence: statues are made from copper which is potentially a statue though not actually. So three things are needed for generation: something potential of existence—the material or matter, its lack of actualization—a lacking of being, and something to give it actualization—a form. When statues are made from copper, copper is the material potential of statue-form, its shapelessness or unworked state is the lack, and the shape of the statue is the form. That shape is not a substantial form, since copper already actually exists before it receives shape or form and does not depend for existence on the shape; like all artificial forms, it is a non-essential form, since art or artifice operates on material which already of its nature completely exists. [2] So there are three *principles* [or origins] of nature: matter, form, and lack of form; one, namely, form, is where generation is going to, and the other two characterize where generation comes from.

[Lack of form]

But matter and lack of form characterize the same subject in different ways: before form arrives the same thing is both bronze and shapeless but bronze for one reason and shapeless for another. Lack of form, then, is a principle not in its own right but incidentally, because it coincides with matter; just as doctors build houses only incidentally, since they build them not as doctors but as builders, doctor and builder happening to coincide in one subject.

But even what is incidental can sometimes be necessary and inseparable (as a sense of the ridiculous is to being human), and sometimes unnecessary and separable (as whiteness is to being human). And in this way, lack of form, though an incidental principle, is still necessary to generation, since the material must lack the form to start with; as existing under one form it lacks another and vice versa, as fire lacks that of air and air that of fire.

Note too that though generation starts out from non-existence we don't locate its origin in absence, but in lack; for absence doesn't imply a subject. Even things that don't exist can be said *not to see*—chimeras don't see, and things like stones too that aren't meant to see. But only things meant to see are called *blind*: lack implies some type of subject meant to have what is lacking. So because generating doesn't start from non-existence (period!) but from non-existence in some subject, and not just any subject but a particular type of subject—you can't generate fire from any non-fire thing but only from a non-fire thing open to being fire—it is lack[, not absence,] of form that we call the principle or origin.

Lack differs, however, from the other origins. The others are principles of being and of coming to be: for a statue to come to be you need bronze and, at the end, shape, two things still needed when you already have the statue; lack, on the other hand, is a principle only of coming to be, not of being: for while coming to be a statue it must be not-statue (otherwise it couldn't come to be, since only before-and-after things [like time] are their own coming to be); but once the statue exists there is no longer a lack of statue, since lack and having can no more coexist than is and isn't. Another difference, as we explained earlier, is that lack is a principle coincidentally, whereas the other two are principles in their own right.

Clearly then matter differs by definition from form and from lack of form, and can be understood as taking on either: copper can be understood to have shape or shapelessness. And sometimes the material's name implies lack of form and sometimes not: calling a statue's material bronze doesn't imply lack, for the word *bronze* doesn't imply any unworked or shapeless state; but calling bread's material flour does imply lack of the form of bread, for the word *flour* implies an unworked and unstructured state opposed to the form of bread. And because, in generation, the subject material persists whilst the lack and the complex of material and lack don't, material implying lack passes away whilst material not implying it persists.

[Ultimate matter]

But note that some matter is already formed: bronze, for example, though it is statue-material, is itself formed matter; it contains its own material and so cannot be called ultimate material. Only material subject to form and lack of form but having no particular form or lack of form in itself can be called *ultimate material* [first matter], because it presupposes no other material; and another name for it is *yle*. But since we define and know things by way of their forms, ultimate matter can't be known or defined as such, but only by an analogy, as that which relates to all forms and lack of forms as bronze does to statues and to shapelessness, and so is ultimate (period!). One might talk of matter ultimate in a particular genus—water, for example, as the ultimate liquid—but that wouldn't be ultimate (period!), for, being itself formed matter, it presupposes some matter.

Note that neither forms nor ultimate matter are generated or decompose, since all generation must start and end somewhere, starting from matter and ending with form. If matter and form themselves were to be generated, matter would need matter and form form without end. So properly speaking only things composed of matter and form are generated.

Note also that there is only one ultimate matter underlying everything. But a thing can be one by having a single determinate form—the way Socrates is one, but not ultimate matter since in itself it is without form—or by having nothing to make it more than one—and this is the way ultimate matter is one, because it is understood without anything that would make it more than one.

And note that although matter in its nature is neither formed nor formless (as bronze in its nature is neither shaped nor shapeless), it never exists stripped of form and lack of form, but sometimes takes on one form and sometimes another. By itself it can never exist for it has no form of its own and so—because actual existence comes with forms—matter by itself never exists actually but only potentially. Nothing actually existent then can be called ultimate matter.

[Agency]

[3] So now we have shown nature to have three principles: matter, form, and lack of form; but these are still not enough for generation to occur. For what potentially exists can't bring itself to actualization: copper is potentially a statue, but can't make itself into a statue: it needs a workman to draw the statue's form out of potentiality into actuality.

For the form too can't draw itself out of potentiality into actuality—and I am talking of the form of the thing generated, the end-product of generation, as we said—for the form won't exist until the thing is made, whereas the maker exists in the coming to be, that is, while the thing is coming to be. So besides matter and form there must be some active principle or origin, which we call the efficient cause or mover or agent, from which the change originates.

[Goal]

And because to be active, as Aristotle[1] says, what is acting must tend towards something, there must be yet a fourth thing towards which the agent tends, called the goal. Note that every agent, whether it acts by nature or by will, tends towards a goal, though it doesn't follow that every agent is aware of a goal or deliberates about it. Something that hasn't a fixed way of acting but can go either way—as willing agents can—must consider a goal and use that to decide how to act; but natural agents act in fixed ways and don't need to choose the means to their goals. Ibn Sīnā[2] gives the example of a guitar-player who doesn't have to think about every pluck of the strings because they are now second nature to him; otherwise he would pause between each pluck and ruin the sound. And since [the guitar-player] who acts by will is more likely to deliberate than things that act by nature, we can argue *a fortiori* that natural agents can tend to goals without deliberating, where tending towards is simply having a natural bias towards something.

[Principles, causes, and elements]

So now we see there are four causes: material, efficient, formal, and final. And although Aristotle[3] says the words *origin* and *cause* are interchangeable, in another place[4] he lays down four causes and three origins or principles. The causes he accepts are both intrinsic and extrinsic—matter and form being a thing's intrinsic, constitutive parts, whilst agent and goal are outside the thing and extrinsic; but as principles he accepts only intrinsic causes, and lack of form, which is not accounted a cause because, as we said, it is only incidentally a principle. What we call the four causes are causes in their own right to which all incidental causes lead back, since anything coincidental must lead back to something essential. And although here Aristotle calls intrinsic causes principles, strictly speaking—as Ibn Rushd[5] says elsewhere—principles are extrinsic causes, elements are intrinsic, constitutive causes, and both are called causes. But sometimes we use the terms interchangeably, calling all causes principles and all principles causes.

All the same, we seem to mean more by *cause* than we usually mean by *principle* or origin, for any beginning, whether followed by existence or not, can be called an origin. Thus we say the knife originated from the smith, meaning he was the source of the knife's existence, but also that a change from black to white originates in blackness (generally calling anything where a change starts its origin) though blackness is not the source of the following whiteness's existence. A beginning is only called a *cause*, however, if it gives existence to what follows, for a cause, we say, is that from the existence of which another follows. So a beginning where a change starts cannot of itself be called its cause, even it is called its origin; and that is the reason lack of form, which is where generation starts, is called an origin but not a cause. Though it can also be called a cause coincidentally, as coinciding with the matter in the sense explained earlier.

Elements, however, are strictly speaking causes which form part of a thing's make-up: material causes, then, strictly speaking, and again not every material cause but those which are part of a thing's ultimate make-up. Thus the elements of a human being are not limbs, since limbs in turn are composed of other things; but earth and water are called elements because they are not made up of further bodily components, but themselves ultimately make up all natural bodies. So Aristotle[6] defines an element as *what things are ultimately made up of, existing in the things, and indivisible in its own nature*. The first phrase—*what things are ultimately made up of*—is explained by what we have said. The second—*existing in the things*—is there to distinguish elements from the sort of matter that disappears during generation. Bread, for example, is material for blood, but to build up the blood you must break down the bread, so that bread doesn't persist in the blood and you can't call it an element of blood. Elements must persist in some way since, as Aristotle[7] says, they can't be broken down. The third phrase—*indivisible in its own nature*—is there to distinguish elements from things that contain heterogeneous parts differing in nature, like hands made up of flesh and bone (which differ in nature). Elements, however, don't divide into heterogeneous parts: every bit of water is water. For elements can be quantitatively divided into parts, as long as those parts are homogeneous; though sometimes elements are completely indivisible: letters, for example, are the elements of syllables.

So now we can see how a *principle* is something wider than a *cause*, and a *cause* something wider than an *element*; as Ibn Rushd says.[8]

[Mutual relations between causes]

[4] Now that we have seen the four classes of cause, note that it is possible for one thing to have many causes (copper and the craftsman both cause the statue, but the craftsman as producer, the copper as material), and for one cause to have opposed effects (a steersman can save or sink a ship by his presence or absence).

Note too that it's possible for one thing to be both cause and effect of another, though in different respects: walking is a productive cause of health, and health is sometimes the goal of walking and its cause in that sense; and body is material for soul, whilst soul is form of body.

Productive causes cause goals inasmuch as what an agent does realizes a goal, and goals cause productive causes inasmuch as the agent can't do anything except by tending towards a goal. So a productive cause causes the thing that is the goal—health, for example—but doesn't cause it to be a goal, doesn't cause the goal-causality of the goal, doesn't give it its goalness. For example, a doctor makes health actually exist, but doesn't give health its drawing power. Goals, on the other hand, don't cause the things that are productive, but do cause their productiveness. Health isn't what makes the doctor exist[9]—I am talking of the health his doctoring produces—but it does cause him to be productive. So the goal is the cause of the producer's causality, the cause of his productiveness. In the same way the goal makes material material and form form, since material only takes on form and form only makes something out of the material because of the goal. This is why the goal is called the cause of causes: because it causes the causality of all other causes.

Matter causes form inasmuch as forms only exist in matter; and similarly form causes matter inasmuch as matter can only actually exist under a form. As Aristotle[10] says, matter and form are correlatives, related as simple parts to the composite whole they together make up.

[Priority among causes]

But since causes as such are always prior in nature to what they cause, note that, because of the two senses of *prior* that Aristotle[11] distinguishes, something can be said to be both prior and posterior to one and the same thing, both cause and caused. For prior can mean occurring earlier in the temporal process of generation, or, again, ranking first in completeness of being. Because activity in nature moves from the incomplete and unachieved to completeness and achievement, the unachieved is prior to the achieved in the temporal process of generation, though the achieved is prior in completeness. So we say adults come before children in completeness of being, though children come before adults in the temporal process of generation.

But though unachieved potential precedes actual achievement in things that are generated—seeing that each such thing is first unachieved then achieved, first potential then actual—nevertheless, simply speaking, achieved actuality comes first, for the actual actualizes the potential and the achieved brings the unachieved to achievement. Matter precedes form in the temporal process of generation, because what takes on is prior to what is taken on; but form precedes matter in achievement, because matter is incomplete without form. In the same way, agent precedes goal in the temporal process of generation, since the agent initiates the movement towards the goal; but goal precedes agent (as agent) in completeness of being, since the agent's activity fulfils itself in the goal. So these two causes—matter and agent—are prior in the temporal process of generation, but form and goal are prior in regard to achievement.

Note too that necessity has two senses: absolute and hypothetical necessity. Absolute necessity results from causes prior in the process of generation: matter and agency; thus, death's necessity arises from matter and the inherent conflict between [its] components. And it is called absolute because nothing can stop it; and we also call it material necessity. Hypothetical necessity results from causes posterior in the process of generation: form and goal; thus, conception is necessary if a human being is to be born. And it is called hypothetical because it is not necessary (period!) that this woman should conceive, but only on the hypothesis that a human being must be born; and we also call it necessity for a goal.

[Coincidence among causes]

Note that three of these causes—form, goal, and agent—can coincide: when fire produces fire, fire is the agent cause (the producer), the form that realizes the potentiality, and the goal that the agent tends towards in which its activity is fulfilled. However, there are two senses of goal: the goal of production and the goal of the product: in the production of knives, for example, the goal of production is the form of a knife, but the goal of the product—the knife—is the knife's own activity—cutting. So the goal of production sometimes coincides with the other two causes: namely, in reproduction of species, human being reproducing human being and olive-tree olive-tree; but there can't be coincidence with the goal of the product. Note, moreover, that goal and form can coincide in the same individual, since the goal of production is the individual form produced; but agent can't coincide in the individual but only in species: maker and made can agree in species but can't be the same individual; when human beings produce human beings, one individual produces another like to it in species. Matter never coincides with other causes since it exists potentially and is by nature unachieved, whereas other causes exist actually and are by nature achieved; the achieved and the unachieved cannot coincide.

[Subdivisions of causes]

[5] Note that there are several ways of subdividing each of these four types of cause—agent, material, form, and goal.

For we distinguish primary and secondary causes. Thus the doctor and his skill are both agents of health, but skill is the primary agency and the doctor secondary; and the same distinction can be made in forms and in the other types of cause. Note that we should always press questions back to the primary cause: to the question 'What cured him?' and the answer 'The doctor', we should ask 'How did he do it?' and answer 'By his skill'. Note too that the distinction between proximate and remote causes is the same as this one, the proximate cause being secondary and the remote cause primary. And observe that the more general cause is always the more remote, and the more specialized one the more proximate: the proximate form of a human being is what defines him—a mortal animal with reason, his animality being more remote, and his substantiality still more so. For the more general is a form of the less general. In the same way copper is the statue's proximate material, metal is more remote, and body most remote of all.

Again, we distinguish inherent and incidental causes. The inherent cause is the cause of something as such: builders the agents of houses and wood the material of stools. An incidental cause is something coincidental to the inherent cause: a grammarian builder, for example, since a grammarian is an agent of buildings incidentally, not as grammarian but as builder—who happens to be a grammarian. And similarly for other causes.

Again, we distinguish simple and composite causes. A simple cause is a cause mentioned on its own, be it inherent or incidental: the simple agent of the house is the builder, or this doctor. The composite cause is both mentioned together: the agent is this doctor-builder. Or we can adopt Ibn Sīnā's explanation and say a simple cause is what can cause on its own, as copper without any additional material can make a statue, or doctors cure, or fire heat. But a cause is composite when several things are needed to cause something, as many men are needed to move a ship, and many stones to provide material for a house.

Again, we distinguish actual and potential causes. An actual cause is something actually engaged in causing, as a builder when building and copper when providing material for a statue. A potential cause is able to cause but is not actually engaged in doing so, as a builder when not building. Note that where actual causes are concerned cause and caused must exist simultaneously: if one exists so must the other; when a builder is an actual builder actual building must be going on, and vice versa. But this doesn't have to be so for potential causes.

[Generality and particularity applied to causes]

Note, however, that we compare general causes with general effects and individual causes with individual effects: builders are the cause of houses, this builder of this house.

[6] Note too that when talking of intrinsic principles like matter and form, whether they are the same or different is determined by whether what they are principles of is the same or different. For certain things are individually the same, like Socrates and *this man* (pointing at Socrates); others are different individuals of the same species, like Socrates and Plato, who are both human beings but different individuals; others differ in species but not in genus, like human beings and donkeys, which are both animals; others differ in genus and are only proportionately or analogically the same, like substance and quantity, which are different genuses of being, and the same only by analogy, for they share being, and that is not a genus and is attributed to things not univocally but analogically.

To understand this last point note that what is attributed to a set of things may be attributed univocally, equivocally, or analogically. It is attributed univocally if the same word is used with the same meaning or definition every time it is attributed, as when human beings and donkeys are both called animals: the same word *animal* is used with the same definition: a living thing endowed with sensation. It is attributed equivocally if the same word is used but with different meanings, as when something which barks and a star in the heavens are both called *the dog*: the word is the same but its meaning or definition is different (for the meaning of names is their definition, as Aristotle[12] says). It is attributed analogically if it is attributed to several things with different meanings but all having reference to some one thing, as when we call organisms and medicines and complexions all healthy: the meaning is not altogether the same, for complexions are called healthy as indications of health, organisms as subject to it, and medicines as causing it, but all the meanings have reference to the one health that is their goal. Sometimes the reference binding the meanings together analogically (in a proportion or relation or agreement) is to a single goal, as in the example just quoted; sometimes to a single agency, as when skilled doctors and unskilled old women and even their tools are all called *healing* by reference to the one agency of the healing art; and sometimes to a single subject, as when we call substances, quantities, qualities and all the other [Aristotelian] categories *beings*, for although quantity and the others are not beings in exactly the same sense as substance is being, still each of the others is called *being* because of its relation to substance as its subject. So being is attributed first to substance and only secondarily to other attributes, and that means being is not a genus comprising substance and quantity [and the rest]—since genuses are predicated equally of their species—but is attributed analogically. And that is why we said earlier that substance and quantity are different genuses, the same only by analogy.

So the matter and form of one and the same individual—of Tully and Cicero[13]—are the same individually; the matter and form of different individuals of the same species—of Socrates and Plato—are the same in species but differ individually; and in the same way the principles of things that are generically the same are themselves generically the same—the bodies and souls of donkeys and horses differ in species but are the same generically; and in the same way the principles of things that are only analogically the same are themselves only analogically or proportionately the same. Thus, matter, form, and lack of form, or potentiality and actuality, are the principles of all the categories—substance and the rest—but the matter of substance and of quantity, and their form and lack of form, differ in genus and agree only proportionately: as the matter of substance is material to substance, so also the matter of quantity to quantity. However, substance is also the cause of the other categories, so that substance's principles are also principles for every other category.

Passage 5

Substance and Accidents, Action and Passion

Source: Thomas's commentary on Aristotle's *Physics*, 3.3 (202^{a}22–202^{b}29). Text from *In Aristotelis Libros Physicorum*, 3.5 (*Opera Omnia*, Leonine edn., vol. ii).

Date: 1268, Italy, aged 43.

Type of passage: Commentary with digression (see Introduction).

How to read: With one finger on the commentary and one on Aristotle's text, which has been inserted, italicized, in short paragraphs. Aristotle's text has been translated in such a way that it can be compared on the one hand with modern translations of Aristotle's text, and on the other with the extracts Thomas quotes in his commentary.

After declaring that change is an actualization both of what is causing the change and of what is changed, Aristotle raises a difficulty: and first [at *This view has a dialectical defect*] he proposes the difficulty, and then, at *It is not absurd*, he solves it.

[Aristotle's text, 202^{a}22–202^{b}4]

This view has a dialectical defect. Perhaps agents must be actualized in some way, and patients actualized in some way. What actualizes an agent is called action, and what actualizes a patient passion: the activity and goal of agents is action, and of patients passion. Since then they are both changes, if different they must be in a subject: either both in the patient undergoing change, or action in the agent and passion in the patient. If someone were to call this latter action he would be equivocating. Now in the latter case there will be change in what causes change. For the same argument must hold for what causes change and what undergoes change, so either everything causing change will change, or something in which there is change will not change. If on the other hand both are in the patient undergoing change, both action and passion, and teaching and being taught though they are two are in the learner, then first a thing's actualization will not exist in it, and then a second absurdity: one same thing will undergo two changes like one subject undergoing two modifications towards one form, which is impossible. Is the actualization one? Someone could say it is absurd that one and the same thing would actualize two things which are different in kind. Then action will be identified with passion and teaching with learning, to act will be the same as to undergo and to teach the same as to learn, all teachers will be learning and all agents undergoing.

[A difficulty]

And in proposing the difficulty, first he prefaces the difficulty with a preliminary remark, and then, at *Since then they are both*, expounds the difficulty. He starts by saying that *This view has a dialectical defect*, i.e. a logical difficulty, since there are plausible reasons for and against it. And he makes a preliminary remark, saying that *agents [of change] are actualized in some way, and patients [of change] actualized in some way* (which parallels what he said earlier: that both what causes change and what undergoes change are actualized in some way). *What actualizes an agent is called action, and what actualizes a patient passion*. This he proves: since what actualizes and achieves things is their activity and goals, and since, self-evidently, *the activity and goal of agents is action, and of patients passion*, it follows that action actualizes agents and passion patients, as he has said.

Next, when he says *Since then they are both*, he expounds

the difficulty. Clearly *both* action and passion *are changes*, for both are identified with change. So action and passion are either the same change or different changes. *If different* each must exist *in a subject: either both in the patient undergoing change, or* one of them (namely, *action*) *in the agent, and* the other (namely, *passion*) *in the patient. If someone were to* say the opposite—that passion is in the agent and action in the patient—clearly *he would be equivocating*, simply *calling* passion *action* and vice versa. A fourth alternative seems to be overlooked: namely, that both are in the agent; but he passes this over because he has shown change to take place in what is changed, which excludes this alternative of neither being in the patient and both in the agent.

Of the two alternatives mentioned he first pursues the second, saying *Now in the latter case*. For since as we have said action is a kind of change, if someone says action is in the agent and passion in the patient, *there will be change in what causes change. For the same argument must hold for what causes change and* for *what undergoes change*, namely, that everything in which there is change must change. (Or, *the same argument must hold for what causes change and what undergoes change* as holds for patient and agent.) Anything in which there is change, then, must change; *so* it follows *either* that *everything causing change will change, or* that *something in which there is change will not change*; both of which seem absurd.

Next, when he says *If on the other hand*, he pursues the first alternative. If someone says *both action and passion, though they are two* changes, *are in the patient undergoing change, and* that *teaching* (the teacher's side of things) *and being taught* (the learner's side) *are* both *in the learner*, there are two absurd consequences. *The first* [a] comes from our having said that action actualizes the agent. If then action is in the patient, not the agent, it will follow that *a thing's* own *actualization will not exist in it*, the thing that it actualizes. And *then* there will follow *a second absurdity*: namely, that *one* and the *same thing* will be undergoing *two changes*. For at the moment we are supposing action and passion to be two changes. Now whatever change exists in will be changed by that change. So if what can change has both action and passion in it, it will follow that what can change will be changed by two changes. This would be *like one* and the same *subject undergoing two modifications towards one* and the same *form*—one subject turning white twice at once—*which is impossible*. There's no absurdity about one subject undergoing two modifications at once towards different forms—turning white and turning hot, for instance. But action and passion clearly tend towards the same form, since what the agent does is what the patient undergoes.

Next, when he says *Is the actualization one?*, he goes back to the beginning of the difficulty. *Someone could say* that action and passion are not two changes but one; but this has four *absurd* consequences. First [**b**], *one and the same thing would actualize two things which are different in kind*. For action has been said to actualize the agent and passion the patient, and these differ in kind. If then action and passion are one change, that change must actualize two things different in kind. The second absurdity that follows if action and passion are one change is [**c**] that *action will be identified with passion and teaching* (the teacher's part) *with learning* (the learner's part). The third absurdity is [**d**] that *to act will be the same as to undergo and to teach the same as to learn*. And the fourth consequence is [**e**] that *all teachers will be learning and all agents undergoing*.

[Aristotle's text continued, 202^{b}5–22]

It is not absurd that the actualization of one thing should exist in another, for even if teaching actualizes the teacher, it tends into another thing without break; it belongs to this thing yet exists in that. Nor is there anything to prevent something that actualizes one thing from actualizing another, as long as it differs in being, like what exists potentially to an agent. Nor is it necessary for all teachers to be learning even if to act and to undergo are one and the same: provided they're not the same by definition, as raiment and dress are, but as the road from Thebes to Athens and the road from Athens to Thebes are the same, as was said earlier. For things which are the same in a certain respect don't have to be altogether the same, but only if they are the same by definition. Nor even if teaching was identified with learning would to teach be to learn; just as when one distance separates two things this's distance from that and that's from this are not one and the same thing. Altogether it should be said that it doesn't follow that action and passion are the same, or teaching and learning, but only that the change they presuppose is one and the same change; for it is defined in one way as the actualization of this thing received in that, and in another as the actualization of that thing issuing from this.

[Aristotle's solution of the difficulty]

Next, when he says *It is not absurd*, he solves the preceding difficulty. For from what we have said it is already clear that action and passion are not two changes but one and the same change, called action in so far as it is caused by an agent, and passion in so far as it takes place in a patient. So we don't need to solve the absurdities that follow from supposing action and passion to be two changes, except for one absurdity [**a**] that needs solution even if action and passion are one and the same change: for since action is an actualization of an agent as we have said above, if action and passion are one and the same change, it follows that what actualizes the agent is somehow in the patient, and that means what actualizes one thing exists in another. But there were four absurdities consequent on the other supposition; so five await solution.

So first he says that *It is not absurd* [**a**] *that the actualization of one thing should exist in another, for even if teaching actualizes the teacher,* it is something coming from him and *tending into another thing without break* or interruption; so that the same actualization *belongs to this thing*, namely, the agent, as that from which it comes, and *yet exists in the patient*, as that in which it is received. This would only be absurd if what actualized one thing were to exist in the other in exactly the same way in which it actualized the first thing.

Next, when he says *Nor is there anything to prevent*, he solves another absurdity, namely [**b**], that one and the same thing would be actualizing two different things. *Nor*, he says, *is there anything to prevent something that actualizes one thing from actualizing another, as long as*, however one it is in reality, *it differs in* some aspect of its *being*, just as it was earlier said that one and the same interval relates two to one and one to two, and *what exists potentially to an agent* and vice versa. One and the same actualization in reality relates to each of the two in a different respect: to the agent as coming from it, and to the patient as existing in it.

To the remaining three absurdities, which are deduced one from another, he responds in reverse order. Firstly, to the one he mentioned last, as the most absurd. So his third response is to the fifth absurdity [**e**]. Nor, he says, *is it necessary for all teachers to be learning* or all agents undergoing *even if to act and to undergo are one and the same*: *provided* we're not saying *they're the same by definition, as raiment and dress are, but* only that they're the same in subject and differ in definition, *as the road from Thebes to Athens is the same as the road from Athens to Thebes, something he said earlier. For things which are the same in a certain respect don't have to be altogether the same, but only if they are the same* both in subject (or in reality) and *by definition*. So, even were we to suppose that acting and undergoing were the same thing, because, as we have said, they would not be defined the same way, it wouldn't follow that whatever is acting must also be undergoing.

Next, when he says *Nor even if teaching*, he replies to the fourth absurdity [**d**]. And he says that it wouldn't follow, *even if teaching was identified with learning*, that *to teach would be to learn*, since teaching and learning are abstract concepts, but to teach and to learn concrete actions. That means they are pursuing goals and ends and as such receiving the different definitions of action and passion. *Just as* we talk of *one distance separating two things* abstractly considered, though if we orient it towards one end or the other, calling it *this's distance from that and that's from this*, these *are not one and the same thing*.

Next, when he says *Altogether it should be said*, he replies to the third absurdity [**c**], demolishing the argument that if action and passion are one and the same change then action and passion are one and the same. And he says that in the final analysis *it should be said that it doesn't follow that action and passion are the same, or teaching and learning, but only that the change they presuppose is one and the same change.* This change is defined in one way as action and in another as passion. *For it is defined in one way as the actualization of this thing received in that, and in another as the actualization of that thing issuing from this.* Change is called action inasmuch as it actualizes an agent by being **from** it; and it is called passion inasmuch as it actualizes a patient by being **in** it.

Thus it is clear that change, belonging both to what causes the change and to what is changed by it, is still one thing which abstracts from these different respects, whereas action and passion differ because they include these different respects in their meaning.

[Further difficulties: a digression by Thomas]

The above shows that change, since it abstracts from what defines action and passion, cannot belong in either the [Aristotelian] category of action or in that of passion, as certain people have asserted. However, two difficulties remain about this. Firstly, if as we have said action and passion are one and the same change and differ only in the way the change is defined, then it seems they shouldn't name two categories, since categories are classes of things. Again, if change is either action or passion then how can there be change in [the other categories of] substance, quality, quantity, or place, as we have said there are? Surely there can only be change in action and passion?

[Preliminary discussion by Thomas of the Aristotelian categories]

For clarity on these matters note that being is divided [by Aristotle] into ten categories not as a genus is divided into species, univocally [as though being had one meaning], but according to different senses of being. These senses of being correspond to the ways in which something can be said to be something. When we say: This is thus, we ascribe [predicate] one thing to another; and so the ten genuses of being are called ten ascription-categories [predicaments].

Now there are three ways of ascribing. Firstly, we can ascribe to a subject something that is of its essence, as when we say: Socrates is a human being, or: A human being is an animal; and this is the category that ascribes **substance.** Secondly, we can ascribe to a subject something not of its essence, but nevertheless existing within it. And that will either be something consequent on the subject's material—the category that ascribes **quantity,** for quantity is a characteristic consequence of materialness: thus Plato saw bigness as something material—or something consequent on the subject's form—the category that ascribes **quality,** so that qualities presuppose quantity, like colours a surface and shapes lines and surfaces—or something relating the subject to other things—the category that ascribes **relationship,** for when I call this human being a father I ascribe to him not something he has as standing alone, but something which though intrinsic to him yet relates him to something outside him.

There is a third way of ascribing, in which we ascribe to a subject something existing outside it, but which still qualifies it in some way. For even intrinsic[1] accidents are ascribed to substances in that way [as qualifying]: not by saying a human being is whiteness but by saying a human being is white. Such qualification by something outside is in one way[2] common to every sort of thing, but in another way special to human beings. The common way in which something external can qualify a subject is as a cause or as a measure, for things are qualified as caused or measured by things outside them. Now there are four kinds of cause. Two of these—matter and form—are parts of the thing, of its essence; so any ascription to a subject made on their account will fall into the category that ascribes substance: as when we say that human beings are rational or have bodies. And goals don't cause except through agents, for a goal counts as a cause in so far as it moves an agent. So we are left with agents as the only causes which can give rise to qualification of a subject by something outside. To qualify something by its agent cause falls into the category that ascribes a **passion** [or change suffered], for suffering or undergoing change is nothing more than taking on something from an agent; and the opposite qualification of an agent cause by its effect falls into the category of **action**, for action is an actualization from an agent in something external, as we have said above. As to measures, some are extrinsic and others intrinsic. Intrinsic measures are things like a subject's own length, breadth, and depth, which qualify it by what inheres in it intrinsically, and so belong under the category that ascribes quantity. External measures are a thing's time and place. To qualify a thing by its time belongs to the category **when**; to qualify it by its place belongs to the category **where**, and also to the category **position**, which adds to place how the subject's parts are disposed in that place [sitting, standing, etc.]. Such an addition is not needed in the case of time, since being in time already implies a disposition of parts in time: time being the measure of the before-and-afterness of changes. So stating a thing's when or where qualifies it by its time or place.

What is left is the special case of human beings. Other animals are sufficiently equipped for survival by nature—they have horns to defend themselves, thick hairy skin to cover them, and hooves or the like for getting about without injury. And so when we call such animals armed or clothed or equipped with hooves, we are not in a way qualifying them by anything external but by parts of themselves. So this will belong to the category that ascribes substance, just like calling human beings handed or footed. But nature can't give human beings the same sort of equipment as animals, partly because that wouldn't go with the more subtle constitution of their bodies, partly because nature couldn't devise fixed tools to suit the variety of things that reason enables human beings to do. So instead of such equipment human beings must use the reason they have to devise for themselves external substitutes for what in other animals is intrinsic. As a result, when we call human beings armed or clothed or shod we are qualifying them by something external to them which is neither cause nor measure, and so belongs in a special category that ascribes **equipment**. But note that this category does also apply to other animals, not of their own nature, but as used by human beings: as when we call horses caparisoned or saddled or armoured.

[Thomas's solution of his difficulties]

So now we see how change can be one single thing, and yet give rise to two categories of ascription ascribing qualifications by different external things. For the agent, to which the category ascribing passion refers, is one external thing qualifying the subject; whilst the patient, referred to when qualifying something as an agent, is another. And so the first difficulty is solved.

The second difficulty is easy to solve. For our notion of change is made up not simply of what corresponds to it in the real world, but also of what our reasons have made of that. In the real world there is no more to change than an incomplete actualization, the start of some complete actualization in what is changing: in something turning white there is some beginning of whiteness. But this incomplete actualization can be seen as change only if we understand it as a kind of transition between two things: something preceding (which relates to it as potential to actual, so that change is seen as an actualization) and something following (which relates to it as complete to incomplete or actual to potential, so that change is seen as [actualization] of something that exists in potentality, as we said earlier). Unless incomplete actualizations are seen as tending to further completeness, they will be seen as results of change, not as changes that something is still undergoing: as, for example, the state of something which had started to turn white but got interrupted immediately. With respect then to what is real in it, change belongs reductively to whatever genus the result of the change belongs to, in the way anything incomplete is reductively what it would be if complete, as we have said. But with respect to what our reasons have made of change, namely, a sort of transition between two extremes, the notions of cause and effect are already implied, since without an agent cause nothing can be brought from potentiality to actualization. In this respect change belongs to the categories of action and passion; for these two categories derive from the notions of agent cause and effect, as we have seen.

[Aristotle's text, 202^{b}23–29]

What then change is we have stated both generally and in particular. It is not difficult to see how to define each of its species. A modification of properties is an actualization of what is capable of modification of properties precisely as such: more clearly that change actualizes the potentialities of both agent and patient, generally and also in particular, building and healing, and the same of other changes.

[Summing up]

Next, when he says *What then change is*, he defines change in particular. And he says that *we have stated what change is both generally and in particular*, since from what has been said about how to define change in general *it is not difficult to see how to define its species*. For if change is an actualization of what is capable of change precisely as such, then *a modification of properties is an actualization of what is capable of modification of properties precisely as such*, and so on for other types of change.

And because a difficulty was expressed about whether change actualized what caused it or what underwent it, and it was shown that it actualized the agent by being from it, and the patient by being in it, to remove every difficulty let us say a little *more clearly that change actualizes the potentialities of both agent and patient*. And that *also* can be said *in particular*: *building* actualizes both builder and what he builds as such. *And the same with healing, and other changes.*

Passage 6

Essence and Existence

Source: On Being and Essence (complete). Text from *De Ente et Essentia* (*Opera Omnia*, Leonine edn., vol. xliii).

Date: 1252–6, first stay in Paris, aged about 30.

Type of passage and how to read: The work reads like an attempt to summarize and mediate between remarks made by past masters on the subject of essence and universals: especially Ibn Sīnā and Ibn Rushd. It marks an early stage in the rejection by Thomas of a form–matter composition in non-bodily substances; and the consequent ascription of an essence–existence composition to them.

Notes on translation: The words translated as 'being', 'existence', and 'essence' all derive from the Latin verb *esse* ('to be'). St Thomas conceives the being of a thing on the model of an activity which that thing exercises: call it the activity of being be-ing being. The quasi-activity of 'be-ing' he refers to as *esse* or *actus essendi*, the 'to be' or the 'act of be-ing', and it is customary to translate it 'existence', though that English word is not as flexible as the Latin. What exerts this quasi-activity, the 'being' which is, he refers to as *ens*, a sort of bastard present participle of *esse*. And the complement, the 'being' that a being is, what it is, is referred to by many terms, of which *essentia* is one, a sort of abstract noun derived from yet another bastard present participle of *esse*. It corresponds to a similarly derived Greek word: *ousia*. An English equivalent might be 'beingness'. So this work should really be called 'On Being and Beingness', or 'On Beings and their Being'. I have given way to custom and translated: 'On Being and Essence'.

Parallel reading: Cf. Passage 21: God is his own existence.

[Prologue]

Since Aristotle[1] says big mistakes grow from small beginnings and Ibn Sīnā[2] says understanding begins with the notion of being [what is] and essence [isness], lest ignorance of these notions lead us astray, we must dispel their difficulty by saying what is meant by the word *essence* (and *being*), the various forms in which we come across it, and its relation to logical notions like genus, species, and differentiating characteristic. And because human beings get their knowledge of simple, primary things from what is later and more complex, it will be best to start from what is easiest for us, learning first about being [what is] and then about essence [isness].

[Being]

[1] Note then that Aristotle[3] says there are two proper uses of the term *being*: firstly, generally for whatever falls into

one of Aristotle's ten basic categories of thing, and secondly, for whatever makes a proposition true. These differ: in the second sense anything we can express in an affirmative proposition, however unreal, is said to be; in this sense lacks and absences are, since we say that absences are opposed to presences, and blindness exists in an eye. But in the first sense only what is real is, so that in this sense blindness and such are not beings.

[Essence]

The word *essence* [isness] then refers to what is in the first sense, not the second; for things like lacks that can be in the second sense still don't have [isness or] essence. Hence Ibn Rushd[4] comments that *being* in the first sense expresses the isness of things. And because, as we have just said, being in this sense applies generally to all ten categories, essence must be something all the natures that sort different beings into their various genera and species have in common: being human is the essence of human beings, for example, and similarly for other things. Now what sorts things into their proper genus and species are the definitions that express what they are; so some philosophers have used the word *whatness* for *essence*, Aristotle himself frequently calling it the what-it-is-to-be-that: i.e. that which makes something what it is. The word *form* is also used, which Ibn Sīnā[5] says means what gives a thing its stable identity. And yet another name is *nature*, in the first of four senses assigned to that word by Boethius:[6] as meaning whatever understanding can grasp; for it is definition of essence that makes things understandable. In this sense Aristotle[7] called every substance a nature. However, nature so understood seems to express essence as what underlies a thing's characteristic behaviour (for nothing lacks a characteristic behaviour), whereas whatness expresses it as underlying the thing's definition, and essence refers to it as that through which and in which a being has existence.

But because *being* is used in a primary unqualified sense of substances, and in a secondary qualified sense of incidental properties, essence too belongs properly and truly to substances, but to incidental properties in a qualified sense. And though composite and non-composite substances both have essence, simple non-composite things have it more truly and excellently since they exist in a more excellent way, as the cause of composite things (this is true of God at least, who is the first of all simple substances). But because the essence of such substances is more hidden from us, it will be best if we start with what is easier, learning first about the essence of composite substances.

[Essence in composite substances]

[2] Note that what composes composite substances is material and its form (humans, for example, contain body and soul), and neither of these by itself can be the thing's essence. This is clear enough for anything's material, because things are known and sorted into species and genus by their essence, but a thing isn't known by its material, and we determine its species or genus not by its material but by the way that material is actualized. But neither can form alone be a composite substance's essence, though some think so. For a thing's essence, we have said, is expressed by its definition, and unless the definition of a physical substance included not only its form but its material, definitions of natural objects wouldn't differ from those of mathematical objects. It won't do to say that the material only enters the definition of a physical substance as something added to its essence from outside, since that kind of definition characterizes incidental properties, which have an incomplete essence and need to refer in their definitions to their subject, lying outside their own genus. Clearly then essence involves both material and form. But it doesn't simply express a relationship between material and its form or something supervening on both, because this would be incidental and extraneous to the thing and not identify it to the mind, as essence must. For form actualizes its material and makes it into a this-thing, actual and existent, so that anything that supervenes can no longer actualize the material, simply speaking, but only in this or that way as incidental properties do: whiteness making it actually white, for example. Acquiring such a form is not

coming to be, simply speaking, but only in this or that respect.

So what is left is that in composite things essence expresses a composite of material and form. This agrees with Boethius' comment[8] that *ousia* means the composite, where *ousia*, as he also tells us,[9] is Greek for *essence*; and with Ibn Sīnā's assertion[10] that the whatness of composite substances is their very compositeness of form and material, and also with Ibn Rushd's comment[11] that *the nature that species of generable things have is a sort of mixture*, i.e. composite *of material and form*. And it also agrees with reason, since the existence of a composite substance belongs not just to its form or to its material but to the composite itself. Now it is by having essence that things exist; so the essence which allows us to call it existent must consist not of form alone or material alone but of both; even though form alone causes—in its own way—that existence. For things composed of several elements are always named in this way: not because of any single element but because of the complex of both; a sweet taste, for example, is caused by the action of digestive heat on moist matter, but though heat causes sweetness we don't call hot bodies sweet, only bodies with that complex of hot and moist that constitutes a sweet taste.

But now, because their material makes things individual, it could seem that an essence made up of material and form together would not be general but particular, and that, since definitions express essence, nothing could be given a general definition. So note that what makes things individual is not material as such but demarcated material, by which I mean material thought of as underlying certain defined dimensions. Now material thought of in this way doesn't enter the definition of human being as human being (though it would enter Socrates' definition if he had one); what enters the definition of human being is undemarcated material, not this flesh and these bones but flesh and bones in general, the undemarcated material of human beings. Clearly then Socrates' essence differs from human essence only by being demarcated. *Socrates*, as Ibn Rushd[12] says, *is nothing more than animality plus rationality; those are what he is.*

And the specific essence of something also differs from its generic essence by being demarcated, though the method of demarcation is different: for individuals are demarcated within species by dimensionally defined material, but species within genus by a defining differentiation taken from the form. This determination or demarcation of species within genus is not because of anything existing in the specific essence that was totally absent from the generic essence; indeed everything present in a species is present in the genus in a non-determined way. For if only part of a human being and not the whole was animal, human beings wouldn't be animals, since wholes aren't named after parts.

To see how this is possible, contrast body as component of an animal with the genus of bodies, for they must be different. The word *body* has several senses. As naming a substance, it names something of such a nature as to occupy three demarcated dimensions, the three dimensions demarcated being body-as-quantity, [the solid body of mathematics]. Now things with one perfection are not excluded from further perfections: human beings, able by nature to sense, are further able by nature to understand. And in the same way things by nature able to occupy three demarcated dimensions can add to that perfection others like life or the like. So this word *body* sometimes means a thing of a form such that it can occupy three dimensions, but stopping there: in other words the form produces no further perfection, so that anything extra lies outside the meaning of body so understood; and in this sense body names a component and material part of animals, with its animating soul lying outside the meaning of body so defined and supervening upon it, so that the animal is made up of two component parts, body and soul. But the same word *body* sometimes means a thing of a form such that it can occupy three dimensions, whatever form that be, whether producing further perfections or not; and in this sense body names a genus that includes animals, since now there is nothing in animal that isn't already implicit in body. For the animating soul isn't a different form from the one enabling the thing to occupy three dimensions, and when we said *body is anything of a form such that it can occupy three dimensions* we were meaning *whatever form that be*: be it an animal soul, or stone-ness, or anything else. And in this way the animal form was implicit in the form of body, body being its genus.

The same relation holds between animal and human. If animal names only things perfect enough to be able to sense and move about of themselves, stopping short of any further perfections, then any supervening perfection would be a fellow component with animal and not something already implicit in the notion of animal, and animal would not name a genus. Animal as genus means anything of a form able to sense and move about, whatever form it be: a soul that only senses, or one that both senses and understands. In this way then a genus expresses non-determinately the whole of what the species expresses (not only the material), and in the same way a differentiating characteristic expresses the whole (not only the form), and the definition or species also expresses the whole: but all in different ways. The genus expresses the whole through a name which determines the thing's material but falls short of the [full] determination proper to the form: though not itself that material, it bases itself on the material; body is a clear example, naming something of a perfection such that it can occupy three dimensions, a perfection which is a sort of material for further perfections. A differentiating characteristic on the other hand names something by its determinate form, abstracting at first from the material it determines; living is a clear example, meaning endowed with soul, for this doesn't determine what is living, a body or something else; which is why Ibn Sīnā[13] says genus is not part of the essence of a differentiating characteristic but something extraneous to it in the way subjects enter the definitions of their incidental properties, and also why Aristotle[14] remarks that genus is not predicated of differentiating characteristics as such except perhaps in the way subjects are predicated of their properties. But a definition or species comprehends both the determinate material expressed by the name of the genus and the determinate form expressed by the name of the differentiating characteristic.

And now we can see why genus, species, and differentiating characteristic correspond to material, form, and composite in the natural world, though differing from them; for a thing's genus is not its material but a name for the whole derived from its material, and its differentiating characteristic is not its form, but a name for the whole derived from its form. Thus we call humans logical animals made up of body and soul, but not made up of animality and logicality; for a human being is a third thing composed from two components, body and soul, both differing from the whole (for a human being is neither soul nor body). Whereas if human being were said in some sense to be composed of animal being and logical being, that would not be two component things making a third thing, but two component concepts making a third concept. The concept animal expresses a thing's nature without determining its specific form, seeing it only as material for that final perfection; the concept logical, the differentiating characteristic [of a human being] provides the determination to that specific form; and the concept of the thing's species or definition puts these two concepts together. And just as a thing made up of two others is not identified with them, so a concept isn't identified with any of its component concepts: the definition is neither the genus nor the differentiating characteristic.

Now the fact that a genus expresses the whole essence of its species doesn't mean that all its different species have one and the same essence. For the genus's unity is precisely one of non-determination and undifferentiation: what the genus expresses is not one single nature present in the different species upon which some other thing—the differentiating characteristic—supervenes, determining it like a form determining a single material; but the genus expresses a form without determining it to be this or that form, and the differentiating characteristic expresses it determinately, the form being the same one expressed non-determinately by the genus. This led Ibn Rushd[15] to say that the ultimate material of things has the unity of total formlessness, whereas a genus has the unity of the commonness of the form it expresses. Clearly then adding differentiating characteristics removes the non-determination that unified the genus and what we are left with is species differing in essence.

And because, as we said earlier [pp. 94–5], a thing's specific nature leaves undetermined which individual it is (just as its generic nature leaves undetermined what species it is), the species of an individual expresses—indistinctly—the whole essence of that individual (just as the genus of a species expresses implicitly but indistinctly the whole of what the species expresses determinately). And because this is the way the phrase *human being* expresses the essence of his species, we say Socrates is a human being. But if the same specific nature were to be expressed in a way that explicitly excluded the demarcated material which made him an individual, then the specific nature would be conceived of as a component part: the way the word *humanness* expresses it, since humanness means what makes humans humans. Now demarcated material isn't something which makes humans humans, and can't be included among what makes humans humans. Humanness, however, is a concept including only what makes humans humans, so that demarcated material is clearly cut out or excluded from its meaning; and consequently, since we don't call the whole its part, we don't say a human being (or Socrates) is his humanness. That is why Ibn Sīnā[16] says no composite is its own 'whatness', even though that whatness is itself composed; humanness, though composite, is not a human—it needs to be taken on by something, namely, demarcated material.

But because, as we have said [pp. 94–5], form demarcates species within a genus whereas material demarcates individuals within a species, our word for the generic in a thing—cutting out the form as determinately perfecting the species—names a material part of the whole (in the way *body* names the material part of humans). In contrast, our word for the specific in a thing, cutting out demarcated material, expresses a formal part. So *humanness* expresses a sort of form called the form of the whole: not meaning something added over and above a thing's entitative parts—its form and material—as the form of house is added over and above its component parts, but rather meaning the form which is the whole, the complex of form and material cutting out only what serves to demarcate the material.

So human essence is expressed by both words: *human*

being and *humanness*, but differently, as we have said [p. 98]. For the phrase *human being* expresses it as a whole (not cutting out demarcated material but including it implicitly and indistinctly in the way we said a genus includes its differentiating characteristics): so individuals can be called human beings. But the word *humanness* expresses it as a part (including in its meaning only what belongs to humans as humans and cutting out all demarcation), and so we don't call an individual human being humanness. This is why the word essence is sometimes asserted of things (Socrates, we say, is an essence of sorts) and sometimes denied (Socrates' essence, we say, is not Socrates).

[How essence relates to logical notions like genus, species, and differentiating characteristic in composite substances]

[3] So now that we have seen what the word *essence* means in composite substances, we must see how it is related to the notions of genus, species, and differentiating characteristic.

Now notions like genus, species, and differentiating characteristic attach to something that can be attributed to this demarcated singular. So general notions like genus or species can't attach to essence as a component part (expressed by words like *humanness* or *animalness*). This is the reason Ibn Sīnā[17] says logicalness is not a differentiating characteristic but a source of differentiation, and for the same reason humanness is not a species and animalness not a genus. In the same way a notion like genus and species can't attach to essence as something existing outside singulars in the way Platonists propose, for then genus and species could not apply to this individual: one can't say Socrates is something separated from him, nor would that separate thing help you to know this singular. So the only alternative is that notions like genus and species attach to essence as the whole (expressed by words like *human being* or *animal*), as implicitly and indistinctly including the whole of what is present in the individual.

However, nature or essence so understood can be considered in two ways. Firstly, on its own, considering what properly defines it, so that only what belongs to it as such is true of it and everything else attributed to it false. Thus, being logical and animal and whatever else defines human beings belongs to them as human, but being white or black or anything else not included in humanness doesn't belong to human beings as human. So, asked whether nature considered in this way is one or many, one should answer neither, since neither is contained in what we understand by humanness though both can belong to it coincidentally: if manyness was contained in humanness it could never be one as it is in Socrates, and if oneness was part of its definition then Socrates would be Plato and the nature couldn't be realized more than once. The second way of considering nature is as existing in this or that: and considered in this way something can be attributed to it coincidentally by reason of what possesses the nature, as a human being can be called white since Socrates is white though white doesn't attach to human beings as human. Nature in this sense exists firstly in singulars and secondly in the mind: in both cases certain things are true of it coincidentally, and in singulars it also exists more than once in a diversity of singulars. None of these existences belong to nature in the first sense, considered on its own. For it is false to say that human being as such exists in this singular: if existing in this singular belonged to human beings as human no humans could exist outside it, and if not existing in this singular belonged to human beings as human that singular could never be human. But it is true to say that human being—though not as human being—exists in this or that singular or in the mind. Clearly then human nature considered on its own abstracts from all these existences but cuts none out, and it is nature considered in this way that is predicated of all individuals.

Nevertheless, one can't say general notions attach to nature so understood, since the notion of generality involves unity and commonness, neither of which belong to human nature considered on its own: for if commonness were part of what we understood by human, then wherever humanness was found commonness would be found too, which is false: for we don't find commonness in Socrates but everything in him is individuated. Nor can one say that notions like genus and species attach to human nature as it exists in individuals, since human nature is not present in individuals as a single unified something attaching to all in the way the notion of generality requires. So the only alternative is that notions like species attach to human nature as it exists in our understanding.

For human nature itself exists in our understanding abstracted from all individuation, but with a definition uniformly applicable to all individuals outside the mind, since it is a likeness of them all equally, and leads us to know them all as human beings. And out of this relationship the nature has to all individual human beings, our understanding constructs the notion of species and attributes that to the nature; so that Ibn Rushd[18] says *it is our understanding that works generality in things*, and Ibn Sīnā[19] says the same. And although nature in the understanding possesses this generality in regard to things outside the mind (being a single likeness of them all), it still, as existing in this or that understanding, is a particular mental idea. And that shows up Ibn Rushd's mistake[20] in wanting to argue from the generality of the form in the understanding to a unity of mind in all men; because the generality attaches to the form not as existing in this understanding but as referring by way of likeness to things; just as the image or species present in one bodily statue and representing many men would undoubtedly have its own single existence in the statue's material despite its relationship of commonness as a common representation of many.

And because it is human nature considered on its own that is attributed to Socrates, and the notion of species doesn't attach to the nature considered on its own but is something coincidentally true of it as existing in understanding, the word *species* can't be attributed to Socrates (you can't say *Socrates is a species*). This you couldn't avoid doing if the notion of species attached to human being as existing in Socrates, or to human being as human, considered on its own, for whatever attaches to human beings as human can be attributed to Socrates. Nevertheless, attributability to things is an essential property of a genus, forming part of its definition. For attribution is something mind brings to completion by constructing propositional connections and disconnections, basing itself on the real-world unity possessed by the things being attributed to one another. So the notion of attributability can form part of the logical notion of genus which is likewise brought to completion by an act of mind; though what mind attributes the notion of attributability to, what it connects it with, is not the notion of genus itself, but rather that to which it also attributes the notion of genus, e.g. what it means by *animal*.

This then explains the relationship between essence or nature and the notion of species: the notion of species is not something attaching to essence considered on its own, nor something coincidentally true of it as existing outside the mind (as whiteness and blackness would be), but something coincidentally attached to it as existing in the mind. And this is also the way the notions of genus and differentiating characteristic attach to it.

[Essence in simple non-composite substances]

[4] At this point, we still have to see how essence is present in separated [immaterial] substances like human minds, [angelic] intelligences, and the first cause.

[The simpleness of intelligences]

Now, though everyone concedes simple non-compositeness to the first cause, some people have wanted to introduce a compositeness of material and form into intelligences and minds, a position apparently first adopted by Ibn Gebirol.[21] It contradicts the common opinion of philosophers, who had called such substances separated, i.e. from material, and proved them to exist without any material. The strongest such proof is drawn from their power of understanding. For we see that forms are only actually understandable when separated from material and material conditions, and the only thing that can make them actually understandable in this way is the power of some intelligent substance taking them in and acting on them. But if that is so all intelligent substances must be entirely free from material, neither containing it nor even being the sort of form material takes on (i.e. forms of matter). Nor can one say that intelligibility is impeded only by bodily material, not all material; for if only bodily material did it, since bodiliness comes from taking on bodily form, material's impeding of intelligibility would come from that form. But that can't be true, because this form too is actually intelligible, just like other forms, when abstracted from material.

So in minds and intelligences there is no composition of material and form to give them the same kind of essence that bodily substances have, but they are composed of form and existence, as we read in the book of Causes:[22] *intelligence is what has form and existence*, where form means the simple whatness or nature they have. How this can be is easy to see, for when things are so related that one causes the other to exist, the cause can exist without what it causes but not vice versa. Now material and form are so related, form giving existence to the material. Material then can't exist without form, but form, precisely as form, is not dependent on material. When we do find forms which can't exist except in material this is incidental to them and due to their distance from the ultimate pure actualization which is their first source; forms nearest to that first source subsist by themselves without material (for the whole genus of forms doesn't need material, as we have said), and such forms are the intelligences, in which essence and whatness doesn't have to differ from the form itself.

The difference then between the essence of composite and the essence of simple substances is that the former is not just form but a complex of material and form, whereas the latter is just form. And two other differences follow from this. The first is that, because of demarcated material as we have said, the essence of composite substances can be expressed as a whole or as a part, so that you can't say a composite thing is in all respects its own essence: a human being is not his whatness. But the essence of simple things—their form—can only be expressed as a whole, since there is no other thing taking the form on. So a simple substance is its own essence in every sense, and Ibn Sīnā[23] can say: *the simple's whatness is its very self*, nothing else takes it on. The second difference is that entities of composite things when taken on by demarcated material are multiplied by the material's dividedness, and many individuals can exist in the same species. Because the essence of simple things is not taken on by material it cannot be multiplied in this way, and in such substances one can't have many individuals in one species, but each individual is a species, as Ibn Sīnā[24] explicitly asserts.

[The compositeness of intelligences]

Such substances then are just forms without material. However, they are not totally simple, not pure actualizations, but have potentiality mixed in. And this can be shown as follows. No essence or whatness can be understood without its parts. So what isn't contained in our understanding of an essence must be something extraneous added on to it. But all entities and whatnesses can be understood without understanding their existence: I can understand what humans or phoenixes are without knowing whether such things really exist; so clearly a thing's existence differs from its essence or whatness. A possible exception would be something whose essence was its own very existing, but there could only exist one primary thing like that; for, to be many, things must add some differentiating characteristic to a genus to make many species, or one form must be taken on by different material to make many individuals in a species, or one must exist on its own while the other exists in something (in the way heat, if it could exist separately, would by its very separateness differ from heat existing in something). Now the thing we are positing—something that just is existence, so that its very existing subsists—can't add on differentiating characteristics without ceasing to be just existing and becoming existence plus form; and even less can it add on material, because then it would straight away be not subsistent but materialized existence. So there is no alternative: only one thing that is its own existence can exist, and all other things must have an existence differing from their whatness or nature or form. Intelligences then must have existence over and above their form; and that explains the saying: *intelligence is what has form and existence.*

Now a thing's attributes are caused either from within its nature (like a human being's sense of the ridiculous) or by some extrinsic source (like light in the atmosphere by the sun). But the very existence of a thing can't be caused by its own form or whatness—I am talking of agent causality—because then something would be causing itself and bringing itself into existence, which is impossible. So everything in which existence and nature differ must get its existence from another. And because all getting from another must eventually lead to something possessing of itself, there must be something which can ultimately cause everything's existence because it is its own existence; otherwise the causes would go on for ever, with everything which is not just existence requiring a cause of its existence, as we have said. Clearly then intelligences are form and existence, and get their existence from a first existent which is just existence: the ultimate cause which is God.

Now whatever acquires something from another has a potentiality for what it acquires, a potentiality that what is acquired actualizes; so the very whatness or form which an intelligence is has a potentiality for the existence it acquires from God, and the acquired existence actualizes it. So there is potentiality and actualization in intelligences, though if we called that form and material we would equivocate in the way that Ibn Rushd[25] says we would equivocate were we to say intellectual substances, like bodily substances, underwent change, or took on or were subject to form (all of which seem to apply to material things as such). Now because, as we have said, the whatness of an intelligence is the intelligence itself, the whatness or essence is that which exists, and the existence it receives from God is that by which it really subsists in nature; so some people say such things are composed of that which and that by which, or from that which exists and existence, as Boethius[26] says. But because there is this potentiality and actuality in intelligences, there is no difficulty about having more than one of them, something that would have been impossible in the absence of potentiality. As Ibn Rushd[27] says: if we hadn't known mind could be 'possible' [i.e. receptive] we wouldn't have been able to have more than one separate substance. So they are distinguished among themselves by their degree of potentiality and actualization, higher intelligences nearer to their source being more actualized and less potential, and so on down until you finally reach the human mind, the lowest ranked of intellectual substances. According to Ibn Rushd,[28] our receptive mind is related to forms that can be understood, as ultimate material (lowest ranked of what can be sensed) is related to forms that can be sensed; and Aristotle[29] for that reason compares it to a blank slate. And, being of all intellectual substances the most potential, it so borders on material things that it even draws one of them in to share its own existence, and from mind and body there results a single existent composite thing, although mind's possession of that existence is not dependent on body. And below the form which is our mind we find other forms more potential, so close to material that they can't exist except as forms of material; and these are ordered in degree right down to the first forms of elements, nearest of all to material, and active only in the sense of clothing material with the active and passive and other qualities needed to dispose it for form.

[Essence in God, intelligences, and material things]

[5] What we have been saying explains the diverse ways things have essence. For there are three ways substances possess essence.

[God]

God's essence is identified with his own very existence; so that some philosophers have denied any essence or whatness to God at all, because he hasn't essence distinct from his existence. As a result he isn't a member of any genus: for all members of genuses must have whatness distinct from their existence, since they are not diversified in their generic or specific whatness or nature as nature, although each differs in existence. Saying God is simply existence doesn't force us into the error of those who say God is the existence in general by which each thing exists. Existence in God is of such a sort that it can't be added to, distinct therefore from all other existence by its very purity; as the book of Causes[30] says: *its own pure goodness makes the first cause, pure existence, individual.* But existence in general is not conceived as either including addition or prohibiting addition; for otherwise nothing that added anything to existence could be conceived of as existing. In the same way, that God is simply existence doesn't mean he has to lack other perfections and excellences. Rather he possesses every perfection of every genus—his perfection is without qualification, as Aristotle[31] and Ibn Rushd[32] both say—possessing them more excellently than anything else can because in him is unified what in others is diverse. And this is because all these perfections belong to him simply as existing; just as someone exercising the activities of all qualities through one quality would possess all qualities in that one, so God in his very existing possesses all perfections.

[Intellectual substances and essence]

Created intellectual substances realize essence in a second way: in them essence, though immaterial, differs from existence. So they don't have a stand-alone existence, but an acquired existence, circumscribed and limited to what the acquiring nature can take on; though they have a stand-alone nature or whatness, not acquired by any material. And so intelligences are described in the book of Causes[33] as *unlimited below but limited above*: limited in existence which they acquire from above, but unlimited below since their forms are not limited to what some acquiring material can take on. Consequently, in such substances there is only one individual in a species, as we have already said [p. 104]. The exception is the human mind, because of the body it is joined to. And here, though its individuality depends to start with on what body it happens to be joined to (since it acquires individual existence only in the body it actualizes), nevertheless its individuality doesn't have to perish when the body is taken away, because the existence it has in its own right—an existence individuated by it being made the form of this body—from then on always stays individuated. As Ibn Sīnā[34] says: *that minds are one or many depends on bodies in the beginning but not in the end.*

[Intellectual substances and genus and species]

Again, because whatness in these substances differs from existence, they are categorizable, and can be assigned genus and species and characteristic differences, though what those differences really are we can't see. Even when things can be sensed we don't know what really differentiates them but use consequent incidental differences as symptomatic of differences in essence, in the way effects are symptomatic of causes: two-legged, for example, to distinguish humans. But even incidental characteristics of immaterial substances are unknown to us, and so we can't distinguish them either in themselves or through incidental differences.

Note, however, that genus and differentiating characteristic don't arise in the same way in these substances and in substances we can sense. In the substances we sense genus arises from what is material in a thing and the differentiating characteristic from what is formal in it. Thus Ibn Sīnā[35] says that *in things composed of material and form the form is a simple differentiation of what it forms* (though, as Ibn Sīnā[36] himself says, the form makes rather than is the differentiation), where the differentiation is called simple because it arises from a single part of the thing's whatness, namely, its form. Immaterial substances, however, are their own simple whatnesses, and differentiation in them must derive from the whole of their whatness and not just a part of it, and so Ibn Sīnā[37] says that *only species whose essence is composed of material and form have a simple differentiation*. And in such things genus too derives from their whole essence, but in a different way. For immaterial substances agree with one another in immateriality but differ in perfection measured on a scale running from potentiality to pure actualization. So genus derives from features like intellectuality, consequent on their immateriality, whilst differentiation derives from their degree of perfection, something unknown to us. You can't argue that such differences of degree are incidental because not differences of kind: true, taking on one and the same form more or less perfectly doesn't make a difference in kind (white and less white are degrees of the same whiteness), but when the shared forms and natures themselves are of different degrees of perfection we get difference in kind, as in Aristotle's[38] account of nature advancing by degrees from plants through intermediate things to animals. Nor must intellectual substances always be pairwise divided by true differentiations, since Aristotle[39] notes that this can't be the case for everything.

[Composite substances]

Substances composed of material and form realize essence in yet a third way, in which both existence is taken on and thus limited by being acquired from another, and their nature or whatness too is taken on by demarcated material. Such substances then are limited both above and below; and already, because of the divisions in demarcated material, have more than one individual in a species. And how essence in such things is related to logical concepts we have said earlier [p. 99].

[How essence is realized in incidental properties]

[6] Now that we have explained how essence is realized in all substances, it remains only to see how it is realized in incidental properties.

And since, as we have said [p. 92], essence is what is expressed in a definition, incidental properties will have essence in whatever way they have definition. Now they are not completely definable; any definition of them must mention their subject too, because they cannot exist on their own apart from their subject but incidental property and subject join together to yield something that exists in an incidental sense. In the same way, form and material join to yield something that exists as a substance, so that forms and material of substances also have incomplete entities; for in defining forms of substances too we must mention what is formed, adding in something outside their genus, just as in defining incidental forms: thus a natural philosopher's definition of mind will mention body, since his interest in mind is its role of giving form to the physical body.

However, substantial and incidental forms differ to this extent: not only does substantial form have no existence of its own apart from the material upon which it supervenes but the material doesn't either, so that existence of a self-subsistent thing waits on the joining of the two into something essentially one, a joining, therefore, which yields an essence. Form then, though having no complete essence of its own, forms part of a complete essence. But that which incidental properties supervene on already exists complete in itself, subsisting in its own existence, an existence naturally prior to anything that incidentally supervenes. So when what supervenes is joined to that, it produces not the kind of existence in which things subsist as self-existent, but a kind of secondary existence: an existence that the subsistent thing can be conceived to exist without, in the way we can conceive anything that comes first without what comes second. From subject and incidental property, then, we get something incidentally, not essentially, one, and the joining doesn't yield an essence as the joining of form and material does. So an incidental property neither has complete essence nor does it form part of a complete essence: because it exists only in a qualified sense it has essence only in a qualified sense.

But because what is most fully and truly of a certain kind is the source of all later instances of the kind (fire, the supremely hot, is the source of the heat of hot things, as Aristotle[40] says), substance, as primarily existent, most fully and truly having essence, must be the source of incidental properties, which are existent in a secondary and qualified sense. Now this happens in different ways, for a substance has parts—its material and its form—and certain incidental properties derive principally from form and certain from material. Now there is one form—mind—which can exist independently of any material, but no material can exist except as formed; so, among incidental properties consequent on form, one—understanding—has nothing in common with material, making use of no bodily organ as Aristotle proves,[41] while others consequent on form—sensing—have their material side; but, among incidental properties consequent on material, all have their formal side. Yet there are differences among these incidental properties consequent on material: some of them are consequent on material in a certain specific form—male and female, for example, on material in animal form, according to Aristotle[42]—and persist only equivocally in the absence of animal form; but others are consequent on material in its general form, so persist in the absence of the specific form—the African's black skin derives not from his human form but from a chemical compounding of elements which persists after death. And because material makes things individual, and form gathers them into genus and species, incidental properties consequent on material are incidental to individuals, distinguishing them within the same species, whereas incidental properties consequent on form characterize genuses or species and are common to all members of the genus or species: a sense of the ridiculous, for example, which is consequent on the human form, since the ridiculous is something only human minds can grasp.

Note too that a substance is sometimes the source of incidental properties in full actualization—the heat of fire never fails to be hot—and sometimes the source only of a susceptibility which some exterior agent must actualize—as an independently shining light must actualize the transparency of the atmosphere; and that in the latter case the susceptibility is an inseparable incidental, but the completion by a change or the like is separable, because it has a source outside the thing's essence or not forming part of it.

[How essence relates to logical notions like genus and species in incidental properties]

Note too that genus, differentiating characteristic, and species arise in a different way in incidental properties and in substances. Since form and material in substances yield something essentially one, joining into a single nature categorizable in the strict sense as a substance, the concrete nouns expressing the composite thing—e.g. human, animal—express its strict genus and species; form and material themselves, however, are not categorizable in this way, but only reductively in the way elements of a thing are said to belong to its genus. But subject and incidental property yield nothing essentially one, their joining resulting in nothing to which the concept of genus or species can be strictly applied. So incidental properties as expressed by concrete nouns—whites, musicians—belong to a category reductively, and not as species or genus unless they are expressed abstractly—whiteness, musicality.

Note too that incidental properties aren't composed of material and form, so genus in them can't derive from the material nor differentiating characteristic from form as in composite substances. Their primary genera [or categories] must derive from their very mode of existing, in the way existing is divided into a hierarchy of senses by Aristotle's ten categories: quantity as measuring substances, for example, and quality as modifying them, and so on for the others.[43] The differentiating characteristics of incidental properties on the other hand derive from the diversity of sources causing them. Properties peculiar to a subject derive from intrinsic factors peculiar to that subject, so the subject itself takes the place of a differentiating characteristic in definitions of the property abstractly expressed and strictly categorized—snubness is curvedness of nose. But conversely, in definitions of the property concretely expressed, the subject takes the place of the genus, and it is then defined as composite substances are, by deriving the genus from the matter—the snub is a curved nose. A similar thing happens when one accident is the source of another, as acting, being acted on, and quantity cause relationships, and so are referred to by Aristotle[44] when distinguishing relationships. But because the exact cause of incidental properties is not always clear, we sometimes differentiate incidental properties by their effects, differentiating colours, for example, as dark and light, which are effects of the abundance or scarceness of light that diversifies colours.

[Summing-up]

In this way, then, it is clear how essence is realized in substances—composite and simple—and in their incidental properties, and how logical concepts of generality arise in all except the first supremely simple [being], whose simpleness refuses to be placed in either genus or species, and cannot therefore be defined, in whom may this discourse have its end and its fulfilment. Amen.

Part III
The Ladder of Being

Passage 7
General Overview

Source: *Summa contra Gentiles*, 4.11. Text from *Summa contra Gentiles* (*Opera Omnia*, Leonine edn., vol. xv).

Date: 1264, Italy, aged 39.

. . . Different kinds of things produce in different ways, those on a higher level producing in a more interior way.

The lowest level of all is that of non-living bodies, in which production is only possible when one body acts on another: fire produces fire when some outside body is so affected by fire that it takes on the quality and nature of fire itself.

The living things closest to these are the plants, in which there is already some interior production, turning the inner juices of the plant into seed which, committed to earth, grows into a plant. So here already we have a first level of life, since living things move themselves whilst non-living things can only move things outside themselves. In plants then there is this sign of life: that something within them moves towards some form. Nevertheless, the life of plants is not perfect, for although what they produce comes from inside, still it gradually emerges from within and ends up entirely outside. For the tree's juice as it comes out of the tree first makes a flower, then later a fruit separate from the bark of the tree though joined to it, a fruit which, when mature, separates entirely from the tree and falls to the ground, there producing by virtue of its seed another plant. And if one thinks more deeply about even that, the first beginnings of production are also outside: for the inner juices of the tree are sucked up by the roots from the earth which nourishes the plant.

There is another level of life above that of plants: that of animals endowed with sense-awareness so that they have a form of production peculiar to themselves, starting indeed from outside but ending up inside, and getting more interior the further it progresses. For something outside that can be sensed impresses its form on the external senses, and from there goes on to the imagination, ending up stored in memory. But at each stage of this process the beginning and end differ: no sense-power reflects on itself. So this level of life is higher than that of plants to the extent that it is more interiorly contained; but it is still not altogether perfect, since the production always is from one thing to another.

So the highest, most perfect level of life is that of the intellect, for intellect can reflect upon itself and understand itself. But here too there are different levels. The human mind, even though it can come to self-awareness, must still start by knowing outside things, and they can't be understood without sense-images... More perfect then is the intellectual life of angels, in which intellects know themselves not from outside but by knowing themselves in themselves. And yet their life isn't yet the acme of perfection, for although the idea in their mind is altogether within them it isn't what they are, since in them to exist is different from to understand... The acme of perfection in life, then, belongs to God, in whom to exist is to understand... so that in God the idea in his mind is what God himself is.

When I say 'the idea in the mind' I am talking of what is conceived in the mind by the mind out of the thing it is understanding. In us this isn't the thing understood itself, nor is it our own mind's substance, but a sort of representation conceived by the mind out of the thing it understands, and which is expressed externally in speech (so that the idea itself can be thought of as an interior word expressed by our exterior word). And that in us this idea we are talking of is not indeed the thing itself is clear from the fact that understanding things is not the same as understanding ideas, which mind does when it reflects on its own workings, and that the sciences of things differ from the science of intellectual ideas. And that in us this idea is not the mind itself is clear from the fact that for ideas to exist is nothing more or less than to be understood, whereas for our minds existing differs from being understood. But in God existing and understanding are one and the same, so that in him the idea in his mind is his very mind itself; and because in him understanding is the thing he understands, in understanding himself he understands everything else... so that God in understanding himself is identical with his understanding intellect and with the thing he is understanding and with the idea by which he understands...

Passage 8

How Elements are Present within Compounds

Source: On Compounds of Elements (complete). Text from *De Mixtione Elementorum* (Leonine edn., vol, xliii).

Date: Uncertain.

How to read: I have added three short headings in bold type to pick out the stages of the discussion. The *elements* in question are a sort of pure fire, pure air, pure earth, and pure water; their behavioural qualities (or active and passive qualities) come in opposed (contrary) pairs, of which two pairs are primary: hot/cold, moist/dry. Pure fire is hot (+ dry), pure air moist (+ hot), pure earth dry (+ cold), and pure water cold (+ moist). Though this physics and chemistry is now antiquated, the philosophical question Thomas is asking would still have to be asked today by an Aristotelian philosophy of substance: in a compound what is the substance: only the elements, or both the elements and the compound, or only the compound?

Notes on translation: For *accidens* I have used (supervening) properties; for *contraria* opposed properties. Elsewhere in these translations I sometimes anachronistically call the active and passive elemental qualities the physico-chemical properties of things.

Parallel reading: Cf. Aristotle, *De Generatione et Corruptione*, book 2.

[As independent actualities?]

Often people ask how elements are present within compounds. Some think elements remain present in substance but with their behavioural properties modified and averaged out somewhat; for if they weren't present in substance wouldn't that mean they had been destroyed rather than formed a compound? Again, if matter in a compound is actualized immediately by the form of the compound rather than through the intermediary of the elements' forms, the simple component parts of the compound could no longer be called elements. For an element is *what things are ultimately made of, existing in the things and indivisible in its own nature*;[1] but if the substance of the elements has disappeared the compound is no longer made up of indivisible things *existing in it.*

Nevertheless, this can't be how things are. For one and the same matter can't take on the forms of different elements. If then the elements are to be preserved in substance within the compound it will have to be in different parts of the matter. Now matter can have different parts only if we think of it as already having quantitative extension (for without extension a substance would stay indivisible, as Aristotle[2] explains). But extended matter that has taken on the form of a substance is already a physical three-dimensional body, so that the different parts of matter that have taken on the forms of the elements are so many several bodies. Now several bodies can't occupy the same place. So the four elements won't be present in every part of the compound, and as a result the compound will not be real but only apparent, like a mixture of particles too small for the senses to distinguish. Furthermore, each different substance, if it is to exist, needs matter specially conditioned in a way appropriate to that substance, and this is done by the modifications of qualitative properties which lead up to the formation (and destruction) of substances. However, the special conditions required for fire and the special conditions required for water can't coexist in the same matter, because they are opposed conditions, and opposed things can't coincide. So fire and water can't possibly exist in the same part of any compound. If then elements remain in substance within the compound, the compound is only apparent, not real, consisting of juxtaposed particles too small for our senses to distinguish.

[In a half-existent state?]

Some people, in avoiding these difficulties, fell into worse problems. In order to distinguish the compounding of elements from their destruction they said that in some way the elements remain in substance in the compound. But again, to avoid saying the compound was apparent and not real, they suggested that the elements didn't remain totally distinct in the compound but were averaged out in some way; for they said that elements could be more or less themselves and balance each other out. Now this clearly contradicts both common opinion and also Aristotle's[3] statement that substances don't have [balancing] substances opposed to them and don't more or less exist; so they expanded it by saying that elements exist in a very imperfect way, close to ultimate unformed matter, and so are intermediate between substances and supervening properties [in which we do find opposition and balance], so that it was this closeness in nature to supervening properties that enabled them to more or less exist.

But this is an unlikely suggestion on many counts. Firstly, because it is altogether impossible for there to be something intermediate between substances and supervening properties: it would have to be intermediate between an assertion and its denial. For the characteristic of properties is to exist in a subject, and the characteristic of substances is precisely not to do so. The forms of substances are not [like properties] forms of some [already formed] subject, but of [unformed] matter: a subject is a this thing, and the form of a substance makes it a this thing rather than presupposing a this thing already existing. Again, an intermediary between completely heterogeneous extremes is an absurdity, as Aristotle[4] proves. Ends and middle must share something in common. Between substance and its properties then there can be nothing intermediate. On top of that, the substance of elements can't more or less exist. For anything that can be more or less actual is, at least incidentally, divisible into parts, inasmuch as some subject can have more or less of it. But things that have parts, incidentally or of their own nature, are characterized by gradual change, as Aristotle[5] notes: thus local movement and growth or shrinkage are found where there is extension and place, which are by nature divisible into parts; and qualitative modifications are characteristic of those qualities you can have more or less of like hotness and whiteness. If then elements too could exist more or less, then their formation and destruction would be a gradual change; and that is ruled out since, as Aristotle[6] proves, there are only three types of gradual change: change in quantity, in quality, and in place. Further, every difference in the form of substances is a difference in kind. But in what exists more or less, the more differs from the less and opposes it, as, for example, more white and less white. If then fire's substance could be more or less, the more and the less would have to differ in kind, and then they wouldn't be the same substance but different ones. And this is why Aristotle[7] said substances varied in kind like numbers, by addition and subtraction.

[Virtually?]

So we have to find some other way of maintaining the reality of compounds: one which doesn't involve total destruction of the elements but lets them exist somehow in the compound. Observe then that the behavioural properties of elements do oppose one another, and can exist more or less. From such opposed properties existing more or less we can construct an intermediate property that retains a taste of what each extreme is like: grey, for example, intermediate between black and white, and tepid, intermediate between hot and cold. So then, when the extreme properties of elements have been damped down, there remains an intermediate property characteristic of the compound, differing in each compound because of different proportions of the component elements. It is this intermediate property that specially conditions matter to the form of the compound in question, just as each element's simple quality disposes matter to the form of that element. Just as any intermediate retains part of the nature of the two extremes, so the characteristic quality of the compound retains something of the qualities of its elements. But the qualitative property of an element is not its substance, though it is active with the substance's power; unless that were so heat would only heat, and not by its action also bring new substances into existence, for nothing can do what transcends its own kind of reality. So the powers of the elemental substances are preserved in the compound substance in this way. The substances of the elements then are present in the compound, but virtually—through their powers—not actually. And that is what Aristotle[8] says: *Thus they neither persist actually* (the elements, namely, in the compound) *as body and white do, nor are they destroyed (either one of them or both); for their power is preserved.*

Passage 9
Life, or Soul and its Abilities

Source: Thomas's public disputation on Created Spirits, 11. Text from *Quaestio Disputata de Spiritualibus Creaturis*, in *Quaestiones Disputatae de Potentia* (Marietti edn., Turin, 1953).

Date: 1269, Italy, aged 44.

Type of passage and how to read: Disputed question. Note that Objections 4 to 7 have been indented to show that they are not simply a linear sequence, but depend on one another: the bachelor respondent's answers led to new questions (see Introduction).

Notes on translation: 'Soul' translates *anima*, and means the animating principle of the body; it should not be given any religious overtones. 'Incidental' translates *accidens*, 'characteristic' *proprium*; 'ability' *potentia*. Since here, as often elsewhere, Thomas uses *substantia* and *essentia* to all intents and purposes synonymously, 'substance' and 'essence' do not always translate their etymological counterparts.

The subject for debate is **Created Spirits.**

... [**Article 11**] And finally we are asked: **Do the soul's abilities constitute its substance?**

It seems so:

For . . . [2] the *De Spiritu et Anima*[1] says *everything in God is God, but in the soul some things—its abilities—are soul whilst other things—its virtues—are not.*

Moreover, [3] incidental properties don't define types of substance. But abilities to sense or to reason do define types of substance. So the senses and reason and other like abilities, are not incidental properties, but must be what soul essentially is.

But it was said [by the respondent] that abilities are neither incidental to soul nor of its essence, but are natural characteristics of its substance, a half-way house between the subject and its incidental properties.

But against that: [4] substance and incidental properties differ like yes and no, since incidental properties require a subject and a thing's substance doesn't. Now there is no half-way house between yes and no. So there is no half-way house between a thing's essence and what is incidental.

Moreover, [5] to call soul's abilities natural characteristics of its substance means either that they constitute its essence or derive from what constitutes its essence. If the former then they belong to soul's essence, because a thing's essential constituents are of its essence. If the latter then even incidental properties can be called essential, since they too derive from what constitutes the subject. So, if soul's abilities are not to be incidental, they must belong to its essence.

But it was said [by the respondent] that though incidental properties derive from what constitutes substance, not everything so derived is incidental.

But against that: [6] what is in the middle must differ from either extreme. So if soul's abilities are half-way between essential and incidental they must differ from both. Now things can't differ by what they have in common: and since deriving from what constitutes substance—which was said to make abilities essential—

applies also to what is incidental, there seems to be no distinction between soul's abilities and its incidental properties; and no half-way house between what's essential and what's incidental.

But it was said [by the respondent] that the distinction is this: that we can understand soul without its incidental properties but not without its abilities.

> But against that: [7] we understand things by taking in their essence: for the object of understanding, according to Aristotle,[2] is the what-a-thing-is. So, if *A* can't be understood without *B*, *B* must be of *A*'s essence. Now soul can't be understood without abilities, so they must be of its essence, and no half-way house exists between what's essential and what's incidental . . .

Moreover, [12] if soul's abilities are not the same as its essence they must derive from its essence. But this is impossible: the effect would be more immaterial than the cause, since soul of its essence actuates a body, whereas understanding—an ability—actuates no body. So our premiss must have been faulty: namely, that soul's abilities are not its essence . . .

Moreover, [14] soul is joined to body not by way of any ability, but as its form, directly actuating it in some way. Not, however, by giving it existence, for things can exist without souls; nor by giving it life, for things can be living without rational souls. So it must be by giving it understanding, which is what we say ability to understand gives. So ability to understand must be the soul's essence.

Moreover, [15] soul is more perfect and excellent than the ultimate material of things. Now ultimate matter is its own potentiality: being potential can't be incidental to it—for then an incidental property would pre-exist in matter before it took on the form of any substance (since, as Aristotle[3] shows, potentiality precedes its own actualization in time); nor can it be the substance's form—for potentiality is the opposite of form; nor can it be what matter and form combine to make—for that can't precede form. Matter's potentiality then must be matter's very essence. *A fortiori* then must soul's powers be soul's essence...

Moreover, [17] freedom from matter makes a substance intellectual, according to Ibn Sīnā.[4] Now soul is by essence immaterial, so by essence intellectual. Intellect then is its essence, and other abilities likewise.

Moreover, [18] in the absence of matter, Aristotle[5] says, understanding is one thing with what it understands. But what it understands is soul's essence; so soul's essence must also be the understanding that understands, and other abilities likewise.

Moreover, [19] a thing's parts belong to its substance. But soul's abilities are called its parts. So they belong to its substance.

Moreover, [20] the soul is a non-composite substance, as we said earlier, but with many abilities. If these are not its essence but incidental to it, then something non-composite will have a diversity of incidental properties, which doesn't seem plausible. So soul's abilities are not incidental to it but its very essence.

But against that:

[1] Pseudo-Dionysius[6] says higher beings divide into *substance, power, and activity*. Much more then in souls must essence differ from power or ability...

Moreover, [4] abilities are in the middle, joining substances to their activity. Now soul's substance and activity differ. So its abilities must differ from both, for a middle must differ from either extreme.

Moreover, [5] an agent isn't the same thing as his tool. But soul's abilities relate to its essence as tools to an agent: Anselm[7] says will—an ability of soul—is like a tool. So soul is not its abilities...

In reply

Some people identify soul's abilities with the soul itself, the same soul as source of sense-activity being called our ability to sense, as source of understanding activity our ability to understand, and so on. Ibn Sīnā thinks people were led to believe this mainly by the non-compositeness of soul, which seemed at odds with the diversity displayed in its abilities. But the opinion is altogether impossible: firstly, because no created substance can be identified with its power to act. For clearly, distinct potentialities require distinct actualities—actualizations must match what they actualize. Now existence actualizes, so to say, a thing's essence, whereas activity actualizes its active powers and dispositions: to be actual essences must exist but powers must act. So, since no creature's doing is its being (that is God's prerogative), no creature's power to act is its essence (that too is the prerogative of God). Secondly, this is particularly impossible in the soul's case, for three reasons: firstly, because essence is one whereas abilities must be many because of the variety of their activities and objects: abilities are diversified by their activities in the way all potentialities are by what actualizes them. A second reason is a difference between abilities, some of which actualize parts of the body (all our sense-abilities and nutritive powers) whilst others do not (mind and will). Now if abilities were nothing but soul's essence this couldn't be so, for one and the same thing can't both actuate a body and exist separated, except by some diversity it has. A third reason is the hierarchical order of abilities among themselves, one moving another: reason moves our aggressive and affective emotions, for example, and mind will. But if abilities were nothing but soul's essence this couldn't be so, for nothing can move itself in the same respect, as Aristotle[8] proves.

So we are forced to conclude that soul's abilities are not its essence.

Now some people concede this, but say abilities aren't incidental to soul either, but are its essential or natural characteristics; which is acceptable on one interpretation and impossible on another. To be clear about this we should note two ways in which philosophers use the word *incidental*. Firstly, as a general description for the nine [Aristotelian] categories other than substance. In this sense the above opinion is impossible, for in this sense there is no half-way house between what is substance and what is incidental: they differ as yes and no, since substances characteristically don't exist in subjects, and incidental properties do. So if soul's abilities are not its essence—and clearly they are not other substances—they must belong in one of the [Aristotelian] categories of incidental property: in fact in the second [of the four] types of quality, that of natural abilities or inabilities. But there is a second use of the word *incidental* as a name for one of Aristotle's[9] four predicables, or Porphyry's[10] five types of general concept. In this sense *incidental* doesn't express something common to the nine categories, but a particular relationship a proposition's predicate can bear to its subject, or a class to a member of that class. In this sense *incidental* is contradistinguished against genus and species, so can't be used in the same sense as previously; otherwise nothing in the nine categories could ever be given a genus or a species, which is clearly false since whiteness is in the genus of colour and twoness in that of number. Now in this sense of *incidental* there is a half-way house between substance and incidentals, i.e. between predicates which define a thing's substance and predicates ascribed to it incidentally: namely, predicates characteristic of it. Such characteristic predicates resemble the predicate defining a thing's substance in deriving from the thing's specific nature: which is why, by appealing to a subject's definition, we can prove it to have such and such characteristics.[11] But they also resemble properties predicated incidentally in being neither a thing's substance nor part of it, but something added. Incidental predicates, however, differ from characteristic predicates in not deriving from a subject's specific nature: they are incidental to individuals in the way characteristics are to species, though sometimes they accompany all individuals and sometimes not.

Soul's abilities then are something half-way between its essence and what is incidental to it: they are, so to speak, natural or essential characteristics of soul, natural consequences of its essence.

Hence: . . .

to 2: The *De Spiritu et Anima* is an apocryphal work of unknown authorship[12] containing more than one false or inaccurate statement. Whoever wrote it didn't understand the words of the holy men he was attempting to make his own. However, if we must make a case for him, note that there are three kinds of whole. The first is the general, sharing itself and its potentiality with each of its subdivisions and therefore predicable of them: human beings are animals. The second is the composite, sharing neither itself nor its potentiality with any of its component parts, and so in no way predicable of them: walls are not houses. And the third is the functional whole, midway between the other two, sharing itself with part of its potentiality to each subfunction, and so sometimes predicable of them, but improperly. And this is the way soul is sometimes said to be its own abilities and vice versa.

to 3: We know the form of no substance directly, but get to know it through its characteristic properties. So often we define types of substances by such properties—two-legged, for example, or mobile—rather than by any form of substance they reveal. And this is the way ability to sense or to reason differentiate substances. Or one could say that ability to sense and to reason, when used to differentiate substances, name not the abilities but the souls that have the abilities.

to 4: This argument understands *incidental* as a generic description for the nine [Aristotelian] categories [other than substance], and in that sense there is no half-way house between substance and incidental properties; but in the other sense of *incidental* referred to above, there is.

to 5: Soul's abilities are called essential characteristics not because they constitute its essence but because they derive from it. That doesn't distinguish them from the incidental properties contained in the nine [Aristotelian] categories, but it distinguishes them from incidental predicates which do not derive from a thing's specific nature. And this also provides the answer to **6**.

to 7: Aristotle[13] says we exercise understanding in two ways: firstly, by taking in what something is, and secondly, by making propositional connections and disconnections. Exercising understanding in the first way we can take in a thing's essence without either its characteristic or its incidental properties, since neither enter its essence (and the objection used this sense of understanding). But exercising understanding in the second way, substance can be understood without its incidental accompaniments, even when they always accompany it in fact: thus we can understand a crow to be white, since the concepts are not incompatible and the specific nature of the named subject [crow] doesn't imply the contrary predicate [black]. But substances can't be understood in this way without their characteristic properties: we can't understand human beings not to have a sense of the ridiculous, or a triangle not to have its internal angles equal to two right-angles. Here there are two incompatible concepts, since the nature of the subject implies the contrary predicate. With the first sort of understanding, then, we can understand soul's essence—what it is—without its abilities; but with the second sort of understanding, we can't understand soul to exist without such abilities...

to 12: That an ability actuating no body can derive from soul's essence happens only because soul contains in its essence more than body requires, as we said earlier. So we can't conclude that the power is more immaterial than the essence, since it derives its immateriality from that of the essence...

to 14: Soul, being essentially body's form, gives body existence (being the form of its substance) and that sort of existence we call life (being the sort of form we call soul) and that sort of life we call understanding or intellectual (being the sort of soul we call intellectual). For *understanding* sometimes names an activity (and then its source is an ability or disposition), and sometimes names our very existence as creatures of an understanding nature (and then its source is the very essence of our intellectual soul).

to 15: Matter's potentiality is not a potential to act but potential to exist as a substance, and so can be classified as [potential] substance; but soul's powers are potentials to act and can't...

to 17: It is precisely because soul's substance is free from matter that it has a power of intellect, but that power is not its substance.

to 18: Understanding isn't just an ability to understand but much more a substance acting through that ability; and so what it understands is not just its own ability but also the substance.

to 19: Soul's abilities can be called parts of soul's total potential, but not of its essence, just as one could say the king's officer's power is part of the total power of the king.

to 20: Many of soul's powers don't have soul for their subject but the composite of body and soul, and the multiplicity of these powers matches a multiformity of bodily parts. The powers that have for subject only soul's substance are our agent and receptive mind and will. And for that multiplicity of powers the compositeness of potentiality and actuality that even soul's substance has is enough.

Passage 10
Levels of Life

Source: Thomas's public disputation on the Soul, 13. Text from *Quaestio Disputata de Anima* (ed. Robb, Toronto, 1968), with corrections from the Leonine text in preparation.

Date: 1269, second stay in Paris, aged 44–5.

Type of passage and how to read: Disputed question (see Introduction).

Notes on translation: For remarks on the word 'soul' see previous passage on Created Spirits. 'General root sensitivity' translates *sensus communis*: 'common-sense' has come to mean something else in modern English.

The subject for debate is **Soul.**

. . . **[Article 13]** And in the thirteenth place we are asked: **What distinguishes soul's abilities: is it their objects?**

And it seems not:

For . . . [2] difference in substance—as between human beings and rabbits—is greater than incidental difference—between sound and colour. Yet one and the same ability perceives human beings and rabbits. So *a fortiori* should it perceive sound and colour. No difference of objects then should need different abilities...

Moreover, [4] same cause, same effect: so if a difference in object were to diversify abilities here it should diversify them everywhere. But that's not what we observe: rather differences in object—sound and colour—correspond sometimes to different abilities—hearing and sight—and sometimes to only one—imagination, or mind. So differences in object don't cause diversity in abilities...

Moreover, [6] a gift is what the recipient makes of it. Now soul's abilities are received into body's organs; for abilities are actuations of organs. So bodily organs differentiate abilities, rather than objects.

Moreover, [7] soul's abilities don't constitute its substance but flow as natural characteristics from its essence. Now from unity without intermediary flows only unity, so only one ability can flow from soul's essence to begin with, and others from that in a hierarchy. Abilities then differ by origin, not by object...

Moreover, [11] everything desirable can be either sensed or understood. Now what can be understood fulfils our understanding, and what can be sensed fulfils our senses; and since by nature everything desires its fulfilment, understanding and sense between them must desire by nature everything that is desirable. So we need no other ability to desire than our abilities to sense and understand.

Moreover, [12] desire is either willing or a feeling of aggression or affection, where will is desire of intellect and aggressive and affective feeling desire of the senses, as Aristotle[1] says. So we need no ability to desire other than our abilities to sense and understand.

Moreover, [13] Aristotle[2] proves that local movement in living things is caused by sense (that is to say, imagination), understanding, and desire. But in living things what causes their movement is called motive power. So there is no motive power other than the abilities to know and desire...

Moreover, [15] the higher a power the more extensive and yet integrated it is. But the soul's living powers are higher than the powers in nature. If then one and the same power in nature can give a body existence and proper size and preserve it in existence, it seems soul should *a fortiori* do all this through one power. So there shouldn't be different reproductive, nutritive, and growth functions...

Moreover, [17] every genus has its fundamental pair of opposing properties. So if we are going to differentiate sense-powers by diverse genera of passive qualities, there should be different sense-powers wherever there are diverse pairs of opposing qualities. Now sometimes this is so—sight sees black and white, hearing hears booms and squeaks—but sometimes not—touch senses hot and cold and wet and dry and soft and hard and much else. So abilities are not distinguished by their objects...

Moreover, [19] understanding knows everything sense knows and more besides. So if our sense-powers are distinguished by different objects, understanding too should be diversified into the same kinds of power as the senses, which is clearly false.

Moreover, [20] agent intellect and receptive intellect are, we say, different abilities. But both have the same object. So abilities are not distinguished by difference in object.

But against that:

[1] Aristotle[3] says we distinguish abilities by their activities and activities by their objects.

Moreover, [2] ways of being fulfilled are distinguished by what fulfils them. But abilities find fulfilment in their objects. So that's what distinguishes them.

In reply:

An ability or potential is nothing else than an openness to actualization, so what the actuality is must define the potentiality, and potentials for diverse actualities must be distinct. Now the actuality is defined by the actuating object: and abilities to be receptive are actuated by objects that act on them, and abilities to be active are actuated by goals. Activities then can be defined in either way: heating is distinguished from cooling because the initiating object is heat rather than cold, or—since agents act to imprint likenesses of themselves on others—because heat is the activity's end-goal. So to distinguish abilities of soul [i.e. potentials of living things] we must distinguish their objects. However, the distinction of objects required must be one relevant to them as objects of soul's activities, not any other sort, since a genus doesn't divide into species except by way of differences relevant to the genus as such: white/black doesn't constitute different species of animal, but reasoning/non-reasoning does.

Now there are **three levels** to soul-activity. For soul-activity [life-activity] transcends the activities of nature at work in non-living creatures; and this in two ways: in manner of acting and in what gets done. In manner of acting all soul-activity transcends the action or workings of nature in non-living things, because soul-activity is life-activity and living means self-moving, so that all soul-activity comes from interior agency. But as to what gets done, not every soul-activity transcends the working of non-living nature. For bodies, whether animate or inanimate, must have existence in nature and whatever is required for that; in inanimate bodies this is the function of exterior agencies, but in animate bodies it is a function of interior agencies: and the soul's potentials for such activities we call its **vegetative powers.** These comprise generative powers which bring individuals into existence, powers of growth which cause them to attain their proper size, and nutritive powers which conserve them in existence. But since all of this in inanimate bodies is brought about by external natural agents, these powers of soul are [often] called natural powers.

However, there are other higher-level life-activities which transcend the working of natural forms also in regard to what gets done: those, namely, that are based on soul's ability to give everything immaterial existence within itself, for soul as sentient and intelligent is in a sense everything. But this immaterial existence has different levels. At the first level things exist in the soul without their own material but accompanied by the singularity and conditions of individuality which that material has conferred on them; and this is the level of the senses, which take in individual natures without their matter but into bodily organs. A higher and more perfect level of immateriality is intellectual understanding, which takes in natures altogether abstracted from matter and material conditions, and without any bodily organ. And just as things are endowed by natural form with tendencies to some goal and the movements and activity that pursue the goal, so too by a form sensed or understood they are endowed with tendencies towards the thing (or object of understanding) taken in, tendencies which are functionings of an ability to desire; and also here there must follow movements pursuing the desired thing, functionings of a motive power.

So at **the level of sense-awareness,** which suffices for animal life, five things are needed. Firstly, sense must take in the form of what it senses, and that is the function of **particular senses.** Secondly, the different sense-perceptions must be discriminated and distinguished one from the other, and that needs some central power to which everything sensed is brought, and which we call the **general root sensitivity.** Thirdly, the forms taken in have to be stored—for animals need to be aware of what can be sensed not just when it's present but also when it's absent—and that needs another ability or power: for what makes bodies impressionable is not what makes them retentive: something easily imprinted may retain imprints badly. This other power we call **imagination** or **fancy.** Fourthly, certain notions are needed which are not the sort senses can take in, like danger, usefulness, and so on. Human beings learn these by research and discussion, but other animals by a sort of natural instinct: sheep by nature flee wolves as dangerous. So where other animals have a power of natural **judgement,** human beings have a sort of calculation that pieces together particular experiences and is therefore called particular reasoning or passive mentality. Fifthly, what has been taken in by the senses at some earlier time and stored internally needs to be recalled to actual consideration. And this is the function of

memory, which in other animals works without enquiry, but in human beings with enquiry and study: so that human beings have not only memory but reminiscence. And this needs a power distinct from the others, since other sense-activity moves from things to soul whereas memory moves from soul to things, and different movements need different motive principles or powers.

Since the particular senses—the first in this range of sensitive powers—are the ones immediately stimulated and affected by what is sensed, differences in these stimulations force differentiation of these powers. And since the senses take in the forms of what they sense without matter, we order and grade these affections of sense by what is sensed by comparing them with material changes. Now certain forms of things we sense, although taken in by the senses immaterially, nevertheless also change the sensing animal materially. These are the qualities which cause change in all material things: hot and cold, wet and dry, and so on. Because what we sense in this way also changes us by material action, and material change works through contact, necessarily such sensing is done by contact. And for this reason the sense-power that takes in all such objects of sense is called **touch**. Other objects of sense don't as such induce material change, but nevertheless affect us in connection with some material change: and this can happen in two ways. Sometimes the connected material change affects what is sensed and what senses, as in **taste**: for though taste doesn't affect the sense-organ by making the organ itself tasty, still the affection of taste depends on change in both the tasty substance and the organ of taste, chiefly change in their wet-or-dryness. Sometimes, however, the connected material change affects only what is sensed: either by some break-down or modification of what we sense, as in the case of **smell**; or simply by vibration in it, as in **hearing**. Which is why hearing and smell, involving material change only in what is sensed and not in what senses, don't sense by immediate contact but through an external medium; whereas taste, involving material change also in what senses, only senses by contact. Yet other objects of sense affect our senses without any connected material change, in the way light and colour affect our sense of **sight**. For this reason sight is sensing at its highest and most general, able to sense qualities that earthly and heavenly bodies have in common.

We must also differentiate in a similar way the ability to desire that depends on our powers of sense. This power divides into two: for things are desirable either because they themselves delight and suit the senses, and these require a capacity for **affective emotion**; or because they empower us to enjoy things delightful to the senses, though they in themselves sometimes sadden the senses, as when an animal fights to repel obstacles and gain access to what he naturally enjoys; and this requires a capacity for **aggressive emotion.**

But **motive power**, directed to movement, is differentiated only by diversity of movements: movements special to various animals—some crawling, some flying, some walking, some moving in other ways—or even characterizing different parts of one animal, for every part has its own proper movement.

At **the level of intellectual powers** there is a similar distinction into powers of knowing and powers of desiring, but motive power is something shared between sense and intellect, for the same body is moved to the same movement by both. And intellectual knowing requires two powers, as we saw above: the **agent intellect** and the **receptive intellect.**

Clearly then there are **three levels** among powers of soul, or living abilities: those of vegetable life, of animal life, and of rational life. But there are **five sorts** of ability: namely, nutritive, sensitive, intellectual, appetitive, and locomotive, some of these containing several powers under them, as we have said.

Hence: . . .

to 2: Colour and sound may be incidental properties, but, as we have said, they stimulate our senses in essentially different ways. Human beings and rabbits, on the other hand, stimulate our senses in an identical way, and, though essentially different as substances, differ only incidentally as sense-objects. For there is no reason why differences essential in one context shouldn't be incidental in another, as white and black things differ essentially in colour but not in nature...

to 4: Higher-level abilities extend over wider fields and are defined by a more general concept of object; so things that share a higher ability's definition of object may constitute distinct objects of lower-level abilities...

to 6: Organs serve abilities and not vice versa; so organs are distinguished by their objects rather than the reverse.

to 7: Each soul has a primary goal—for the human soul what it understands to be good—which all its other goals serve—so that what is sensed as good serves what we understand to be good. Now soul is ordered to its objects by means of abilities, so that our ability to sense exists in us to serve our ability to understand, and so on. So one ability flows from another as from a goal, according to their respective objects, and distinction of soul's abilities by origin[4] is not therefore opposed to distinction by object...

to 11: By nature understanding desires the understandable as something to understand, for it has a natural desire to understand as the senses have to sense. But we desire what can be sensed and understood not only for sensing and understanding but also for other reasons; so we must have an ability to desire over and above our abilities to sense and understand.

to 12: Will is a desire of reason in the sense of following reason: its activity belongs at the same level of ability in the soul but is not of the same sort. And the same is true of aggressive or affective feelings and the senses.

to 13: Knowledge and desire move by commanding movement, but there must be motive power to execute the movement, moving limbs to implement the commands of desire and understanding or sense...

to 15: Inanimate things in nature acquire form and proper size together, but living things can't do that, since they are reproduced from seed and must begin small. So their reproductive function must be accompanied by a growth function to bring them to their proper size. This can only be done by converting additional material into the substance of the growing thing, and such conversion needs heat, which not only converts external but breaks down internal material. So, to preserve individuals by continually replacing lost matter and adding matter lacking to their full size and needed to produce seed, an ability to assimilate food is needed: that serves both the growing and reproductive functions, and also preserves the individual...

to 17: Because the opposed qualities of which touch is aware don't all belong to one genus in the way the opposed visible qualities belong to the genus of colour, Aristotle[5] decided touch was not one sense but several, which had this in common: that they sensed without any external medium and so were all called touch, one sense generically but several specifically. But one could also say touch is one sense simply speaking, since all the opposed qualities it senses [use the same organ][6] and belong in one [common] unnamed genus (as indeed the immediate genus of hot and cold is unnamed)...

to 19: Sense takes the forms of the things we sense into bodily organs and is aware of them in their particularity; understanding takes in things' forms without using bodily organs and so is aware of them in their generality. As a result certain diversities of object may differentiate sense-powers without differentiating our powers of understanding. In the material world different materials are needed to receive and to retain impressions, but not in the immaterial world; and in a similar way different sorts of sense-stimuli diversify our senses but make no difference to understanding.

to 20: One and the same object—the object actually understood—is made understandable by agent intellect and then actualizes receptive intellect. And so the same object is not related to agent and receptive intellect in the same respect.

Passage 11
Inner and Outer Senses

Source: Thomas's *Commentary on Aristotle's De Memoria et Reminiscentia*, $449^b30-450^a25$. Text from *Sentencia Libri de Sensu (de Memoria)* (*Opera Omnia*, Leonine edn., vol. xlv.ii).

Date: 1269–70, second stay in Paris, aged 45.

Type of passage: Commentary with digressions (see Introduction).

How to read: Cf. remarks on Passage 5 above.

Aristotle has already explained what memory is; now he goes on to explain what part of us remembers. And he does this in two parts: firstly [at *The subject of imagination*], making preliminary remarks necessary to his explanation; and secondly, at *It is now clear*, giving the explanation itself.

[Aristotle's text, $449^b30-450^a10$]

The subject of imagination has already been considered in the De Anima, and without images understanding is impossible. For the same thing happens in understanding as in geometrical diagrams, where we draw a triangle of a certain size, even though we don't use the particular size. So likewise when we want to understand anything we conjure up before our eyes something of a certain size but the mind understands it not as having that size. And if it is of its nature quantitative but indeterminate we conjure it up as of determinate size though the mind understands it only as a quantity. It is another question why human beings can't understand except in space and time.

[Preliminary remarks]

Here there are three parts: firstly [1], he states what he means to do; secondly [2], at *For the same thing happens*, he clarifies what he has said with an example; and thirdly [3], [at *It is another question*] he indicates something needing another type of explanation. So firstly [1], he says that *the subject of imagination*—what it is—*has already been con-*

sidered in his De Anima:[1] imagination is a change wrought in us by actual sensing. And in the same book[2] he says that *without images* human *understanding is impossible*.

Next [2], when he says *For the same thing happens*, he clarifies what he has just said. For it might seem absurd to say that there is no human understanding without images when images are representations of bodily things and understanding is of universals abstracted from all particular things. So to clarify this he offers an example, saying that *the same thing happens in understanding as in geometrical diagrams, where we draw a triangle of a certain size, even though we don't use the particular size* in our proofs. *So likewise when we want to understand anything we conjure up before our eyes something of a certain size*, something particular; when we want to understand a human being there comes up the image of some six-footer, for example. *But the mind understands* human being as human being *not as having that size*. However, because what the mind may be wanting to understand is the nature of size, he goes on to say that if what is to be understood *is of its nature quantitative*—a line, say, or a surface or a number—*but indeterminate*—that is, not in its determinate particularity—we nevertheless *conjure up* before our eyes an image *of determinate size*; when we want to understand a line there comes up the image of a line two-foot long, for example, *though the mind understands it only* in its nature *as a quantity*, not as being two-foot long.

Next [3], when he says *It is another question*, he declares what he will leave for consideration [elsewhere]. And he says that *it is another question why human beings can't understand except in space and time*.

[Thomas's first digression]

Now in fact this happens because human beings can't understand in the absence of images; for images must involve space and time, being likenesses of individual things in the here and now. And the explanation of why human beings can't understand without images would be easy enough if it was only a question of where ideas come from, since Aristotle[3] makes it clear that we abstract these from images.

But experience shows that even people who already have knowledge, having acquired ideas in this way, can't actually think about what they know in the absence of images. For this is the reason why, when we damage our [brain, the] organ of imagination, we are debarred not only from any new understanding, but even from thinking about what we previously understood, as we see in cases of madness.

One might hypothesize that human minds, having acquired ideas, retain them only while actually thinking of them, and that if they stop actually thinking of them the ideas vanish from the mind like light vanishes from the air when the source of light is removed. Consequently, when the mind wants to understand something again it must turn again to images and acquire ideas afresh. But this hypothesis expressly contradicts Aristotle's words[4] where he says that 'as soon as the receptive mind is formed by what is able to be understood', taking in its species, 'it has the potential to actually understand it'. And it also goes against reason, since mind's actual acquisition of species must share in the sort of thing mind is, namely, something unchanging.

Now the fact that ideas persist in the acquiring mind even when it isn't actually thinking about them is not like what happens in sense-perception where, because of the bodily constitution of our organs, receiving the sense-impressions by which we actually perceive is one process, and retaining them even when we are not actually perceiving is another, as Ibn Sīnā[5] maintains. Rather it happens due to the diverse levels on which forms that can be understood exist: as purely potential before we learn and discover, as totally actual when we are actually thinking of them, or at a level intermediate between potentiality and actuality in our habitual knowledge. So human minds don't only need images as a source of ideas, but also as something in which they can be observed: as Aristotle[6] puts it: 'Our mind understands the species of things in their images.'

And the reason for this is that activity must be proportionate to the acting power and nature. Now in humans mind exists within a sensing entity, as Aristotle[7] says. So its characteristic activity is understanding what can be understood through images; just as the activity of intellect in immaterial substances is understanding what can be understood through itself. And so we have to look to the metaphysician [i.e. elsewhere] for the reason, since different levels of intellect are his subject.

[Aristotle's text, 450^{a}10–25]

It is now clear it must be the same part of us that is aware of extension and movement and of time. Imagining is a being affected by our common root sensitivity. Clearly then these are perceived by that common root sensitivity. Memory, however—even of what we understand—doesn't happen without images, and so is an ability only incidentally intellectual, but belonging in itself to our primary common sensitivity. Hence not only human beings and beings possessing opinion and discretion possess memory, but also certain other animals. If memory was one of our understanding abilities it would not be found in many other animals and perhaps not in any other mortal creature; since even as the case stands not all animals possess memory but only those who are aware of time. For whenever someone actually remembers, as we have said, it senses at the same time that it saw or heard or learnt this before: before and after, however, characterize time. It is now clear what part of us remembers, namely, the part that imagines. And what is imaginable is memorable in itself, whereas we incidentally remember what cannot be grasped without the help of images.

[The explanation: what part of us remembers]

Next, when he says *It is now clear*, he explains what part of us remembers. Firstly [1], he argues the point; secondly [2], at *Hence not only human beings*, offers some indications from experience; and thirdly [3], at *It is now clear*, comes to his conclusion.

So firstly [1], he says that *it must be the same part of us that is aware of extension and movement and of time*. These three belong together both because they are all divisible into parts, and because all are able to be limited or unlimited, as he proves in the *Physics*.[8] Now we perceive extension with our senses: extension being one of those objects common to all the senses; and we perceive changes—especially movements—in the same way, by being aware of near-and-far in extension, and time by perceiving a before-and-afterness in change; so these three things we perceive with our senses.

However, sense-perception takes place at two levels: firstly, when our senses are actually stimulated by what they sense, as when particular senses perceive their own particular objects, and the common root of sensitivity in us perceives objects the senses have in common; and secondly, when that first stimulation of our senses by what they sense leaves in us a sort of secondary change, which persists even in the absence of what has been sensed, and is located in the imagination, as Aristotle[9] says. *Imagining*, then, because it emerges from this secondary stimulus, *is a being affected by our common root sensitivity*; for it results from the completed stimulation of our senses, beginning with the particular senses and ending up in the common root of our sensitivity. *Clearly then these* three things: extension, change, and time, as features of our images, are *perceived by that common root sensitivity*.

Memory, however, not only of what we sense (as, for example, when we remember having had some sense-perception), but *even of what we understand* (as, for example, when we remember having understood something), *doesn't happen without images*. For absent objects of sense can only be perceived in our imaginations; and, as we have just said, understanding can't happen in the absence of images. So we conclude that memory *is an ability only incidentally intellectual, belonging in itself to our primary common sensitivity*. For we have already said that understanding, which of itself understands things in the abstract, conjures up before it images of a certain size. Now memory grasps time as a certain time in the past, this far distant from the present moment. Memory then, of itself, is a kind of imaginative appearance, though incidentally it can involve mental judgement.

[Thomas's second digression]

What has been said here, however, could lead someone to think that imagination and memory are not abilities distinct from our common root sensitivity, but just certain ways in which it is affected. But Ibn Sīnā[10] has plausibly argued that they are separate abilities. For our abilities to sense are actualizations of bodily organs, and so our abilities to take in the forms of what we sense (our sense-powers) must differ from our abilities to retain them (imagination and memory), just as taking on and retaining bodily form require different materials: moist material to take on form well, dry, hard material to retain it well. In the same way taking in and retaining the forms of what we sense require different abilities from those required for taking in significances the senses do not perceive; these, even in other animals, are perceived by an instinctive power of judgement and retained by a power of memory, which remembers things not in the abstract but as taken in in the past by our senses or our understanding. Nevertheless, one ability can sometimes turn out to be a root or source of others, the actualizations of those others presupposing the actualization of the first power. This is the way our ability to feed is the root of our abilities to grow and to reproduce, both of which utilize food; and it is in this way too that our common root sensitivity is the root of our imagination and memory, which presuppose the actualization of the common sensitivity.

[Return to commentary]

Next [2], when he says *Hence not only human beings*, he illustrates what he has said with two indications from experience. The first is drawn from animals possessing memory. And he says that, because memory of itself is an ability of our primary sensitivity, *not only human beings and beings possessing opinion* (which can refer to theoretical understanding) *and discretion* (which refers to practical understanding) *possess memory, but also certain other animals. If memory was one of our understanding abilities it would not be found in many other animals* that clearly do possess memory but not understanding; *and perhaps* it would *not* be found *in any other mortal creature* but humans, since humans alone among mortal creatures possess understanding. He says *perhaps* because of people who wonder whether intelligence shouldn't also be attributed to some non-human animals—monkeys and animals of that sort—because of their apparently rational behaviour.

He gives a second indication at *even*, drawn from animals that don't possess memory. And he says that what makes clear that memory is in itself a sense-ability is that *since even as the case stands*, when we are supposing that only human beings among mortal creatures possess understanding, *not all animals possess memory but only those who are aware of time*. For certain animals perceive nothing except in the presence of something they can sense; certain animals, for instance, are immobile and therefore have fuzzy imaginations, as Aristotle says,[11] and so are unaware of before-and-after, and therefore of time, and as a result have no memories. For always, *whenever* the soul *actually remembers, as we have said, it senses at the same time that it saw or heard or learnt this before: before and after, however, characterize time*.

Next [3], when he says *It is now clear*, he comes to his conclusion. And he says that *it is now clear what part of us remembers, namely, the part that imagines; and what is imaginable is memorable in itself*, namely, what we can sense, *whereas we incidentally remember what* we understand, which *cannot be grasped* by human beings *without the help of images*. And this is why things which need subtle spiritual consideration are less easy to remember than the gross things we can sense, and why, as Cicero[12] teaches us, if we want to remember intellectual things more easily we must as it were tie them to some other images. However, there are people who regard memory as intellectual, understanding by memory all habitual retention of things intellectual.

Passage 12

Mind [*a*]

Source: *Summa Theologiae*, 1a.79.2–3. Text from *Summa Theologiae* (*Opera Omnia*, Leonine edn., vol. v).

Date: 1266–8, Italy, aged 42.

Type of passage and how to read: Modified disputed question (see Introduction).

Notes on translation: Where *intellectus* must have a special meaning I use 'understanding', where the meaning is more general 'mind'. 'Receptive mind' translates *intellectus possibilis*.

Parallel reading: For a similar treatment of the word 'passive' cf. Passage 15 below.

[Question 79] We are asking about **Our Intellectual Powers . . .**

[Article 2] The second question [**If mind is an ability, is it a passive ability?**] we approach as follows:

It seems that mind is not a passive ability:

For [1] matter is what makes things passive, and form what makes them active. But mind is an ability belonging to things immaterial in substance. So mind it seems is not a passive ability.

Moreover, [2] minds are imperishable, as we have said. But Aristotle[1] says that *intellect, if passive, is perishable*. So mind is not a passive power.

Moreover, [3] Augustine[2] and Aristotle[3] say *acting is a more excellent thing than being acted on*. Now the lowest-level powers of living things—vegetative powers—are all active powers. So *a fortiori* the highest-level power of living things—understanding—must be active.

But against that:

Aristotle[4] says *understanding is being acted on in some way*.

In reply:

The word *passive* [patient, suffering, undergoing] is used firstly, in the strictest sense, to describe things undergoing loss of something natural or congenial to their inclinations: human beings undergoing sickness or sadness, or heated water undergoing loss of its [natural] coolness. It is used secondly, and less strictly, of things altering or changing in any way, undergoing loss of anything, congenial or not: in this sense one can be patient not only of sickness but also of health, suffer the passion not only of sadness but also of joy. And thirdly, and most broadly of all, it is used when anything acquires what it had a potential to acquire, without losing anything at all: in this sense every potentiality can be said to undergo the actualization that in fact brings it to fulfilment. And in this last sense understanding is a kind of undergoing.

This is shown by the following argument. We said already that the object of mind's activity is what exists in general. So to find out whether mind is something actual or something potential we must ask how it relates to what exists in general. For there is a mind related to what exists in general as actualizing everything that exists: God's mind, identical with his substance, in which originally and virtually as in its primal cause everything that exists pre-exists. So God's mind is not a potential but sheer actualization. But no created mind can be related as actualization to everything that exists in general: for that it would have to exist without limit. So every created mind, by the very fact of being what it itself is, is not an actualization of everything that can be understood, but is related to every such thing as a potential which they actualize.

Now potentialities are actualized in two ways. The potentiality of some things—the matter of heavenly bodies, for example—is always perfectly actualized. But the potentiality of other things—things that are born and die—is not always actualized but moves from potentiality to actuality. Angelic minds are always actualized by what they understand, because of their closeness to that first understanding, the sheer actuality of which we have spoken. But human minds, being the lowest and furthest away from God's perfect mind, are sheer potentials of understanding—what Aristotle[5] calls *blank pages on which nothing is written*. And this is clear from the way we start with only a potential to understand and later become people with actual understanding. Human understanding then is clearly a being acted on in some way, an undergoing in the third sense above. And so mind is a passive ability.

Hence:

to 1: This objection understands passive in the first and second sense, characteristic of matter. But anything potential of actualization is passive in the third sense.

to 2: Some people understand *passive intellect* to refer to the seat of our passions, the sense-appetite, which elsewhere[6] Aristotle says *shares in reason* by *obeying reason*. Others take it to mean the native cunning sometimes called *particular reason*. And on both interpretations *passive* has its first two meanings since intellect in those senses is an actualization of a bodily organ. But mind as potential of what it can understand, which Aristotle[7] calls, for that reason, *receptive*, is passive only in the third sense, not being the actualization of any bodily organ. And so it is imperishable.

to 3: Acting is a more excellent thing than being acted on if the acting and being acted on relate to the same thing, but not always if they relate to different things. Now mind is passive in relation to all that exists in general, whereas vegetative powers are active in relation only to one particular existent thing, namely, the associated body. So there is no reason why that passivity can't be more excellent than this activity.

[**Article 3**] The third question [**If mind is a passive ability, must we also acknowledge the existence of an agent mind?**] we approach as follows:

It seems that we need acknowledge no agent mind:

For [1] the mind relates to what it understands as the senses to what they sense. But because the senses are potential of what they sense we don't posit an agent sense but simply receptive ones. So because mind is potential of what it understands it doesn't seem we ought to posit an agent mind, but simply a receptive one.

Moreover, if you say that in sensing too there is an agent, namely, the light, then against that: [2] seeing needs light only to make the intervening medium actually transparent, for colour itself as such then acts through the transparent. But there is no such medium in mind that needs to be actuated. So there is no need for an agent mind.

Moreover, [3] what is acted on receives the agent's imprint in the way suited to it. Now the receptive mind is an immaterial ability, and so its own immateriality suffices to ensure that forms received in it are received immaterially. But immateriality of form makes it actually understandable. So there is no need to posit an agent mind to make the received forms actually understandable.

But against that:

Aristotle[8] says that *in the mind, just as in the rest of nature, besides what is receptive of existence there is what makes things exist.*

In reply:

In Plato's view there was no need for an agent mind to make things actually understandable, but only perhaps to give us light to understand by. For according to Plato the forms of things in nature exist on their own account outside matter, constituting objects for our understanding, since immateriality is what makes things actually intelligible. He called them *forms* or *ideas*, and said that both bodily matter and mind were formed by *participating* in these ideas: matter being formed into particular things having their own specific and generic natures, and mind into knowing such species and genera. According to Aristotle, however, the forms of things in nature don't exist on their own account outside matter, but in matter; and since forms as they exist in matter are not actually understandable, it follows that the natures and forms of the things we sense and understand are not actually understandable. Now only something actual can actualize a potential: only what is actually there to be sensed can actualize our senses. So our minds need to have a power to make things actually understandable by abstracting their forms from their material conditions. And this is why we have to acknowledge the existence of an *agent mind*.

Hence:

to 1: Things outside us are already actually able to be sensed, so we don't need an agent sense. So we see that our nutritive powers are all agent powers, our sense-powers all receptive powers, and our intellectual powers part active and part receptive.

to 2: There are two opinions about what light does. Some people say that seeing needs light to make the colours actually visible; and if that is so understanding needs an agent mind in the same way and for the same reasons that seeing needs light. But other people like Ibn Rushd[9] say that light is needed for seeing, not to make the colours actually visible, but to make the medium actually transparent. And if this is so, Aristotle's[10] comparison of the agent mind with light is true to the extent that understanding needs one as seeing does the other, but not for the same reason.

to 3: Given an agent, of course its imprint will be received into different things in ways determined by their different dispositions. But if there's no agent there's nothing disposition in the receiver can do. Now the natures of the things we sense don't exist as actually understandable anywhere in nature, since those things exist in matter. So the immateriality of a receptive mind is of no use to understanding without an agent mind to make things actually understandable by a process of abstraction.

Passage 13
Mind [*b*]

Source: *Summa contra Gentiles*, 2.77. Text from *Summa contra Gentiles* (*Opera Omnia*, Leonine edn., vol. xiii).

Date: 1264, Italy, aged 39.

That it is is not impossible to combine in the one substance of soul both receptive mind and agent mind.

Now to some it may seem impossible that one and the same substance, namely, our soul, should be both a receptive mind, potential of everything we understand, and an agent mind, making everything actually understandable, for agents must be actual not potential. So it might seem impossible to combine in the one substance of soul both an agent and a receptive mind.

But if we examine this aright, there is no difficulty or inappropriateness. For there is no reason why *A* can't relate to *B* in one way as potential and in another as actual; we see it in nature, where air is actually damp and potentially dry whereas earth is the reverse. Now this is how our understanding mind relates to images. For in one respect the mind is actually what images are potentially; and in another images are actually what the mind is potentially. For the substance of the human soul is immaterial and consequently, as we saw, is of an intellectual nature: all immaterial substances are. But this doesn't yet make it a mind representing determinately this or that thing, which it must be if it is to know determinately this or that thing: for all knowledge arises from a representation of the known in the knower. So the mind is still potential in regard to determinate representation of the sort of things we can know, namely, the natures of things sensed. Now it is exactly these determinate natures of things sensed that are presented to us in our images. And yet there they are not yet understandable, since they represent things sensed in the materiality of their individual properties, and exist in our own material sense-organs.

So they are not yet actually understandable. However, because the human being represented to us in these images possesses a nature common to all human beings when divested of features individual to this one, the images are potential of understanding. And so the images are understandable potentially and determinate representations of things actually; whereas exactly the reverse is true of the mind. So the mind is able to act on our images to make them actually understandable, and this ability of mind is called the agent mind; and it is also capable of being determined by the representations of things sensed, and this capability is the receptive mind.

But there is a difference between what we find in mind and what we find in nature, where one thing can potentially be what another actually is in an identical way—the material of air can take on the form of water in exactly the way water has the form—so that bodies in nature, because they share matter, act on and are acted on by each other at one and the same level. But the mind is not potentially able to assimilate representations of things in images in exactly the way they exist there, but needs them raised to a higher level, that of being abstracted from all individual material features so as to be actually understandable. So the agent mind must act on the images before they can be received by the receptive mind. For this reason the primacy of activity is ascribed not to the images but to the agent mind, so that Aristotle[1] says it is *related to the receptive as craft to its material.* A perfect parallel would be an eye that was not only a transparent medium for receiving colours, but itself possessed enough light to make those colours actually visible, as certain animals are reputed to have light enough in their own eyes for them to see better at night than they see during the day (for they have weak eyes that a little light stimulates but much light dazzles). Our minds are like that, related to *what is clearest as owls' eyes are to the sun,*[2] so that the little light our understanding has by nature is enough for our understanding.

That our mind's natural light of understanding is enough to do what the agent mind has to do is clear if we examine why we need the agent mind. For mind is potential of what it understands in the way the senses are potential of what they sense: just as we aren't always sensing so we aren't always understanding. Now the things the human mind understands were thought by Plato to be understandable in themselves (the Platonic Ideas), and so there was no need to postulate an agent mind to make them understandable. But if this were true, the more understandable a thing was in itself the more we would understand it, and that is clearly untrue. For we find things more intelligible the closer to the senses they are, yet those things are less understandable in themselves. It was this that led Aristotle to say that the things we understand are not things existing as understandable themselves but things we sense and then make understandable. And so he had to postulate a power to do this: the agent mind. So the agent mind is there to make things proportionate to our understanding; and since this is something our own natural light of understanding is enough for, there is no reason to ascribe the action of the agent mind to anything else than the natural light of our own mind, especially since Aristotle himself compares the agent mind to light.

Passage 14

Mind [*c*]

Source: Thomas's public disputations on Truth, 8.6. Text from *Quaestiones Disputatae de Veritate* (*Opera Omnia*, Leonine edn., vol. xxii).

Date: 1257–8, first stay in Paris, aged 32–3.

Type of passage and how to read: Disputed question (see Introduction). This passage is included to redress the balance of the previous two passages: they describe something incidental to understanding as such but characteristic of human understanding—the existence of agent and receptive mind; this passage crucially distinguishes understanding as such from the activity of either of these.

Notes on translation: 'Action' translates *actio*, and 'activity' *operatio*.

[**Question 8**] The subject for debate is **Knowledge in Angels.**

... [**Article 6**] And in the sixth place we are asked: **Do angels know themselves?**

It seems not:

For ... [3] the same thing can't both actively cause and passively undergo a change, except in the way Aristotle[1] says animals do, one part of them actively causing a change and another part passively undergoing it. But understanding and understood are like what acts and what it acts on. So an angel can only understand a part of itself ...

Moreover, [6] for an angel to understand itself by its own substance, its substance would have to be in its mind. But this can't be! Rather, its mind is in its substance; and since things can't be mutually inside each other, an angel doesn't know itself by its substance.

Moreover, [7] an angel's mind is potential in some way, and nothing can actualize its own potentiality. So, since it is what a mind knows that makes it actually knowing, no angel can possibly understand itself ...

Moreover, [11] activity lies between an agent and what it acts on. Now understanding and understood are like agent and acted on. Since then nothing can lie between a thing and itself, it doesn't seem angels can understand themselves.

But against that:

[1] What lesser powers can do, greater can too, as Boethius[2] says. But we know ourselves, so how much more angels?

Moreover, [2] as Ibn Sīnā[3] says, the reason mind knows itself and senses don't is that senses use bodily organs and mind doesn't. But angels' minds are even further divorced from bodily organs than ours. So angels too must know themselves ...

Moreover, [5] in the book of Causes[4] we read: *Everything knowing knows its own nature and reflects completely on it.* Angels too then, since they are knowing.

In reply:

Action is of two sorts: one sort—action in a strict sense—issues from the agent into something external to change it (to illuminate it, for example), but the other sort—properly called activity—doesn't issue into anything external but remains within the agent itself perfecting it (glowing, for example). What both have in common is that they issue only from things actually existent precisely as actualized; a body neither illuminates nor glows unless actually alight.

Now activities like desiring and sensing and understanding are not activities that issue into external matter but activities that dwell within the agent itself, perfecting it. So, though understanding when understanding must be actualized, it needn't be related to what it understands as an agent to something it is acting on, but the understanding and what it understands, having become one thing (the actualized understanding), constitute a single source of the activity we call understanding. By *constituting one thing* I mean that what we understand is joined to what understands it either in substance or by some likeness. So understanding is an agent or is acted on only coincidentally, in so far as the joining of what is understood to what understands presupposes acting and being acted on: acting, for example, in so far as our *agent mind* makes actually understandable the species [of what is to be understood], and being acted on, in so far as our *receptive mind* takes in that understandable species (as sense-powers take in perceptible appearances). But the activity of understanding is something that follows on such acting and being acted on, as an effect following on its cause. So, just as bodies that can glow, once actually alight, will glow, so understanding, once something understandable is actually present within it, will understand it.

Note then that there is no reason why something can't be actually one thing and potentially another, as transparent bodies are actually bodies but only potentially coloured. In the same way things can be actually existent but only potentially understandable: for just as in the realm of existence there are degrees of actuality and potentiality—ultimate matter entirely potential, God entirely actual, and everything between both actual and potential—so too in the realm of understanding—God's nature being entirely actual, but our own receptive mind entirely potential (for, as Ibn Rushd[5] says, our mind in the realm of understanding is like ultimate matter in the world of the senses). And all angelic substances lie in between, part potential and part actual, not only in the realm of existence but also in the realm of understanding. Now ultimate matter can't exercise activity until it takes on a form (and then the action is the form's doing rather than matter's), whereas things actually existent can exercise activity to the extent that they are actual. In the same way then our receptive mind can't understand anything until it takes in the form of something actually understandable (by which it then understands things of that form), and so can't understand itself except when it has such an understandable form present in it. The mind of an angel, on the other hand, has its own substance present in it—as something actually understandable—and so can understand its nature—present in it as something understandable—not through the medium of a likeness but immediately by way of itself.

Hence: . . .

to 3: Understanding and understood are not like what acts and what it acts on—even if grammatically we seem to treat them as active and passive—but both together make up one agent, as we have said . . .

to 6: There is no reason why things can't be mutually inside each other in different senses of inside, as a whole is in its parts and its parts are in it. And the present case is similar: the angel's substance is in its mind as something to be understood by its understanding, its mind in its substance as a power of that substance.

to 7: The angel doesn't potentially understand its own substance; though it potentially understands other things, it always understands itself actually. And in any case a mind in potentiality doesn't always need an external agent to actualize it, but only when it is essentially potential, before it has learnt anything; when the mind is only accidentally potential—possessing knowledge it is not attending to but is able to consider—then it can actualize itself, unless you prefer to say it is actualized by the will that moves it to actually consider . . .

to 11: The activity of understanding doesn't really lie between understanding and what it understands, but issues from both conjoined.

Passage 15
Feelings

Source: *Summa Theologiae*, 1a2ae. 22–3. Text from *Summa Theologiae* (*Opera Omnia*, Leonine edn., vol. vi).

Date: 1269–70, second stay in Paris, aged 45.

Type of passage and how to read: Modified disputed question (see Introduction).

Notes on translation: 'Feeling', 'passion', and 'emotion' all translate *passio*.

Parallel reading: For a similar treatment of the word 'passion' cf. Passage 12 above.

Our first consideration [**feelings in general**] divides into four:

first, [Question 22] What in us is subject to feelings?
second, [Question 23] the classification of feelings . . .

[**Question 22**] The first question [**What in us is subject to feelings?**] divides into three:

Can soul be subject to passions?
Are passions desires rather than perceptions?
Are they desires of the sense-appetite rather than of the intellectual appetite we call will?

[**Article 1**] The first question [**Can the soul be subject to passions?**] we approach as follows:

It seems that the soul can't be subject to passions:

For [1] *passion* means *being acted on*, which characterizes material. But we showed in book 1 that the soul is not constituted of formed material. So it can't be subject to passions.

Moreover, [2] passion is change, according to Aristotle.[1] But in the *De Anima*[2] he proves that the soul is not subject to change. So it can't be subject to passions.

Moreover, [3] passion leads to decomposition, for Aristotle[3] says that *as passion intensifies substance decays*. But the soul can't decompose. So it can't be subject to passions.

But against that:

Paul says [Romans 7: 5] that *while we still lived in a fleshly way the sinful passions law aroused were at work throughout our bodies*. But sins affect our souls, properly speaking. So the passions here called sinful affect our souls.

In reply:

The word *passion* [being a patient, suffering, undergoing] is used firstly, in a broad sense, to describe any acquiring, even if the acquirer loses nothing thereby, as if we talked of the atmosphere undergoing illumination, though *being fulfilled by* would be the better term in this case. It is used secondly and properly when something is lost in the acquiring, and that can take two forms. Sometimes what is lost is uncongenial to the thing—an animal body undergoes healing, acquiring health, and losing sickness; but sometimes the opposite happens—we undergo a sickness, acquiring ill health and losing health—and this is passion in its strictest sense, since passion implies being drawn by some external agent, and this is most apparent when a thing is drawn away from some state congenial to it. Aristotle[4] makes a similar point: generating higher forms of life from lower forms is called generation without qualification, even though in a sense it is also decomposition; and the opposite terms are used when lower forms are generated from higher forms.

Now the soul can be subject to passions in all three senses. In the sense of simple acquiring, *sensation and understanding are passions of a sort*. Passion with loss, though, is a characteristic of bodily changes, so that passions in the strict sense characterize the soul only incidentally in so far as the whole animal, body and soul, is subject to them. But here too a distinction should be made: exchanges for the worse are more properly passions than exchanges for the better: feeling sad is more properly passion than feeling pleased.

Hence:

to 1: Passion with change and loss characterizes material, and occurs only in wholes constituted of formed matter, but passion which is simple acquisition occurs wherever there is a potentiality of some sort, whether that be material or not. So although the soul is not constituted of formed matter, it has potentiality to acquire and undergo the sort of passion Aristotle[5] says understanding is.

to 2: Though the soul as such is not subject to passion and change, it is subject to them incidentally, as Aristotle[6] says.

to 3: This argument holds for passion that changes for the worse. The soul is only incidentally subject to such passions; as such they affect the whole animal, body and soul, and that does decompose.

[**Article 2**] The second question [**Are passions desires rather than perceptions?**] we approach as follows:

It seems that passions are perceptions rather than desires:

For [1] Aristotle[7] says the first in any field seems to be supreme in that field and cause of the others. Now passions occur first in perception and then in desire, since we can't undergo desire until we have undergone perception. So passions are perceptions rather than desires.

Moreover, [2] the more active the less passive, it would seem, for action and passion are opposites. Now desire is more active than perception; so passion, it would seem, is more characteristic of perception.

Moreover, [3] sense-desire and sense-perception are both located in organs of the body. Now passion of soul in the strict sense requires bodily change. So desires can no more claim to be passions than perceptions can.

But against that:

Augustine[8] says *the movements of soul the Greeks called* pathe *and Roman authors like Cicero* agitations, *some call* feelings *or* affections *and some—following the Greek more explicitly—call* passions. So passions, feelings, and affections are all identical. Now affections are clearly desires, not perceptions. So passions are desires rather than perceptions.

In reply:

We have already said that passion implies being drawn towards some agent. Now things draw us through desire and affection rather than through perception; for desire is attraction to things themselves existing in their own reality (Aristotle[9] says *good and bad*, the objects of desire, *exist in things*), but perception isn't attraction to something in its own reality, but awareness of it through some representation of it in the mind, innate or acquired depending on the type of mind (so that Aristotle[10] says that *true and false*, objects of awareness, *exist not in things but in mind*). So passions are desires rather than perceptions.

Hence:

to 1: Perfections and deficiencies behave in exactly opposite ways. Things get more perfect the closer they approach some first starting-point, as a thing gets brighter the nearer it gets to some supremely bright light-source. But things get more deficient not by getting closer to something altogether deficient, but by getting further away from something perfect; for this is what lack and deficiency mean. So the closer to the starting-point the less deficient, which is why we find big mistakes grow from small beginnings. Now passions are a sort of deficiency due to a thing's potentiality. So the closer a thing is to the first and most perfect of things, God, the less potentiality and passion it displays, and vice versa. And this holds also for the higher powers of soul—its perceptive powers—which are less passive in nature.

to 2: Desire is thought more active because it motivates our external activity; but this characterizes it precisely because it is more passible and responsive to things as they exist in their own reality; for external activity pursues things.

to 3: In book 1 we said that bodily organs can undergo two kinds of modification. The first is non-physical, the acquiring of a representation or intention of something, and characterizes sense-perception: for the object of sight doesn't induce colour in the eye but representation of colour. The second is physical modification of the organ affecting its natural constitution: heating or cooling it or some change like that. Such modifications are incidental to the act of sense-perception (eye-strain from excessive concentration, for example, or the dazzle of a bright light), but are essential to emotion, so that every passion is defined as involving materially physiological modification of an organ: *being angry is the heart's blood boiling.*[11] So clearly acts of sense-desire are more truly passions than acts of sense-perception, even though both are acts of bodily organs.

[**Article 3**] The third question [**Are passions desires of the sense-appetite rather than of the intellectual appetite we call will?**] we approach as follows:

It seems that passions belong as much to our intellectual appetite as to our sense-appetite:

For [1] pseudo-Dionysius[12] says that Hierotheus was taught by a certain divine inspiration *that brought him not only knowledge but a passion for divine things.* Now a passion for divine things can't be a matter of sense-appetite, which responds only to good that we can sense. So passions can affect our intellectual as well as our sense appetite.

Moreover, [2] the more powerful the action of the agent the greater the passion of the patient. Now good in general—the object of our intellectual appetite—is more powerful than particular goods—the objects of our sense appetites. So passion is more truly found in intellectual appetite than in sense-appetites.

Moreover, [3] joy and love are called passions, and they are found in our intellectual appetite as well as our sense-appetites; otherwise scripture would never ascribe them to

God and spirits. Passions then characterize our intellectual appetite as much as our sense-appetites.

But against that:
John Damascene[13] describes soul's passions as *movements of sense-appetite towards what is imagined, good or bad,* or, translated differently, *movements of our non-logical soul caused by awareness of good or bad.*

In reply:
As we have said already, passions properly belong where there is bodily change, and that is found in the acts of our sense-appetite where there is not only the non-physical kind of modification found in our powers of sense-perception, but also physiological modification. But the acts of our intellectual appetite require no change in our body at all, since this kind of appetite doesn't act through a bodily organ. Clearly then passion more truly exists in acts of sense-appetite than in those of intellectual appetite, as also emerges from Damascene's definition above.

Hence:

to 1: The passion for divine things mentioned here is a desire for divine things and a union with them through love, all of it happening without physiological change.

to 2: Greatness of passion depends not only on agent-power but also on patient-passibility, since what is very sensitive is greatly affected by even small active stimuli. So although the object of intellectual appetite is more active than the objects of sense-appetites, our sense-appetites are more passible.

to 3: When we talk of God and spirits or our own human wills loving and enjoying and so on, this is a metaphorical description of pure acts of will lacking passion but having a similar [external] effect. Thus Augustine[14] says: *The holy angels punish but without feeling anger, and help us without feeling compassion. But our ordinary human language applies these passion-words to them too, because what they do is similar though without the weakness of feelings.*

Next [Question 23] we consider the classification of feelings; and that divides into four:

Should we distinguish affective from aggressive feelings?
Are the antitheses between aggressive feelings always antitheses between good and bad?
Has every feeling an antithetic feeling?
Within each division of feelings, affective or aggressive, is all difference of kind due to antithesis?

[**Article 1**] The first question [**Should we distinguish affective from aggressive feelings?**] we approach as follows:

It seems that there is no distinction between affective and aggressive feelings:

For [1] Aristotle[15] says feelings *are accompanied by joy or sadness*. But joy and sadness are affective in nature. So all feeling is affective in nature, and there is no distinction between affective and aggressive feelings.

Moreover, [2] Jerome glossing Matthew 13: 33: *The kingdom of heaven is like yeast, etc.*, says: *Reason is given prudence, our aggressive spirit a hatred of vice, and our affective a desire of virtue*. But Aristotle[16] tells us that hatred is as much an affective feeling as its antithesis, love. So the same feelings are aggressive and affective.

Moreover, [3] passions and actions are differentiated in kind by their objects. But aggressive and affective passions have the same objects, namely, good and bad. So there is no distinction between aggressive and affective feelings.

But against that:

Actions realizing different abilities to act are different in kind: seeing and hearing, for example. But as we said in book 1, the sense-appetite consists of two abilities: the affective and the aggressive. So, since feelings, as we have said, are movements of sense-appetite, feelings exercising our affective ability will differ in kind from those exercising our aggressive ability.

In reply:

Aggressive and affective feelings do differ in kind. For, as we said in book 1, abilities differ because their objects differ, so that feelings that realize different abilities must have different objects. As a result feelings that realize different abilities must be more than normally different in kind, since greater difference of object is needed to differentiate abilities than to differentiate acts or passions. It is like the situation in nature: there generic differences depend on different material capabilities and differences in species within a genus on one and the same material taking on different forms. In the same way when the acts of living things exercise different abilities they differ not only in species but also in genus, whereas acts or passions that have different specialized objects within the one common object of some ability differ as species within that genus.

So to find out which feelings are affective and which aggressive we need to know the object of these abilities. In book 1 we said the object of our affective ability was anything sensed as straightforwardly good or bad, pleasurable or painful. But sometimes the animal has a hard struggle attaining such good or avoiding such bad things, because they are not within its immediate power, and then good or bad, seen as challenging or requiring effort, becomes an object of our aggressive ability. So any straightforward feeling for good or bad as such is an affective feeling, like feeling joyful or sad, loving or hating, or the like; and any feeling for good or bad as something challenging, the attaining or avoiding of which will require effort, is an aggressive feeling, like feeling bold or afraid or hopeful, and the like.

Hence:

to 1: As we said in book 1 the function of aggressive feelings in animals is to remove obstacles preventing affective feelings from pursuing their objective, obstacles that make good difficult to attain or bad difficult to avoid. So all aggressive feelings end up in affective feeling, so that even aggressive feelings *are accompanied by* the affective feelings of *joy or sadness.*

to 2: Jerome locates hatred of vice in our aggressive ability, not because it is hatred—for that is an affective feeling—but because it involves struggle and aggressiveness.

to 3: As pleasurable the good attracts our affections, and as hard to attain it repels them, so we had to have another ability called our aggressibe ability, enabling us to pursue such good and avoid such bad. So affective and aggressive feelings differ in kind.

[Article 2] The second question **[Are the antitheses between aggressive feelings always antitheses between good and bad?]** we approach as follows:

It seems that antitheses between aggressive feelings are always antitheses between good and bad:

For [1] aggressive feeling serves affective feeling, as we said. Now antitheses between affective feelings are antitheses between good and bad: loving versus hating, feeling joyful versus feeling sad, and so on. So the same will apply to aggressive feelings.

Moreover, [2] passions are differentiated by objects in the way movements are by destinations. Now Aristotle[17] shows that what differentiates antithetic movements are antithetic destinations. So what differentiates antithetic passions must be antithetic objects. Now good and bad are the objects of our appetite. So all antitheses between passions in appetitive powers will be antitheses between good and bad.

Moreover, [3] Ibn Sīnā[18] says that *every emotion approaches or retreats*. Now approach is attraction to good, and retreat is repulsion from bad; for just as Aristotle[19] says that *good is what everyone desires*, so bad is what everyone recoils from. So all antitheses between animal passions must be between good and bad.

But against that:

Aristotle[20] makes an antithesis between feeling afraid and feeling bold. But this isn't a difference of good and bad:

both are reactions to something bad. So not every antithesis between aggressive feelings is an antithesis between good and bad.

In reply:

Passions, says Aristotle,[21] are changes of a sort. So antitheses between passions must be modelled on those between changes or movements. Now Aristotle[22] distinguishes two sorts of antithesis between changes or movements: sometimes the antithesis is between moving towards or away from one state, as in changes of substance where birth moves to existence and death moves away; and sometimes the antithesis is between movements that lead towards antithetic states, as in changes of quality where getting whiter moves from black to white and getting blacker moves from white to black. In our animal passions too then we find these two sorts of antithesis: one due to antithetic objects, in this case good and bad, and another between tending towards or away from the same object. In our affections we see only the first sort of antithesis—the antithesis of object—but in aggressive feelings we see both sorts.

The reason is that affections, as we have said, respond to what is sensed as straightforwardly good or bad. Now good as such cannot repel but only attract, so as such can only be moved towards, not away from; and bad as such cannot attract but only repel, so as such can only be moved away from, not towards. Consequently, all affections related to good (like loving or desiring or enjoying it) tend towards it, and all affections related to bad (hating it, rejecting it, or being sad at it) tend away from it. Affections cannot be antithetic in the other way of moving towards and away from the same object.

Aggressive feelings, however, as we have said, react to what is sensed as good or bad not straightforwardly, but as challenging and requiring effort. Now challenging difficult goods can both attract us as goods (so that we feel hopeful) and repel us as difficult (so that we feel despairing); and challenging evils can both repel us as evils (so that we feel afraid) and attract us to face up to the challenge and thus escape the evil (so that we feel bold). In aggressive feelings then we find both types of antithesis: the antithesis due to the antithetic objects of good and bad that distinguishes hope from fear; and the antithesis between confronting and shunning one and the same object that distinguishes boldness from fear.

And these considerations are enough to answer the initial objections.

[Article 3] The third question [**has every feeling an antithetic feeling?**] we approach as follows:

It seems that every feeling has an antithetic feeling:

For [1] every feeling is either affective or aggressive, as we have said, and each of these have their own kinds of antithesis. So every feeling has an antithetic feeling.

Moreover, [2] every animal passion has either good or bad for its object, since these are the objects common to appetite as such. But to any passion for good there must be an antithetic passion for bad. So every passion has its antithetic passion.

Moreover, [3] every emotion either approaches or retreats, as we just said. But every approach has its antithetic retreat, and vice versa. So every emotion must have its antithetic emotion.

But against that:

Anger is a feeling, and Aristotle[23] says it has no antithesis. So not all feelings have antitheses.

In reply:

Anger is peculiar in being the only feeling that can't have an antithesis, whether on the model of approach–recoil, or due to the antithesis of good and bad. For anger is provoked by evils already done to us and hard to repel. Either we yield to such evils sadly (an affective feeling) or we are impelled to confront the harm done us angrily. But no feeling can impel us to avoid the evil, since the evil is already present or past. So anger has no antithetic feeling on the approach–recoil model. Nor any based on the antithesis of good and bad. For evil already done to us is like good already achieved: it can't any longer be thought of as challenging or difficult. Once good is achieved the only movement remaining is resting of desire in the achieved good, that is to say, its affective enjoyment. So the movement of anger can't have any antithetic movement, but simply absence of movement: as Aristotle[24] says *the only opposite to being angry is calming down*, which is not its antithesis but its absence or lack.

And these considerations are enough to answer the initial objections.

[**Article 4**] The fourth question [**Within each division of feelings, affective or aggressive, is all difference of kind due to antithesis?**] we approach as follows:

It seems that within each division all difference of kind is due to antithesis:

For [1] animal passions are differentiated by object. Now the objects of passion are good and bad and they differentiate passions by antithesis. So unless the feelings within each division of feeling are antithetic they will not differ in kind.

Moreover, [2] difference in kind is difference of form, and Aristotle[25] says all differences of form involve antithesis. So feelings within the same division which are not antithetic will not differ in kind.

Moreover, [3] since every emotion is an approach to or a recoil from good or bad, differentiation of emotions must come either from the difference between good and bad, or from that between approach and recoil, or from that between more or less approach and recoil. Now the first two differences do introduce antitheses between feelings, as we have seen; whilst the third doesn't differentiate kinds of feeling, for then there would be unlimited species of feeling. So one can't differentiate species of feeling within a genus except by antithesis.

But against that:

Loving and feeling joyful are both affective feelings and differ in kind, yet they are not antithetic; rather one causes the other. So some feelings within the same division differ in kind but are not antithetic.

In reply:

Passion [being acted on] is differentiated by the agent acting, which is the object in the case of the soul's passions. But active agents differ in two ways: in nature or kind, as fire differs from water, and in strength of activity. This difference of movers by their power to move offers a natural model for the differentiation of animal passions, for agents that move things either attract or repel them. Now attraction has three effects: first of all, the agent gives an object an inclination or bias towards itself, as, for example, light bodies whose place is above generate light bodies, that is to say, bodies with an inclination or bias upwards; secondly, if the generated body is not already in its proper place the agent moves it there; and thirdly, when it is there, the agent brings it to rest, for the cause of a thing's rest in a place is the same cause that moved it there. And a similar analysis applies to causes that repel.

Now in movement of appetite good attracts and bad repels. So good first provokes an inclination or bias or affinity to itself, called loving (having an antithetic movement, hating, in regard to evil); then secondly, if the good is not yet possessed it provokes a movement towards getting it, called desiring (opposed to aversion or disgust, as regards evil); and thirdly, when the good is finally achieved, it provokes a repose of desire in the good achieved, called feeling pleased or enjoyment (and opposed to pain or feeling sad, as regards evil). And aggressive feelings presuppose the same bias or inclination towards seeking good and avoiding evil that underlies affective feelings directed straightforwardly at good and evil. And if the good is not yet acquired this provokes hope or despair and if the evil is not yet upon us fear or boldness. But good acquired provokes no aggressive feeling because, as we have said, it no longer offers a challenge; while evil already upon us provokes anger.

So we see that there are three groupings of affections: loving and hating, desiring and aversion, feeling pleased and feeling sad; and three of aggressive feelings: hoping and despairing, feeling afraid and feeling bold, and feeling angry (which has no antithesis). That makes eleven distinct species of feeling—six affective and five aggressive—which comprise every animal feeling there is.

And these considerations are enough to answer the initial objections.

Passage 16
Will as Rational Desire

Source: *Summa contra Gentiles*, 2.47–8. Text from *Summa contra Gentiles* (*Opera Omnia*, Leonine edn., vol. xiii).
Date: 1264, Italy, aged 39.
Notes on translation: In this extract 'desire' translates *appetitus*; 'freedom to decide' translates *liberum arbitrium*.

[Chapter 47] That substances with understanding must have wills.

There is a desire for good in everything: *good*, the philosophers tell us, *is what all desire*. In things without awareness this desire is called natural desire: the attraction a stone has for downwards, for instance. In things with sense-awareness it is called animal desire, and divides into capabilities of affective and aggressive feeling. In things with understanding it is called intellectual or rational desire: will. So created intellectual substances have wills . . .

In addition, a thing's activity originates in the form by which it actually exists: behind activity always lies actuality. So the way agents have form determines the way they are active. Thus, from forms that are in agents but not from them, there issues activity of which its agent is not master. But if there could be agents acting through a form they themselves produced, then such agents would also be masters of the consequent activity. Now the natural forms behind natural changes and activities aren't produced by the things they form but by entirely external agents, since in nature things exist by such natural forms and nothing can cause its own existence. So things that move by nature don't move themselves: heavy objects don't move themselves downwards but are moved downwards by what produced them and gave them their forms. In the lower animals too the sensed or imagined forms that move them are not thought up by the lower animals themselves, but received into them from external things acting on their senses and there evaluated by an instinctive judgement of nature. So although we say they move themselves—meaning one part is moved and another does the moving—that very moving comes, not from them, but partly from the external things they sense and partly from their nature: we say they move themselves inasmuch as their appetite moves their limbs (and this is an advance over non-living things and plants), but inasmuch as that appetite itself is necessitated by forms received from their senses and subject to an instinctive judgement of nature, they don't cause themselves to move themselves; and so are not masters of their action. But the understood form by which intellectual substances are active issues from the intellect itself, as something conceived and in a sense thought up by itself: as we see in the forms that craftsmen conceive and think up and operate according to. So intellectual substances move themselves to activity, and are masters of their own action. They therefore have wills . . .

[Chapter 48] This shows that those substances are free to decide their own actions.

. . . Moreover, things lack freedom to decide either because they lack all judgement, like stones and plants which lack awareness, or because their judgements are fixed by nature, like non-reasoning animals. For sheep judge wolves harmful and consequently flee by instinctive natural evaluation, and similarly in other cases. But wherever judgement of what to do is not fixed by nature, there is freedom to decide. And all creatures with understanding are of this sort. For understanding takes in not only this or that good but the notion of good as such. So, since will is moved by forms taken in by understanding, and what moves and what is moved must be proportioned to one another, the will of creatures with understanding is not fixed by nature [on any particular good] but only on good as such. The will, then, can tend towards whatever is presented to it as good, with no fixed opposed tendency of nature prohibiting it. So all things with understanding have freedom of will deriving from understanding's judgement, and that is freedom of decision, which is defined as free judgement of reason.

Passage 17
Free Will

Source: Thomas's public disputations on Evil, 6. Text from *Quaestiones Disputatae de Malo* (*Opera Omnia*, Leonine edn., vol. xxiii).

Date: 1270–2, second stay in Paris, aged 46.

Type of passage and how to read: Disputed question. Note that some objections have been indented to show that they depend on one another: the bachelor respondent's answers led to new questions (see Introduction).

[**Question 6**] The subject for debate is **Human Choice**; and we ask: **Can human beings choose their actions freely, or are such choices compelled?**

And it seems that they are compelled, not free:

For [1] we read in Jeremiah 10 [23]: *No one's ways are his own, nor can he guide his steps as he goes.* But whatever a human being is free to do is his own, of which he is master. So it seems human beings have no free choice over their ways and actions.

But it was said [by the respondent]: this refers to the implementation of a choice, which is sometimes not in our power.

But against that: [2] Paul says in Romans 9 [16]: *It* (namely, willing) *does not depend on who wills or* running on *who runs but on God having mercy.* Now running is the external implementation, but willing is internal choice. So even internal choices aren't in a human being's power but come to him from God.

But it was said [by the respondent]: God himself moves us to choose by a sort of internal stimulus, infallibly but without compromising our freedom.

But against that: [3] all animals move themselves by their appetites; but the lower animals can't choose freely, because that appetite itself is moved by something outside them, the power of the heavens, for example, or action by some other body. If then human will is infallibly moved by God, humans can't choose their actions freely either.

Moreover, [4] violence is defined as exercise of power from outside without the victim's co-operation. If then choice in the will comes from outside—from God—it seems that our wills are moved violently and under compulsion, and cannot freely choose their own actions.

Moreover, [5] human will can't diverge from God's will, as Augustine[1] says, for even if it does not will what God wants, God implements what he wants by way of what it wills. But God's will can't be changed. Neither then can human will. So all human choices derive from an unchanging choice.

Moreover, [6] no power can act except in pursuit of the object that defines it: sight can only direct its activity at what can be seen. But will's object is what is good, and so it cannot will anything but what is good. It is compelled then to will the good, and can't freely choose between good and bad.

Moreover, [7] any ability to be acted on by its object is a passive ability, the activity of which consists in being affected. The senses, for example, are acted on by their objects and are therefore passive abilities, and the activity of sensing is a kind of being affected. Now will's object acts on it, for Aristotle[2] says that *what we desire moves but is not moved, whereas our desire moves and is moved.* So will is a passive ability, and the activity of willing a being affected.

Passive abilities, however, can be compelled to change by something sufficiently active. So will it seems can be compelled to change by what it desires: humans can't freely will or not will.

But it was said [by the respondent]: our will is compelled by our ultimate goal (since we all compulsively will total happiness), but not by the means of achieving it.

But against that: [8] goal and means are both objects of will, being both goods. So if will moves to its goal compulsively, it seems it should move to means compulsively too.

Moreover, [9] when what is moved and what moves it are the same, then the way of being moved must be the same. But in willing goals and willing means what is moved—will—is the same, and also what moves it, since means are willed by willing the goal. So the way of being moved must be the same: and just as our ultimate goal is willed compulsively, so must the means be too.

Moreover, [10] will, like mind, is an immaterial power. But mind is compelled by its object: we are coerced into assent to a truth by reason's violence. In the same way then will must be compelled by its object . . .

Moreover, [13] will's love moves us more ardently than mind's knowledge, since knowledge assimilates but love transforms, as pseudo-Dionysius[3] says. So will is more able to be moved than mind. If then mind can be compelled to move, *a fortiori* will.

But it was said [by the respondent]: mind's activity is movement into the soul and will's a movement out, so that mind is more passive and will more active and less under compulsion from its object.

But against that: [14] mind assents and will consents, assent yielding to the thing it assents to and consent yielding to the thing it consents to. So will's movement is no more a movement out from the soul than mind's.

Moreover, [15] if there are things will is not compelled to move to, we shall have to say it is open to conflicting possibilities, since what needn't be can possibly not be. But what is potential of conflicting alternatives can realize one of them only if something already actualized actualizes its potential, and what actualizes it we call its cause. So if will is to determinately will anything it must be caused to will. But, as Ibn Sīnā proved,[4] given a cause the effect follows; for if a cause was given and it still remained possible for the effect not to exist, something else would be needed to actualize that potential, and the first cause wouldn't have been a sufficient one. So the will is compelled to move towards what it wills . . .

Moreover, [17] sometimes our will starts to choose after not previously choosing. Either then its previous disposition has changed or not. If not, then it must still be as it was before, not choosing, and so something not choosing is choosing, which is impossible. If, however, it has changed its disposition, something must have caused that; since everything that is moved is moved by something else. But a mover compels what it moves to move, otherwise it wouldn't be sufficient to cause movement. So will is compelled to move.

But it was said [by the respondent]: such arguments apply to natural powers in material things, but not to immaterial powers like will.

> But against that: [18] all our knowledge comes through the senses, and so nothing can be known unless it or its effects can be sensed. But we can't sense the power itself, open to conflicting ways of acting; and among its effects which can be sensed we never find two conflicting activities existing together, but always see determinately the one or the other. So we have no way of judging whether such a power of acting in conflicting ways exists in humans . . .

Moreover, [20] Augustine[5] says that nothing causes its own existence; and for the same reason nothing causes its own movement. So will doesn't move itself but needs to be moved. For it starts into activity from inactivity, and that needs movement (which is why we don't say God starts into willing things when previously he hasn't, because God doesn't change). Will then must be moved by something else;

and since what is moved by something else is placed under compulsion by it, will must will under compulsion and not freely.

Moreover, [21] the variable depends on the constant. Now human actions are many and variable, and must depend causally on the constant movement of the heavens. But what the heavens cause happens under compulsion, for all natural causes compel their effects unless interfered with. But nothing can interfere with the effects of the heavens' movement, since the interfering factor also causally depends on that movement. So it seems that human movements are compelled, and not freely chosen...

Moreover, [24] Augustine[6] says that unless one resists habit it compels one. So it seems that at least the wills of people acting out of habit are acting under compulsion.

But against that:

[1] We read in Ecclesiasticus 15 [14]: *God made human beings in the beginning, then left them to their own deliberations.* But that means they had free choice, which Aristotle[7] defines as *a deliberated desire.* So human beings can choose freely.

Moreover, [2] Aristotle[8] says that reasoning powers can entertain opposite objects. Now will is a reasoning power, a power in reason as Aristotle[9] calls it. So will can entertain opposites and is not compelled to embrace one of them.

Moreover, [3] Aristotle[10] says human beings are masters of their own actions, able to act or not to act. But this can only be so if they can freely choose. So human beings can freely choose their actions.

In reply:

Some have suggested that human will is compelled to choose what it does, though not coerced. For not all compulsion is violent, only external compulsion: the movements of nature are compelled but not violent, since violence—originating outside—is incompatible with both the natural and the willed—both of which originate inside. The suggestion, however, is heretical since it destroys the notion of human action as deserving or undeserving: somebody so compelled to act that he can't avoid it doesn't seem to be doing anything deserving or undeserving. The opinion is also philosophically anarchic, not only opposed to the faith but destroying the foundations of ethics. For if we are not in any way free to will but compelled, everything that makes up ethics vanishes: pondering action, exhorting, commanding, punishing, praising, condemning. Opinions like these, which destroy the foundations of a branch of philosophy, are called anarchic: the opinion that nothing changes, for example, which does away with natural philosophy. People are led to embrace them, Aristotle[11] says, partly by brinkmanship and partly by sophistical reasoning to which they can't find the answers.

To clarify the truth in this matter let us note firstly that like other things human beings originate actions. The active or motive principle peculiar to them is, as Aristotle[12] says, mind and will, which is partly like the active principles in nature and partly unlike. Like, because action in nature originates from things' forms, which give them natural tendencies (called desires of their nature) leading to action, just as in human beings from forms taken in by mind there follow willed tendencies leading to external activity; but also unlike, because forms in nature are forms taken on and made individual by matter, so that the resultant tendency is fixed on one course, whereas forms taken in by mind are general forms covering a number of individual things, so that the willed tendencies remain open to more than one course of action—actions being individual and none matching the generality of the power. The architect's concept of house, for example, is general enough to cover many different house-plans, so that his will can tend towards making the house square or round or some other shape. The active principle in lower animals lies somewhere in between: the forms their senses take in are individual like the forms of nature and give rise to tendencies to react in fixed ways as in nature; yet the form taken in by their senses is not always the same as it is in nature (where fire is always hot) but varies, pleasant at one moment, painful the next, so that the animal flees at one moment and pursues the next, behaving like a human being.

Secondly, note that abilities can be affected in two ways: subjectively and objectively. Sight, for example, is affected subjectively when a change in the eye's disposition affects our clarity of vision, and objectively when we see white one moment and black the next. The first kind of affection relates to exercising an action (whether you do it or not, or do it well or badly), and the second to what sort of action it is (for actions are defined by their objects). So note that in nature classification of action comes from form, but its exercise comes from an agent causing the action in pursuance of a goal, so that the first source of an activity's exercise is some goal. And if we take note of the objects of mind and of will we will find that mind's object is what holds first place in the world of form—namely, being and truth—whilst will's object is what holds first place in the world of goals—namely, good; and that good applies to all goals just as truth applies to all forms mind takes in, so that good itself as taken in by mind is one truth among others, and truth itself as goal of mind's activity is one good among others. If then we think of the way soul's abilities are affected by the object that defines them, the first source of such affection is mind; for this is the way even will itself is affected by good: as taken in by mind. But if we think of the way soul's abilities are affected in the exercise of their action, the first source of such affection is will; for it is always the ability pursuing the goal that activates abilities that pursue the means (the military man puts the manufacturer of bridles to work). For this is the way in which will puts itself and all other abilities to work: I think because I want to, I use all my other abilities and dispositions because I want to, so that Ibn Rushd[13] defines a disposition as what is ready to be used when wanted. If then we are going to show that will is not compelled to act, we must consider acts of will both as to their exercise and as to their determination by some object.

As to the **exercise** of acts of will, clearly will moves itself just as it moves our other powers. This doesn't mean will is potential and actualized in the same respect, for, just as mind in knowing moves itself to discovery, progressing from known to unknown, from what it actually knows to what it can come to know, so by way of actually willing one thing we move ourselves to actually willing another; from willing health, for example, to willing medicine, since, because we want to be healthy, we start to deliberate about what will make us healthy, and eventually, coming to a decision, want to take our medicine. The willing of the medicine is thus preceded by deliberation, which has itself issued in turn from the willer's will to deliberate. Now, because will moves itself by way of deliberation—a kind of investigation which doesn't prove some one way correct but examines the alternatives—will doesn't compel itself to will; but, since it hasn't always been willing deliberation, something must have moved it to will deliberation, and if that was itself, then deliberation must have preceded that movement too, and preceding that deliberation, yet another act of will. Now this can't go on for ever; so we are forced to admit that, in any will that is not always willing, the very first movement to will must come from outside, stimulating the will to start willing.

So some people think the outside stimulus comes from the heavens; but that can't be. For will is a power in reason, as Aristotle[14] calls it, and reason or mind is not a bodily ability; so the bodily power of the heavens can't directly influence will as such. To think the heavens can affect human will as they can the appetites of animals is to think mind no different from sense-awareness, as did the people to whom Aristotle[15] attributes the quote that *human will follows the lead of the father of men and gods*, namely, of the heavens or the sun. We are left then with Aristotle's conclusion in the *De Bona Fortuna*[16] that what first moves mind and will must be something above mind and will, namely, God, who—just as he moves everything in the way natural to it, light up and heavy down—moves will in the way will is disposed to be moved, not compelling it to one course, but as open to more than one possibility. Clearly then, as far as exercising will is concerned, will is not compelled to move.

If now we turn to consider the way will is moved by the object that determines what it is we will, note that the object moving will is something apprehended as both good and appropriate. Goods proposed as good but not apprehended as appropriate will not move will. And since decisions and choices bear on particular circumstances—where actions take place—what is apprehended as good and appropriate must be seen as good and appropriate in these circumstances and not just in general. Something apprehended to be good and appropriate in any and every circumstance that could be thought of would, to be sure, compel us to will it; and this is the reason human beings compulsively will total happiness, which, according to Boethius,[17] is the perfect state in which every good is collected together. (And I am talking of a compulsive determination of *what* is willed so that one can't will the opposite; not a compulsive *exercise* of that will, since someone can will not to think of total happiness just now, since even acts of mind and will take place in particular circumstances.) But something not found to be good in any and every circumstance that can be thought of will not compel the will, even as regards determination of what to will; because then, even when thinking about it, someone can will its opposite, because of some other particular circumstance in which the opposite perhaps is good or appropriate, as, for example, when what is good for health is not good for pleasure. And here there are three ways in which will can be attracted by one particular circumstance of what is offered rather than by another: firstly, because it is of greater weight, so that reason moves the will towards it: something that serves health, for example, is preferred to something that serves pleasure;[18] secondly, because one circumstance is thought of and the other not: and this often happens when some chance occurrence, external or internal, draws attention to the circumstance; and thirdly, because of some disposition in the one willing, since, as Aristotle[19] says, *what you want depends on what you are*. The will of an angry man won't agree with that of a peaceable one; the same thing is not appropriate to both, just as the same food won't appeal to the sick and the healthy. When the disposition to see something as good and appropriate is innate, not subject to will, will is compelled to prefer it in the way everyone naturally desires existence, life, and knowledge. But if the disposition is subject to will and not innate—some acquired disposition or passing emotion disposing us to see something in these particular circumstances as good or bad—then will won't be compelled by it since the disposition can be removed and things seen differently; for example, someone can calm down his own anger so as not to judge something while still angry. Though emotions are easier to get rid of than habitual dispositions.

So then sometimes the will can be compelled by an object, but not always; but to exercise its act it can never be compelled.

Hence:

to 1: This authority is open to two interpretations. One is that Jeremiah is talking of implementation of choice: for it is not [always] in a human being's power fully to implement what he has in mind. The second is that even our internal willing is stimulated by a higher source, God. So that St Paul is saying [in argument 2 above]: willing *does not depend on who wills or* running on *who runs* for its first stimulation, *but on God having mercy*. And that is an answer to 2.

to 3: Lower animals are moved by the higher agent's stimulus towards something determinate, in accordance with the particularity of the form they conceive and which draws their sense-appetite; but God moves wills—though infallibly because his moving power can't fail—freely and without compulsion, in accordance with the nature of what he is moving, which is open to more than one possibility. Just as his providence works infallibly in everything, yet in such a way that effects follow contingently from contingent causes; for God moves everything proportionately, each in its own way.

to 4: Will does in a sense co-operate when moved by God, since it itself does the willing under God's influence. So though the movement is from outside as regards its first source, it is not violent.

to 5: Human will can diverge from God's will in a sense, by willing something God doesn't will it to will—sin, for example (though God doesn't will human will not to sin either, since *the Lord does whatever he wills*, so that, were he to will no sin to be committed, none would be). But though actual movement of will can diverge from God's will in this way, the final outcome can never diverge, for the outcome human will always brings about is that God's will for humans gets done. But as to mode of willing, human will can't be expected to conform to God's will, since God wills things eternally and infinitely and human will can't; and so Isaiah 55 [9] says: *But as high as the heavens above the earth, so high are my ways above your ways.*

to 6: Because will's object is the good it follows that nothing can be willed except as good. But many and various things are good, and you can't conclude from this that wills are compelled to choose this or that one.

to 7: Active objects compel change only when they are more powerful than what they act on. Now will is an ability to be moved by good in general; so no good will be powerful enough to compel will to will unless it be good in every respect, the only perfect good, total happiness. This our wills cannot not will, if that means willing what conflicts with it; but they can avoid actually willing it by avoiding thinking of it, since mental activity is subject to will. In this respect then we aren't compelled to will even total happiness, just as one is not compelled to get hot if one can shut down the heat when one wants.

to 8: The goal is the reason for willing the means, so will doesn't relate in the same way to both.

to 9: When there is only one way to achieve a goal then we will the means for the same reason we will the goal; but this doesn't apply in the case being considered. For total happiness can be reached by many paths; so though a human being may compulsively will total happiness, none of the paths to it are willed compulsively.

to 10: Will is like mind in one way and unlike it in another. As regards the exercise of its act it is unlike, since will moves mind to act but is not itself moved by any other power than itself. As regards object it is like, for just as will is compelled by an altogether good object but not by objects that can appear bad in some respect, so too mind is compelled by necessary truths that can't be regarded as false, but not by contingent ones that might be false . . .

to 13: Love is said to transform lover into beloved because it moves a lover towards the actual thing loved, while knowledge assimilates by bringing a likeness of what is known into the knower; the former is the way agents seeking goals move, the latter the way forms move.

to 14: Assent names a movement of mind not so much towards a thing as towards a conception of it present in the mind, to which the mind assents when it judges it a true conception.

to 15: Even a sufficient cause doesn't always compel its effect, since it can sometimes be interfered with so that its effect doesn't happen: natural causes, for example, produce their effects not always but more often than not, being occasionally interfered with. And so what causes us to will need not compel us to will, since will itself can interfere with the process either by refusing to consider what attracts it to will or by considering its opposite: namely, that there is a bad side to what is being proposed as good . . .

to 17: When a will starts to choose it is changed from its previous disposition of being able to choose into actively choosing, and that is caused by will moving itself to act and by movement from an external agent, namely, God. But [in neither case] is it compelled to move, as we have said.

to 18: All our knowledge comes through the senses, but that doesn't mean that everything we know is sensed or known through some immediate sensed effect: mind itself is known to itself through its activity and that can't be sensed. In the same way will's interior activity is known to mind, as something put in movement by mind's act, and, in another way, as something causing mind to act, as we have said: as effects are known through causes and causes through effects. But even granting that a power of will open to conflicting possibilities has to be known by effects we can sense, the argument still doesn't hold. For just as universal notions which hold always and everywhere are known to us through here-and-now particular things, and just as the ultimate material of everything able to take on diverse forms is known to us by the succession of forms it can take on (though not simultaneously), so we can know that the power of will is open to conflicting possibilities not by opposing actions occurring simultaneously but by the way they follow each other yet derive from the same source...

to 20: A thing can't move itself unless it moves and is moved in different respects. Mind, for example, by actually knowing premisses actualizes its own potentiality for knowing conclusions; and will by willing a goal actualizes its own potentiality for willing means.

to 21: The many varying movements of will have a single constant source, and that, as we have said—if we are talking of what directly moves the will—is God, not the heavens. But if we are talking about those willed movements occasionally stimulated by some external thing we sense, then their ultimate cause is the heavens. But the will is not compelled to move, for it doesn't have to want the pleasant things set before it. Nor is it true that what the heavens directly cause happens under compulsion. As Aristotle[20] says, if every effect had a cause, and all causes compelled their effects, then everything would happen under compulsion; but both premisses are false. Some causes, even sufficient ones, don't compel their effects, because they can be interfered with; and all natural causes are of this sort. And it is not true that every happening has a natural cause, for chance happenings have no active natural cause, since they don't actually exist as unified things. So interfering occurrences which happen by chance are not caused by the heavens, since the heavens act as natural causes do...

to 24: Habit doesn't altogether compel one, but mainly when one is taken unawares; for however habituated you are, given time to ponder you can go against a habit.

Passage 18
Soul in Human Beings

Source: Thomas's public disputation on the Soul, 1. Text from *Quaestio Disputata de Anima* (ed. Robb, Toronto, 1968), with corrections from the Leonine text in preparation.

Date: 1269, second stay in Paris, aged 44–5.

Type of passage and how to read: Disputed question (see Introduction).

Notes on translation: For remarks on the word 'soul' see notes on translation to Passage 9. The phrase 'itself a thing', frequently repeated during this passage, translates Thomas's Latin phrase *hoc aliquid* (literally, a this-thing), itself a translation of Aristotle's *tode ti*.

The subject for debate is **Soul.**

[Article 1] And in the first place we are asked: **Can the human soul be both a form and itself a thing?**

And it seems not:

For [1] if human soul is itself a thing, then it subsists and has complete existence in its own right. Now anything attached to something after it has a complete existence is attached incidentally, as whiteness or clothing is attached to human beings. So body joined to soul will be joined to it incidentally. If then soul is itself a thing, it isn't the substantial form of the body . . .

Moreover, [4] since God made things to manifest his own goodness in their various levels, he instituted as many levels of being as nature could carry. If then human soul can subsist—as it must if it is itself a thing—it follows that separately existing souls constitute one level of being. But forms, without their matters, are not a separate level of being. So soul, if it is itself a thing, is not the form of any matter . . .

Moreover, [7] if the soul is itself a thing able to subsist in its own right, it doesn't need a body except as some sort of perfection. Such perfection would either be essential [to the soul] or something supervening. Now not essential to it, since the soul can subsist without a body. And not supervening, for the chief perfection body might seem to offer in that way is the soul's knowledge of truth, drawn from the senses, which require bodily organs. However, people say that the souls of children who die in the womb have a perfect knowledge of things, and this they certainly can't have drawn from their senses. If then the soul is itself a thing, it has no reason to unite to a body as its form . . .

Moreover, [9] what is itself a thing subsists in its own right, whereas it is characteristic of forms to exist in something else, which seems the opposite. So it seems that a soul which is itself a thing won't be a form.

But it was said [by the respondent] that when the body decomposes, soul remains as itself a self-subsistent thing, but its formhood is lost.

> But against that [10]: whatever is lost to something of which the substance remains is incidental to it. So if soul, remaining after the body, loses its formhood, formhood must be incidental to it. But it is as form that it is joined to body to constitute a human being. So its unity with body is incidental, and human beings exist only incidentally, and that is unacceptable.

Moreover, [11] if human soul is itself a thing existing in its own right, it must have an activity of its own peculiar to it, since everything that exists in its own right has its own activity. But human soul has no activity of its own, since even understanding—the most likely candidate—is not an activity of soul but of human beings because of their souls, as Aristotle[1] says. So the human soul is not itself a thing.

Moreover, [12] if the human soul is the form of a body, it must depend in some way on the body, for form and matter are mutually dependent. But what depends on something else is not itself a thing. So if the human soul is a form it is not itself a thing.

Moreover, [13] if soul is body's form, body and soul must share one existence, for matter and form make one existent thing. But body and soul can't share one existence, since they belong to different genuses: soul to the genus of the non-bodily and body to that of the bodily. Soul then can't be body's form.

Moreover, [14] body's existence is decomposable and made up of extended parts, whereas soul's existence is non-decomposable and non-composite. So they can't share one existence.

But it was said [by the respondent] that the very existence as body of the human body comes through soul.

> But against that [15]: Aristotle[2] says *soul is the actualization of an organized physical body*. So what relates to soul as matter to actualization is already an organized physical body, which it can't be unless some form is already constituting it a body. So the human body has its own existence apart from that of the soul . . .

Moreover, [17] existence actualizes soul's substance and is therefore soul's highest point. But lower-order things don't join up with higher-order things at their highest point but at their lowest, for pseudo-Dionysius[3] says God's wisdom links the ends of first things to the beginnings of second things. Body then, which is of a lower order than soul, doesn't join soul in its existence, its highest point . . .

But against that:

[1] what decides a thing's species is the form characteristic of it. But what makes human beings human is reason, so their characteristic form is a soul that reasons. But since, as Aristotle[4] says, understanding needs no bodily organ, the human soul can act in its own right, and so must be able to subsist in its own right as itself a thing. So the human soul is itself both a thing and a form.

Moreover, [2] the human soul's ultimate perfection consists in knowing truth with the mind. But to achieve this perfection soul needs to be joined to a body, because it understands by way of images which only the body can provide. So even if soul is itself a thing it has to be united to a body as its form.

In reply:

By *itself a thing* is properly meant an individual substance: for Aristotle[5] says that without a doubt *substance* primarily means what is itself a thing, though secondarily—even if it seems to mean what is itself a thing—it rather means the sort of thing that thing is. Now an individual substance not only subsists—i.e. exists in its own right—but does so as a whole instance of some species and genus of substance. Thus Aristotle[6] adds that hands, feet, and suchlike don't so much name substances, primary or secondary, as parts of substances: for though they don't need something else as a subject to exist in (thus possessing one characteristic of substances), they aren't complete instances of any specific nature of thing, and so belong to a species and genus only indirectly.

Now certain people deny to the soul or life-principle of human beings both of these requisites for being itself a thing, saying the principle of life is equilibrium (Empedocles) or complexity (Galen) or something similar. In this case the life-principle could neither subsist in its own right nor be a whole instance of some species or genus of substance, but would simply be a form of matter like all others. Yet this is already impossible for the life-principles of plants, the activities of which—like digestion and growth—must spring from a source transcending the physico-chemical reactions those activities employ as tools, as Aristotle[7] shows. Complexity and equilibrium don't transcend the physics and chemistry of the elements. It is equally impossible for the life-principles of things living lives of sense-awareness, the activities of which stretch to taking in the appearances of things without their matter, as Aristotle[8] proves; physico-chemical behaviour can't stretch beyond matter and arrangement of matter. And it is *a fortiori* impossible for the life-principles of things which reason, the activities of which involve abstracting the species of things not only from matter but from every material condition of particularity, so as to know them in general. And there is something further still to consider, which is peculiar to reasoning souls: not only do they take in species that can be understood without their matter and material conditions, but, as Aristotle[9] proves, they cannot share that special activity of theirs with any bodily organ, in the sense of having a bodily organ for thinking as an eye is the bodily organ for seeing. And so the life-principle of a thing with understanding has to act on its own, with an activity peculiar to itself not shared with the body. And because activity flows from actuality, the understanding soul must possess an existence in and of itself, not dependent on the body. For forms that depend for existence on the material or subject [they form] don't have activities of their own: it is not heat that heats but hot things. For this reason then later philosophers have judged that the understanding part of the soul is something that subsists of itself. Thus Aristotle[10] says that mind is a sort of undecomposable substance. And Plato's saying that soul is immortal and subsists of itself because it moves itself amounts to the same. For he is using movement broadly to mean any activity, and the mind moving itself must be interpreted to mean that it is active of itself.

Plato, however, went further, saying not only that the soul subsisted on its own but that it possessed a complete specific nature of its own. For he thought the whole nature of human beings resided in their souls, defining them not as body–soul composites but as souls using bodies, as though souls inhabited bodies like sailors do ships, or people their clothes. But this is impossible. For clearly the life-principle is what gives life to the body. But being alive is existing as a living thing. So the soul is that by which the human body actually exists: in other words, it is the sort of thing a form is. So the human soul is the form of the human body. Further, if soul inhabited body like a sailor his ship, it wouldn't give body or its parts their specific nature; yet clearly it does since when it leaves the body the various parts lose the names they first had, or keep them in a different sense; for a dead man's eyes are eyes only in the sense that eyes in a picture or a statue are, and the same goes for other parts of the body. Moreover, if soul inhabited body like a sailor his ship the union of body and soul would be accidental, and when death separated them it wouldn't be decomposition of a substance, which it clearly is.

So our conclusion is that soul is itself a thing in the sense of being able to subsist by itself, but one which does not possess a complete specific nature of its own; rather it is something which completes a human being's specific nature by being the form of a human body. So that the soul is at one and the same time a form and itself a thing.

And this fits with the hierarchy of forms in nature. For forms of lower-order bodies are higher the closer they approximate and resemble higher causes. For consider the activities peculiar to forms. The activities of elemental forms—the lowest and closest to matter of all—don't transcend the physico-chemical level of expanding and contracting and what seem other ways of arranging matter. But above these come forms of compounds, which, over and above such elemental activities, display behaviour specific to their own natures derived from heavenly bodies; as, for example, the magnetic properties of iron, which derive not from heat and cold and properties like that but from sharing the powers of the heavens. Above these again come plant-forms or plant-souls, which resemble not simply the heavenly bodies but the [spirit] movers of those heavenly bodies, inasmuch as they too cause movement: moving themselves in certain ways. Above these again come the souls of lower animals, which resemble the substances that move the heavens not only in moving themselves around but in having knowledge of their own, though such animals know only material things in a material way, and so require bodily organs. Above these further still are the life-principles of human beings, which resemble the higher substances even in their kind of knowledge, since they can know and understand immaterial substances. But they differ from them still in that human souls by nature acquire immaterial intellectual knowledge from knowledge of material things through the senses. And in this way then we can know the mode of existence of the human soul from examining its activity. Inasmuch as it has an activity transcending that of material things, it has a higher existence than the body and doesn't depend on it. But inasmuch as by nature it acquires immaterial knowledge from material it clearly needs to be united to a body in order to have a complete specific nature; for nothing has a complete specific nature unless it possesses everything required for the activity that characterizes that species. In this way then, inasmuch as the human soul is united to a body as its form and yet also has an existence transcending that of the body and not dependent on it, clearly it exists on the boundary between bodily and separate substances.

Hence:

to 1: Even if soul has a complete existence it doesn't follow that body is joined to it incidentally. For one reason, soul shares that very same existence with body so that there is one existence of the whole composite; and for another, even though soul can subsist of itself, it doesn't have a complete specific nature, but body is joined to it to complete its nature...

to 4: Although a human soul can subsist by itself it hasn't a complete specific nature of its own. So separate souls don't constitute one of the levels of being...

to 7: The soul is joined to a body for its own perfection, both its essential perfection—the completion of its species—and a supervening perfection—the knowledge it draws from the senses, for this is the human being's natural mode of understanding. If separated souls of children and other human beings use another method of understanding, that's no objection: for that belongs to them as separate, not as having a human nature...

to 9: To exist in something else in the way incidental properties exist in a subject is against the nature of what is itself a thing. But existing in something else as a part in a whole, in the way soul exists in human beings, doesn't altogether exclude what exists in something else from being called itself a thing.

to 10: When body decomposes, soul doesn't lose the nature that enables it to be a form, though it is not actually perfecting matter as a form.

to 11: Understanding is an activity which as regards its source is the soul's alone: for soul doesn't use a bodily organ to understand, as it does the eye to see. Body, however, shares in the activity by providing its object, since the images we understand can't exist without the bodily organs.

to 12: Even soul depends somewhat on body, since it can't achieve its complete specific nature without body. But it doesn't so depend on body that it can't exist without it.

to 13: If soul is body's form, body and soul must share one existence in common, the existence of the thing they compose. And the different genus of soul and body is no obstacle to this: for neither body nor soul exists in a species or genus of its own, but belongs as a part to the species or genus of its whole.

to 14: What decomposes, properly speaking, is neither form nor matter nor existence, but the composite of formed matter, the thing. We talk of body having a decomposable existence inasmuch as body through decomposition loses the existence it shared in common with soul, an existence which remains in the subsistent soul. And to that extent the body's existence can also be said to result from the coming-together of its parts, since the coming-together of its parts make it into something that can receive existence from soul.

to 15: When defining a form we include its subject, sometimes as unformed—as when we define change as the actualization of what can come to be—and sometimes as formed—as when we define change as the actualization of what is changing and light as the actualization of what is lit. And this is the way soul is defined as the actualization of an organized physical body, for it is soul that gives body its organized existence just as it is light that makes something lit...

to 17: Though existence is of everything the most formal, yet it is also of everything the most shareable, though not shared in the same way by things of lower and higher order. So body shares soul's existence, but not as excellently as soul...

Passage 19

My Soul is not Me

Source: Thomas's commentary on St Paul's first letter to the Corinthians, 15: 17–19. Text from *Super Epistolam Pauli Apostoli* (Marietti edn., Turin, 1953).

Date: 1269–73, second stay in Paris, aged 45.

Type of passage and how to read: Commentary (see Introduction).

[St Paul's text]

If Christ has not been raised your faith is pointless . . . If our hope in Christ has been for this life only, we are of all people the most pitiable.

. . . But is what Paul says here altogether true? Can Christians *hope only for this life* [if there is no resurrection]? Body may have to be content with the goods of this mortal life, but can't soul still hope for many goods in the life to come? To this there are two answers. Firstly, if we deny the resurrection of the body it isn't easy—indeed it becomes very difficult—to defend the immortality of the soul. The union of body and soul is certainly a natural one, and any separation of soul from body goes against its nature and is imposed on it. So if soul is deprived of body it will exist imperfectly as long as that situation lasts. Now how can a normal situation in accord with nature come to an end, having lasted no time at all, and a situation imposed against nature then last for ever! But this is what must happen if the soul is to go on existing without its body for ever. It is for this reason that the Platonists who believed in immortality believed also in reincarnation, though that is heresy. And this is why Paul says: if the dead don't rise we have only this life to hope for. Secondly, what human beings desire by nature is their own well-being. But soul is not the whole human being, only part of one: my soul is not me. So that even if soul achieves well-being in another life, that doesn't mean I do or any other human being does. Moreover, since it is by nature that humans desire well-being, including their body's well-being, a desire of nature gets frustrated.

Part IV

God in Himself

Passage 20

There Exists a God

Source: *Summa Theologiae,* 1a.2.1–3. Text from *Summa Theologiae* (*Opera Omnia*, Leonine edn., vol. iv).

Date: 1266–8, Italy, aged 42.

Type of passage and how to read: Modified disputed question (see Introduction).

Notes on translation: 'Self-evident' translates *per se nota,* and 'can be made evident' translates *demonstrabile.* 'What need not be and what must be' translates *possibilia et necessaria.*

Parallel reading: See the note on parallel reading attached to Passage 33.

[Question 2] We consider first whether God exists . . . and that divides into three:

Is it self-evident that God exists?
Can it be made evident?
Does God exist?

[Article 1] The first question [Is it self-evident that God exists?] we approach as follows:

It seems self-evident that God exists:

For [1] things of which we are innately aware—first principles, for instance—are said to be self-evident to us. But, as John Damascene[1] says, *the awareness that God exists is implanted by nature in everyone.* So it is self-evident that God exists.

Moreover, [2] propositions are self-evident when we acknowledge them immediately we know what is meant by their terms: a characteristic according to Aristotle[2] of the first principles of demonstration. Thus, once we know what wholes and parts are, we acknowledge wholes to be always bigger than their parts. But once we understand what the word *God* means, it follows that God exists. For the word means *that than which nothing greater can be meant*. Consequently, since existing in thought and in fact is greater than existing in thought alone, and since, once we understand the word *God*, he exists in thought, he must also exist in fact. So it is self-evident that God exists.

Moreover, [3] it is self-evident that truth exists, for even denying it admits it. For if it doesn't exist, then it's true it doesn't exist, and if something's true, truth exists. Now God is truth itself: in John 14 [6], [Jesus says] *I am the way, the truth, and the life*. So it is self-evident that God exists.

But against that:

No one can think the opposite of a self-evident proposition, as Aristotle's[3] discussion of the first principles of demonstration makes clear. But the opposite of the proposition that God exists can be thought, for *the fool* in Psalm 51 [1] *said in his heart: There is no God*. So it is not self-evident that God exists.

In reply:

A self-evident proposition, though always self-evident in itself, is sometimes self-evident to us and sometimes not. For a proposition is self-evident when the predicate forms part of what the subject means: thus it is self-evident that human beings are animals, since being animal is part of what being human means. If then it is evident to everyone what it is to be this subject and what it is to have this predicate, the proposition itself will be self-evident to everyone; and this is clearly so for first principles of demonstration, which use common terms known to all, such as *be* and *not be*, *whole* and *part*. But if there are people to whom the meanings of subject and predicate are not evident, then the proposition, though self-evident in itself, will not be so to such people. Which is why Boethius[4] says *certain notions are* self-evident and *commonplace only to the learned, as, for example, that what isn't a body won't occupy space.*

I maintain then that the proposition *God exists* is self-evident in itself, since its subject and predicate are identical: God, I shall argue later, is his own existence. But because what it is to be God is not evident to us the proposition is not self-evident to us. It needs to be made evident by things less evident in themselves but more evident to us, namely, God's effects.

Hence:

to 1: The awareness that God exists is implanted in us by nature in no clear or specific way. Man is by nature aware of what by nature he desires: a happiness to be found only in God. But this is not, simply speaking, to be aware of God's existence, any more than to be aware of someone approaching is to be aware of Peter, even if it is Peter approaching; many, in fact, believe the perfect good which will make us happy to be riches, or pleasure, or some other such thing.

to 2: Someone hearing the word *God* may very well not understand it to mean *that than which nothing greater can be thought*; indeed, some people have believed God to be a body. And even if the word *God* were generally recognized to have that meaning, nothing thus defined would thereby be granted existence in the world of fact, but merely in thought. Unless one is given that something in fact exists than which nothing greater can be thought—and this nobody denying God's existence would grant—the conclusion that God in fact exists does not follow.

to 3: It is self-evident that truth exists in general, but not self-evident to us that there exists a first Truth.

[**Article 2**] The second question [**Can God's existence be made evident?**] we approach as follows:

That God exists can't, it seems, be made evident:

For [1] God's existence is an article of faith, and since St Paul in Hebrews 11 [1] says that faith is concerned with *the unseen*, its propositions can't be demonstrated, that is, made evident. So we can't demonstrate that God exists.

Moreover, [2] the central link in a demonstration is a definition. But as John Damascene[5] says, we can't know what God is but only what he isn't. So we can't demonstrate that God exists.

Moreover, [3] if we could demonstrate God to exist, it could only be by arguing from his effects. Now God and his effects are incommensurable, he being limitless and his effects limited and the limited not being able to measure the limitless. So, since effects incommensurate with their cause can't make it evident, it doesn't seem possible to demonstrate that God exists.

But against that:

In the words of St Paul in Romans 1: 20 *the hidden things of God can be clearly understood from the things that he has made*. If so, we must be able to demonstrate that God exists from the things that he has made, for the first step in understanding a thing is to know that it exists.

In reply:

There are two kinds of demonstration: those that argue from cause to effect, following the natural order of things themselves and showing *why* things are as they are; and those that argue from effect to cause, following the order in which we know things and simply showing *how* things are—for when effects are more apparent to us than their cause we come to know the cause through its effects. Now any effect that is better known to us than its cause can demonstrate that its cause exists: for effects are dependent on their causes and can only occur if their causes already exist. From effects evident to us, therefore, we can demonstrate something that is not self-evident to us, namely, that God exists.

Hence:

to 1: The truths about God which St Paul says we can know by natural reasoning—that God exists, for example—are not articles of faith but presupposed by them. For faith presupposes some natural knowledge just as grace does nature and any perfection what it perfects. However, there is nothing to stop an individual accepting on faith some truth he can't demonstrate, even if it be in itself something that demonstration can make evident.

to 2: When we argue from effect to cause, the effect must take the place of a definition of the cause in the proof that the cause exists; and especially so when the cause is God. For when proving anything to exist the central link is not what the thing is—we cannot even ask what it is until we know that it exists—but rather what we use the name of the thing to mean. Now, as we shall see, what the word *God* means derives from his effects; so when demonstrating from effects that God exists we are able to start from what the word *God* means.

to 3: Only effects commensurate with their cause can give comprehensive knowledge of it, but, as we have said, any effect whatever can make it clear that the cause exists. God's effects then are enough to prove that God exists, even if they are not enough to help us comprehend what he is.

[**Article 3**] The third question [**Does God exist?**] we approach as follows:

It seems there is no God:

For [1] if one of two mutually exclusive things were to exist unbounded, the other would be totally destroyed. But the word *God* implies some unbounded good. So if God existed, no evil would ever be encountered. Evil is, however, encountered in the world. So God does not exist.

Moreover, [2] when a few causes fully account for some effect it doesn't need more. But it seems that everything we observe in this world can be fully accounted for by other causes, without assuming a God: natural effects by natural causes, and contrived effects by human reasoning and will. There is therefore no need to assume that God exists.

But against that:

Exodus 3 [14] represents God as saying: *I am who am.*

In reply:

There are five ways of proving there is a God:

The first and most obvious way is based on change. For certainly some things are changing: this we plainly see. Now anything changing is being changed by something else. (This is so because what makes things changeable is unrealized potentiality, but what makes them cause change is their already realized state: causing change brings into being what was previously only able to be, and can only be done by something which already is. For example, the actual heat of fire causes wood, able to be hot, to become actually hot, and so causes change in the wood; now what is actually hot can't at the same time be potentially hot but only potentially cold, can't at the same time be actual and potential in the same respect but only in different respects; so that what is changing can't be the very thing that is causing the same change, can't be changing itself, but must be being changed by something else.) Again this something else, if itself changing, must be being changed by yet another thing; and this last by another. But this can't go on for ever, since then there would be no first cause of the change, and as a result no subsequent causes. (Only when acted on by a first cause do intermediate causes produce a change; unless a hand moves the stick, the stick won't move anything else.) So we are forced eventually to come to a first cause of change not itself being changed by anything, and this is what everyone understands by *God*.

The second way is based on the very notion of agent cause. In the observable world causes are found ordered in series: we never observe, nor ever could, something causing itself, for this would mean it preceded itself, and this is not possible. But a series of causes can't go on for ever, for in any such series an earlier member causes an intermediate and the intermediate a last (whether the intermediate be one or many). Now eliminating a cause eliminates its effects, and unless there's a first cause there won't be a last or an intermediate. But if a series of causes goes on for ever it will have no first cause, and so no intermediate causes and no last effect, which is clearly false. So we are forced to postulate some first agent cause, to which everyone gives the name *God*.

The third way is based on what need not be and on what must be, and runs as follows. Some of the things we come across can be but need not be, for we find them being generated and destroyed, thus sometimes in being and sometimes not. Now everything cannot be like this, for a thing that need not be was once not; and if everything need not be, once upon a time there was nothing. But if that were true there would be nothing even now, because something that does not exist can only begin to exist through something that already exists. If nothing was in being nothing could begin to be, and nothing would be in being now, which is clearly false. Not everything then is the sort that need not be; some things must be, and these may or may not owe this necessity to something else. But just as we proved that a series of agent causes can't go on for ever, so also a series of things which must be and owe this to other things. So we are forced to postulate something which of itself must be, owing this to nothing outside itself, but being itself the cause that other things must be.

The fourth way is based on the levels found in things. Some things are found to be better, truer, more excellent than others. Such comparative terms describe varying degrees of approximation to a superlative; for example, things are hotter the nearer they approach what is hottest. So there is something which is the truest and best and most excellent of things, and hence the most fully in being; for Aristotle[6] says that the truest things are the things most fully in being. Now *when many things possess a property in common, the one most fully possessing it causes it in the others: fire,* as Aristotle says, *the hottest of all things, causes all other things to be hot*. So there is something that causes in all other things their being, their goodness, and whatever other perfections they have. And this is what we call *God*.

The fifth way is based on the guidedness of nature. Goal-directed behaviour is observed in all bodies in nature, even those lacking awareness; for we see their behaviour hardly ever varying and practically always turning out well, which shows they truly tend to goals and do not merely hit them by accident. But nothing lacking awareness can tend to a goal except it be directed by someone with awareness and understanding: arrows by archers, for example. So everything in nature is directed to its goal by someone with understanding, and this we call *God.*

Hence:

to 1: As Augustine[7] says: *Since God is supremely good, he would not allow any evil at all in his works if he wasn't sufficiently almighty and good to bring good even from evil.* It is therefore a mark of his unbounded goodness that God allows evils to exist and draws from them good.

to 2: Natural causes pursue fixed goals under the direction of some superior cause, and so their effects must also be traced back to God as the first of all causes. In the same manner contrived effects must also be traced back to a higher cause than human reasoning and will, for these are changeable and can cease to exist, and, as we have seen, everything that can change or cease to exist must be traced back to a first cause which cannot change and of itself must be.

Passage 21

God is his Own Existence

Source: Thomas's public disputations on the Power of God, 7.2. Text from *Quaestiones Disputatae de Potentia* (Marietti edn., Turin, 1953), with corrections from the Leonine text in preparation.

Date: 1266–7, Italy, aged 42.

Type of passage and how to read: Public disputation (see Introduction).

Notes on translation: Read the notes on translation for Passage 6. The verbs 'to be' and 'to exist' both translate the verb *esse*. Throughout I have used 'substance' for *substantia* and 'essence' for *essentia*. The student will notice (1) that these two words are used synonymously (the Greek background of both is the word *ousia*), and that (2) the distinction between *esse* (existence) and *essentia* (essence) here asserted of creatures and denied of God is carefully nuanced: sensitive to *essentia* as an abstract form of *esse* (see objection [7] and answer), to existence as meaning actually having essence (see **Hence to 1**), and to essence as causally involved in existence (compare objection [10] and its answer with the **In reply** of Question 5, Article 3, in Passage 1, and with related passages in other works of Thomas, e.g., *Metaphysics*, 4.2. [558], and *Summa Theologiae*, 1a.3.4).

[Question 7] The subject for debate is **The Simpleness of God's Substance...**

[Article 2] And in the second place we are asked: **Is it God's substance or essence to exist?**

It seems not:

For [1] John Damascene[1] says that *it is clear that God exists, but what he is in substance or nature is altogether beyond comprehension and unknown.* Now the same thing can't be both known and unknown. So God's existing is not the same as his substance or essence.

But it was said [by the respondent] that God's existing is just as unknown to us as his substance is.

But against that: [2] whether God exists and what he is are quite different questions, to one of which we know the answer and to the other of which we don't, as is clear from the authority already quoted. So what responds to the question whether God exists is not the same as what responds to the question what he is. But God's existing answers to the whether question, and his substance or nature to the what question.

But it was said [by the respondent] that God's existing is known not in itself but by what resembles it in creatures.

But against that: [3] creatures have both existence and substance or nature, both come from God and both must resemble him, since what agents do reflect what they are. So if we know God's existence by created existence's resemblance, we must be able to know his substance by created substance's resemblance: and in that case we must know not only that God exists but what he is.

Moreover, [4] things differ from each other in substance. But they can't differ by what they have in common: so, as Aristotle[2] says, you don't mention existence in definitions because it won't distinguish what you're defining from anything else. So the substance of anything distinguished from other things can't be its existing, since that is what everything has in common. Now God is something distinct from all other things. So existing can't be his substance.

Moreover, [5] things are different only if they have differing existence. But this thing's existing doesn't differ from that thing's existing as existing, but only as existing in this or that a nature. So any existing which is not in a nature added to existing itself wouldn't differ from any other existing. If to exist is God's substance then, it will follow that he is the existing all have in common.

Moreover, [6] being (period!) is the being everything has in common. But if God were his own existing, he would be being (period!). He would be what everything has in common and could be attributed to everything: God would be compounded of all things. Now that is a heresy, and also contradicts the opinion of Aristotle,[3] who said that *the first cause rules everything and is mixed in with nothing.*

Moreover, [7] non-abstract terms don't properly apply to what is absolutely simple. But existing is this sort of term: for existing seems to relate to essence as white to whiteness.[4] So saying God's substance is existing uses terms badly.

Moreover, [8] Boethius[5] says that *Everything existent shares in existence in order to be, and in something else in order to be something.* But God is; so over and above his existence there must be something else in him by which he is something.

Moreover, [9] one shouldn't attribute to God, who is utterly perfect, what is utterly imperfect. Now existing, like ultimate matter, is utterly imperfect: ultimate matter is indeterminate relative to every form, and in the same way existing is utterly imperfect and indeterminate relative to every special category [of being]. So, if ultimate matter doesn't belong in God, neither should one attribute existing to God's substance.

Moreover, [10] what is thought of as an effect can't be attributed to the first of all substances, which is uncaused. But that is what existence is like, since everything that exists has existence through its essence. So God's substance can't be said to be existence itself.

Moreover, [11] a proposition is self-evident if its subject and predicate are identical. Now if God's substance is his own very existence, then the subject and predicate of the proposition *God exists* will be identical. And then it will be a self-evident proposition, which is clearly false since it needs proving. So God's existence can't be his substance.

But against that:

[1] Hilary[6] says that *Existence isn't incidental to God but his subsistent truth*. But what subsists is a thing's substance. So God's existence is his substance.

Moreover, [2] Moses Maimonides[7] says that *God is existent not by way of some essence, living not by way of some life, powerful not by way of some power, wise not by way of some wisdom*. So God's essence is not other than his existence.

Moreover, [3] the name that properly designates a thing derives from its quiddity: for Aristotle[8] tells us that names properly signify substance and quiddity. Now God's most proper name, as Exodus [3: 14] makes clear, is *He who is*. This name, however, derives from his existence, so it seems God's existence is his substance.

In reply:

God's existing doesn't differ from his substance. To be clear about this, note that when several causes producing different effects have also, besides those differing effects, one effect in common, then they must produce that common effect in virtue of some higher cause to which it properly belongs. For the effect properly belonging to a cause is determined by the cause's own proper nature and form; so that effects properly belonging to causes of diverse nature and form must differ, and any effect produced in common must properly belong not to any one of them but to a higher cause in virtue of which they act. Thus since pepper, ginger, and other differently structured spices with their own specific effects are all hot, this common effect must properly belong to some prior cause, in this case elemental fire. In the movements of the heavens, too, each planetary sphere has its own proper movement, and the movement which they all share must properly belong to some higher containing sphere rotating them all daily.[9] Now all created causes, distinguished by the effects that properly belong to each of them, have also one effect in common, namely, existence: heat, for example, causes things to be—or exist as—hot, and builders cause there to be—or exist—houses.[10] So they agree in causing things to exist, but differ in this: that heat causes heat and builders houses. So there must be some cause higher than all of them in virtue of which they all cause existence, a cause of which existence is the proper effect. And this cause is God. Now the proper effect of any cause issues from it by reproducing its nature. So existing must be God's substance or nature. And that is why the book of Causes[11] says that *intelligence gives existence only if it is divine*, and that *the first of all effects is existence, and nothing created precedes that.*

Hence:

to 1: According to Aristotle[12] we use the verb 'to be' in two ways: sometimes to signify the essence of a thing, its act of existing, sometimes to signify the truth of a proposition, even where there is lack of existence, as when we say that blindness exists since it is true that some men are blind. When Damascene says it is clear that God exists he uses 'exist' in the second way and not the first. Used in the first way God's existing is his substance and as unknown to us as his substance is. But used in the second way we know that God exists, since that is a proposition we can conceive in our mind through his effects. And that makes clear the answers to 2 and to 3.

to 4: God's existing—his substance—is not the existing common to other things, but an existing distinct from all other existing. So by his very own existing God differs from all other beings.

to 5: As we read in the book of Causes,[13] God's existing is individually distinguished from all other existing by the very fact that it is an existing subsistent in itself, and not one supervening on a nature other than existing itself. All other existing, as non-subsistent, must be individually distinguished by some nature or substance that subsists with that existence. And of such things it is true that this thing's existing differs from that thing's existing by belonging to a different nature. Just as if heat existed alone of itself without matter or subject, that very fact would distinguish it from all other heat; though all instances of heat existing in subjects would have to be distinguished [from each other] by way of those subjects.

to 6: The being everything has in common is being (period!), though not in the sense that additions can't be made to it. But God's existing is being (period!) in the sense that no addition can be made to it. So God's existing is not the existing everything has in common. Just as the genus animal neither includes the addition rational in its definition, nor yet excludes it; for that defines irrational animals, a species of animal.

to 7: The way words we use express things is determined by the way we understand the things, for, as Aristotle[14] says, *words express mental conceptions*. Now our mind understands existing in the way we see it on earth where our knowledge starts, and there existing is not subsistent but attaches to things. Our reasons, however, discover that there is a subsistent existing, and so—although our word for existing is a non-abstract term—our mind in attributing it to God goes beyond the way it expresses, attributing to God what the word expresses but not in the way it expresses it.

to 8: We must understand Boethius to be talking of things that share in existence rather than exist by essence; for what exists by its essence, if we give due weight to the words we use, should not be said to be something existent, but rather to be existence itself.

to 9: What I am calling *esse* [being in being] is of all things the most perfect. Clearly this is so, since actualizing potentiality perfects it, and no form whatever can be understood actualized except by thinking of it as in being. Human-being or fire-iness can be thought of as existing[15] potentially in some material, or virtually in some cause, or even in mind, but only by being in being is it made actually existent. So clearly what I am calling *esse* is the actualization of all actuality, and consequently the perfection of all perfections. Nor should we think anything is ever added to what I am calling *esse* in the way forms are added [to matter], or actualization to potentiality: for anything added in that way is different in essence from that to which it is added, but nothing outside existence can be added to it, since nothing exists outside existence except the non-existent, and that can't be either form or matter. So existing is determined by other things not as potentiality by actualization, but rather as actualization by potentiality, in the way we include in definitions of forms their appropriate matter to differentiate them, saying, for example, that the soul is the actualization of a natural organic body; it is in this way that we distinguish this existence from that existence, as existence in this or that sort of nature. And this is why pseudo-Dionysius[16] says that *though living things are more excellent than existent things, existence is more excellent than life*: for living things don't only have life but, together with life, have existence.

to 10: Goals are ordered in the way agents are, the ultimate goal being that of the first agent, and the other goals belonging proportionately in an ordered way to the other agents. For think of the city-ruler, his army-commander, and a private soldier: clearly the city-ruler is the first agent sending the army-commander off to war, and the army-commander sets the private soldiers under him to do the actual fighting. The soldier's goal is to lay low the enemy, a goal which is subordinate to the army-commander's goal, the victory of his army, which in turn is subordinate to the ruler or king's goal, the good state of the city or kingdom. Existence then, the proper effect and goal of the first agent's activity, must be the ultimate goal. Now goals, though intended first, are implemented last, and thus are effects of later causes. So that caused existence, the proper effect corresponding to the first agent, is caused through secondary causes, whereas the first [agent's] existence is a causing existence, first and uncaused.

to 11: A proposition self-evident in itself need not be so to this or that person: to someone, for example, unaware that its predicate forms part of its subject's definition. Thus the proposition that every whole is bigger than its part isn't self-evident to someone who doesn't know what a whole is, for, as Aristotle[17] says, we know such propositions by knowing their terms. Now the proposition that God exists is self-evident in itself since its subject and predicate are identical, but it isn't self-evident to us because we don't know what God is: so it needs to be made evident to us, but not to those who can see God's essence.

Passage 22

Eternity and Time

Source: *Summa Theologiae*, Ia.10.1, 4. Text from *Summa Theologiae* (*Opera Omnia*, Leonine edn., vol. iv).

Date: 1266–8, Italy, aged 42.

Type of passage and how to read: Modified disputed question (see Introduction).

Notes on translation: 'The aeon' translates *aevum*, originally another word for eternity, but here used to distinguish the 'duration' of heavenly creatures from time, on the one hand, and the Creator's eternity, on the other.

[Question 10] We next consider **Eternity**, and that divides into six:

What is eternity? . . .
Does eternity differ from the aeon and time? . . .

[Article 1] The first question **[What is eternity?]** we approach as follows:

It seems that Boethius'[1] definition of eternity won't do:

For [1] he defined eternity as *the simultaneously whole and complete possession of endless life*. Now *endless* is a negative term such as belongs only in the definition of defective things; eternity, however, is no defect. So the word *endless* is out of place in a definition of eternity.

Moreover, [2] *eternity* names a sort of duration, and duration measures existence rather than life. So the word *existence* should be used in the definition in place of *life*.

Moreover, [3] the word *whole* describes something having parts. Now eternity is simple and has no parts. So *whole* won't do.

Moreover, [4] several days or times can't be simultaneous. But in speaking of eternity we talk of *days* and *times* in the plural. For Micah 5 [2] says *his going forth is from the beginning, from the days of eternity*, and St Paul in Romans 16 [25] talks of *the revealing of the mystery kept secret through times eternal*. Eternity then is not simultaneously whole.

Moreover, [5] wholeness and completion are the same. Given then that eternity is whole it is redundant to add that it is complete.

Moreover, [6] possession has nothing to do with duration, and eternity is a sort of duration. So eternity is not a possession.

In reply:

Just as we derive our knowledge of simple things from composite ones so we derive our knowledge of eternity from time, which is *the measure of before and after in change*. For in all change there is successiveness, one part coming after another, and from our numbering antecedent and consequent parts of change there arises the notion of time, which is simply the numberedness of before and after in change. Now something that lacks change and never varies its mode of existence will not display a before and after. So just as numbering before and after in change produces the notion of time, so awareness of invariability in something altogether free from change produces the notion of eternity. A further point: time is said by Aristotle[2] to measure things that begin and end in time, and that is because you can always find a beginning and an end in changing things. But things altogether unchangeable can no more have a beginning than show successiveness.

Two things then characterize eternity: firstly, things existing in eternity are *endless*, lacking both beginning and end (for both may be called *ends*); and secondly, eternity itself exists as a *simultaneous whole*, lacking successiveness.

Hence:

to 1: We often use negations to define simple things, saying points have no parts, for example. This is not because they are negative in substance but because our minds first grasp composite things and only come to know simple things by denying compositeness of them.

to 2: That which exists in eternity is, in fact, also alive. Moreover, life covers activity too, which existence doesn't, and the flow of duration is more apparent in activity than in existence: time, for example, measures changes.

to 3: Eternity is called whole not because it has parts but because it has nothing lacking to it.

to 4: Just as scripture described God metaphorically in bodily terms though he is not a body, so it describes eternity in temporal and successive terms though it exists simultaneously.

to 5: Note two things about time: time itself is actualized successively, in a present instant which is never complete. So to deny that eternity is time Boethius calls it *simultaneously whole*, and to deny that it is temporal instantaneity he calls it *complete*.

to 6: To possess something is to hold it firmly and unmovingly. So to signify eternity's unchangeableness and constancy Boethius used the word *possession* . . .

[Article 4] The fourth question [**Does eternity differ from the aeon and time?**] we approach as follows:

Eternity doesn't seem to differ from time:

For [1] two measures of duration can only exist simultaneously if one is part of the other: thus two days or hours can't occur simultaneously, but an hour and a day can, since an hour is part of a day. Now eternity and time, both of which signify some sort of measure of duration, exist simultaneously. So since eternity is not a part of time but exceeds and contains it, time must seemingly be a part of eternity and not differ from it.

Moreover, [2] according to Aristotle[3] the present moment of time persists unchanged throughout time. But the nature of eternity seems to consist precisely in remaining unbrokenly the same throughout the whole course of time. Eternity then must be the present moment of time. But the present moment of time is in substance identical with time itself. So eternity must be in substance identical with time.

Moreover, [3] Aristotle[4] says the measure of the most fundamental change measures all other changes. In the same way it seems that the measure of the most fundamental existence should measure all other existences. But eternity measures God's existence, which is the most fundamental existence; so it should measure all existence. Now the existence of perishable things is measured by time. So time is either eternity or part of eternity.

But against that:

Eternity is simultaneously whole, while in time there is before and after. So time and eternity differ.

In reply:

Time clearly differs from eternity. But some people say the reason for the difference is that time began and will end, whereas eternity doesn't begin or end. Now this is an accidental difference, not an intrinsic one, for even if time had always existed and will always exist—as those hold who think the heavens will go on revolving for ever—there would still be the difference Boethius pointed out between time and eternity: that eternity is simultaneously whole, while time is not, eternity measuring abiding existence and time measuring change.

If, however, the suggested difference is applied to the things being measured rather than to the measures themselves, then it has some justification, for, as Aristotle[5] says, time measures only those things that begin and end in time. So, even if the heavens did rotate for ever, time would measure not the whole duration of the movement—since the infinite is immeasurable—but each revolution separately as it began and ended in time.

Or we could justify applying the difference to the measures themselves if we talked of potential beginnings and ends. For even if time lasted for ever it would always be possible to mark off beginnings and ends in it by dividing it into parts, in the way we talk of days and years beginning and ending; and this would not apply to eternity.

However, these differences are secondary. The primary intrinsic difference of time from eternity is that eternity exists as a simultaneous whole and time doesn't.

Hence:

to 1: This would be a valid argument if time and eternity were measures of the same kind, but when one considers the different things they measure, they clearly aren't.

to 2: The present moment persistently underlies time, altering state continuously; just as time corresponds to movement [of the heavens], the present corresponds to what moves, which remains in substance the same throughout time though it alters its position, first here and then there, and, by altering its position, moves. Time consists in the passing of the present moment as it alters state. Eternity, however, remains unchanged both in substance and in state, and thus differs from the present of time.

to 3: Just as eternity is the proper measure of existence as such, so time is the proper measure of change. In so far then as some existence falls short of permanence in its existing and is subject to change, so will it fall short of eternity and be subject to time. So the existence of perishable things, being changeable, is measured by time and not by eternity. For time measures not only the actually changing but also the potentially changeable. It measures, therefore, not only movement but also rest, the state of the movable when not moving.

Passage 23

Do we Have Words for God?

Source: *Summa Theologiae*, 1a.13.1–6, 12. Text from *Summa Theologiae* (*Opera Omnia*, Leonine edn., vol. iv).

Date: 1266–8, Italy, aged 42.

Type of passage and how to read: Modified disputed question (see Introduction).

Notes on translation: 'Names', 'nouns', and 'words' all translate *nomina*. Clearly Thomas does have names and nouns particularly in mind in some of the arguments that follow, but mostly he is talking of words in the sense given by the English question 'Is there a word for that?' The use of the Latin word *nomina* is determined by the history of this discussion, the origins of which lie in a fifth- or sixth-century work of pseudo-Dionysius quoted frequently here by Thomas, the *De Divinis Nominibus*. This work, too, though often called in English 'The Divine Names', would perhaps better be called 'Words for God'. 'Express' and 'mean' translate the verb *significare*.

[Question 13] Next we consider **the words we use for God**, and this divides into twelve:

Can we use words for God?
Do any of the words we use for God express what he essentially is?
Do some of the words we use for God apply to him literally, or are they all metaphorical?
Are these words used for God synonymous?
Are words used of God and creatures univocally or equivocally?
If we say they are used analogically, do they apply primarily to God or to creatures?...
Can we make affirmative statements about God?

[Article 1] The first question [**Can we use words for God?**] we approach as follows:

It seems we have no words for God.

For [1] pseudo-Dionysius[1] says: *of him there is neither name nor opinion.* And Proverbs 30 [4] asks: *What is his name or his son's name? Do you know?*

Moreover, [2] nouns are either abstract or concrete. Neither are appropriate to God: concrete nouns because he is simple, abstract nouns because they don't express complete subsistent things. So no nouns apply to God.

Moreover, [3] nouns express sorts of things, verbs and participles are tensed, pronouns are either demonstrative or relative. None of this is appropriate to God, who is without qualities or incidental properties, exists out of time, can't be ostensively demonstrated to our senses, nor referred to by any pronoun referring back to a noun or participle or demonstrative pronoun. So no sort of word can apply to him.

But against that:

We read in Exodus 15 [3]: *The Lord is a great warrior: Almighty is his name.*

In reply:

Aristotle[2] says *words express thoughts and thoughts represent things*; so clearly words refer mediately to things by way of our mental conceptions: we talk about things in the way we know them. Now we have already seen that in this life we cannot see God's substance but know him only from creatures: as their non-creaturely and transcendent cause. So this is where our words for God come from: from creatures. Such words, however, will not express the substance of God as he is in himself, in the way words like *human being* express the substance of what human beings are in themselves, expressing what defines human beings and declaring what makes them human beings; for the meaning of a word is the definition of some thing.

Hence:

to 1: God is said to have no name or be beyond naming because his substance lies outside what we understand of him or can express in words.

to 2: Because our knowledge and our words for God come

from creatures, the words we use for him express him in ways more appropriate to the kind of creatures we know naturally, and these, as we have said, are material creatures. In such creatures subsistent wholes are composed [of formed material], the form not being a subsistent whole itself but determining what subsists. So all our words for expressing subsistent wholes are concrete terms, appropriate to composite things; whereas to express the non-composite forms we use words that don't express them as subsistent but as determining what subsists: as *whiteness*, for example, names what makes things white. Now God is both non-composite *and* subsistent, so we use abstract terms to express his lack of composition and concrete terms to express his subsistence and wholeness. But neither way of talking fully measures up to his way of existing, for in this life we do not know him as he is in himself.

to 3: To express something as a sort of thing is to express it as a subject subsisting under a determinate nature or form. So just as we have said concrete nouns are used to express God's subsistent wholeness, so too are words that express him as a sort of thing. In the same way, tensed verbs and participles are used to express God's eternity (which includes all time); for just as we can only grasp and express non-composite subsistent things in the way we do composite things, so we can understand and express in words the simpleness of eternity only in terms of things in time: the reason being our mind's kinship with composite temporal things. We use demonstrative pronouns of God in the way we use them of certain other things, pointing them out not to our senses but to our minds, for the way in which we point out things depends on the way we know them. And so because there are ways in which nouns and participles and demonstrative pronouns apply to God, there are ways in which relative nouns and pronouns can express him.

[**Article 2**] The second question [**Do any of the words we use for God express what he essentially is?**] we approach as follows:

It seems that no word used of God can express what he essentially is:

For [1] John Damascene[3] says: *Of necessity each word said of God expresses not what he essentially is but what he is not, or some relationship he has, or something following from his nature or activity.*

Moreover, [2] pseudo-Dionysius[4] says: *You will find that the utterances of all God's holy teachers articulate the names of God, in praise and revelation, in accordance with blessed outpourings of his divinity.* And what he means is that the words the holy teachers use in praise of God differ according to what issues from God. But words expressing what issue from something don't express anything of its substance. So the words we use of God don't express what he essentially is.

Moreover, [3] we talk of things in the way we understand them. But we don't understand God's substance in this life, so no words we use can express God's substance.

But against that:

Augustine[5] says: *The being strong of God is his being, and the being wise, and whatever other phrase we use to express the very substance of that simple being.* So all such names express God's substance.

In reply:

Clearly negative names for God and names relating him to creatures don't in any way express his substance; rather they express an absence of something in him, or a relationship he has to other things (or better, that other things have). Opinions have differed, however, about non-relative affirmative terms like *good* and *wise*.

Some have said that all such names, though ascribed affirmatively to God, are actually designed to exclude something from God rather than to ascribe something positive to him. So, according to them, when we say *God is alive* we mean that God is not like inanimate things, and other propositions are to be understood in the same way. And this was Moses Maimonides' view. Others say that such names are used to express God's relationship to creatures, so that when we say *God is good* we mean that God causes goodness in things, and so on for other propositions.

Both views seem unacceptable, for three reasons. In the first place, neither view explains why some words are used of God rather than others. God causes bodies just as he causes goodness, so if all that we are expressing by saying *God is good* is that God causes goodness, why don't we say *God is a body* because he causes bodies? Or we could say *God is a body* in order to exclude his being merely unformed potentiality like ultimate matter. In the second place, all words used of God would apply to him only secondarily, in the way the word *healthy* applies secondarily to medicine, where it means only that medicine causes bodies to be healthy, that being the primary meaning of the word. In the third place, it isn't what people talking of God want to say. When we talk of the *living* God, we want to say something else than that he causes life in us or differs from non-living bodies.

So we must rather say that such words do express God's substance and say something of what God essentially is, but represent him inadequately. And we explain this as follows. We can only talk of God as we know him, and since we know him through creatures, we only know him as creatures represent him. But we have said above that all creaturely perfections pre-exist in God in one simple all-embracing perfection. So creatures having any perfection represent and resemble him, but not as things of one type or kind represent each other, but as effects partially resemble a cause of a higher kind though falling short of reproducing its form: the way earthly bodily forms, for example, reproduce the power of the sun. We explained all this earlier when talking of God's perfection. So the sort of words we are considering express God's substance, but do it imperfectly just as creatures represent him imperfectly.

So when we say *God is good* we mean neither *God causes goodness* nor *God is not bad*, but *What in creatures we call goodness pre-exists in a higher way in God*. Thus God is not good because he causes goodness; rather because he is good, goodness spreads through things. As Augustine[6] says, *because* he *is good*, we *exist*.

Hence:

to 1: The reason John Damascene says such words don't express what God is is that none of them perfectly express what he is; but each expresses him imperfectly in the imperfect way creatures represent him.

to 2: *Why* a word gets used to mean something differs sometimes from *what* it is used to mean: the Latin word *lapis* derives from *laedens pedem*—hurting the feet, but it doesn't mean any and every kind of thing that hurts our feet, but the particular kind of body we call a rock. And so we answer that *why* certain words get used of God depends on the outpourings of his divinity: for just as creatures represent him, however imperfectly, according to differing outpourings of perfection, so our minds know and name God in accordance with each outpouring. Nevertheless, these words don't mean those outpourings: *God is alive* doesn't mean life pours out from him, but expresses the fact that life pre-exists in him as the source of all things, though in a way surpassing anything we can understand or express.

to 3: We can't know God's substance in this life for what it is in itself, but we can know it as represented by creaturely perfections, and that is how our words for him express it.

[**Article 3**] The third question [**Do some of the words we use for God apply to him literally, or are they all metaphorical?**] we approach as follows:

It seems that no words apply literally to God:

For [**1**], as we have said, all words used of God come from creatures. But to apply names of creatures to God—calling him a rock or a lion, for example—is to use metaphor. So the words we use of God apply to him metaphorically.

Moreover, [**2**] no word applies literally to something of which it is more truly denied than asserted. But all words like *good* and *wise*, pseudo-Dionysius[7] says, are more truly denied of God than asserted. So none of these names apply to him literally.

Moreover, [3] words for bodies can only apply to an incorporeal God metaphorically. But all the words we are considering carry with them features characteristic of bodies: tense, for example, or concreteness, or other bodily conditions. So all these words apply to God metaphorically.

But against that:

Ambrose[8] says *There are certain words which reveal clearly what is proper to divinity, and some which express the evident truth of divine majesty; but others are used of him by simile and metaphor*. So not all words are used metaphorically of God; some apply literally.

In reply:

As we have said, we know God from the perfections that are poured out from him into creatures, and exist in him in a way surpassing the way they exist in creatures. Now our minds apprehend those perfections in the way they exist in creatures, and give them names suiting the way we apprehend them. So in using such words of God we must consider on the one hand the perfections they express—goodness, life, and the like—and on the other their manner of expressing them. In regard to what they express, these words apply literally to God, and indeed more properly to him than to creatures, and so primarily to him. But as regards their manner of expressing it, they don't apply literally to God; for their manner of expression is appropriate only to creatures.

Hence:

to 1: Some words so express the perfections issuing from God into created things that the imperfect way in which the creature shares God's perfection is included in what the word means, as materiality is included in the meaning of *rock*. Such words can apply to God only metaphorically. But other words express the perfections without including in what the word means any particular way of sharing those perfections:

words like *existent* and *good* and *living*, for example. And such words apply to God literally.

to 2: The reason pseudo-Dionysius says we should deny such words of God is that what they express doesn't belong to him in the way they express it but in a surpassing way. Thus in the same place he says that God *exists beyond all substance and life.*

to 3: Words applying literally to God carry with them features characteristic of bodies not in what they express but in the way they express it; whereas words that apply metaphorically to him carry some bodily feature as part of what they mean.

[Article 4] The fourth question **[Are these words used for God synonymous?]** we approach as follows:

It seems that the words we use about God are all synonymous:

For [1] synonyms are words meaning exactly the same thing. Now the words we use about God mean exactly the same thing: for his goodness is his substance, and his wisdom is his substance, and so on. So these words are completely synonymous.

Moreover, if it's said that the words refer to one reality but express different notions,

> then against that: [2] notions not corresponding to reality are empty. So if reality is one and the notions many, it seems the notions are empty.

Moreover, [3] what is really and notionally one is more one than what is really one but notionally complex. Now God is supremely one. So it seems he isn't really one and notionally complex. So the words used of him don't express different notions, and so are synonymous.

But against that:

All joining of synonyms results in tautological triviality, as when one says a *clothing garment.* So if every word used of God was synonymous it wouldn't be acceptable to talk of *the good God* and so on. Yet scripture says: *Most powerful, great, and mighty one, Lord of hosts is your name!*

In reply:

The words we use of God are not synonymous. It wouldn't be difficult to see this if such words were designed to exclude something from God or signify some causal relationship he has to creatures: for they would then differ in meaning according to the different things denied or the different effects referred to. But what we have said about these words expressing, however imperfectly, God's substance, will also make clear, if we recall it, that they express different notions.

For the meaning of a word is our mental conception of the thing meant. Now, because the mind knows God from creatures, the conceptions it forms in order to understand God correspond to the perfections that issue from God into creatures. In creatures these shared perfections are many and various, but in God they pre-exist in a simple unity. So just as the various perfections of creatures correspond to one simple source, which they represent in many and various ways by their different perfections, so too to our many and various mental conceptions there corresponds something altogether one and simple, understood imperfectly by way of these conceptions. And so the words we use of God, though all expressing one thing, do so by way of many and various conceptions, and so are not synonymous.

Hence:

to 1: The answer to this is now clear. Synonyms signify the same thing under the same notion. Words that express the same thing with different notions don't have one meaning in the primary and simple sense of that expression, since words mean things only by way of our mental conceptions of them, as we said earlier.

to 2: The many notions expressed by these words are not useless or empty, for there corresponds to them all one simple reality that they all represent in various imperfect ways.[9]

to 3: The very fact that God contains in one simple unity what other things share in many different ways shows the perfection of God's unity. And it is this that makes him really one and notionally complex, since our minds apprehend him in the many different ways creatures represent him.

[**Article** 5] The fifth question [**Are words used of God and creatures univocally or equivocally?**] we approach as follows:

It seems that words used of God and creatures are used univocally [**i.e. in exactly the same sense**] **of both:**

For [1] the equivocal presupposes the univocal, as manyness presupposes unity (the equivocal use of the word *dog*, for example, to signify things that bark and a type of fish must presuppose its univocal use to signify all things that bark); otherwise we would go on for ever. Now there are univocal agents that share with their effects a single name and definition (human beings, for instance, reproducing human beings), and equivocal agents (the sun, for example, causing heat, though it itself is hot only in an equivocal sense). Seemingly then the first of agents, to which all agency is traced back, will be a univocal agent; and so the words used of God and creatures must be univocal.

Moreover, [2] there is no likeness between things equivocally the same. Since, however, creatures are like God in some respect—*Let us make the human to our own image and likeness*, God says in Genesis 1 [26]—it seems that something is said univocally of God and creatures.

Moreover, [3] Aristotle[10] says that a measure must be generically one with what it measures. Now God is the first measure of everything, and therefore generically one with creatures; so something can be said univocally of God and creatures.

But against that:

[1] When the same word is used but with different meanings it is used equivocally. But no word means the same used of God as it does used of creatures: in creatures, for example, wisdom is a property, but not in God, and such a change in genus alters the meaning, since a thing's genus is part of its definition. The same applies to all other words, so whatever word we use of God and creatures is used equivocally.

Moreover, [2] God is much further from creatures than any creatures are from one another. But some creatures are so far from one another that nothing can be said univocally of them: things not in the same genus, for example. Much less, then, can anything be said univocally of God and creatures, but everything must be said equivocally.

In reply:

Nothing can be said univocally of God and creatures. For effects that don't measure up to the power of their cause resemble it inadequately, not reproducing its nature, so that what exists in simple unity in the cause exists in many various forms in the effects: the uniform energy of the sun, for example, produces manifold and varied forms of effect on earth. And in the same way, as we have said, all the many and various perfections existing in creatures pre-exist in God in simple unity.

In this way then words expressing creaturely perfections express them as distinct from one another: *wise*, for example, used of a human being expresses a perfection distinct from his nature, his powers, his existence, and so on; but when we use it of God we don't want to express anything distinct from his substance, powers, and existence. So the word *wise* used of human beings somehow contains and delimits what is meant; when used of God, however, it doesn't, but leaves what it means uncontained and going beyond what the word can express. Clearly then the word *wise* isn't used in the same sense of God and man, and the same is true of all the other words. No word, then, is said of God and creatures univocally.

But neither are they said purely equivocally, as some people have held. For that would mean nothing could be known or proved about God from creatures, but all such argument would commit the logical fallacy of equivocation. And that contradicts both the philosophers who have demonstrated many truths about God, and St Paul, who said in Romans 1 [20] that *the hidden things of God can be clearly understood from the things that he has made.*

Our answer then is that these words apply to God and

creatures by analogy or proportion. There are two ways in which this happens with words. It happens when two or more things are 'proportioned' to another one: the word *healthy*, for example, is applied both to medicines and to urine because both are related or 'proportioned' to the health of some organism, the one as its cause and the other as its symptom. It also happens when one thing is 'proportioned' directly to another: the word *healthy* applies to the medicine and to the organism itself, since the medicine is cause of health in the organism. And it is in this way that words are used analogically of God and creatures, not purely equivocally and not purely univocally; for our only words for God come from creatures, as we have said, and so whatever we say of God and creatures is said in virtue of the relationship creatures bear to God as to the source and cause in which all their creaturely perfections pre-exist in a more excellent way.

And this way of sharing a word lies somewhere between pure equivocation and straightforward univocalness. For analogical use doesn't presuppose one and the same sense as univocalness does, nor totally different senses as equivocation does, but a word said in senses that differ by expressing different proportions to one and the same thing, as *healthy* said of urine means it is a symptom of the organism's health, and said of medicine means it is a cause of the same health.

Hence:

to 1: In our use of words the equivocal presupposes the univocal, but in activity univocal agents necessarily presuppose a non-univocal agency. Non-univocal causes are general causes of entire species, in the way the sun has been the cause of the whole human race. But univocal causes can't be general causes of entire species—if that were so they would cause themselves as members of the species—but they are particular causes of this or that individual becoming a member of the species. So the general causes of entire species can't be univocal causes. Now the particular causes of individuals presuppose a general cause of the species. Such general causes, though not univocal, are not wholly equivocal either, since they are expressing themselves in their effects; but we can call them analogical causes, paralleling the way our use of univocal terms presupposes the one first non-univocal but analogical term, namely, *being*.

to 2: The likeness of creatures to God is imperfect, since they don't even represent him generically, as we have said.

to 3: God is not a measure proportionate to what is measured, and so God and creatures don't have to be generically one.

As to the arguments against:

They prove that such words are not used univocally of God and creatures, but not that they are used equivocally.

[Article 6] The sixth question [**If we say they are used analogically, do they apply primarily to God or to creatures?**] we approach as follows:

It seems our words apply primarily to creatures, not God:

For [1] we talk about things as we know them: *words express thoughts*, as Aristotle[11] says. But we know creatures before we know God. So the words we use apply first to creatures and then to God.

Moreover, [2] pseudo-Dionysius[12] says that *we name God from creatures*. But names like *lion* and *rock* transferred to God from creatures apply first to the creatures and then to God. So all names used of God and creatures apply first to creatures and then to God.

Moreover, [3] words used in common of God and creatures apply to God as cause of creatures, says pseudo-Dionysius.[13] Now words said of something as cause of something else apply to it secondarily: *healthy* is first said of organisms, and only secondarily of the medicines that cause the organisms' health. So such words apply first to creatures, and then to God.

But against that:

We read in Ephesians 3 [14–15]: *I bow my knee to the Father of our Lord Jesus Christ, from whom all fatherhood in heaven and earth is named*; and why should other words used of God and creatures be any different? Such words then apply first to God, and then to creatures.

In reply:

Whenever words are used analogically of several things, it is because they are all related to some one thing; so that one thing must help define the others. And because, as Aristotle[14] says, the meanings of words are definitions, the word must apply first to what helps define the others and only after that to the others in the order of their approximation to the first thing: thus *healthy* as it applies to organisms helps define *healthy* as used of medicines (called healthy because they cause health in organisms) and of urine (called healthy because it is symptomatic of health in organisms). In the same way then all words used metaphorically of God apply first to creatures and then to God, since said of God they only express some likeness to creatures. Just as talking of a *smiling* meadow expresses a proportion: that flowers adorn a meadow like a smile on a man's face, so talking of God as a *lion* expresses this proportion: that God is powerful in his doings like lions in theirs. And so clearly we can't define what such words mean when used of God unless we refer to what they mean used of creatures.

And this would also be the case with words used of God non-metaphorically, if all they expressed was God's causality, as some have supposed. For then saying *God is good* would mean simply *God causes the goodness of creatures*, and then the goodness of creatures would be helping to define what was meant by the word *good* said of God. So good would apply first to creatures and then to God. But, as we have seen, such names don't simply express God's causality but his substance, for calling God *good* or *wise* doesn't only mean that he causes wisdom or goodness, but that these perfections pre-exist in him in a more excellent way. So taking this into account we say rather that as expressing these perfections such words apply first to God and then to creatures (since the perfections flow into creatures from God); but as applied by us we apply them first to creatures, which we know first. And that is why the way in which they express the perfections is appropriate to creatures, as we already mentioned.

Hence:

to 1: The objection here is talking of our application of the words.

to 2: The case is different with words used metaphorically of God, as we have said.

to 3: This objection would hold if such words expressed only God's causality and not his substance, as *healthy* said of medicine . . .

[**Article 12**] The twelfth question [**Can we make affirmative statements about God?**] we approach as follows:

It seems we can't make affirmative statements about God:

For [1] pseudo-Dionysius[15] says *denials are true of God but affirmations disconnected.*

Moreover, [2] Boethius[16] says *A simple form can't be a subject.* But as we have shown, God above all is simple form; so he can't be a subject. But whatever affirmative propositions are about is accounted its subject. So affirmative propositions can't be made about God.

Moreover, [3] all understanding of things in a way other than they are is false. Now God, as we have proved, is altogether free of compositeness. So since affirmative statements understand things as composite [connecting a subject with a predicate], it seems they can't truly be made about God.

But against that:

Faith can't profess falsehood, yet it makes certain affirmations, as, for example, that God is three persons in one nature, and that he is almighty. So affirmative propositions can be made about God.

In reply:

We can make true affirmations about God.

To make this clear note that in every true affirmative statement subject and predicate signify under different aspects what is in some way identical: and this whether the predicate expresses some incidental property of the subject or what it substantially is. For clearly [if we say *The man is a white man,*] *man* and *white man* refer to one subject under different aspects, the notion of man and the notion of white man being different. And similarly if I say *humans are animals* it is precisely whatever is human that is truly animal—one and the same subject is called an animal because of its sense-nature and human because of its reasoning nature. So here too predicate and subject refer to one subject under different aspects. And this happens in a way even in propositions of identity, for there the mind treats the subject-term as though it referred to some subject the form of which is expressed in the predicate-term, in accordance with the saying: *predicates must be interpreted as forms and subjects as matter*.

To the different aspects then there corresponds the plurality of subject and predicate, and the mind expresses the underlying identity by connecting the two in one proposition. Now God, altogether one and simple in himself, is nevertheless known to us by way of many different conceptions, since we can't see him as he is in himself. But all of these different conceptions we have of him correspond, as we know, to one and the same simple thing. So we represent this conceptual plurality by the plurality of subject and predicate, and God's unity by the mental connecting of subject and predicate.

Hence:

to 1: Pseudo-Dionysius says affirmations about God are disconnected (or unfitting, as another translation has it) because no word used of God expresses him in an appropriate way, as we have said.

to 2: Our minds can't comprehend the way subsistent simple forms exist in themselves, but understands them as though they were composite things, subjects existing under a form. And so simple forms are understood as subjects, and then something is attributed to them.

to 3: This proposition: *All understanding of things in a way other than they are is false*, is ambiguous, because the words *in a way other than* can describe the *understanding* in relation to the thing understood or in relation to the mind understanding. In relation to the thing understood the proposition says that *any understanding of things which understands them to exist in a way other than they do is false*; which is true but irrelevant, since our mind when it composes propositions about God doesn't assert that he is composite but that he is simple. But if the proposition is interpreted in relation to the mind understanding then it is false. For our way of understanding things is clearly different from the way things exist: our mind understands material things below its own level immaterially, not in the sense of thinking *them* immaterial, but in the sense that thinking them is an immaterial act; and in a similar way it understands simple things above its own level in the way natural to it, compositely, but not in the sense of thinking *them* composite. So our minds aren't false because their statements about God are composite.

Passage 24

How we Know One Simple God by Many Concepts

Source: Thomas's commentary on book 1 of Peter Lombard's *Sentences*, Distinction 2, 1.3. Text from Parma edn., vol. vi (1856) (reprinted in American edn., vol. vi, New York, 1948).

Date: 1253–5, Paris, Thomas's first public theology lectures as bachelor, aged 28–9.

Type of passage and how to read: The commentary on the *Sentences* is of the same type as the commentary on Boethius' *De Trinitate*, but with the more complex division into queries described in the preliminary note to Passage 1 on *How to read*, and in the Introduction. The full structure can be seen in Passage 34. But our present passage is a single disputed question extracted from the commentary. It is just possible that it was a later insertion by Thomas into his original commentary.

[Book 1, Distinction 2, Question 1]

[Article 3]: The third question **[Is the difference in meaning between God's attributes something that exists in God or only in our minds?]** we approach as follows:

It seems that the difference in meaning doesn't exist in God, but only in the mind apprehending the meanings:

For [1] pseudo-Dionysius[1] says: *You will find that the utterances of all God's holy teachers articulate the names of God, in praise and revelation, in accordance with blessed outpourings of his divinity.* And what he means is that the words the saints use in praise of God differ according to different outward manifestations of God that issue from his godhead. The difference then is not on God's side but on the side of these different effects by which our mind comes to know and name God in different ways.

Moreover, [2] pseudo-Dionysius[2] says: *if someone sees God and understands what he sees, it is not God he sees but something belonging to God.* If then we understand what our different names for God mean, those meanings must correspond not to anything in God but to the things that belong to him, namely, creatures.

Moreover, [3] Ibn Rushd[3] says this about such names: *the multiplicity they suggest exists in God only as he exists in our mind and not at all in fact.* So it seems the multiplicity is purely in our minds.

Moreover, [4] whatever exists in God is God. So if what these different attributes mean exist in God they are God. Now God is a single non-composite unity. So these meanings, if they exist in God, will not differ.

Moreover, [5] whatever is in every way one in itself cannot be the root of any multiplicity within itself. But God's substance is supremely one and therefore in every way one. So it cannot be the root of any multiplicity within itself. The multiplicity of meaning then isn't rooted in God's substance but purely in our minds.

Moreover, [6] John Damascene[4] says that *everything is one in God, save the non-begottenness* [of the Father], *the begottenness* [of the Son], *and the procession* [of the Holy Spirit]. So if attributes like wisdom and goodness exist in God they are all one in him. So the multiplicity of meanings expressed by these words exists not in God but only in our minds.

But against that:

[1] Pseudo-Dionysius[5] says that *God is perfect and all-embracing*, and Aristotle[6] and Ibn Rushd[7] say the same: *God is called perfect because within him exist all the perfections of every class of thing.* But the perfection God has is real, not purely in our minds. So the attributes that display this perfection are not purely in our minds, but there in the thing which is God...

Moreover, [3] we don't equivocate when we call both God and creatures wise. If we did, created wisdom wouldn't give us any clue to uncreated wisdom. And the same has to be said of power and goodness and so on. But attributes are equivocally ascribed to things if what they mean in each is quite different... So what wisdom means in God and in creatures must be one and the same: not univocally one but analogically; and the same applies to what other attributes mean. Now what wisdom means when ascribed to creatures differs from what goodness means and what power means. So the meanings must be different as ascribed to God too...

In reply:

Though wisdom, goodness, and the like differ in meaning, they name one and the same thing in God; and the differences in meaning are not just thought up by our minds: they respond to something real in God himself. To make this clear, and thoroughly open up the whole matter—since the understanding of practically everything said in this book depends on it—we must look into four points:

Firstly, when we say attributes differ in meaning, what do we mean by meaning?

Secondly, what does it mean to say a meaning exists or does not exist in a thing?
Thirdly, do the different meanings of God's attributes exist in God or not?
Fourthly, does the multiplicity of meaning arise from our own minds or in some way from God himself?

As to **the first point [the meaning of meaning]**, note that meaning here means what the mind takes the word to express; and for definable things that is the definition of the thing named, as Aristotle[8] said: *the meaning expressed by a word is a definition.* But some things have meaning in this sense though they are indefinable; like quantity and quality and other things which can't be defined since they constitute the most general categories of being that there are; and yet quality has a meaning expressed by the word *quality*, something that makes quality quality. So it is not relevant whether what has meaning can be defined or not. Clearly then the meaning of wisdom as said of God is what that word is conceived to express, even though God's wisdom itself can't be defined. Not that the word *meaning* expresses what is conceived, for that is expressed by the word *wisdom* or some other word applicable to things; the word *meaning* expresses the notion of conception, as second-level words like *definition* do.

And this explains **the second point: how meanings can be said to be realized in things.** For we don't mean that this very notion expressed by the word *meaning* is realized in things; or even that the conception to which the notion attaches is realized in something outside the mind, since it is precisely something that has mind as its subject; but the meaning is said to be realized in something outside the mind inasmuch as the mind's conception is matched by something there in the way expressions are matched by what they express. So note that the mind's conception can relate to a thing outside the mind in three different ways:

Sometimes what the mind conceives is a likeness of something existing outside the mind, as when we conceive what the word *human* expresses; and such conceptions have an immediate basis in reality, inasmuch as the thing itself conforms to what we understand, and so makes our understanding true and the word expressing that understanding properly applicable to a thing.

Sometimes, however, what the word expresses is not a likeness of anything outside the mind, but something arising from the way we understand what exists outside the mind, a notion framed by the mind. Thus what is expressed by the word *genus* isn't a likeness of anything existing outside the mind, but a notion the mind attaches to *animal* [for example] when it understands there to be many species of animal. And though the immediate basis of such an idea is not in reality but in the mind, nevertheless the more remote basis is reality itself, so that the mind framing such ideas is not framing a fiction. And this is true of every other idea consequent upon our way of understanding things: for example, the abstract entities studied in mathematics and the like.

But sometimes what the word expresses has no basis in reality either immediate or remote, as the conception of a chimera. This is neither a likeness of anything outside the mind, nor something consequent on the way our minds understand something in nature; and so such a conception is fictitious.

So this explains our second point: for a meaning is said to be realized in something inasmuch as what the word expresses, and which we call its meaning, is realized in something; and this is properly the case when what the mind conceives is a likeness of that something.

As to the third point: whether the meanings of God's attributes are realized in God. Note that there are two opinions about this:

Some people like Ibn Sīnā[9] and Moses Maimonides[10] say that *God's very substance is existence subsistent* and that *in God nothing else exists but existence*: and so they say that *he is existence without nature*, and that whatever else we say about God is true of him either because of what it denies of him or because of his causal activity. Denial works in two ways: sometimes we are removing an opposed lack or defect, as saying *God is wise* removes from him lack of wisdom; sometimes we assert some consequence of a denial, as calling God *one*, because it follows from his being undivided, or *intelligent*, because it follows from his being immaterial. According to them then all these words are framed in order to remove something from God rather than to attribute something to him. Saying something of him as cause also works in two ways: sometimes it is something he produces in creatures, as calling God *good*, because he pours goodness into creatures, and so on; and sometimes because he behaves like a creature, as when he is said to be *willing* or *holy*, because he does things in the way a willing and holy creature might, and *angry*, because he behaves like an angry creature. And according to this opinion everything we say of God and creatures is said equivocally, and calling creatures good or wise or the like expresses no likeness of creatures to their creator. Moses Maimonides says this explicitly. On this view what words for God's attributes are conceived to express is not to be referred to God as though some likeness of it existed in God. And so it follows that the meanings of such attributes are not realized in God in the sense of having any immediate basis in God; but they have a remote basis in him in the way that we maintain historically grounded relationships attributed to God do: for such relationships don't exist really in God but are what we called notions, consequent upon the way we understand him. On this view then the meanings of such attributes exist only in the mind and not in the reality of God himself; and the mind frames such attributes from a consideration of creatures by denial or by causal attribution, as has been said.

But other people like pseudo-Dionysius[11] and Anselm[12] say that whatever perfection exists in creatures eminently pre-exists in God, and that this eminence has three features: universality, collecting together in a unity all the perfections we find dispersed in creatures; fullness, because wisdom and all the other attributes are found here without any of the defects they suffer from in creatures; and unity, because attributes which differ in creatures are all here possessed, caused, known, and produced in an analogic likeness of itself by what is one and the same. On this view then what our mind conceives the names of the attributes to mean are true likenesses of the reality which God is, although imperfect and incomplete, as is the case with anything else that is like to God. So that such meanings don't exist only in the mind but have an immediate basis in the reality which God is, and whatever is implied by having wisdom as such can be truly and properly said of God.

These two views, though superficially different, are not opposed to one another, if one interprets what words say in the context of the reason for saying them. For the first group of people considered the actual created things *upon which* the attribute-words had been imposed: the word wisdom upon a certain quality, the word nature upon something which didn't subsist; and these things are far from God. So they said that God is existence without nature, and that wisdom as such does not exist in him. But the other people considered the modes of perfection *from which* those words arose, and because God in his one simple existence is perfect according to all the modes these words describe, they therefore said that these words positively applied to God. And so it is clear that neither view contradicts what the other wants to say, since the first people don't say God is lacking in any mode of perfection, and the second don't say that there are in God any qualities or non-subsistent things.

So this explains our third point: that the meanings of God's attributes are truly realized in God; for the meaning of a word is more truly that *from which* it arose, than it is that *upon which* it was imposed.

As to the fourth point: does the multiplicity of meaning arise only from our own minds or in some way from the thing itself [namely, God]? Note that the multiplicity of meaning arises from the fact that the reality which is God is above our minds. For our minds can't take in in one conception different modes of perfection: partly because they take in their knowledge from creatures in which the different modes of perfection follow from different forms, and partly because what is one simple thing in God becomes multiplied in our minds even when received immediately from God, just as the issuing of his goodness is multiplied in other creatures. So, since God contains in one and the same reality every mode of perfection, our minds cannot take in totally his perfection in one conception and so cannot give him a name; for that reason we have to have different conceptions of him, with different meanings, and must adopt different words to express these meanings. Such words, then, are not synonymous, for they express different meanings. If, however, our mind could see God in himself then it could give him one name, and since that will happen in heaven Zechariah 14 [9] tells us that *in that day there will be one lord with one name*. That one name, however, will not express goodness alone, or wisdom alone, or anything similar, but will include everything these words express. Nevertheless, if a mind seeing God in his substance names what it sees by way of some conception it has of him, it would still have to give him many names, because the total perfection of God's substance cannot be represented in the conception of a created mind. So it would form different conceptions corresponding to the one thing seen and give it different names, in the same way that Chrysostom[13] says *angels praise God, some as majesty, some as goodness, and so on for the others*, indicating that they don't see him with a vision that comprehends him; for the one and only conception that perfectly represents him is the uncreated Word.

So this explains how our multiplicity of words for God arises from the fact that God himself is greater than our mind; and this depends partly on his fullness of perfection, and partly on our minds' inability to comprehend that. Clearly, then, the multiplicity of meaning derives not only from our minds but also from God himself, inasmuch as his perfection is above every conception of our minds. So there corresponds to this multiplicity of meaning something in the reality that is God: not indeed a multiplicity in him but a fullness of perfection which allows all of these conceptions to be applied to him.

So people who say that this multiplicity derives only from

our minds, or from God's effects, say something true in one sense and false in another. For if they mean to indicate the cause of the multiplicity then there is a sense in which it is true to say that the cause is our minds and God's effects, inasmuch as our minds cannot conceive God's perfection in one conception but only in many, one reason for which is that it is accustomed to created things. But if they mean to indicate the way in which we must attribute the meanings to God, then they speak falsely, for he is not good because he makes or resembles things that are good, but he makes good things because he is good, and they, in sharing that goodness, resemble him. And even if he had never made a creature and never would make one, he in himself would have been such that the conceptions our minds apply to him now would have truly applied to him then.

So this explains our fourth point: that the multiplicity of these words for God derives not only from our mind framing different conceptions of God with different meanings, as we have said earlier, but from God himself, in whom something corresponds to all these conceptions, namely, his own full and all-embracing perfection. For it is this perfection which allows every word expressing one of these conceptions to be truly and properly asserted of God without such assertion attributing any real diversity or multiplicity to God is because of having these attributes.

Having looked into these four points, then, the objections can be easily answered.

Hence:

to 1: Pseudo-Dionysius wants to say that God is named, revealed, and praised according to various goodnesses that he has poured out on creatures. But he is not saying that the meanings of these goodnesses are truly ascribed to him because he has poured them out on creatures, but rather the reverse, as we have already said. For although the structure of effects can reveal the structure of their cause, they are not what gives the cause that structure, but rather the reverse.

to 2: Our mind doesn't understand what it conceives of goodness and wisdom to exist in God in the way it conceives them, since this would be to comprehend his wisdom and goodness. But it understands his goodness, to which what our mind conceives is somewhat alike, to be far above what it conceives of it. So we don't see God as he is in himself through such conceptions, but he is understood as beyond understanding. And that is what pseudo-Dionysius wants to say in this quotation.

to 3: This multiplicity of attributes is not at all to be found in God as if he himself in reality was multiple; nevertheless, he in his own simple perfection matches the multiplicity of these attributes, so that they can be truly said of him. And this is what Ibn Rushd meant.

to 4: Just as the conceived meaning of human being isn't a thing existing in human beings, but exists in the mind as its subject and in human beings as providing the basis of its truth; so the meaning of God's goodness exists in the mind as in its subject, and in God as in something corresponding by a certain likeness to this meaning, making it true. Clearly then this objection has misunderstood what we are saying.

to 5: Saying *A* is based on or rooted in *B* is a metaphor for saying *B* gives *A* its firmness. Now meanings in our mind have two sorts of firmness: the firmness of existing in the mind, in the way all incidental forms exist in a subject; and the firmness of their truth, which comes to them from the thing to which they conform; for what we say and think gets its truth or falsity from whether things are so or not. The meanings of the attributes then are based on or rooted in mind as regards the firmness of their existence, since as we have said they exist in the mind as subject, but rooted in God's nature as regards the firmness of their truth; and that without in any way offending against God's simpleness.

to 6: Everything is really one in God, save the non-begottenness, the begottenness, and the procession which constitute the persons of God as really distinct. But that doesn't mean that everything else we say of God has one and the same meaning. And we must understand Boethius'[14] remark that *relationship alone is multiple in the Trinity* in the same way: namely, in reality multiple. For a thing is in reality one yet in meaning multiple whenever one thing corresponds truly to many conceptions and words; as a single real [geometrical] point may truly correspond truly to several conceptions we frame of it: conceived of in itself, conceived of as a [circle's] centre, conceived of as the end of a line. All these conceptions are in the mind as subject, yet in the point itself as giving a basis to the truth of the conceptions. Admittedly, the example is not altogether suitable, but then no example is when discussing God.

Passage 25

How God Knows Many Things by One Simple Idea

Source: *Summa contra Gentiles*, 1.50, 53. Text from *Summa contra Gentiles* (*Opera Omnia*, Leonine edn., vol. xiii).

Date: 1259, first stay in Paris, aged 34.

Notes on translation: In the extract from Chapter 53, 'representation' translates *species intelligibilis*, 'likeness' *similitudo*, 'conception' *intentio*, 'idea' *ratio*.

[Chapter 50]

... The distinctions between things can't result from chance since they are stably ordered; so they must result from some causal tendency. But not that of a cause acting by necessity of its nature, for nature is determined to one course, and so nothing that acts by necessity of its nature can intend distinction of things as such. So their distinction must result from the intention of a knowing cause; the consideration of distinction seems to be intellect's prerogative, and Anaxagoras attributed distinction to intellect. But the universal distinction of things can't result from some secondary cause's intention, since all such causes are themselves part of the universe of distinct causes. So there must exist a first cause—as such distinguished from all others—intending the distinction of all things. God then knows everything distinctly.

Again, God knows everything he knows most perfectly, for, as we have already said, all perfections exist in him as in a thing perfect without complexity. But things known in general are not perfectly known, for then what is most important in a thing is ignored, namely, those ultimate perfections that perfect it in an existence peculiarly its own; so knowing in general is knowing things potentially rather than actually. If God then in knowing his own substance knows everything in general, he must also have particular proper knowledge of each thing...

[Chapter 53] The question raised [**How can God understand more than one thing?**] is easily answered by close examination of how things understood exist in understanding. We shall start with human understanding, and from there try, as far as that is possible, to come to know God's understanding. So, as a first step, note that nothing external that we understand exists in our understanding in its own proper nature, but its representation exists in our understanding and actualizes understanding so that, existing actually by that representation as by its own form, it understands the thing itself. But note that the act of understanding is not like an action that passes over into what is understood, as heating passes over into what is heated. The action of understanding stays in the person understanding, but relates to the thing understood, because the representation just mentioned, the form from which our activity of understanding starts, is a likeness of the thing.

Further, note that understanding, formed by the representation of the thing, forms within itself, in the act of understanding, a certain conception of the understood thing, and it is that idea of the thing which we express in its definition. Our understanding needs such a conception in order to be able to understand things equally, present or absent, and to this extent understanding resembles imagination. But understanding goes further, for it also understands things in abstraction from those material conditions without which they cannot exist in nature; and this is only possible because understanding forms such a conception for itself. This understood conception in which the act of understanding ends up, so to speak, must be distinguished from the object-representation which is actualizing understanding and must therefore be thought of as beginning the act of understanding; though the conception, like the representation, is a likeness of the thing understood. For since the object-representation forming the understanding and beginning its act of understanding is a likeness of an external thing, understanding forms a conception which is also like that thing: what things do reflects what they are. And because the understood conception is like some external thing, understanding, in forming the conception, understands that thing.

Now, as we showed earlier, God's understanding understands by no other representation than his own substance; nevertheless, that substance is a likeness of all things. Consequently, the conception in God's understanding when he understands himself—his Word—is not only a likeness of the very God he is understanding but also of all those things of which God's substance is a likeness. And so it is that by one object-representation—God's substance—and by one understood conception—God's Word—God can understand many things.

Passage 26
God's Power

Source: Thomas's public disputations on the Power of God, 1.3, 7. Text from *Quaestiones Disputatae de Potentia* (Marietti edn., Turin, 1953), with corrections from the Leonine text in preparation.

Date: 1265–7, Italy, aged 40.

Type of passage and how to read: Disputed question (see Introduction, where the unique structure of Article 7 below is also referred to).

Notes on translation: The word *potentia* is here translated 'power', but also, both here and elsewhere, 'ability'. It is an abstract noun from the verb *posse* 'to be able'. *Possibile*, translated 'possible', derives from the same root, and means, literally, 'able to be able'.

[Question 1] The subject for debate is **God's power in general.**

. . . [**Article 3**] And in the third place we are asked: **Can God do what nature can't?**

And it seems not:

For [1] there is a gloss on Romans 11 [24] which says that God, as author of nature, can't go against nature. But whatever nature can't do is against nature. So God can't do it either.

Moreover, [2] whatever in nature is necessary can be proved, and whatever in nature is impossible can be disproved. Now all conclusions of proofs involve their premisses, and among those premisses there is always the axiom that things cannot be simultaneously asserted and denied. So this premiss is involved in anything in nature impossible. Since, however, as the respondent said, God cannot make anything to be simultaneously and truly asserted and denied, he can't do anything impossible in nature . . .

Moreover, [9] what is essentially impossible is more impossible than what is incidentally impossible. But God can't do what is incidentally impossible, for example, cause the past not to have been. For, as Jerome[1] says, whatever God can do he can't make loss of virginity not to have happened; and Augustine,[2] and Aristotle[3] say the same. So God cannot do what is naturally impossible in itself.

But against that:

[1] [The angel in] Luke 1 [1] says: *No word is impossible for God.*

Moreover, [2] power is limited if it can do this but not that. So if God can do what is possible in nature but not what is impossible, or do these but not those impossible things, it seems his power is limited, which contradicts what we have already proved.

Moreover, [3] nothing real can stand in the way of what nothing real limits. But nothing real limits God's power. So nothing can stand in his way. So neither the truth of the principle that nothing can be simultaneously asserted and denied, nor any similar thing, can stand in the way of God's action . . .

Moreover, [8] to suppose that we could remove from a defined thing something belonging to its definition would imply that contraries could be true together: that a human being could be non-reasoning, for example. Now to be bounded by two points belongs in the definition of a straight line, so that if it were removed from some straight line, contraries would be true together. But God did this when he entered in on his disciples, the doors being closed; for then two bodies occupied the same place so that two lines used the same two points as boundaries, and they didn't each have two. God then can make assertions and denials true simultaneously and as a result can do every impossibility.

In reply:

Aristotle[4] says the words *possible* and *impossible* are used in three different senses: firstly, relative to some ability to act or be acted on (as when we say our human locomotive powers make it possible for us to walk but impossible for us to fly); secondly, in an absolute sense, not relative to any ability (as when possible means anything the existence of which is not impossible, and impossible anything the non-existence of which is necessary); and thirdly, in mathematics the word possible is used relative to the sort of potentiality exemplified in geometry, where a line is called potentially commensurable because its square is commensurable. This latter sense we shall leave aside, considering the two others.

Note then that when we say something is *impossible* in itself, i.e. not relative to any ability, we appeal to some incompatibility in terms, based on some opposition between the terms, all opposition being ultimately one of assertion versus denial, as Aristotle[5] proves. So everything impossible in this sense involves simultaneous assertion and denial. Clearly this can't be the subject of any agent's action. For agents, to have power, must actually exist, and what they do will reflect what they are, so that the end-product of every agent's action is always existence of some sort. For even when action ends in loss of existence, as in decomposition, this is because something else's existence is incompatible with that existence. Hot and cold are incompatible, for instance, so that heat, which principally intends to make things hot, incidentally destroys cold. What is simultaneously asserted and denied, however, can neither exist nor not exist—since existing excludes not existing and not existing existing—so that it can't be the end-product of any agent's action, either as principally intended or as a consequence.

As to the use of *impossible* relative to some ability, we can distinguish a first use referring to some intrinsic deficiency of the ability by which it falls short of that effect (for example, when an agent in nature can't transform certain material), and a second use referring to something external that prevents or stands in the way of the ability.

Altogether then there are three ways in which we say something can't be done: firstly, because of agent inability to transform material or do whatever else is needed; secondly, because of something resisting or standing in the way; thirdly, because the thing that we say can't be done can't be the end-product of any action.

Now things in nature impossible in the first two ways God can do, because his ability is unlimited, is subject to no deficiency, can transform any material at will, and cannot be resisted. But things impossible in the third way God cannot do, because, as the supremely actual source of being, the end-products of his action can only be existence as principally intended and non-existence as a consequence. So he can't make an assertion and its denial simultaneously true, nor anything that would involve such impossibility. And he is said not to be able to do this, not because of some lack of ability in him, but because of some lack of possibility in what is to be done; which is why some say that God has the power to do it but it can't be done.

Hence:

to 1: Augustine's words quoted in this gloss don't mean that God can't do other than nature does, since he often goes against the ordinary run of nature, but that, since he creates and directs nature, anything he does in nature is to be counted natural to things and not as going against nature. For this is the way movements of lower-order things by higher-order things in nature are judged natural, though they don't stem from the lower-order things' own nature. Thus, tidal movements caused by the moon in the sea are natural, as Ibn Rushd[6] points out, even though water's own natural movement is downwards. And in this sense what God does in any creature is so-to-speak natural to it, and we can distinguish a double potentiality in creatures: their natural potentiality to their own actions and movements, and their potentiality to obey whatever they acquire from God.

to 2: Anything impossible, inasmuch as it is impossible, implies some simultaneous assertion and denial. But things like the blind regaining sight and so on, which are impossible because of some deficiency in the powers of nature, aren't impossible in themselves, and so don't in themselves imply that sort of impossibility, but only relative to the natural powers to which they are impossible: as if we said 'nature being able to make the blind see' implies this impossibility, because it attributes to a power something beyond its natural limits . . .

to 9: For Socrates not to have run when he has run is called incidentally impossible, because Socrates running or not running is in itself something that could or could not be so, but something that is made impossible by the extra implication that the past might not have been; so it is called impossible incidentally, that is, by the incidence of something extra. This extra is impossible in itself, and plainly involves a contradiction: for saying that the past has not been is to say both that it was and wasn't, and those are contradictories.

As to the arguments against:

to 1: Words are not only what mouths utter but what minds conceive, and mind, as Aristotle[7] proves, can't conceive of assertion and denial being true simultaneously or of anything that implies that (for, as Aristotle says, since contrary opinions are of contraries,[8] it would mean the same person simultaneously having contrary opinions). So saying God can't do that sort of impossible doesn't contradict what the angel says.

to 2: The reason God's power can't do what is impossible in the sense we are discussing is because it lacks possibility; so we don't say God's power is limited by not being able to do it.

to 3: As we have said, saying God can't do this doesn't mean something stands in his way, but that this cannot be the end-product of any active power's actions . . .

to 8: When Christ entered through closed doors and two bodies occupied the same place nothing contrary to geometrical principles occurred: for there were two lines, not one, and where they ended the two lines ended at two points in two different bodies. For though mathematically conceived lines can only be distinguished by being positioned differently, so that one can't understand two such lines coinciding, two lines in nature can be distinguished by their subjects, so that when two bodies coincide, two lines will also coincide and two points and two surfaces . . .

[**Article 7**] And in the seventh place we ask: [**Query 1**] **Why is God called omnipotent?**

And it seems [Definition 1] that he is called omnipotent because he can do absolutely everything:

For [**1**] God is called omniscient in the same way as he's called omnipotent. But he's called omniscient because he knows absolutely everything; so he must be called omnipotent because he can do absolutely everything.

Moreover, [2] if he's not called omnipotent because he can do absolutely everything, then the implied quantification must be not absolute but accommodated, not universal but restricted in some way. So God's omnipotence will not be unlimited but have some sort of limit.

But against that:

God, as we have said, can't make assertions and denials simultaneously true, nor can he sin or die. But these would be included in quantification taken absolutely. So it shouldn't be taken absolutely, and so God isn't called omnipotent because he can do absolutely everything.

Again, it seems [Definition 2] that he is called omnipotent because he can do everything he wants:

For Augustine[9] says *For there is no other reason to call him truly omnipotent except that he can do whatever he wills.*

But against that:

[1] Those in bliss can do whatever they want, for otherwise their wills wouldn't be fulfilled. But they're not called omnipotent. So it's not enough for God to be omnipotent that he can do whatever he wants.

Moreover, [2] the wise don't will the impossible, so that no one wise wills what he can't do. Yet the wise are not all omnipotent. The same conclusion then.

Again, it seems [Definition 3] that he is called omnipotent because he can do everything possible:

For he is called omniscient because he knows everything knowable, and so by the same token should be called omnipotent because he can do everything possible.

But against that:

[1] If he is called omnipotent because he can do everything possible, either that means everything possible to him, or everything possible in nature. If everything possible in nature, then his omnipotence doesn't transcend nature's power, which is absurd. If everything possible to him, then by the same token we are all omnipotent since we can all do what's possible to us.

Moreover, [2] the explanation would contain a rather disagreeable circularity.

Again we ask: **[Query 2] Why, if God is called omnipotent and omniscient, is he not called omnivolent?**

In reply [to Query 1]:

Some of those wanting to define omnipotence mentioned things belonging not to omnipotence itself but to its cause, or to power's perfection, or ways of possessing power. For some said God is omnipotent because he has unlimited power, which doesn't define omnipotence but says what causes it, just as soul doesn't define human beings but causes their existence. Others said he is omnipotent because he can't suffer or lack anything nor can others act on him: all things belonging to the perfection of his power. Still others said he is called omnipotent because he can do whatever he wills, and has that from himself and through himself, which all belongs to his way of possessing power. And all these definitions are insufficient because they omit any relationship to the objects implied by omnipotence. So we must adopt one of the three ways touched on in the objections, which express its relationship to objects.

We say then, as we have above, that God's power as such extends to all objects that don't imply a contradiction. Things involving deficiencies or bodily changes are irrelevant, since ability to do such things is non-ability in God. But things which imply contradiction God can't do because they are impossible in themselves. So we conclude that God's power extends to anything possible in itself and not implying contradiction. Clearly then God is called omnipotent because he can do everything possible in itself.

Hence:

to 1: God is called omniscient because he knows everything knowable; false things not knowable he does not know. And things impossible in themselves relate to power as false things to knowledge.

to 2: This would be a valid argument if the quantification was less extensive than the realm of possibility, so that it didn't extend to everything possible.

As regards the second definition of omnipotence:

To be able to do everything one wants is not enough to define omnipotence, but it is a good enough sign of omnipotence, and Augustine must be so understood.

As regards the third definition of omnipotence:

God is called omnipotent because he can do everything absolutely possible, so objection [**1**] goes astray in talking of what is possible to God or to nature.

In reply to Query 2 [Why isn't God called omnivolent?]:

The power and knowledge of voluntary agents is determined to action by will, as Aristotle[10] says, so that God's knowledge and power, as if non-determined, are declared universal by calling him omniscient or omnipotent. But will determines and so can't be of everything but only of the things to which it determines power and knowledge; so God can't be called omnivolent.

Part V
God as the Beginning of Things

Passage 27
Creation as God's Doing

Source: Thomas's public disputations on the Power of God, 3.1–3. Text from *Quaestiones Disputatae de Potentia* (Marietti edn., Turin, 1953), with corrections from the Leonine text in preparation.

Date: 1265–7, Italy, aged 40.

Type of passage and how to read: Disputed question (see Introduction).

Notes on translation: In Article 2 'change' translates *mutatio*, 'passage' *transitus*, 'alteration' *motus*, 'modification' *alteratio*.

Parallel passages: Thomas here, especially in Article 3, presupposes Aristotle's views on action, discussed above in Passage 5. It is because Aristotle has said that all action takes place in the things agents act on that Thomas asks whether creation takes place in creatures.

[Question 3] The subject for debate is **Creation—the first effect of God's power.**

[**Article** 1] And in the first place we are asked: **Can God make something from nothing?**

And it seems not:

For [1] God can't do something that contradicts our most general mental conceptions: he can't make a whole smaller than some part of it. But Aristotle[1] says it is a general conception and maxim of philosophers that nothing can be made from nothing. So God can't make something from nothing.

Moreover, [2] everything that comes to exist was able to exist before it existed; for what couldn't exist couldn't come to be: nothing moves towards the impossible. But the ability of something to exist must itself exist in some subject—or perhaps itself be a subject—for no property can exist without a subject. So whatever comes to be must come to be from matter or a subject; nothing can come to be from nothing...

Moreover, [4] Aristotle[2] says the totally unlike doesn't act on the totally unlike: what acts and what is acted on must agree in genus and in material. But unqualified non-being agrees with God in nothing. So God can't act on unqualified non-being, and so can't make something from nothing.

But it was said [by the respondent] that this argument holds only when the activity of an agent is not its substance and so needs to be received into some subject.

> But against that, [5] Ibn Sīnā[3] says that if heat was robbed of its material it would act of itself without its material; yet heat's activity is not its substance. So you can't say it is because God's activity is his substance that he doesn't need material.

Moreover, [6] nothing can be inferred from nothing, and inference is reason's way of bringing things into being. Now reason models itself on nature. So in nature too nothing can come to be from nothing.

Moreover, [7] if something comes to be from nothing, the preposition *from* must denote either cause or relationship. The causes it denotes seem to be either agency or material, but what doesn't exist can't be either the agent or the material of what does; so here *from* doesn't denote a cause. But neither can it denote relationship, for, as Boethius[4] says, being doesn't relate to non-being. So there is no way something can be made from nothing...

Moreover, [10] what is made from nothing exists after not existing; so there was some last moment of non-existence when it ceased not existing, and some first moment of existence when it began to exist. These moments are either the same or different. If the same, then two contradictories coexisted at the same moment; if different, then, since the two moments can only be separated by time, there must be some state of things midway between affirmation and negation: for a thing can't not exist after its last moment of non-existence, nor exist before its first moment of existence. But both things are impossible—contradictories can neither coexist nor have a between state. So it is impossible for something to come to be from nothing.

Moreover, [11] what is made must have been made at some moment, and what is created must have been created at some moment. So was the creature made and being made at the same moment or at different ones? How can one say at different ones? For before it is made no creature exists, so if its being made pre-existed its madeness, there would have to be some other subject of the being made, and that goes against the notion of creation. If, however, the thing was made and being made at the same moment, then it was not being made and being made at the same moment; for what is already made stably exists whereas what is being made does not yet exist. So the whole thing is impossible and something cannot be made from nothing or created...

But against that:

[1] A gloss on Genesis 1 [1]: *In the beginning God created heaven and earth*, says that *create* means make something from nothing. So God can make something from nothing.

Moreover, [2] Ibn Sīnā[5] says that only agents that are incidentally active need material to act on. But God isn't incidentally active: his activity is his very substance. So he doesn't need material to act on, and can make something from nothing...

In reply:

We must firmly maintain that God can make something from nothing and did.

To be clear on this, note that activity flows from actuality, so that the way an agent acts is determined by the way it has actual existence. Now things in nature have actuality which is partial, in two senses of the word. Firstly, relative to themselves, since not all their substance is actual: they are made of formed material, and as a result, they don't act with the whole of themselves but through the form that gives them their actual existence. Secondly, relative to all that actually exists, since nothing in nature contains every actual perfection actually existing in things: the actuality of each is determined to one species of one genus, and, as a result, none is an agent of being as such but only of this being as this being, determinately of this or that species. For what things do reflects what they are, so that the activity of agents in nature doesn't produce being without qualification but determines already existent being in this or that way, for example, to be fire or to be white or something similar. And this is why agents in nature act by causing change, and so need matter as a subject for change or for the actuality [they bring about], and so cannot make something from nothing.

God himself on the other hand is totally actual both relative to himself (since he is pure actuality unalloyed with any potentiality) and relative to actually existent things (since every perfection of being is found in him as in the first and fullest beginning of things). As a result he, by his action, produces the whole substance of things, presupposing nothing but rather being himself the source of all existence with the whole of himself. And this is why he can make something from nothing, an activity of his which is called *creation*. And so we read in the book of Causes[6] that *existence is created, but life and the rest formed*: for the causing of being, unqualified, is traced back to the first universal cause, whilst the causing of anything over and above being or specifying it is attributed to secondary causes, which act by forming so to speak the presupposed effect of the universal cause. And so too nothing can give existence except by sharing God's power; which is why the same book[7] says that *the excellent soul possesses the divine activity of giving existence*.

Hence:

to 1: Aristotle calls *nothing can be made from nothing* a general conception or opinion of natural philosophers because the agents they observe in nature act by causing change, and that needs a subject capable of changing. But, as we have said, an agent outside nature doesn't need this.

to 2: Before the world existed it was able to come to be, but that doesn't mean some pre-existing material possessed that ability; for, as Aristotle[8] says, sometimes we call something possible not because of any ability, but because the proposition expressing it contains no contradiction in terms, possible here meaning not impossible. So we say: Before the world existed it was possible for it to come to be, since subject and predicate in that proposition do not contradict one another. Alternatively, one can say that the possibility is founded on an ability, that of an active agent not of a passive material. Aristotle himself, when talking of generation in nature,[9] uses this argument against the Platonists, who had said separate forms could cause generation in nature...

to 4: When something is made from nothing, the nothing—non-being—is not a sort of passive contributor to the making but a sort of opposite to what the making makes. Even in natural changes there is an oppositeness which doesn't passively contribute, though there it is incidental to a passively contributing subject.

to 5: If heat was robbed of its material it would act without the material through which it acts, but not without the material on which it acts.

to 6: Reasoned inference resembles natural change inasmuch as it moves from one thing to another; and so just as all natural change starts from something, so also all reasoned inference. But just as the understanding of the principles from which the inference starts is not itself inferred from anything, so creation—the beginning of every change—is not creation *from* anything.

to 7: Saying something comes to be from nothing has two senses, as Anselm[10] points out, for the negation in the word *nothing* can either deny the preposition *from* or be governed by it. If it denies the preposition there are a further two senses. In the first both preposition and verb are denied, so that saying something comes to be from nothing means it doesn't come to be at all (like saying a non-talker is talking of nothing); and in this sense we might say—though it's an odd turn of phrase—that God comes to be from nothing because he doesn't come to be at all. In a second sense the negation negates the preposition but the verb remains affirmed, so that saying something comes to be from nothing means it comes to be but not from anything pre-existent (like saying someone sad without cause is heartsick for nothing); and in this sense everything created comes to be from nothing. If, however, the preposition governs the negation there are again two senses, one true and one false. The false sense takes the preposition to denote a cause, for there is no way non-being can cause being. The true sense takes the preposition to denote only a relationship, so that saying something comes to be from nothing means it comes to be after nothing; and this is also true of creation. When Boethius says being doesn't relate to non-being, he must mean that no determinate proportion or real relationship can exist between being and non-being, as Ibn Sīnā[11] says . . .

to 10: When something comes to be from nothing it starts to exist at some moment; and at that moment its non-existence ceases to exist. In fact there was no real moment at which non-existence did exist, but only imaginary ones: for just as there isn't real space outside the universe, but one we imagine when we say God could make something at such-and-such a distance from the universe, so there wasn't real time before the universe began, but one we imagine when we talk of a last moment of non-being. And so the two moments [the first moment of being and the last moment of non-being] don't exist in the same time, since real and imaginary time are not continuous with one another.

to 11: What is made from nothing is *made* and *being made* at the same moment. And this is no different from any instantaneous change: the air, for instance, is lit up and being lit up at the same moment. For in such changes the very madeness is called *being made* at its first moment of madeness. Alternatively we can say that when something is made from nothing we talk of it *being made* at that time not because it is moving from one state to another, but because of the outflow from agent into effect. Both occur when nature generates things (namely, passage from one state to another, and outflow from agent into effect), but only the latter properly exists in creation...

[**Article 2**] And in the second place we are asked: **Is creation a sort of change?**

And it seems so:

For [1] according to Aristotle[12] the word *change* means this existing after that. This fits creation, in which existence comes after non-existence. So creation is a change.

Moreover, [2] everything that comes to be comes to be from non-existence in a sense, since what exists doesn't have to come to be. So the relationship that generation (in which a thing receives [form,] a part of its substance) bears to formlessness (qualified non-being), creation (in which a thing receives the whole of its substance) bears to unqualified non-being. So since formlessness is properly speaking one extreme of generation, unqualified non-being is properly speaking one extreme of creation, and creation therefore properly speaking a change...

Moreover, [4] what is not now as it was earlier has changed. But what is created is not now as it was earlier, for first it did not exist (in the unqualified sense) and later it came to exist. So what is created has changed.

Moreover, [5] what was potential and is now actual has changed. But created things were potential and are now actual, since before creation they existed only in the power of their maker and now actually exist. So created things have changed, and creation is therefore a change.

But against that:

Aristotle[13] lists six kinds of change, and they don't include creation, as you can verify by going through them all. So creation is not a change.

In reply:

In every change the extremes of the change have to have something in common. For if nothing connected the opposing extremes we couldn't talk of one *passing* into the other (the words *change* and *passage* both refer to some same thing being differently disposed now from earlier). Again, unless they referred to the same subject, these extremes wouldn't exclude one another as is required of extremes of a change: for two opposites referring to different subjects can coexist.

Sometimes then the extremes of a change have one actually existent subject in common, giving rise to alterations in the strict sense: modifications of quality, increase and decrease of quantity, and change of place, all of which are alterations in which one and the same actually existent subject changes from one of two opposed extremes to another. Sometimes, however, the subject common to both extremes is not actually existent but something only existing potentially, as happens when things are generated or destroyed in an absolute sense: for the subject of the form which makes a thing exist as a substance (or of the lack of such a form) has to be some ultimate matter which [of itself] doesn't exist actually; so that generation and destruction are changes but not alterations strictly speaking. Sometimes, however, there is no common subject actually or potentially existing, but only a single continuous time in the first part of which one opposite exists and in the second part another, as when one thing is said to come from another in the sense of coming after it like afternoon from morning; and this is change not properly but metaphorically, inasmuch as we imagine time itself to be a sort of subject of what happens in time.

Now in creation nothing is common in any of the above ways: for there is no common subject either actually or potentially existing, and, if we are talking of the creation of the universe, no common time, since before the world there was no time. The only thing in common is imaginary: a single common time imagined to exist before and after the world was made; for just as no real space exists outside the universe though we can imagine one, so no time existed before the world began though we can imagine one. And for this reason creation truly and properly speaking is not a change, though it can be imagined to be one, not properly but metaphorically.

Hence:

to 1: The word *change* means this existing after that in some same subject, as we have said, and this doesn't fit creation.

to 2: In generation, in which a thing receives part of its substance, there exists—though not actually—a subject common to form and formlessness, so that the words *extreme* and *passage* properly apply; but this is not true of creation, as we have said...

to 4: What is not now as it was earlier has changed, given persistence of a subject; otherwise what has no existence at all would change, since what has no existence at all neither exists now as it did earlier nor not now as it did earlier. For change some same thing must be not now as it was earlier.

to 5: The subject of a change is some potential to be acted on, not the agent's power to act; so what was potential of being acted on and is now actual has changed, but not what was in someone's active power and is now actual; so the objection is invalid.

[**Article 3**] And in the third place we are asked: **Does creation name something real in creatures, and if so what?**

And it seems it is not anything real in creatures:

For [1], as the book of Causes[14] says: *what is received into anything exists there in the way the recipient exists*. But, since in creation God makes things out of nothing, what receives his creative action doesn't exist at all. Creation then can't be something really existing in the creature.

Moreover, [2] everything real is either creator or creature. But creation is not the creator, because then it would have existed eternally; nor is it a creature, because then it would have been created by another creation, which would then itself have needed creating, and so on *ad infinitum*. So creation is not something real.

Moreover, [3] whatever exists is either substance or incidental property. Now creation is not a substance, since it is neither matter nor form nor anything combined from the two, as is easy to see. Nor is it an incidental property, because properties follow on their subjects but creation is prior in nature to its only possible subject, the thing created. So creation is not anything real . . .

Moreover, [6] if creation signifies some relatedness of the creature to the God who gives it being, since this relatedness is always there in creatures and not just when they start existing, that means there is not only creation when a thing starts to be but as long as it goes on existing, so that things are being continually created, which seems absurd. Creation then is not a relatedness [in creatures], and we are led to the same conclusion as before . . .

But against that:

[1] If creation isn't real then nothing is really created, and that appears to be false. So creation must be something real.

Moreover, [2] God is master of what he creates because by creating them he brought them into being. Now mastery implies a real relatedness [to God] of creatures. *A fortiori* creation.

In reply:

According to some people creation is something real existing between creator and creatures, and, since what lies between is neither one extreme nor the other, creation would then be neither creator nor creature. But the masters [of theology] have pronounced this mistaken, since whatever exists, in whatever manner, must get its existence from God and so be a creature. So other people say that creation itself is not anything real on the side of creatures: but this too doesn't seem acceptable, for wherever there are things related in such a way that one depends on the other but not vice versa, we find the dependent one related really and the other related only notionally, as Aristotle[15] says is the case of knowledge and what is known. Now the very word *creature* relates it to a creator; and the creature depends on the creator but not vice versa; so creatures must have a real relationship to the creator, but God a notional relationship only. And this Peter Lombard[16] says explicitly.

So one must say that creation can be understood actively

or passively: actively it denotes God's activity—which is his substance—as related to creatures, not really but only notionally; passively creation is not something in the category of *passion*—because, as we have said earlier, creation is not properly speaking a change—but something in the category of relationship. And we can explain this as follows. In all true changes two processes occur: one goes from one extreme of the change to the other, from white to black, for example; and the other goes from agent to what is acted on, from the maker to what is made. Now both these processes feature differently during the change and at its end. During change what is changing is distancing itself from one extreme and approaching the other, but at the end of change what was changing has already started to exist at the last extreme; for clearly something changing from white to black is no longer approaching black at the end of the change but has already started being black. In the same way what the agent acts on or makes is undergoing transmutation by the agent during change, but at the end ceases to undergo transmutation by the agent and takes up the relationship of being from the agent, resembling it in certain respects; what humans generate, for example, takes up at birth the relationship of child. Now we have already said that creation shouldn't be understood as some process preceding the end of change, but as something characterizing what is already made. So creation as such doesn't imply any process of approaching being or any undergoing of transmutation by the creator, but simply a starting to exist, and [consequently] a relatedness to the creator from whom this existence comes. So creation is really nothing other than a relatedness to God consequent on starting to be.

Hence:

to 1: In creation it is not non-being that receives God's action but what is created, as we have said.

to 2: Understood as an action, creation is God's substance understood as bearing a certain relationship [to creatures], and is thus something uncreated. Understood as going on in creatures, as we have said, creation is in reality a certain relatedness [of creatures] conceived as a change because of the beginning or novelty implied. Now this relatedness is in a certain sense something created, if that word means something come from God. But there is no need to go on *ad infinitum*, because the relatedness of creation is not referred to God by some further real relatedness, but in itself: relationships, as Ibn Sīnā[17] says, don't need further relationships to relate them. And if we understand the word *created* strictly, as applying only to subsistent things—made and created in a strict sense because only they exist in a strict sense—then the relationship we are talking of is not something created but *con-created*. For properly speaking it does not exist but rather belongs in existence as all incidental properties do.

to 3: This relatedness is an incidental property, and as existent, inherent in a subject, is posterior to the thing created in the way all incidental properties are, really and notionally; though it is not the sort of incidental property that the subject itself can cause. But if we look at what defines this particular relationship—namely, that it is something arising from an agent's action—then it is in a certain sense prior to its subject, in the way its immediate cause, God's own action, is . . .

to 6: Creation implies the relationship we are talking of together with newness of existing, so that even though things are always related to God it doesn't follow that they're being created as long as they go on existing. Though there's nothing unacceptable in saying that as long as creatures exist this comes from God, just as as long as the air is lit up this comes from the sun, as Augustine[18] also pointed out. Here the difference is only one of words, depending on whether the word *creation* implies newness of existing or not . . .

Passage 28

Did Creation Occur in Time?

Source: Thomas's public disputations on the Power of God, 3.17. Text from *Quaestiones Disputatae de Potentia* (Marietti edn., Turin, 1953), with corrections from the Leonine text in preparation.

Date: 1265–7, Italy, aged 40.

Type of passage and how to read: Disputed question (see Introduction).

[Question 3] The subject for debate is **Creation—the first effect of God's power.**

...**[Article 17]** And in the seventeenth place we are asked: **Has the world always existed?**

And it seems it has:

For [1] what characterizes a thing always accompanies it. But pseudo-Dionysius[1] says that *it is characteristic of God's goodness to call existent things to communion with him*, that is, to give creatures existence. So, since God was always good, it seems he must always have given creatures existence; and the world must always have existed...

Moreover, [6] what stays the same will go on doing the same until stopped. Now God always stays the same—*you never alter*, says Psalm 101 [28]—and because of his unlimited power what he does can't be stopped. So it seems he must always go on doing the same; and thus, since he produced a world once, it seems he must always have been producing it...

Moreover, [10] if the world didn't always exist, then before it existed it was either possible or not. If it wasn't possible, then its existence was impossible and its non-existence necessary and it never was brought into existence. But if it was possible, then a potentiality for a world existed, and that means some subject or material existed, since potentialities can't exist without something to be potential. But if material existed it existed under a form, since altogether formless material can't exist. So something composed of material and form existed, and consequently a whole universe . . .

Moreover, [12] any agent that newly starts to act changes from being able to act to actually acting. Now God can't do that, since he is altogether unchanging. So it seems he can't have newly started to act but must have produced the world from eternity . . .

Moreover, [15] what is always beginning and ending never begins or ends, since things exist after beginning and before ending. But time is always beginning and ending, since the only part of time that exists is the present moment, which ends the past and begins the future. So time never begins and never ends but always exists, and the same must be true of change, and of what changes, and so of the whole world; for time can't exist without change, nor change without what changes, nor what changes without the world.

But [the respondent] said that the first moment of time didn't end a past, and that its last moment won't begin a future.

> But against that: [16] what differentiates the temporal present from the eternal present is that it passes. But what passes passes from one state to another. So all moments must pass from an earlier to a later state. So there can't be either a first moment or a last . . .

Moreover, [20] God, who is prior in nature to the world, is either prior to it also in duration or not. If not, then he resembles those causes that have effects of equal duration to themselves, and it would seem that creatures must have existed from all eternity as God has. But if God is prior in duration to the world, then there must have been a duration prior to the world's duration relating to it as early to late. But duration that has early and late in it is time. So time pre-existed the world, and thus change and what changes; and we have reached the same conclusion as before . . .

Moreover, [25] if time started to exist, did that take time or was it instantaneous? Not instantaneous because in an instant no time as yet exists; nor did it take time, for since nothing exists before it begins to exist, no time could have existed until the time [of its beginning] ended. So time didn't start to exist, and we are led to the same conclusion as before.

But against that:

[1] Proverbs 8 [24] represents God's wisdom as saying: *There was not yet a deep when I was conceived, no springs brimming over with water; before the great mass of the mountains was settled, before the hills I came to birth; when as yet he had made neither earth nor rivers nor the hinges on which earth turns.* So earth and rivers and the hinges on which earth turns did not exist for ever.

Moreover, [2] Priscian tells us that as time goes by people get cleverer. But since cleverness isn't limitless, the time during which cleverness has been growing can't be limitless either; nor can the world.

Moreover, [3] Job 14 [19] says *cloudbursts wear away the earth*. But there isn't unlimited earth. So if limitless time has passed, the earth would have disappeared already; which is clearly false.

Moreover, [4] everyone agrees that God is prior in nature to the world as cause to effect. But in God nature and duration are the same. So God is prior to the world in duration, and the world has not existed for ever.

In reply:

We must firmly maintain that the world has not always existed: catholic faith teaches it and no scientific proof can succeed in proving the opposite. To be clear on this, note . . . that God's actions are determined neither by his material nor by the power available to him nor by some ultimate goal, but only by the form at which his activity is aimed, for this, once presupposed, requires things to exist in a way conformable to that form.

Now we must distinguish the production of an individual creature from the coming out of the whole universe from God. When talking of the production of an individual creature we can say it is as it is because of some other creature or at least because of the order of the universe which all creatures serve as parts do the form of a whole. But when we talk of the bringing into existence of the whole universe, there is no other created thing which can be used to explain why the universe is as it is; and since its arrangements aren't determined by the power available to God—which is infinite—or by his goodness—which would be there even without such things—we must say they depend simply on its maker's will.

If you want to know why the heavens are so big and not bigger, the only answer is that he who made it wanted it that size. And that, according to Moses Maimonides, is why scripture urges us to look at the stars, since their order above all shows how everything is subject to the will and providence of the creator. There is no answer to the question why this star is that far from that star—or any other such question about the order of the heavens—except that God planned it so in his wisdom. And so Isaiah 40 [26] says: *Lift up your eyes to the heavens; consider who created them.* It won't help to say that such and such is the size appropriate to the nature of heavens or heavenly bodies in the way every solid thing has a size fixed by nature, for just as God's power isn't limited to this size rather than that, so it isn't limited to a nature requiring this size rather than one requiring that. So we will have to ask the same question about the nature as we asked about the size, even if we concede that the nature of the heavens requires this size and can't have any other one.

Not even this can be said about time and its duration. For time is as extrinsic to things as place is; so that even heavens which can't have another size or other intrinsic properties than the ones they have can still occupy a different place and position by moving in space, or even a different time; for time succeeds time for ever as movement follows movement and place place, and one can't say, as we said of size, that the nature of the heavens demand this time not that or this place not that. Clearly then it is simply a matter of God's will what length of time the universe lasts, just as its size is. And so there is no proving necessary anything about the universe's duration, as one would have to do to prove the world always existed.

But some people, because they didn't think of the universe as issuing from God, were forced into errors about the world's beginning. Some of the earlier cosmologists, overlooking agent causes and postulating an uncreated matter as a cause of everything, were forced into saying matter had always existed. For nothing can bring itself into existence from non-existence and to begin existing would need some other cause. These cosmologists believed that the world always existed, either continuously (since the only agents they knew of were those in nature with fixed effects which necessarily go on doing the same thing) or discontinuously in the way Democritus believed the world—or rather worlds—to have been built up and broken down many times by chance, by the random movements of atoms. But because it didn't seem right that all the agreements and usefulnesses that occur in nature—always or practically always—should come from chance, as they would have to do if all there is is matter, and especially since certain effects can't be explained by the causality of matter, other people postulated an agent cause: mind for Anaxagoras, attraction and repulsion for Empedocles. These people didn't think of such agents as causes of the universe, but as particular causes acting on matter to change it from one thing to another. So they were forced to say that matter was eternal (having no cause of its existence) but that the world began: for any agent causing by way of change must temporally precede its effect, since the effect comes only at the end of the change, and that comes after the beginning of the change, at which time the agent must already be present to begin the change. Aristotle,[2] however, realized that if the cause you postulated for setting up the world acted through change, an infinite regress would result, for every change would have to have another one preceding it; so he thought the world always existed. He wasn't talking about a universe issuing from a God, but about agents that started acting by changing, in the way particular causes do, though not the universal one. As a result he argued to the eternity of the world from change and the first mover's lack of change. So if you think about this carefully you will see his reasons are reasons attacking a position: which is why, having raised the question of the eternity of change, he begins[3] with the opinions of Anaxagoras and Empedocles that he intends to attack. Those who came after Aristotle did reflect on the issuing of the whole universe from God by an act of will, not by change, and they tried to show the eternity of the world by arguing that will would delay doing what it intended only for reasons of innovation or at least change, so that we have to think of it as a temporal process, wanting to do something at this time rather than earlier But this is the same mistake as that of the people mentioned earlier. The first agent is being thought of on the model of an agent exercising action in time, even though it acts by will, and so as an agent presupposing time rather than causing it. God, however, is the cause of even time itself, for time itself is part of the total universe God made; so when we talk of a universe issuing from God we can't think of him making it at one time rather than another earlier one. Such thinking presupposes time to making instead of subjecting time to making. Rather if we think of God producing the total universe of creatures including time, our question must not be why he made the universe at a certain time, but why he imposed a certain measure on time. And that depended simply on God's will: he wanted the world not to exist for ever but to start sometime, just as he wanted the heavens to be no bigger and no smaller than they are.

Hence:

to 1: Goodness characteristically gives things existence by being willed; so creatures didn't have to be given existence whenever God was good, but whenever God willed it . . .

to 6: What things do reflects what they are, so that the effects that issue from any efficiently operating cause must reflect that cause. In nature agents' effects reflect them by reproducing the agent's form, and in the same way willed effects reflect their agents by reproducing the form the agent has willingly planned them to have, as we see in a craftsman's handiwork. But will plans not only the form of its effects but every other condition too: so that effects follow willing not at the moment of willing but when will plans them to. For effects reflect not the existence of will but its plans. So the willing could last for ever, but the effect won't follow it for ever...

to 10: Before the world existed it was possible for it to come into existence not because something had a passive potentiality to become it but because an agent had an active power to make it. Alternatively, one can say it was possible not because of a potentiality but because the terms of the proposition *A world exists* are not mutually incompatible. In this way something can be called possible without any need for a potentiality, as Aristotle[4] says...

to 12: This argument applies to agents that start to act by way of a new action, but God's action is eternal, since it is his very substance. So he is said to start to act because a new effect of his eternal action starts to exist, as planned by his will, which is then thought of as though it caused the action in relation to that effect. For effects follow from action in ways appropriate to the form determining the action: just as things heated by fire become hot in the way fire is hot...

to 15: Since, as Aristotle[5] says, time's successiveness initially derives from the successiveness of change, whether every moment begins and ends a time depends on whether every moment begins and ends a change; so that if we suppose change did not and will not always exist we won't have to say that every moment begins and ends a time, but there will exist a moment which only begins time and one which only ends it. So this argument is circular and proves nothing, though it serves Aristotle's purpose, who was arguing *ad hominem*, as we said earlier. For many arguments depend upon assumptions made by opponents and so tell against their position, though they are not simply speaking valid.

to 16: Every moment passes but not all pass from one state to another: the last moment of time passes only *from* a state, and the first moment only *into* one...

to 20: God does precede the world in duration, but in eternity, not in time, since God's existence is not measured by time. There was no real time before the world existed, but only imaginary time, in the sense that we, existing now, can imagine that before time began, while eternity existed, unlimited periods of time could have rolled by . . .

to 25: Time isn't a static thing the whole substance of which exists simultaneously. So the whole of time doesn't have to exist when it begins, and there is nothing to stop us saying time began at an instant.

As to the arguments against:

Although they all argue to the truth only the first [1] does so with necessity, by quoting scripture.

[2] The argument from growth of cleverness during the course of time doesn't show time began. It could be, as Aristotle himself says, that scientific studies often get interrupted for long periods and then taken up again as if for the first time.

[3] The earth too is never worn away in one place without being built up again in another by mutual interchange of elements.

[4] And God's duration, though identical with his nature in reality, is still different notionally, so that priority of nature doesn't imply priority of duration.

Passage 29

Providence (*a*): The Ordered Universe

Source: *Summa contra Gentiles*, 3.97–8. Text from *Summa contra Gentiles* (*Opera Omnia*, Leonine edn., vol. xiv).

Date: 1264, Italy, aged 39.

[Chapter 97] What we have been saying clearly shows that **the dispensations of God's providence have their reasons.**

For we have shown that God's providence orders everything to a goal—his own goodness; not as if what happens could expand that goodness in any way, but things are made to reflect and express it as much as possible. Now created things must all fall short of the full goodness of God, so, in order that things may reflect that goodness more perfectly, there had to be variety in things, so that what one thing couldn't express perfectly could be more perfectly expressed in various ways by a variety of things. For human beings too, when they can't express the idea in their minds in one word, resort to many different ones that express the idea in different ways. And this also draws attention to how great God's perfection is: for the perfect goodness that exists one and unbroken in God can exist in creatures only in a multitude of fragmented ways. Now variety in things comes from the different forms determining their species. So because of their goal things differ in form.

And because they differ in form there is an order among things. By dint of having form a thing exists, and by existing it resembles God, who is his own existence pure and simple; so form can be nothing else than God's resemblance in things, which Aristotle[1] well described as *something of divine good.* Now the only possible way in which things can vary in resembling something absolutely simple is by closeness or remoteness, things more closely resembling God being the more perfect. So forms can differ only by degree of perfection. That is why Aristotle[2] compared definitions, which express things' natures or forms, to numbers, which change species by adding or subtracting 1. He was implying that variety in forms requires different levels of perfection. And one has only to look at things' natures to see this. When you look carefully, you find the variety of things is achieved in steps: above inanimate bodies plants, above them unreasoning animals, and above them intelligent creatures; and within each step a variety of perfection such that the top members of a lower genus approach those of a higher genus and vice versa, animals without movement, for example, resembling plants; so that pseudo-Dionysius[3] said: *God's wisdom joins the ends of one domain to the beginnings of the next.* Clearly then variety in things requires an order of levels in things, and not mere equality.

The same diversity of form which makes things differ in species makes their behaviour different too. For since activity follows on actuality and inactivity on potentiality, and since actuality is given by form, a thing's activity must accord with its form. So things differing in form act in different ways. And since special activities pursue special goals, the special goals of things are also various, even though all have an ultimate goal in common.

Variety of forms also brings with it diverse relationships to matter. Since forms differ by degree of perfection, some are perfect enough to exist perfectly in their own right, without support from matter. Others cannot exist perfectly of themselves but need matter as a sort of base, so that what exists in its own right is neither form alone nor matter alone (since matter of itself has no actuality), but something combining the two. Now matter and form couldn't come together to make one thing unless there was some proportion between them, different matters or materials matching different forms. And that is why some forms need homogeneous material and others heterogeneous; and different forms require different organization of the matter fitted to their species of form and its activity. And these diverse relationships to matter bring with them a diversity of agencies and capabilities of being acted on. Form makes things active, matter makes them capable of being acted on and changed; so that less material things with more perfect forms act on things that are more material having less perfect forms. And diversity of form and matter and agency brings with it diversity of characteristic and incidental properties. Because a thing's substance is a source of its properties (as the perfect of the imperfect) diversity of characteristic properties depends on diversity of substance; and because diverse agents affect what they act on diversely, diversity of incidental properties depends on diversity of agents.

Now from all this it is clear that God's providence, when it distributes a variety of properties and activities and changes and spatial arrangements to the things it has created, has its reasons. That is why sacred scripture ascribes the production and management of things to God's wisdom and discretion, saying *In wisdom the Lord laid the earth's foundations, in understanding he set up the heavens, through his wisdom the deeps break out in spring and the clouds distil their dew* (Proverbs 3 [19–20]); and elsewhere that God's wisdom *reaches from pole to pole with strength, arranging everything with sweetness* (Wisdom 8 [1]), and later in the same book (Wisdom 11 [20]): *You have ordered all things by measure, number, and weight*, meaning by measure the amount or mode or degree of perfection in each thing, by number the diversity and plurality of species that results from these degrees of perfection, and by weight the diverse attractions to specific goals and activities, agents and patients, and properties resulting from the diversity of species.

Now in the hierarchy of reasons behind God's providence just described we have placed first God's own goodness: the ultimate goal as it were which first starts activity off; and after that the manyness of things, which in turn required the different degrees of forms and matters, agents and patients, activities and properties. So just as the absolutely first reason behind God's providence is God's goodness, so the first reason within creation is manyness in things, to set up and maintain which everything else seems to be ordered. So that it seems reasonable when Boethius[4] remarks that *everything laid down in the primeval nature of things seems to have been formed by reason of number.*

But now we must note that practical and theoretical reason are partly like one another and partly unlike. They are alike in this: speculative reason starting from some premiss reaches by intermediate steps an intended conclusion, and practical reason, directing our activity, starts from a beginning and reaches by intermediate means some intended activity or product of activity. But the starting-point for theoretical reason is a form and 'what a thing is', whereas in practical matters it is a goal, which is sometimes a form and sometimes something else. Also in theorizing the starting-points compel our assent, but in practical matters they sometimes compel consent and sometimes not: human beings are compelled to will happiness as a goal, but not the building of a house. Again in scientific proofs later steps follow necessarily from earlier ones, but this only happens in practical matters when there is only one way of achieving a goal: someone who wants to build a house must try to get hold of wood, but that he tries to get hold of deal comes from a simple act of his own will, not from the reason: building a house. And in the same way God must love his own goodness, but from this it doesn't follow necessarily that creatures must exist to express it, since God's goodness is perfect without that. So the coming to be of creatures, though it finds its first reason in God's goodness, nevertheless depends on a simple act of God's will. Given, however, that God does will to share his goodness with creatures as far as that is possible by way of resemblance, then that gives the reason for the variety of creatures. But it doesn't necessitate this or that measure of perfection or this or that number of things. Given, however, that God by an act of will decides on this number of things and that measure of perfection for each thing, then that gives the reason for it having such a form and such matter. And so on in the same way down the list.

Clearly then the dispositions of providence have their reasons, but reasons that presuppose God's will. All this allows us to avoid two kinds of mistake. Firstly, the mistake of those who believe everything comes from simple will devoid of reason: the mistake of the sages in Moorish Law of whom Maimonides[5] speaks, who said there was no reason why fire should heat rather than make cold except that God willed it that way; and secondly, the mistake of those who say the causal order is a necessary consequence of God's providence. From what we have said both are clearly false. Certain words of scripture, however, seem to suggest that everything is due to God's will. But not in order to remove all reason from the dispensation of providence but to show that God's will is the first source of everything, as we have said. Thus the psalm [135: 6] says *the Lord does whatever he pleases*; Job 11 [10] asks *who can ask him Why have you done this?* and Romans 9 [19] *who can oppose his will?*; and Augustine[6] writes: *The first cause of health and of sickness, of reward and of penalty, of favour and requital is God's will alone.* So when we ask the why of any natural effect we can give a reason as an immediate cause as long as we recognize that its ultimate cause is God's will. So you can ask: Why does wood become hot in the presence of fire?, and answer: Because heating is an activity native to fire. And this because heat is its characteristic property. And this because of the form that defines fire. And so on till we come to God's will. To answer, because it is God's will, to the initial question about why wood gets hot is appropriate if you want to drive the question all the way back to the ultimate cause, but inappropriate if you are trying to exclude all the other causes.

[Chapter 98] [Is God bound by the order of his providence?]

The foregoing suggests two sorts of order that can be discerned in the world: one universal, dependent on the first cause of everything and embracing everything, and the other particular, dependent on some created cause and extending to whatever is subordinate to that cause. Such particular orders are many, corresponding to the various causes found in creation, and they exist subordinated one to another in the way their causes are. Necessarily then all these particular orders are subordinate to the one universal order, descendants of that order of things which results in them because of their dependence on the first of causes. Political life offers a parallel: for all the members of a household are ordered to one another by subordination to the master of the house, and then that master and all other masters of households in a city ordered to one another and to the ruler of the city; and he with all his fellows in a kingdom ordered to the king.

However, the universal order in which everything is ordered by God's providence can be looked at from two points of view: that of the things ordered by it, and that of the kind of order it is, which depends on its source. Now we already showed in book 2 that the things subjected to his order God did not have to produce by necessity of his nature or some such thing, but that such things come from a simple act of his will, especially when first set up. It follows then that God can always do other things than those that he has done in the order of his providence: his power is not limited to these things. But if we think of the way the kind of order it is depends on its source, then God can't do anything outside of that order. For it is an order deriving as we have seen from God's knowledge and will ordering everything to the goal of his own goodness. Now God can't do anything he doesn't will, since creatures derive from him not by nature but by act of will, as we have shown. Equally he can't do something he does not understand; since one can't will the unknown. Nor again can he create something not ordered to the goal of his goodness, since that goodness is the object defining his will. And likewise, because God is altogether unchanging, he can't will something that previously he didn't, or start to know something new or order it to his goodness. So God can't do anything that escapes the order of his providence, just as he can't do anything he isn't active in! He can do other things than those in fact subject to his providence and activity, considering his power in the abstract; but he can't do anything that hasn't been eternally subject to the order of his providence since he cannot change.

Because they haven't made this distinction people have made various mistakes. Some have tried to extend the unchanging nature of God's order to the things themselves that are subject by it, saying everything must be as it is; so much so that some have said God couldn't do other than he did. This is contradicted by Matthew 26 [53]: *Do you think I cannot appeal to my Father, and he will send me more than twelve legions of angels?* Some, however, have done the opposite, ascribing the changeable character of the things subject to divine providence to God's providence itself, thinking in a fleshly way that God like fleshly human beings had a changeable will. This is contradicted by Numbers 23 [19]: *God is no human being that he should lie, no child of Adam that he should change his mind.* Yet others thought God's providence didn't cover events that might or might not happen. And this is contradicted by Lamentations 3 [37]: *Who is there who has said something might happen without the Lord's command?*

Passage 30

Providence (*b*): Chance and Freedom

Source: Thomas's commentary on Aristotle's *De Interpretatione*, 1.9 ($18^{b}26$–$19^{a}22$). Text from *In Aristotelis Librum Peri Hermeneias*, 1.14 (*Opera Omnia*, Leonine edn., vol. i, reissued as iA).

Date: 1269–72, second stay in Paris, aged 45.

Type of passage and how to read: Commentary with digression (see Introduction). But this passage contains no commentary, but only one of Thomas's digressions.

Note, however, as Boethius does at this point in his commentary,[1] that there are various opinions about possibility and necessity, about *can be* and *must be*. Some people, like Diodorus, distinguish these by reference to what happens, saying that *can't be* never happens, *must be* always happens, and *can be* sometimes happens and sometimes doesn't. The Stoics, however, distinguished them by reference to external obstruction, saying that the truth of *must be* can't be obstructed, of *can't be* is always obstructed, and of *can be* can sometimes be obstructed and sometimes not. Neither way of distinguishing them seems adequate. The first way gets things back to front: it is not that things must be because they always happen, but that they always happen because they must be, and similarly for the other definitions. And the second way appeals to something extrinsic and so to speak inessential: it is not that things must be because nothing obstructs them, but that nothing can obstruct them because they must be.

So other people have formulated a better distinction by reference to the natures of things, saying that *must be* is constrained by nature to exist, *can't be* is constrained by nature not to exist, and *can be* is not entirely constrained to either, but is sometimes inclined more to one than the other and sometimes equally balanced between the two—the so-called 'might be either'. And this is an opinion Boethius attributes to Philo, though clearly it is the one Aristotle adopts here. For he explains *can be* and *might be* in human behaviour as due to our ability to deliberate, and in other things as due to their material's openness to being realized in different ways. However, the explanation seems inadequate. For just as the matter of bodies that can decompose is open to existing or not existing, so in heavenly bodies there is an openness to being here or being there; and yet in the heavens everything happens *as it must* and never *as it might be either*. So we have to say that, in general, matter's openness to either doesn't adequately explain *might be*, unless the powers that act on the matter are also open to either. Because if they are irresistibly determined on one course, then the passive *might be* of matter will always be realized in just that one way as a *must*.

Certain people, realizing this, held that the *might bes* of nature itself are restricted to a *must be* by a cause determined on one course called *fate*. The Stoics, for example, held fate to be a kind of sequence or chain of causes, because of two assumptions they made: that everything that happens in the world has a cause, and that given its cause an effect must follow. (And wherever there was no single sufficient cause, many co-operating causes took on the role of a single sufficient cause.) So they came to the conclusion that everything happens as it must. This argument Aristotle[2] invalidated by demolishing both its assumptions. For he says not everything has a cause, but only what exists in its own right. What exists only incidentally has no cause, since it doesn't properly have existence and, as Plato[3] also said, should rather be counted as not existing. That I am a musician has its cause, and that I am white likewise, but that what is white is a musician has no cause [as such], and all similar cases are the same. Neither is it true that given a cause—even a sufficient cause—its effect must follow; for not all causes—even sufficient ones—are such that their effects can't be obstructed: fire is a sufficient cause of wood burning, but you can stop it burning by drenching it with water. Now if both assumptions had been true the inevitable conclusion would have been that everything that happens must happen. For if every effect has a cause, then an effect about to happen after some specified time, in five days, say, would indicate some cause existing earlier, and that another, until we reached a cause in the present, or one already past. And if, given its cause, an effect must follow, the *must be* would then pass down the chain of causes to the end effect. If, for example, someone who has eaten salt will thirst, and someone thirsty will go out to get a drink, and someone going out will get killed by robbers, then, because he has already eaten the salt, he is bound to get killed. So Aristotle, to avoid this, showed both the assumed propositions to be false, as we have said.

Some people have remained unconvinced by this, arguing that everything incidental presupposes something existing in its own right, so that incidental effects do presuppose causes that cause in their own right. But what they haven't realized is that what the incidental presupposes as existing in its own right is just that thing to which it is incidental: my being a musician presupposes my being me, and every incidental property some underlying subject that exists in its own right. So everything incidental in some effect presupposes that effect to exist in its own right, and as such have a cause that causes in its own right; but what is incidental in the effect doesn't have a cause that causes in its own right, but only an incidental cause. For effects must have causes proportionate to them, as Aristotle[4] says elsewhere.

Nevertheless, certain people, not distinguishing in effects between what is incidental and what exists in its own right, try to trace back every effect that happens here below to a cause existing in its own right, which they call *fate* and identify with the influence of the heavenly bodies, saying fate is a force exerted by the positions of the stars. But that kind of cause can't impose a *must* on everything going on here. For much of what happens here is determined by mind and will, which aren't directly subject in themselves to the influence of heavenly bodies. Mind, which is reason, and will, which is reasonable, are not activities of bodily organs, as Aristotle[5] showed, so that they can't be directly subject to influence from the heavenly bodies: for bodily forces can act in their own right only on bodies. Our sense-powers, because they are activities of bodily organs, can be incidentally subject to the activity of heavenly bodies; which leads Aristotle[6] to say that the people who believe the human will is subject to the movements of the heavens haven't distinguished mind from the senses. Mind and will, however, are indirectly influenced by the heavenly bodies inasmuch as they make use of the senses; but clearly our sensitive passions don't impose a *must* on our mind and will, for, as Aristotle says,[7] *the disciplined man doesn't follow his bad desires.* So the influence of the heavenly bodies doesn't impose a *must* on what we do with mind and will. But neither does it on other bodily happenings in this changeable world, for many things happen by accident. Now the accidental can't be traced back to any natural cause or force as such, since forces in nature are fixed on one course, whereas the accidental has no unity. That is why we said above that *I am a white musician* is not a single proposition, because it doesn't express a single truth. And this is why Aristotle[8] says that many things the heavens predict—clouds and storms, say—never happen because they are incidentally obstructed. And although this obstruction, considered in its own right, can be traced back to some heavenly cause, nevertheless that it converges with what it obstructs is accidental and so cannot be traced back to any cause that acts by nature.

However, we must now note that the merely incidental can be apprehended as a unity by mind: being white and being a musician, which in themselves are two things not one, can be taken as one by a mind framing a single proposition connecting them. And this is the way it can sometimes happen that an event which in itself happens incidentally and by chance can be traced back to a mind that has set it up beforehand: as the meeting of two slaves in a certain place—which as far as they are concerned is incidental and chance because they didn't know about each other—can nevertheless have been intended by their master, who sent them both to the meeting in that place. And in this way some people have said that everything which goes on in this world, including even what seems fortuitous and chance, must be traced back to God's providence, on which they said fate hangs. Other people have stupidly denied this because they have thought of God's mind on the model of ours that doesn't know singularities. But this is not so: for God's understanding and willing is his very existing. So that just as God's existence embraces in its power everything else that exists in any way whatever, thus sharing in a sense in God's existence, so too God's understanding and what he understands embraces all knowledge and all things that can be known, and God's will and what he wills embraces all desiring and all good things that can be desired. So that by the very fact that something is knowable he knows it, and by the very fact that something is good he wills it, just as by the very fact that something exists it is subject to his active influence, which he utterly comprehends since he acts by his mind.

But if God's providence is the cause of everything that happens in the world, or at the very least all good things, it seems that everything *must* happen the way it does: firstly, because he knows it and his knowledge can't be mistaken, so what he knows must necessarily happen; and secondly, because he wills it and his will can't be ineffective, so everything he wills, it seems, must necessarily happen. But these objections depend on thinking of knowledge in God's mind and the working of God's will on the model of such activities in us, when they are in fact very different.

For firstly, in regard to knowledge we should note that a mind contained in some way within time relates differently to the knowing of what happens in time from a mind altogether outside time. A convenient illustration may be drawn from space, since, according to Aristotle,[9] the successiveness of time derives from that of change and movement, and that from extended successiveness in space. So if we imagine many people travelling a road, all those travelling will have knowledge of the people in front and behind them, according to their beforeness and afterness in space. And so each traveller will see the people next to him and the people in front, but not the people behind. But if someone is outside the whole travelling situation, standing in some high tower, for example, from which he can see the whole road, then he will have a bird's-eye view of every traveller, not seeing them as in front or behind in relation to his own seeing, but seeing them all together in front and behind each other. Now since our knowing occurs within time, either in itself or incidentally (so that when making propositional connections and disconnections we have to add tense, as Aristotle[10] points out), things are known as present or past or future. Present events are known as actually existing and perceptible to the senses in some way; past events are remembered; and future events are not known in themselves—because they don't yet exist—but can be predicted from their causes: with certainty if their causes totally determine them, as with things that must happen; conjecturally if they are not so determined that they cannot be obstructed, as with things that happen usually; and not at all if they are only possible and not determined either to one side or the other, as with things that *might be either,* for we know things not by their potentialities but by what is realized in them, as Aristotle[11] says. God's knowing, however, is altogether outside time, as if he stands on the summit of eternity where everything exists together, looking down in a single simple glance on the whole course of time. So in his one glance he sees everything going on throughout time, and each as it is in itself, not as something future to himself and his seeing and visible only as it exists within its causal situation (although he sees that causal situation). But he sees things altogether eternally, each as it exists in its own time, just as our own human eye sees John sitting there himself, not just as something determined by causes. Nor does our seeing John sitting there stop it being an event that might not have been when regarded just in relation to its causes. And yet while he is sitting there we see him sitting there with certainty and without doubt, since when a thing exists in itself it is already determined. In this way then God knows everything that happens in time with certainty and without doubt, and yet the things that happen in time are not things that must exist or must come to exist, but things that might or might not be.

A similar difference must be noted in regard to God's will; for God's will is to be thought of as existing outside the realm of existents, as a cause from which pours forth everything that exists in all its variant forms. Now *what can be* and *what must be* are variants of being, so that it is from God's will itself that things derive whether they must be or may or may not be and the distinction of the two according to the nature of their immediate causes. For he prepares causes that must cause for those effects that he wills must be, and causes that might cause but might fail to cause for those effects that he wills might or might not be. And it is because of the nature of their causes that some effects are said to be effects that must be and others effects that need not be, although all depend on God's will as primary cause, a cause which transcends this distinction between *must* and *might not*. But the same cannot be said of human will or of any other cause, since every other cause exists within the realm of *must* and *might not*. So of every other cause it must be said either that it can fail to cause, or that its effect must be and cannot not be; God's will, however, cannot fail, and yet not all his effects must be, but some can be or not be.

In the same way some people strive to uproot the other root of *may or may not be*—that which Aristotle here identifies with our ability to deliberate—wanting to show that will when it chooses is compelled to move by what it desires. For since the object of willing is what is good, it doesn't seem possible to turn away will from desiring what seems to it good, just as reason can't be turned away from assenting to what seems to it true. And so it seems that any choice consequent on deliberation will always be made under compulsion; so that everything which takes its rise from our deliberation and choice will be done under compulsion. But the answer to this is that goods differ just as truths do. Certain truths like the first unprovable premisses of all proofs are self-evident and compel the assent of mind; but certain truths are not self-evident but evident for other reasons. And there are two sorts of such truth. Some follow necessarily from the premisses, and given the truth of the premisses can't be false, and these are all provable conclusions; the mind must assent to such truths once it has perceived their relation to the premisses, though not before.

Other truths don't follow necessarily from the premisses and even given the truth of the premisses they can be false; they are matters of opinion and the mind doesn't have to assent to them, although it may, for some motive or other, incline to one side or the other. Now in the same way there is also a certain good which is desirable for its own sake, namely, happiness, which has the nature of ultimate goal, and the will is compelled to adhere to that good, for there is a sort of natural compulsion on everyone to want to be happy. But there are other goods which are desirable for the sake of the goal, and can be compared to the goal as conclusions are to premisses, in the way Aristotle[12] explains. If then there were goods which were *sine qua nons* of happiness, these too would compel desire, and most of all in a person that perceived the connection: and existence, life, understanding, and the like are perhaps goods like these. But the particular goods to which human activity is directed are not like this, and are not seen as *sine qua nons* of happiness: eating or not eating this food or that, for instance; but something in them attracts desire according to the good we see in them. And so our wills are not compelled to choose them. And it is worthy of notice for this reason that Aristotle identified the root of *might or might not be* in what we do with deliberation, which is concerned with as yet undetermined means to a goal. For, as Aristotle[13] says, when the means are already determined there is no role for deliberation.

We have been saying all these things in order to defend Aristotle's identification here of the roots of *might and might not be*; though we have trespassed beyond the borders of a logician's business.[14]

Passage 31
Providence (*c*): How Evil is Caused

Source: *Summa contra Gentiles*, 3.10. Text from *Summa contra Gentiles* (*Opera Omnia*, Leonine edn., vol. xiv).

Date: 1264, Italy, aged 39.

Parallel reading: Passage 35 on moral action.

Notes on translation: 'Vice' is used to translate *vitium* and give the required opposition to 'virtue', *virtus*. But *vitium* has a broader connotation: that of something being vitiated; and *virtus* has the ordinary Latin meaning of 'strength' still present in it. Moral words and words about nature were not so absolutely separated as they misleadingly are today.

[Chapter 10] We can conclude from what we have said that **only good can cause evil.**

For even if evil causes evil, since we have proved that evil acts only by the power of some good, that good will have to be the primary cause of the evil.

Further, what doesn't exist can't cause anything. So all causes must be some or other existent thing. But we have proved that an evil is not an existent thing. So evil can't cause anything. If then there is a cause of evil it must be a good.

Again, whatever is in and of itself a cause tends towards an effect proper to it. If then evil of itself caused, it would tend towards some evil effect proper to it. But this is false for we have shown that all agents tend towards good. So evil can't cause anything of itself but only incidentally. Incidental causes, however, must be traced back to what is of itself a cause. Now only good is of itself a cause; evil can't be. So evil must be caused by good.

Moreover, a cause is either an effect's material, the form [that the material takes on], an agent [imposing form on the material], or a goal [drawing the agent to impose the form]. But evil can't be matter or form, for we showed above that potential being was good and actual being was good. Again, it can't be an agent, for an agent's activity issues from its actuality and the form it has; nor again can it be a goal, since as we have proved evil is never intended. So evil can't be a cause of anything. If evil, then, has a cause, it must be caused by good.

However, since good and evil are opposites, and one opposite can't cause another except incidentally, as Aristotle[1] says *cold causes heat*, it follows that **good can actively cause evil only incidentally.**

In nature this incidentalness can be on the agent's side or on the effect's side. On the agent's side when the agent is deficient in power and so acts defectively and produces a deficient effect: for example, a weak stomach can lead to imperfect digestion and bile, which are natural evils. But deficiency is incidental to the agent as agent; for it is not active inasmuch as it lacks power but inasmuch as it has some: if it had no power at all it wouldn't act. So on the agent's side evil is caused incidentally because of the agent's deficiency in power. And this is why evil is sometimes said to have a defective rather than an effective cause, since evil follows from an agent only in so far as it is lacking in power and to that extent non-effective. It comes down to the same if the defect in action and effect comes from a defect in a tool or anything else that the agent's action requires, as when our motive powers produce limping because our leg is crooked: for the agent acts by way of both, by his power and his tool. On the effect's side, good incidentally causes evil relative to the effect's matter or relative to its form. For if the matter is not disposed to receive the agent's imprint a defect will follow in the effect, as when monsters are born because of unprepared matter: the fact that it doesn't transform and actualize the indisposed matter can't be laid at the door of the agent, for agents have powers proportioned to their natures and their inability to go further can't be called deficiency in power; we can say that only when its power falls short of the measure laid down by nature. Relative to the form of the effect, evil can occur incidentally because the form that is there is necessarily accompanied by lack of another form, so that the generation of one thing entails the decomposition of another. But this evil is not evil to the effect intended by the agent, as is clear from the foregoing, but to some other thing. In nature then evil is clearly caused incidentally by good; and the same is true in things artificially made, for *craft imitates nature*[2] in its activities, and faults occur in the same way in both.

But **in moral matters** things seem to happen differently.

For moral vice doesn't seem to follow from deficiency of power, since weakness of power either totally removes moral vice or at least diminishes it. Weakness doesn't deserve the penalties culpable acts deserve but rather mercy and pardon: moral vice must be voluntary not necessary. However, if we examine matters closely we will see similarities and dissimilarities. The dissimilarity is this: moral vice is ascribed only to actions, not to effects, for moral virtues are virtues of doing, not making, whereas crafts are virtues of making in which, as we have just said, faults happen just as they do in nature. So moral evil is not ascribed to the matter or form of an effect, but follows only on the agent.

Now in moral actions we come across in order four causes of action. There is first the executive or motive power that moves our limbs to execute the command of will. So this power is moved by a second cause, will. Will in turn is moved by a judgement of our perceptive power, which judges things to be good or bad, good and bad being objects of will, one moving the will to follow and the other to flee. And our perceptive power in turn is moved by what it perceives. So the first source of movement in moral actions is what is perceived, the second the perceiving power, the third the will, and the fourth the motive power executing reason's command. Now the executive power's action already presupposes moral goodness or badness, for external action is only thought moral if it is voluntary: so when will is good the external action is good, and when evil evil. If the external act was deficient with some non-voluntary defect there would be no moral evil there at all; limping, for example, isn't a moral fault but a natural one, and such a defect in the executive power totally or partially excuses us from moral fault. Again, the action of what is perceived on the perceptive power is free of moral fault, for what we see influences our sight in the natural order, and similarly with any object's action on a passive power. And even the act of the perceptive power as such, considered in itself, lacks moral fault, since defects there excuse or diminish moral fault just as in the executive power: weakness and ignorance equally excuse or diminish sin.

What remains then is that moral fault is first and foremost found only in acts of will, and that seems reasonable since actions are called moral only when they are voluntary. So the root and origin of moral faults must be sought in acts of will. Now a difficulty seems to attend such an enquiry. If action is deficient because of a defect in its active source a defect in the will must pre-exist the moral fault. If that is a natural defect it will always be there and the will will sin morally whenever it acts; but acts of virtue show that to be false. But if the defect is voluntary then its existence is already a moral fault, the cause of which must be sought in its turn. And that enquiry will go on for ever. So we are forced to say that the defect pre-existing in the will is not natural—lest the will sin in every act—nor fortuitous or chance—for that would not be a moral fault of ours since chance things are unpremeditated and outside reason. So the defect is a voluntary one and yet not itself a moral fault lest we be forced into an infinite regress. So how this can be must now be considered.

Now perfection in power of any active principle at all depends on some higher agent: for secondary agents act through the power of primary agents. Now as long as a secondary agent remains ordered to the primary agent it can act without deficiency; but it will act defectively if it is turned aside from its orderedness to the primary agent, as we see when tools fail to respond to their user's movements. Now we have said that in the orderedness of a moral action two causes precede will, namely, our perceptive power and what it perceives as a goal. But since the ability of one thing to be moved corresponds to the ability of another thing to move it, not any perceptive power moves any appetite, but this this and that that: the due mover of our sensual appetite is our power of sense-perception, and the due mover of will is reason. Again, since reason can perceive many goods and goals, whereas everything has its own due goal, there will be a goal and first mover of the will which will not be any good but a certain determinate one. When then will tends to action moved by a reasoned perception representing to it its due good, right action will result. But when will breaks out in action under the stimulation of sense-perception, or of reason itself but presenting the will with some other good than its due good, morally faulty action will ensue. What precedes the faulty action in the will is thus a defect of orderedness to reason and a due goal: to reason, when some sudden sense-perception draws will towards a good pleasurable to the senses; to a due goal, when reason decides by reasoning on a good which isn't good at this moment or in that way, and yet will is drawn to it as to its due good. Now this defect of orderedness is voluntary, for will has in itself the power to will or not to will, and also the power to make reason actually consider or stop considering, or to consider this rather than that. But the defect is not a moral fault, for reason can consider this good or that good or nothing at all without any fault until the moment comes when the will tends towards the undue goal; and then we already have an act of will.

Both in nature and in moral matters then evil is clearly caused by good only incidentally.

Passage 32

Providence (*d*): Does God Cause Evil?

Source: Thomas's public disputations on Evil, 3.1–2. Text from *Quaestiones Disputatae de Malo* (*Opera Omnia*, Leonine edn., vol. xxiii).

Date: 1270–2, second stay in Paris, aged 46.

Type of passage and how to read: Disputed question (see Introduction).

Notes on translation: 'Sin' translates *peccatum*, which often has the broader notion of 'fault' or 'failure', moral or non-moral, as Thomas points out in this passage. See previous passage, notes on translation.

[**Question 3**] The subject for debate is **What causes sins.**

[**Article 1**] And in the first place we are asked: **Does God cause sins?**

And it seems he does:

For [1] St Paul says in Romans 1 [28]: *God has given them up to their own foul desires and filthy practices*, and the gloss—taken from Augustine[1]—comments: *Clearly God is at work in human hearts bending their wills to whatever he wants, good or evil.* But the bending of will towards evil is sin. So God causes sins . . .

Moreover, [3] guilty acts run counter to the goodness of God's grace, and punishments to the goodness of nature. But God punishes despite being nature's source, so he can cause guilty acts despite being the source of grace.

Moreover, [4] what causes a cause causes its effect. So since God causes our free choice and that causes sin, God causes sins.

Moreover, [5] whatever powers tend towards God causes. But some God-given powers tend towards sin: our aggressive capacity to murder, our affective capacity to adultery. So God causes sins . . .

Moreover, [7] pseudo-Dionysius[2] says the causes of evil lie in God. But they can't be there in vain. So God must cause evils: sins among them.

Moreover, [8] Augustine[3] says grace in the soul is like a light by which we work good and without which we can't work any good. In this way grace causes good works, and so, conversely, taking away grace causes sins. But it is God who takes away grace. So God causes sins.

Moreover, [9] Augustine[4] says: *That there are evils which I have not done, I ascribed to your grace.* But that someone doesn't do evil wouldn't be ascribed to grace if he could avoid sin without grace. So it is not sin that deprives us of grace, but rather being deprived of grace that causes us to sin. And so we conclude, as before, that God causes sins.

Moreover, [10] whatever we praise in creatures must be attributed most of all to God. But Ecclesiasticus 31 [10] praises just men for *being able to sin and not sinning*. Much more then must this be true of God. So God can sin, and in consequence cause sins . . .

Moreover, [17] whoever commands sin causes sins. But we find God commanding sin in 3 Kings 22 [22], for example, when, after the lying spirit had said *I will go out and be a lying spirit in the prophets' mouths*, God said: *Go and do it*; and in Hosea 1 where God orders Hosea to take a whore and have children by her. So God causes sins . . .

But against that:

[1] Augustine[5] says God is never responsible for men getting worse. But sin makes men worse. So God is never responsible for sin.

Moreover, [2] Fulgentius[6] says that God is not responsible for what he avenges. But God avenges sin. So he is not responsible for it.

Moreover, [3] God only causes what he loves, since Wisdom 11 [2] says *You love everything that exists and hate nothing you have made*. But he hates sin, as Wisdom 14 [9] says: *God hates equally the impious and their impiety*. So God is not responsible for sin.

In reply:

People cause sins in two ways: by sinning themselves and by causing others to sin, and neither way can apply to God.

That God can't sin is clear whether we understand sin broadly to mean fault or narrowly to mean moral fault. [In Latin usage] sin is broadly used to mean any failure of activity, natural or designed, to reach its goal. Such failure results from a defect in a thing's ability to act: in the grammatical skill of someone who makes a mistake in writing (given that he intended to write correctly), in the semen's ability to transmit the genes when malformation of offspring occurs in nature. But the meaning of sin proper to morals is of culpable failure of will to reach a due goal because it is drawn towards an unsuitable one. Now in God neither his power to act can fail—since his power is unlimited—nor his will fail to reach its due goal—since his will, identical with his nature, is itself the supreme good, ultimate goal, and first standard for every will. So his will by nature cleaves to supreme good, and can no more fail to reach it than the desire natural to any other thing can fail to desire its own natural good. So God can't cause sin by sinning himself.

But neither can he cause others to sin. For sin as we are now talking of it consists in a created will turning away from its ultimate goal. Now it is impossible for God to make a will turn away from its ultimate goal since he is that goal. For what all created agents share must derive from a reflection in them of the first agent, who makes everything as like himself as they are capable of being, as pseudo-Dionysius[7] says. But every created agent acts in such a way as to attract other things to itself in some fashion and shape them to its own likeness, either by natural likeness (as when heat heats) or by turning towards its own goal (as when a man commands others to pursue the goal he has in mind). So it must be fitting for God too to turn everything to himself, turning nothing away. But he is the supreme good. So it cannot be he who causes will to turn away from the supreme good, which is what makes a culpable fault of the kind we are now talking about.

God then cannot cause sin.

Hence:

to 1: God is said to give people up to foul desires or to bend their wills to evil not by acting on them and moving them, but by deserting them and not interfering, in the way someone who doesn't put out his hand to help a falling man might be said to cause the fall. But God's judgement that he will not help some who fall is just . . .

to 3: Punishment runs counter to some particular good, and to take away a particular good may not run counter to the highest good, since its place may be taken by another maybe better good. Thus though water may go, fire takes its place, and in the same way though punishment takes away what is good for some particular nature, a better good—God's just ordering of things—takes its place. The evil of a guilty act on the other hand runs counter to the highest good, and from that the highest good cannot turn away. God then can punish but not cause guilty acts.

to 4: What an effect does precisely as effect can be traced back to the cause, but whatever else effects do can't. Movement of a leg can be traced back to the animal's power to move it, but a limp in the walk isn't due to the animal's power but to the leg's own inability to respond to the animal's movement. And our free choice causes sin by a lack of response to God. God then causes the free choice but not the sin.

to 5: Sins aren't caused by our aggressive or affective tendencies as God set them up in us, but by disorders in those tendencies. He set them up to obey reason, and any tendency to sin, against reason, is not from God...

to 7: The causes of evil are particular goods which can fall short in some way. As good such particular goods lie in God in the way all effects lie in their causes. And in this sense the causes of evil lie in God, but not in the sense that he himself causes their evil.

to 8: God on his side gives to everything as much of himself as it can take in; and if something falls short of its share in God's goodness, that must be because it presents some obstacle to the sharing. If grace then is not present in someone, the cause is not God but some obstacle to grace presented by the recipient, who turns away from a light that never turns itself away, as pseudo-Dionysius[8] says.

to 9: We must say different things about the state of human nature when created and its state after Adam's fall. When created nothing pulled human beings towards evil, though their natural goodness was not enough to win them heaven; so they needed the help of grace to deserve heaven but not to avoid sin: what they had been given in their nature was enough for them to be able to hold their ground. But after Adam's fall they were pulled towards evil and needed grace's help to avoid falls, and it is in this state that Augustine ascribes to grace that there were evils he didn't do; but this state is caused by a previous sin.

to 10: Lesser things can be praised for something that would be out of place in greater ones: pseudo-Dionysius[9] says we praise dogs for savagery but not humans. In the same way not sinning when they could is praise that suits humans, but falls short of the praise due to God . . .

to 17: God saying *Go and do it* mustn't be understood as commanding but permitting, like Jesus saying to Judas in John 13 [27] *What you are to do, do quickly*, in the sense in which we talk of God's will permitting things. But God telling Hosea to take himself a whore is a command, and as a divine command it makes what would otherwise have been a sin not a sin. For as Bernard[10] says, God can dispense the second tablet of commandments which deal with man's relations with his neighbour, since the good of the neighbour is a particular good, but he can't dispense the first tablet of commandments which deal with man's relationship to God . . .

[Article 2] And in the second place we are asked: **Does God cause sinful actions?**

And it seems he doesn't:

[1] For we are said to sin only because of the sinful actions we cause: as pseudo-Dionysius[11] says, nobody ever does evil intentionally. But God is not responsible for sins, as was said above. So God doesn't cause sinful actions.

Moreover, [2] a thing's cause is the cause of everything that belongs to it by definition: to cause Socrates is to cause a human being. Now there are certain actions that are sins by definition. If then God caused the sinful action he would be responsible for the sin . . .

Moreover, [4] sinful action is freely chosen action, called free because self-moved. But actions caused by someone else are moved by another, not self-moved and not free. So sinful actions are not caused by God.

But against that:

[1] Augustine[12] says God's will is the cause of every nature and every movement. But a sinful action is a certain freely chosen movement. So it comes from God.

In reply:

There were two opinions about this in the old days. The earliest opinion was that sinful actions were not caused by God, since God didn't cause the evilness as such of the sins. But others said sinful actions were caused by God, since the actual being of any action must come from God, and that for two reasons. Firstly, for the general reason that since it is God's very nature to exist he exists of his substance, and that means he must be the source of everything else's existence. For nothing else is its own existence: everything else is said to exist by sharing, and what shares derives what it shares from something that has it of its substance: just as everything on fire is derived from what is fire in its substance. Clearly then, since a sinful action exists in some sense and belongs in one of the categories of being, it comes from God. Secondly, this is also true for a special reason. All movements of secondary causes must be caused by a primary cause, in the way all movements here below are caused by the movement of the heavens. Now in the way the heavens are the first cause of all bodily movement, so God is the first source of all movement whatever, bodily and spiritual. Since then sinful actions are certain freely chosen movements, we have to say that sinful actions, as actions, come from God.

Note, nevertheless, that the movements of the first mover are not received into everything moved by them in exactly the same way, but in ways appropriate to each. The heavens move inanimate objects, which don't move themselves, in one way, and animals, which do move themselves, in another. And under the influence of the heavens plants that are genetically perfect grow perfect seed, whilst those genetically imperfect produce seed that is sterile. When a recipient is rightly disposed to receive the first mover's movement it will produce activity perfectly in accordance with the first mover's intentions, but when it is not rightly disposed and ready to receive that movement it will produce imperfect activity, which as activity can be traced back to the first mover, but as flawed cannot be so traced back. For the flaw in the action results from the agent precisely as not rightly ordered to its first mover, as we have said: just as movement of a limping animal comes from its motive powers, but the flawedness of movement comes not from the motive powers but from the leg's inability to profit from those motive powers. What we must say then is that God is the first source of all movements, and that some things are so moved by him that they also move themselves, having free choice. If such things are rightly disposed and ordered in the way needed to receive God's movements there will result good actions that can be totally traced back to God's causality; but if they are not properly ordered then there will result a disordered or sinful action, in which what there is of action can be traced back to God's causality but what there is of disorder and deformity does not have God as cause but our free choice.

For this reason then we say that God is responsible for sinful actions but not for sins.

Hence:

to 1: Although sinners don't will the evilness of their sin as such it is still included in some fashion in what they will, since they rather choose to incur that evilness than stop acting. But sin's evilness isn't in any way included in God's will, but is a consequence of our free choice abandoning its relationship to God's will.

to 2: The evilness of sin doesn't belong to actions as defined in nature (which is how God causes them) but as defined morally (which is how free choice causes them); and this we said in an earlier question...

to 4: In self-movement what is moved also does the moving; in movement by another what does the moving is different. Now clearly when something is moved by another, that other, just because it is doing the moving, is not necessarily the first source of the whole movement: it could be that it in turn is being moved by another, and does its moving precisely as moved by that other. In the same way then, when something is self-moved, it can still be being moved by another and doing its moving precisely as moved by that other. And in that way God being the cause of our freely chosen actions isn't incompatible with their freedom.

Passage 33

Is God at Work in Nature and in Will?

Source: Thomas's public disputations on the Power of God, 3.7–8. Text from *Quaestiones Disputatae de Potentia* (Marietti edn., Turin, 1953), with corrections from the Leonine text in preparation.

Date: 1265–7, Italy, aged 40.

Type of passage and how to read: Disputed question (see Introduction).

Parallel reading: The reader should compare the first four proofs of God's existence in Passage 20 with the four ways in which God is active in nature in this passage: Proof 1 with Way 3, 2 with Way 4, 3 with Way 2, 4 with Way 1.

[Question 3] The subject for debate is **Creation—the first effect of God's power.**

... [**Article 7**] And in the seventh place we are asked: **Is God at work within every activity of nature?**

And it seems not:

For [1] nature is provided with what it needs, neither more nor less. Now nature's activities need only agent powers to act and recipients to be acted on. So they don't need God's power working within things...

Moreover, [3] if God does act in every activity of nature, then God and nature exercise either one and the same activity or distinct activities. Now not one and the same, for single activities derive from single natures—Christ with two natures exercises two activities—and God is clearly not of one nature with creatures. But not distinct activities either, for distinct activities can't yield the same end-product, since what differentiates movements and activities is their destination. So there is no way God can act in nature...

Moreover, [7] if God acts in natural activity his action must contribute something to natural things, for in doing a doer must do something. Now either the contribution is enough to enable the thing to act by itself, or not. If it's enough, then why, by the same token, isn't the natural power God has already given nature enough for action? Why once that was given did activity need anything further from God? But if it's not enough, then God will have to contribute something else, and if that's not enough something else, and so on endlessly. And impossibly, for a single effect can't depend on an infinite number of actions, which could never get finished since *you can't bridge the infinite*. So rather than start on this path let us admit that natural powers are enough for natural activity, and don't need God acting further within them . . .

Moreover, [9] things of an utterly different sort can be separated one from another. Now God's activity and nature's are of an utterly different sort, the first willed and the second necessitated. So God's activity can be separated from nature's, and God needn't be active in the activities of nature . . .

Moreover, [12] Ecclesiasticus 11 [14] says *God made man and left him in the hands of his own counsel*. But if he is always active within our wills he hasn't left us. So he isn't active within willed activity.

Moreover, [13] the will is mistress of its own acts. Now that wouldn't be so if it could only act when God acted in it; for the will is not mistress of God's activity. So God isn't active in our willed activities . . .

Moreover, [16] given action by a sufficient cause, we don't need to postulate action from any other cause. But unquestionably, if God is active in will and nature, his activity is a sufficient one: *The works of God are perfect* according to Deuteronomy 32 [4]. So no activity of will or nature would then be necessary, and since nature contains nothing unnecessary in nature, neither nature nor will would do anything, but only God. But this can't be right, so neither can the premiss that God is active in will and nature.

But against that:

[1] Isaiah 26 [12] says *Lord, you work in us every work we do*.

Moreover, [2] nature presupposes God, just as craft presupposes nature. But nature acts in a craftsman's handiwork, for without nature's activity the craftsman couldn't himself act: unless iron was softened by fire the smith couldn't hammer it out. So God too acts in natural activity.

Moreover, [3] Aristotle[1] says that *human reproduces human with co-operation from the sun.* Now just as the human activity of reproduction requires the sun's action, so too, and much more, does nature's activity require God's. So whatever nature does God does also.

Moreover, [4] nothing can act unless it exists. But nature can't exist without God's activity: it would fall away to nothing unless God's power maintained it in existence, as Augustine[2] makes clear. So nature can't act without God's activity.

Moreover, [5] God's power exists in every natural thing, for *God exists in everything by substance, power, and presence.* But we can't say God's power exists in things for no reason. So it must do something in nature. Nor can we say that what it does is different from what nature does, since we see only the one activity. So God acts in every natural activity.

In reply:

We must unequivocally concede that God is at work in all activity, whether of nature or of will. But some misunderstand this, mistakenly attributing every natural activity to God in such a way that things in nature do nothing at all by their own power; a position espoused for various reasons.

Thus, according to Moses Maimonides,[3] some sages in Moorish Law said all natural forms were incidental properties, and thought that because such properties can't move across from one subject to another there was no way anything in nature could use its own form to introduce like forms into other subjects: so it is not fire that heats, they said, but God who creates heat in the thing heated. And to the objection that the heating always occurs when fire is being applied to the thing to be heated—except when external factors thwart the fire—which shows that of itself fire heats, they used to reply that God has ordained things to take that course, so that he never causes heat except in the presence of fire, though the fire present contributes nothing to the heat. Now this position clearly conflicts with our senses: our senses sense only when affected by what they sense (this is clearly true of touch and the other senses, even if sight seems doubtful to those who say it works by emitting something), so we would not feel fire's heat unless fire acted to reproduce a likeness of its heat in our sense-organs. If that specific likeness of heat was something else's doing, touch would feel heat but not the fire's heat: it would not feel the fire to be hot though that is its judgement, and senses do not make mistakes in judgement about their own defining sense-object. The position also conflicts with reason, which tells us nothing in nature is without a function. But unless things in nature actually did something, the powers and forces they have in them by nature would be without function: if it is not the knife that cuts, of what use is its sharpness? And of what use is the fire's presence under the wood if God is burning the wood without it? The position also conflicts with God's goodness, which in sharing itself out causes things not only to resemble him in existing but also to resemble him in being active. In fact, the reason adduced for this position is altogether trivial. For when we say an incidental property can't move across from one subject to another we mean numerically the same property can't, not that a property in one natural thing can't cause a property of the same kind to be introduced into some other subject: something which must happen in every activity of nature. Moreover, the supposition that all forms are incidental properties is itself false: for then there would be no substances in nature (which are constituted by substantial, not just incidental, forms), and thus no birth, no death, and many suchlike inconveniences.

Another position is taken up by Ibn Gebirol:[4] namely, that it is not bodies that act, but a spiritual force spread through all bodies acts within them, and bodies are more active the purer and subtler they are, the more able to be penetrated by this spiritual force. He relies on three arguments: firstly, that all agents after God require some subject-matter to act on, but that there is no subject-matter outside body on which it could act; secondly, that quantitative bulk hinders activity and movement (increase in bulk slows movement and makes bodies heavier), so that body (which is by definition bulky) can't act; and thirdly, that body is furthest distant from the primary agent of all that acts but is never acted on, that in between must come agents that act and are acted on, and body—the last in line—must be acted on but never act. But the fallacy here is obvious: body is being regarded as numerically one and the same substance, as though it was merely accidentally various and not made up of distinct substances. As soon as you accept a variety of substantially distinct bodies, then not every body is the last in line or the most distant from the primary agent, but some are above others and nearer the primary agent and so can act on others. Again, what he says pays attention only to the matter of body and not its forms, though it is composite of both. It is because of their matter that bodies come last in line and have no further subject-matter to act on, but in regard to their form every other body in which matter can potentially take on the form this body already actually has is further subject-matter for it, and so bodies can engage in mutual activity, the matter of one potential of the form of another, and vice versa. And if the form isn't enough for activity, neither, for the same reason, would this spiritual force be, since of necessity it would be taken in by bodies in a bodily mode. Again, quantitative bulk doesn't stop things acting or moving, for Aristotle[5] proves that without quantity nothing can move. Nor is it quantitative bulk that makes things heavy—Aristotle[6] disproved that. Quantity makes natural movements faster: the bigger a heavy body the faster it falls, and the bigger a light one the faster it rises. Though quantity is not itself a source of activity it acts as a tool of the qualities that make things active; there is nothing in quantity to hinder their activity, except in so far as the embedding of those qualities in matter of a certain quantity restricts their existence to that particular matter and prevents them being active in other matter. However, though they exist particularized in matter they still possess their specific character, the like of which they can reproduce, even if they numerically cannot exist in another subject.

So one must not understand the statement that God is at work in everything in nature as if that meant the thing itself did nothing; rather it means that God is at work in the very activity of nature and free will. And how that can be we will now explain. Note that there are several ways in which one thing can be said to cause another's activity. **Firstly**, by providing it with its power to act. Thus Aristotle[7] says that the parent producer of something heavy or light produces movement in it by producing its power to move. And God does everything that nature does in this sense since he gives all things in nature the powers to act. And he does this not merely as the parent of something heavy or light gives it a power and then maintains it no further, but as a continual maintainer of those natural powers in existence. For he is the cause not only of the occurrence of those powers, as the parent is, but of their existence. So God can be said to cause activity not only by causing a thing's power but by maintaining it in existence, and this is a **second** way in which things are said to cause activity in others, by maintaining their active power: like medicine that maintains one's sight is said to cause one to see. But because nothing can act or initiate movement of itself unless it can act without being acted on, there is a **third** way in which one thing can be said to cause another's activity: by moving it to act. Here we are not thinking of either the production of power or its maintenance, but of its application to activity, in the way a human being causes a knife to cut by applying its sharpness, moving it to actual cutting. And because lower agents in nature act only when moved, causing alteration only by being altered, and because the heavens, which can cause alteration without being altered, can't move without being moved, and because this chain only ends when we reach God, it must follow that God causes every activity of things in nature by initiating it, applying the thing's power to act to its activity.

But we find, further, that just as causes are ordered so are effects: necessarily, since effects resemble their causes and secondary causes can't of their own power produce the effect of the primary cause, although they can act as tools of the primary cause in producing that effect. For tools do in some sense cause the effect the principal cause is producing, though not by their own form or power; they do it by being moved by the principal cause and sharing in the principal cause's power that way, as the adze doesn't cause the carpentry by its own form or power but by the carpenter's power moving it, which in a way it shares. So a fourth way in which one thing causes another's activity is the way a principal agent causes a tool's activity. And in this way too we must say that God causes the activity of things in nature. For the higher a cause is [in an order of causes] the more extensively effective it is, and the more effective it is the deeper it acts within the effect bringing remoter potentialities to realization. Now everything in nature exists, and is a thing of nature, and a thing of this or that nature: the first being common to everything there is, the second to everything in nature, the third to everything of one species, and a fourth—adding in incidental properties—peculiar to a particular individual. This individual then when acting cannot produce another individual of the same species unless it acts as a tool of what causes that species as a whole, and beyond that of what causes the existence of all lower nature. For this reason nothing can cause species here below unless by the power of the heavenly bodies, and nothing can cause existence unless by the power of God. For existence itself is the most shared effect and the primary one deepest within all other effects. That effect only God can produce of his own power; as the book of Causes[8] says, not even [the heavenly] intelligences can give existence unless God's power is in them. So God causes every activity inasmuch as every agent is the tool of God's active power. And in this way then, as regards the acting subjects, each particular agent causes its effect without intermediary, but as regards the powers by which they act, the higher agent's power is more immediate to the effect than that of any lower cause, since the power of the lower cause is only present to its effect through the power of the higher cause. So the book of Causes[9] says that the first cause's power acts first in the effect and enters more vehemently into it. This presence of God's power within every acting thing is like the way the power of the heavenly bodies must be present in every acting elemental body. The difference is this: wherever God's power is God's very substance is, but the substance of heavenly bodies is not wherever their power is; and again God is his own power, but the heavenly body is not. So one can say that God is active within everything inasmuch as everything needs his power in order to act; but one can't say that the heavens [themselves][10] act within the elements even if the elements are active through the heavens' power.

God then causes everything's activity inasmuch as he gives the power to act, maintains it in existence, applies it to its activity, and inasmuch as it is by his power that every other power acts. And when we add to this that God is his own power and therefore exists within everything, not as a part of its being but as holding it in existence, it follows that he is at work without intermediary in everything that is active, but without excluding the activity of nature or of free will.

Hence:

to 1: Powers to act and be acted on are all that things in nature need for activity at their own level; nevertheless, they need God's power for the reasons already given . . .

to 3: Nature isn't at work in the activity by which God initiates nature's activity, but God's power is at work in nature's own activity in the way a principal agent's power is at work in the activity of a tool. Nor is there anything to stop God and nature producing the same effect, since God and nature are hierarchically related . . .

to 7: The natural powers given to things in nature when first instituted belong to them as forms existing stably and firmly in nature. What God contributes to a natural thing to make it actually active is only a something-in-transit, so to speak, existing incompletely, like colours do in the transmitting air or a carpenter's skill in the tool he uses. Such skill can contribute sharpness to a saw as a lasting form, but its own influence could only be contributed to the saw as a lasting form by giving the saw a mind of its own. In the same way a natural thing can be given its own power as a lasting form, but the influence of the primary cause under which the thing acts as a tool to bring things into existence could only be given it by making it the source of all existence. Nor can God make a natural power that applies itself, or maintains itself in existence. Just as you can't make a tool that acts without being moved by the carpenter's skill, so you can't have things in nature that act without God acting in them...

to 9: Though nature and will exist in utterly different ways they nevertheless act relatedly. For willed activity presupposes nature's activity—the willed activity of arts and crafts needs the activities of nature—and nature's activity presupposes God's will as source of all natural change, so that all natural activities need his activity...

to 12: God is not said to leave human beings in the hands of their own counsel as if that meant he didn't act in their wills; rather it means that he has given them a mastery over their actions whereby they aren't forced to one or other opposing course of action, a mastery he has not given to nature where a thing's form determines it to one course of action.

to 13: The will is said to be mistress of its own action, not as if a primary cause was excluded, but because the primary cause doesn't act in our wills as it does in nature, determining us to one course of action. That determination of the action is left in the power of reason and will...

to 16: God acts perfectly as primary cause, but needs nature's activity as secondary cause. God could of course produce the effects of nature without nature, but nevertheless wills them to be done through nature so that order be preserved in things.

[Article 8] And in the eighth place we are asked: **Is God at work in nature creating? Or, equivalently: Is creation intermingled in the workings of nature?**

And it seems so:

[1] Because of Augustine's[11] words: *The apostle Paul, distinguishing God creating and forming from within from*

the workings of nature applied from without, uses an agricultural simile: 'I planted, Apollo watered, but God produced the growth.'

But it was said [by the respondent] that *create* is here used broadly to mean any kind of producing.

But against that: [2] Augustine appeals to Paul's authority in order to distinguish God's activity from that of creatures. Now he can do that if creation is interpreted strictly but not if it is broadly interpreted to mean any sort of production, for in that sense nature also creates: it produces an effect, as we showed in the previous question. So Augustine must be talking of creation in a strict sense.

Moreover, [3] Augustine continues: *Just as in our own lives only God can set hearts to rights though even human beings can preach the gospel externally, so God works within the things we see, creating them, and then—in the way agriculture is applied to the soil—applies to that nature of things within which he creates everything the external work of good and bad angels and men and animals of all sorts.* Now God sets hearts to rights by an act of creation in the strict sense, for grace is said to be created. So natural forms must also be created by an act of creation in the strict sense.

But it was said [by the respondent] that natural forms differ from grace in having a cause in the subject that acquires them, so that to that extent grace can be said to be created in a strict sense whereas natural forms aren't.

But against that: [4] the gloss on Genesis 1 [1] says creation means making something from nothing. Now the preposition *from* sometimes indicates an agent cause (as in 1 Corinthians 8 [6]: *From whom and through whom all things*) and sometimes a material cause (as in Tobias 13 [21–2]: *all the surrounding walls were made from clean white stone*). Saying something is made from nothing denies a material cause but not an agent cause (for we don't deny God to be the agent cause of created things). Now natural forms may differ from grace in having their agent cause in the subject acquiring them, but they resemble grace in existing in some material. So that having a cause in their subject doesn't make creation any less applicable to them than to grace.

Moreover, [5] the forms of artefacts have no cause within their subjects but are wholly imposed from outside. So that if grace is to be called created because it has no cause in its subject then for the same reason the forms of artefacts must be created.

Moreover, [6] what doesn't contain matter can't come from matter. Now forms don't contain matter (for Aristotle[12] says they differ both from matter and from all composites [of matter and form]); yet they come into existence, newly starting to exist. So it seems that they don't come from matter but from nothing, and must therefore be created.

But it was said [by the respondent] that though there is no matter in natural forms from which they came, there is nevertheless a matter in which they exist, and because of that they are not created.

But against that: [7] human souls, like the forms of other things in nature, are forms existing in matter, and yet they are said to be created. So why can't one say the same of all other forms in nature?

But it was said [by the respondent] that the human soul is not a realized potentiality of matter like other natural forms.

But against that: [8] you can't bring out what isn't in. Now until reproduction is complete the form to be reproduced doesn't exist in the matter, for if it did opposing forms would be coexisting in the matter. So natural forms can't be brought out of matter.

Moreover, [9] the form to be reproduced appears only when reproduction is complete. So if it existed beforehand it existed hidden, and that implies Anaxagoras' thesis that everything lies hidden in everything, a thesis Aristotle[13] disproved.

But it was said [by the respondent] that until reproduction is complete the natural form exists in matter but incompletely, not completely as Anaxagoras held.

But against that: [10] if form exists in any way in matter before reproduction is complete, some part of it pre-exists there, and if it isn't there completely, some part of it doesn't pre-exist there. This would mean form has parts and is composite, which contradicts the first words of the *Six Principles*.[14]

Moreover, [11] if it doesn't completely pre-exist in the matter and must be completed later, the completion must come through reproduction. Now the completion didn't pre-exist in the matter, for then the form would have been there completely. So at least this completion will have been created.

But it was said [by the respondent] that it partially pre-existed in the matter not by some part of it being there, but because it was there in a different way before and after: first potentially and then actually.

But against that: [12] whatever changes its way of being is being modified not reproduced. If then all nature does is to make actual a form that is already there potentially, then there is no reproduction in nature but only modification.

Moreover, [13] the only sources of natural activity here below are incidental properties: fire, for example, acts through its property of heat, and so on. Now activity of properties can't cause substantial forms, since no agent can transcend its species: effects can't surpass their causes in the way substantial forms surpass incidental properties. Substantial forms then can't be the product of natural activity here below, and so must be created.

Moreover, [14] the imperfect can't cause the perfect. Now soul's power is present only imperfectly in animal semen; so the natural activity semen is capable of can't produce an animal's soul. That must be created, and so, by the same token, must all other natural forms.

Moreover, [15] what itself is inanimate and non-living can't cause an animate living thing. But rotting matter produces animals that are animate living things; and yet we can't find any natural living things giving them life. So their souls must come from the first living thing; and by the same token so must all other natural forms.

Moreover, [16] what nature does reflects what it is; but the nature of some generated living things doesn't reflect any generating nature: mules don't resemble in species horses or donkeys. So a mule's form can't come from natural activity but requires creation; which leads to the same conclusion as before.

Moreover, [17] Augustine[15] says that *things in nature would not have forms that formed them unless there was some first source of their forming*. But that is God himself. So all forms are created by God.

Moreover, [18] Boethius[16] says forms in matter derive from forms not in matter. In the context forms not in matter must mean ideas in God's mind, for angels—which might also be called forms not in matter—don't cause natural forms, as Augustine[17] says. So forms in nature don't come from the activity of nature but from the creator giver.

Moreover, [19] we read in the book of Causes[18] that existence is created. But for that to be true forms must be created, since it is forms which determine things to exist. Forms then are created. So God works in nature by creating something, namely, the forms.

Moreover, [20] things that don't exist of themselves are caused by things that do exist of themselves. Now the forms of natural things don't exist of themselves but only in matter; their cause then must be a form that stands by itself. So the forms of nature must be created by an external agent, and this it seems is God's work in nature: to create the forms.

But against that:

[1] We distinguish God's work of creation from his work of management and propagation. But natural activity is part of this work of management and propagation. So there is no creation involved in the workings of nature.

Moreover, [2] only God can create. If then forms are created, they must come straight from God, which means all activity of nature—the goal of which is form—is useless.

Moreover, [3] incidental forms, just like substantial forms, have no matter in them. So if that was a reason for saying substantial forms are created, it must also mean incidental forms are. Now just as things generated are completed by their substantial form, so they are disposed by accidental forms. So a thing in nature won't have any part in generation, whether completing it or disposing to it, and so all natural activity will be useless.

Moreover, [4] nature is procreated like from like: what is generated is like what generates it in species and form. So the very form of what is generated must be being produced by the act of generation, and not by creation.

Moreover, [5] the same effect doesn't come from different agents. But what is made from matter and form is one thing. So it can't be that one agent disposes the matter and another brings the form. Now what disposes the matter is natural agents. So they must bring the form. Thus forms are not created, and creation isn't intermingled in the work of nature.

In reply:

All the various answers given to this question seem to be based on one and the same principle: that nature can't make something from nothing. This principle led some people to believe things come into existence only by being drawn out of hidden pre-existence in some other thing: an opinion Aristotle[19] attributed to Anaxagoras. He seems to have been led astray by confusing potential with actual existence, believing anything nature produces must actually pre-exist. Now it must exist potentially (so that it doesn't come into existence from nothing), but it needn't actually pre-exist (that would stop it coming to exist, since what exists can't come to exist).

But because products exist potentially in their material and actually when that material acquires a form, some people hold that the material pre-exists and things come into existence only as to their forms. So, since nature can't produce from nothing but must presuppose something, these people believe nature's only work is to dispose material for a form, the form itself—which isn't presupposed and must come into existence—coming from an agent which presupposes nothing and produces from nothing: an agent beyond nature, called by Plato the form-giver, identified by Ibn Sīnā with the lowest intelligence among the separate substances, but said by several modern followers of theirs to be God. Now this doesn't seem right. Since things are such that what they do reflects what they are—an agent must actually be what the object of its activity potentially is—no natural parent would need to resemble its offspring in form of substance unless by its action it produced that offspring's substantial form. Moreover, because what the offspring is to acquire actually exists in the natural parent (and what things do reflects what they are) it seems wrong to look for another agent beyond and outside the parent.

So note that just as the former opinion arose from ignorance of what matter is, these opinions seem to arise from ignorance of what forms are. Forms don't exist in nature in the same sense as products of nature do: for these products exist in the strict sense, possessing an existence of their own in which they subsist, whereas forms don't subsist with an existence of their own, existing not in the strict sense but only in the sense that something exists because of them. Thus incidental properties exist only in the sense that they qualify or quantify substances, not in the sense that they make substances exist simply speaking as substantial forms do, so that incidental properties are better said to belong in existence than to exist, as Aristotle[20] says. Now things come into existence in the same sense in which they exist, since existence is where coming into existence ends up. So what comes into its own existence in the strict sense is the thing composed of matter and form; in the strict sense form is not what comes into existence but that by which or by acquiring which [the composed] thing comes into existence. So the principle that in nature nothing comes into existence from nothing doesn't stop us saying that nature produces substantial forms, for what comes into existence is not the form but the thing composed [of matter and form], and that doesn't come from nothing but from matter; and it comes indeed from matter potential of that composite because potential of that form, so that it is not strictly correct to say form comes into existence in the matter, but rather that it is brought out of matter's potentiality. Now from this very fact that it is not forms but things composed [of matter and form] that come into existence, Aristotle[21] shows that forms come from natural agents; for since what is made must reflect what makes it and what is made is a composite of matter and form, so too what makes it must be composite and not, as Plato said, a form existing by itself. Thus, just as what is made is composite but comes into existence by having its form realized in its matter, so its natural cause is composite—not a form by itself—though it acts through its form: and I mean through the form as it exists in this matter, in this flesh and these bones and other like parts.

Hence:

to 1: Augustine's words ascribe to God a work of creation within the workings of nature, because nature's powers were imprinted in matter when God first created it, not because something is created every time nature is at work.

to 2: Augustine uses the word *create* strictly; not, however, with reference to the effect of nature, but to the powers by which nature acts and which were imprinted in nature when God created it.

to 3: Grace is a form and not a subsistent entity, and so it's not strictly true to say that it itself exists or comes into existence; nor then is it created in the way subsistent substances are. However, the instilling of grace is akin to creation in having no cause in its subject, neither an agent cause, nor the sort of material natural forms have, in which they exist potentially and can be brought to realization by some natural agent's activity.

So now the answer **to 4** is obvious. When we say something is made from nothing we deny it any material cause. And when a form can't be brought to realization out of the natural potentiality of its material, that is akin to not having any matter.

to 5: Although no natural agency gives rise to the forms of artefacts, such forms don't transcend nature's level as grace does; indeed they exist at a lower level, since to exist in nature is a more excellent thing than to exist as an artefact.

to 6: If forms came to exist in the strict sense that self-subsistent things do, then, since they don't contain matter, they would have to be created.

to 7: Although human souls exist in matter they are not realizations of some potentiality of matter, for their mental activities show that by nature they transcend the whole realm of matter. Moreover, such forms are self-subsistent things able to go on existing when their bodies decompose.

to 8: Until reproduction is complete the form to be reproduced doesn't actually exist in the matter, but it does exist there potentially. And there's nothing wrong with one form existing actually and its opposite existing potentially.

And that makes obvious the answer **to 9**, for Anaxagoras believed forms did actually pre-exist in matter but in a hidden way.

to 10: Form pre-exists in matter imperfectly, not by one part being actually present and another absent, but by the whole pre-existing potentially and then the whole being brought to actuality.

And that makes obvious the answer **to 11**, for clearly form's existence in matter is not perfected by adding something else that wasn't potentially there in the matter.

to 12: Potential and actual existence are not the sort of incidentally different modes of being that make modification possible, but substantially different ways of existing, for substances too exist potentially or actually just as other categories of being do.

to 13: Incidental properties act as tools of substantial forms in the way Aristotle[22] says fire is a tool of our digestive powers, so there's nothing wrong with activity of properties resulting in a substantial form.

to 14: In semen too the semen's heat acts as a tool of the power of soul present in the semen (imperfectly present but deriving from a perfect presence in the parent) and also as a sort of tool of the power of the heavenly bodies. This is why we don't say semen does the reproducing, but animals with the co-operation of the sun.

to 15: The animals generated in rotting material are less perfect than other animals, so that in their generation the power of heavenly bodies acting on earthly matter is sufficient to do what in the generation of more perfect animals is done by a co-operation of that same heavenly power with the semen's power.

to 16: Although mules are not the same species as either horses or donkeys they are close family, and that family resemblance enables a sort of intermediate species to be generated from differing species.

to 17: Just as God's power is the first of agents and yet doesn't exclude the power of nature, so too God is the first pattern of things and yet doesn't exclude things deriving their form from other lower forms acting to produce forms similar to themselves.

And that makes clear the answer **to 18**, for Boethius understands forms in matter to derive from forms not in matter as from an ultimate, not an immediate, pattern.

to 19: Existence is said to be created in the sense that every secondary cause that gives existence has that power as a tool of the first creator cause, existence being the first of all effects which presupposes nothing else.

to 20: Natural forms in matter can't be derived from any form of the same species existing by itself, since natural forms all contain matter by definition, but they are derived from forms existing by themselves in the way we have said.

Part VI

God as the End of Things

Passage 34

God as Goal of Human Living

Source: Thomas's Commentary on book 4 of Peter Lombard's *Sentences*, Distinction 49.1. Text from Parma edn., vol. vii (1858) (reprinted in American edn., vol. vii.ii, New York, 1948).

Date: 1253–5, Paris, Thomas's first public theology lectures as bachelor, aged 28–9.

Type of passage and how to read: See the preliminary note to Passage 24 and the Introduction.

Notes on translation: 'Bliss' translates *beatitudo*, which Thomas on the whole reserves for the revealed happy state of heaven, whereas 'happiness' translates *felicitas*, which covers both heaven and Aristotle's *eudaimonia*. Note, however, that 'happiness' means a happy or blessed or flourishing state of being, rather than the feeling of happiness or joy (*delectatio*) which accompanies it.

[Book 4, Distinction 49] Five questions need debate:

bliss . . .

[Question 1] The first question divides into four:

Where should bliss be sought?
What is it?
Does everyone desire it? . . .

[Article 1] The first question **[Where should bliss be sought?]** we approach as follows:

[Query 1] It seems bliss should be sought in material goods.

For [1] Ibn Rushd[1] says *widely held views can't be altogether false*, and Aristotle[2] that *No word on many people's lips is wholly lost.* Now most human beings have as their goal bodily pleasures and material goods. So the goal of human life we call bliss consists in material goods. Bliss, then, should be sought in material goods.

Moreover, [2] the goal ultimately achieved is the one first intended and desired. Now human beings desire material before spiritual goods, since, as Gregory[3] says, *we are led to love of the unseen through our love of the material.* So material goods are our ultimate goal: bliss. Bliss then should be sought in material goods . . .

Moreover, [4] everyone agrees that bliss is the end of virtue. But virtues have material as well as spiritual ends: moderation, for example, preserves us from even bodily harm. So bliss isn't to be sought only in spiritual goods, but also in material ones.

Moreover, [5] Aristotle says[4] that *happiness and good fortune seem to belong together*. But fortunes consist in material goods. So happiness and bliss consist in material goods . . .

But against that:

[1] Everything to do with body human beings have in common with other animals, whereas bliss is peculiarly human. So bliss won't be found in bodily or material goods.

Moreover, [2] bliss is the supreme human good, and should be sought among whatever human goods rank highest. Now just as soul ranks higher than body, so what is good for the soul ranks higher than bodily goods. Bliss then should be sought in what is good for the soul . . .

Further, [Query 2] **It seems bliss is more a matter of will than of understanding.**

For [1] bliss is the supreme good. But good is the object that defines will, not understanding. So bliss consists in willing rather than in understanding.

Moreover, [2] according to Aristotle,[5] bliss needs delight; and its Greek name means enjoyment. Delight is, however, a matter of will or the affections. Bliss too then.

Moreover, [3] Aristotle[6] says that happiness or bliss consists in the exercise of our highest virtue. But the most excellent of all virtues, as St Paul makes clear in 1 Corinthians 13, is charity. So, since charity is a virtue of will, bliss should be sought there...

Moreover, [5] human bliss consists in perfect union with God, and will unites human beings to God more closely than understanding: thus Hugh of St Victor commenting on the words of pseudo-Dionysius[7] *Moving and sharp*, writes: *Love surpasses knowledge and is greater than understanding, for God is loved rather than understood, and love enters where knowledge is left outside.* So bliss consists in love rather than in knowledge, in willing rather than in understanding.

But against that:

[1] John 17 [3] says: *this is eternal life, to know you, the true God, and Jesus Christ whom you have sent.* But eternal life is bliss. So bliss consists in knowing...

Moreover, [3] Aristotle[8] says that ultimate human bliss consists in exercise of contemplative virtue. Now that's a matter of understanding. So bliss consists mainly in understanding...

Further, **[Query 3] It seems bliss consists in practical understanding rather than in contemplation.**

For [1], according to Aristotle,[9] the more general a good is the more godlike. But contemplation is to the good of the individual doing the contemplating, whereas practical understanding can be to the general good of many. Bliss then consists in practical understanding rather than in contemplation.

Moreover, [2] bliss is ultimate human perfection. But being able to cause other things is more perfect than being complete in oneself: as pseudo-Dionysius[10] says: *the most godlike thing of all is to become God's fellow worker in guiding others.* Now contemplation perfects human beings in themselves, but practical understanding causes perfection in others. Bliss then consists in practical understanding rather than in contemplation...

Moreover, [4] human bliss consists in what ranks highest in human life. But practical understanding ranks higher than contemplation, since it lays down laws for contemplation: government policy determines the place of the contemplative sciences in education. So bliss consists in practical understanding rather than in contemplation.

But against that:

[1] Bliss, being our ultimate goal, is sought for its own sake and not as a means to something else. Now practical knowledge is a means to a goal outside itself: getting things done, whereas we seek contemplation for its own sake. So bliss consists in contemplation rather than in practical understanding.

Moreover, [2] our bliss consists in unity with God. But we are united to God by contemplation, not by practical understanding. So bliss consists in contemplation rather than in practical understanding . . .

Further, **[Query 4] It seems we can attain to bliss in this life.**

For . . . [3] our present human life is more perfect than that of other animals. Yet the ultimate goal of other animals is contained within their present life. So our goal, bliss, must be contained within our present life.

Moreover, [4] by nature everything desires to attain its goal, and from that arises desire of the means to that goal, and especially of those means which are a *sine qua non* of its attainment. Now if bliss can't be attained in this life, death becomes a *sine qua non* of bliss. So man would by nature desire to die, which is disproved by experience and by St Paul's authority in 2 Corinthians 5 [4]: *I do not wish to put off this body but to be further clothed*. Human bliss then can be attained in this life.

But against that:

[1] Nobody can be blissful if he lacks what he rightfully desires. But the blissful have a right and balanced desire not to be able to lose their bliss; so without that there is no true bliss. Now no one can have that in this life, for, however

blissful this life, it ends at death. So bliss can't be had in this life.

Moreover, [2] no one has attained his ultimate end if something remains to be desired, for bliss, Aristotle says, must be satisfying in itself. Now, however perfect in knowledge or virtue or anything else a person is in this life, there always remains something to be desired: many things he doesn't know, for example. Indeed the goodness of the perfection itself remains uncertain during this life, since even the wisest and most perfect men can lose their minds because of bodily infirmity. So bliss can't be had in this life . . .

In reply to Query 1 [Should bliss be sought in material goods?]:

Bliss, since everyone desires it by nature, names the ultimate goal of human life. Now a thing's goal is either something it characteristically does, or something it attains by what it does. What things do is determined by their form, and in our case the form which makes us human is mind; so bliss consists either in something mind does or in something mind's activity relates us to. Such things we call spiritual goods, and even philosophers hold bliss must consist in spiritual goods. Those who thought it consisted in material goods did so because they were ignorant of their own natures and judged themselves not by what was best in themselves and defined them most fully, but by external appearances; and so sought bliss in external goods.

Hence:

to 1: Widely held views needn't be absolutely true, only true in part. The many people who identify bliss with material goods are correct to this extent: that they identify bliss as they see it with what is best for them as they see it. But though the part of their opinion identifying bliss with what is best for human beings is right, the part identifying it with material goods doesn't have to be right, for that part is rooted in a false assessment of themselves as first and foremost bodies.

to 2: Material goods happen to be desired before spiritual ones because, as Aristotle[11] explains, we know generalities before details; so we start knowing our human goal only in general as something very good, and we desire it in the way we know it. Consequently, we think it to be one of those goods we are first aware of, and since these are the goods we can sense, we start by thinking them the greatest goods. But in the end, when we know perfectly and distinctly, we discriminate our human goal from other goods; and then we desire the highest good as it really is, that is, as a spiritual good. The argument, however, talks as if material goods were desired before spiritual ones in themselves . . .

to 4: We must distinguish the end of an activity from the intended end. Material good can be an end of virtue in the sense of an end-result of virtuous activity, but it is not what virtue's intention comes to rest in; for virtue perfects soul, which is superior to body, and since nothing acts for the sake of something inferior to itself virtue's intention won't rest content with material goods.

to 5: Where happiness and good fortune belong has two meanings. If we mean who enjoys them, then happiness and fortune belong together because only rational creatures can enjoy either. If we mean where are they to be found, then happiness and fortune can't belong together, for fortune is something unintended that happens on the way to a goal, whilst happiness or bliss is intended by everybody and is never on the way to anything else. So though material goods can be called a fortune in this latter sense, it won't follow that they constitute happiness . . .

In reply to Query 2 [Is bliss a matter of will rather than of understanding?]:

A matter of will may mean an object of will, and because bliss is our ultimate goal and goals define goods and goods are what we will, in this sense bliss is certainly a matter of will. But it may also mean an activity of willing, and in this sense bliss is not a matter of will. For by bliss we mean our ultimate human goal, and that can be understood as either internal to us or external: the internal goal of anything being its characteristic activity (since things exist in order to act), and its external goal what is attained by that activity. Now we don't call every activity a goal but only that which first unites a thing to its external goal. And I am talking of the situation in which a thing has an external goal, for then the internal goal serves the external goal: the external goal acts as ultimate goal to which the thing's activity—its internal goal—is ordered. We see this in nature where things by their activity attain their external goal, God's goodness, by imitating it so to speak. Now no one's activity of willing can be their ultimate goal in this way, for willing is willing of a goal: willing as such (like any other act of will) orders things to a goal, and therefore presupposes a goal other than itself; so that though we may will willing itself that must presuppose some previous object of willing. For we can't understand a power turning back on its own activity unless the activity on which it turns back is first completed by an object of its own, different from such activity: otherwise we will go on for ever. Thus, if understanding understands itself understanding, it must understand itself understanding something; and if you say it understands itself understanding this—itself understanding—then we again need some other object, and so on *ad infinitum*. Clearly then understanding can't be what understanding first understands, and in the same way willing can't be what will first wills. And since what will first wills is its ultimate goal, no activity of willing can be will's ultimate goal.

Nor can we say we attain our external goal by the immediate means of an act of willing it; for before attainment of the goal our act of willing is seen as moving us to the goal, and after attainment as a sort of resting in the goal. But a will that has been tending towards a goal can't suddenly start resting in it unless it and the goal are now related differently, and whatever it is that changed will's relationship to the goal so that it now rests in it is the ultimate internal goal which first unites us to our external goal: if, for example, our external goal was money, then our internal goal would be possession of that money, which would relate us to the money in such a way that our will rests in it. Since then the ultimate goal external (in some sense) to human willing is

God, the ultimate internal goal can't be any act of willing, but whatever act first relates us to God in such a way that our will is at rest in him. Now this is the act of seeing God with our understanding, which brings God and our understanding into contact so to speak, since everything we know exists as known in us; in the same way bodily contact brings us a bodily delight in which our affections rest. So our ultimate human goal is an act of intellect, and bliss—our ultimate goal—consists in understanding. Nevertheless, the will's part in this—the resting in the goal which we call delight—is a sort of formal completion of the notion of bliss, supervening on the seeing of God that constitutes its substance. So that we ascribe to will our first relationship to the goal, that of desiring to attain it, and our last, that of resting in it when already attained.

Hence:

to 1: This argument proves bliss is an object of will but not that it is an act of will.

to 2: Bliss needs delight as a sort of formal completion. For *delight completes activity as a sort of end supervening on it in the way beauty supervenes on youth as its adorning grace.*[12]

to 3: Charity is said to be a higher virtue than any other in this life precisely because it directs everyone to God, and in heaven it will enjoy ultimate rest in God. But that doesn't make its activity the very substance of bliss, but either, as in this life, an attraction towards it, or, as in the next, a resting in it...

to 5: The affections unite us to God more perfectly than understanding, inasmuch as affective unity supervenes as an adorning perfection on the perfect unity understanding has achieved; but the first unity is always that of understanding. For love inclines us to desire perfect unity before understanding perfectly achieves it (but not before understanding achieves some knowledge, since one can't desire what one doesn't know at all). And that is why Hugh says that *love enters where knowledge is left outside.*

In reply to Query 3 [Does bliss consist in practical understanding rather than in contemplation?]:

We have already explained that human bliss consists in that intellectual activity which first unites us to our ultimate external goal by giving us knowledge of it. But practical understanding can't give us knowledge of our ultimate external goal; for practical knowledge is related to what it knows as a cause to its effects, and a cause's effects can't be its ultimate goal since it is not causes which depend on effects for perfection but rather the reverse. So bliss can't consist in the activity of practical understanding but only in the activity of contemplation: and that is why practical knowledge is desired always for the sake of something else, whereas contemplation is desired more for its own sake.

Hence:

to 1: The good to which contemplative knowledge unites us is more abstracted from the individual and therefore more general than that to which practical understanding unites us, for practical knowledge reaches completion in activity and that is always individual. It is true that attainment of the goal of contemplation as such is restricted to the attainer, whereas attainment of the goal practical understanding aims at can be both individual and general; for the practical understanding of someone like a ruler can direct both himself and others to a goal, whereas someone's contemplation directs only himself to the goal of contemplation. But so superior is that goal of contemplation to the good of practical understanding that its individual achievement outweighs common achievement of the good of practical understanding. So the most perfect bliss consists in contemplation.

to 2: Having perfection that also overflows into others is more perfect than just having it oneself; and that's the only way the comparison made in the argument can be understood, since causing perfection without being perfect oneself isn't possible. Now sometimes it happens that a thing is more perfect in itself than it is as a cause, because the perfection it communicates is not the same or not as great as the perfection it possesses; thus God has greater perfection in himself than he communicates to others. So we say that the perfection contemplation gives to the contemplator himself is greater than that of a smith making a knife, but that someone who by contemplation made others into equal contemplators with himself would be more perfect than someone who contemplated alone . . .

to 4: Contemplation, simply speaking, ranks higher than practical knowledge, since we seek it for its own sake whereas practical knowledge is sought for the sake of getting something done. Nor does practical understanding lay down laws for contemplation, since contemplation doesn't judge truth by any criteria provided by practical understanding; rather practical understanding by deciding how someone should attain contemplative perfection legislates on behalf of contemplation, as Aristotle[13] says, and that itself shows practical understanding to be at the service of contemplation.

In reply to Query 4 [Can we attain to bliss in this life?]:

In willing desire of the goal and the means to it is related to the goal's achievement as movement is to destination in nature; and just as a thing stops moving when it arrives at its destination, so will's desire subsides when it attains what it was seeking, and turns into love or enjoyment. Bliss then, as the goal of all desire, must be something which when possessed leaves nothing to desire, and since everyone desires to exist and to hold on to good possessed it is generally agreed that bliss must persist without fluctuation. But not everyone has agreed about what that actually means. Some have said bliss doesn't have to persist for ever but only as long as human life lasts, and that though it mustn't actually fluctuate the possibility of fluctuation will always be there; and according to Aristotle[14] this was Plato's opinion. For Plato thought a human being blissful in this life if his bliss lasted till he died, though, because human beings, however perfect, suffer vicissitudes in this life, and cannot know with certainty what the future holds, whether any particular human being's perfection will last till death can't be known until he has actually died. Consequently, no one can be called blissful till he is dead. This view Aristotle rejected, since it doesn't seem right to say that someone can be called blissful only when he doesn't exist and can't when he does. For if bliss belongs in this life, being blissful is being blissful while alive and not when dead, and human beings should rather be called blissful when alive than when dead.

So Aristotle goes on to give his opinion about bliss or happiness: namely, that bliss to be perfect must last for ever without changing, but that human beings can't achieve perfect bliss. They can imitate it a little and to that extent be called blissful, so that human bliss does not have to last for ever without fluctuation in the ordinary sense, but only in so far as the human condition permits: and that is what he calls being *humanly blissful.* And this is the lack of fluctuation that attaches to a human being because firmly established virtuous dispositions won't allow him to be easily turned away from the practice of virtue. But this view also seems unreasonable. For all agree that happiness or bliss is a good of rational or intellectual natures and so wherever such natures truly exist, not by imitation, we should find true bliss and not just an imitation of it. Now human beings don't simply echo understanding (in the way other animals echo reason, imitating planning in some way in their behaviour), but are truly rational and intellectual; so we must believe they can sometimes attain true bliss and not simply an imitation of it; for otherwise the natural desire of their intellectual nature will have no function.

However, because of the many vicissitudes to which human life is subject, true bliss can't be located in this life, but as the goal of human life must be located after this life. And this is conceded by all philosophers who hold the soul that gives form to the human body to be itself an intellect; for they hold the soul to be immortal. But philosophers who hold the soul that forms the human body to be not itself an intellect but some sort of echo of a separate single intellect shared in by all say that the soul which forms our body will die, and attains not perfect bliss but only an imitation of it such as has been described. Now this view, as we showed in book 2, is absurd. So we simply concede that there is a true human bliss located after this life; though we don't deny that a certain imitation of bliss is possible in this life if human beings perfect themselves in the goods firstly of contemplative and secondly of practical reason. This is the happiness Aristotle discusses in his *Ethics* without either advocating or rejecting another bliss after this life.

Hence:...

to 3: The goal of human life surpasses that of other animals even more than the one life surpasses the other, and what gives human life its greater excellence is precisely the greater excellence of the goal it is ordered to. So it doesn't have to contain its ultimate goal in the way the lives of other animals do.

to 4: Though human beings desire their goal by nature they don't have by nature a desire for everything they need to attain that goal, but acquire that desire by reasoning, debating what they need and making choices. Also, there's nothing odd about desiring something hateful in itself as a means to an end, in the way we desire amputation of a limb for health's sake. And this is the way death, which everyone flees from by nature, can be desired for the sake of bliss; as St Paul also says in Philippians 1: 23: *I desire to be dissolved and live with Christ.*

[Article 2] The second question **[What is bliss?]** we approach as follows:

[Query 1] It seems bliss is something uncreated:

For... [3] Augustine[15] defines the enjoyable as what is desirable for itself alone. But bliss, according to Aristotle,[16] is desirable for itself alone, and so is enjoyable. Augustine goes on, however, to say that only God is enjoyable. So bliss can't be anything else but God...

Moreover, [5] everything in us belongs either to our substance or is incidental. Now bliss doesn't belong to our substance, for then we would all always be blissful; so, if bliss does exist in us, it will be something incidental to us. But incidentals can't be a substance's goal, since the substance ranks higher than the incidental. So bliss can't be something existing in us, and must be something uncreated.

But against that:

[1] Boethius[17] explains that human beings are blissful by sharing [God's] bliss, just as they are set to rights by sharing his rightness. But our rightness is something God creates in us. Bliss then too.

Moreover, [2] Aristotle[18] says the more goods it accumulates, the more attractive happiness becomes. But God is not made more attractive by accumulation. So happiness is something other than God, and so something created in us.

Further, **[Query 2] It seems happiness is not an activity.**

For [1] Boethius[19] defines *bliss as a state made up of all goods gathered together*. But a state is not an activity. So bliss is not an activity.

Moreover, [2] our activities are caused by us.[20] So if bliss consists in some activity of ours we will cause our own bliss, which is absurd.

Moreover, [3] if something within us is to be our ultimate goal, it must above all be something sought just for itself. But pleasure is sought just for itself, not as a means to anything else. Bliss then must above all consist in pleasure. Pleasure, however, is a feeling, not an activity. So happiness isn't an activity . . .

But against that:

[1] Aristotle[21] says *happiness is the active exercise of perfected virtue*.

Moreover, [2] that for which a thing exists is its ultimate goal. But Aristotle[22] says everything exists for the sake of its activity. So the activity proper to human beings is their ultimate goal, and human bliss is some sort of activity.

Moreover, [3] human bliss lies in becoming as like God as possible. But actually acting makes us most like God, actualizing our potentialities to the utmost. So human bliss consists in human activity.

Further, **[Query 3] It seems human bliss differs from eternal life.**

For . . . [2] a comment in the book of Causes says life implies movement and change. But bliss implies lack of change. So bliss differs from eternal life.

Moreover, [3] human beings can share bliss, but not eternal life, since what is made in time can't be eternal. So eternal life differs from bliss.

Moreover, [4] things that last for ever share eternity in the broad sense of everlastingness. Now the damned last for ever in the eternal fire to which they have been committed, as Matthew 25 [41] says; not in bliss, however, but in utmost misery. So bliss differs from eternal life.

But against that:

[1] Whatever is the goal of human life is bliss. But according to Romans 6 [22] eternal life is the goal of human life: *your harvest will be holiness and your goal eternal life*. So . . .[23]

Moreover, [2] ultimate human bliss consists in seeing God, as we said above. But that is what eternal life consists in, as we read in John 17 [3]: *This is eternal life: to know you, the only true God, and Jesus Christ whom you sent*. So bliss is the same as eternal life . . .

In reply to Query 1 [Is bliss something uncreated?]:

Boethius[24] says that the good thing everything desires is to exist. So the ultimate thing everything desires is as perfect an existence as its nature allows. Now anything dependent on others for existence will depend on others for the perfecting of its existence; for the more closely united it is to the source of its existence the more perfect an existence it will receive: earthly bodies are subject to decomposition, Aristotle[25] explains, because they are so far away from their first source.

So things dependent on others for their existence have a twofold ultimate goal: an external goal, the source of the perfection they desire; and an internal one, namely, the self-perfection that derives from union with their source. Bliss then, the ultimate human goal, will be twofold: one within, the ultimate perfection human beings can attain, a created bliss; and one without, union with which causes that bliss within, and this is God himself, an uncreated bliss.

Hence: . . .

to 3: Love has two types of object: objects loved with good will—persons to whom we will good for their own sake in the way we love friends without thought of return; and objects loved with desire, be they internal goods like pleasure or things that cause internal good like the wine that gives the pleasure. Now the ultimate thing we love can't be something loved with desire, since that is good only in relation to something else, namely, the person for whom[26] it is desired; but the ultimate thing we love must be loved with good will . . .

So then: our internal created bliss we love only with desire, loving it in relation to ourselves, and thus in relation to God since we too are to be loved in relation to God; it cannot therefore be the ultimate thing we love, though, as the greatest good deriving from union with God, it can be the ultimate thing we desire. In that sense we can say we seek or desire it for its own sake, since this suggests its ultimacy among things loved with desire; for even though we desire God, our desire for God is the same as our desire for the greatest good coming to us from God, just as our desire for wine is the same as our desire for the pleasure it causes in us . . .

to 5: Although incidentals as such rank lower than substances, still a certain incidental in a certain respect may rank higher. As supervenient on the thing and thus by definition incidental to it, incidentals will always rank lower than a thing's substance; but if it relates the thing to something external it can sometimes rank higher: namely, when it unites it to something of higher rank than itself. And this is the way bliss and grace and suchlike things rank higher than the nature of the soul upon which they supervene. And in another respect all incidental properties of a thing rank higher, as actualizations of what exists in the substance only potentially.

In reply to Query 2 [Is happiness an activity?]:

We have said that a thing's ultimate internal goal is what unites it to its ultimate external goal, the source of its perfection. Now things can be united to God, who is their ultimate goal, in two ways: by imitating him, and by coming into contact with him. The things most united to God in the first way are those most like him, and their ultimate internal goal is that in them which is most like God. Now things are more like God the more actualized they are, and less like him the more they are potential, so that a thing's ultimate goal is what most actualizes them. The second way of being united to God—making contact with him—is open only to reasoning creatures, by way of knowledge and love: for God can be an object of such activities but of no other creature's activities.

Now in whichever of these ways we think of the ultimate goal of human perfection we have to regard it as a sort of activity. When we think of it in the way that applies to all creatures uniting with God, we see that activity actualizes the mere capability of acting, so that the ultimate perfection of things lies in their own perfect activity; and this is why we say things exist for the sake of their activity. And again when we think of it in the way that is peculiar to reasoning creatures uniting with God, ultimate human perfection also consists in activity; for a disposition to act only unites with its object when it actually acts. Bliss then must be a sort of activity. Though the second way of thinking of it is more relevant to bliss than the first, since bliss is found only in reasoning creatures.

Hence:

to 1: At every level the means to a goal work together for an ultimate goal, and since in human beings as in other creatures that ultimate goal is perfect activity, every human good contributes to the perfecting of human activity. Thus in this life acquired dispositions, natural abilities, and externally needed tools are all goods contributing to perfect human activity, and bliss, therefore, is said to gather together all such goods so that they can contribute to what is the substance of human bliss, the most perfect human activity. And all these goods also contribute to our heavenly bliss, for it is the use we make of these goods that deserves such bliss. In that bliss not all such goods will still exist in their own natures, but they will exist in what has taken their place: faith, for example, in the sufficiency of eternal goods.

to 2: We must distinguish the essence of an activity from the ways in which it can be perfected. Its essence is determined by some native ability, but it is perfected by dispositions. When these are acquired dispositions the activity is totally our doing, but when they are instilled the activity's perfection derives from the external cause of our dispositions. Now our activity is only called bliss when it is perfected with a perfection uniting us to our external goal. So our bliss is not our doing, but God's.

to 3: Pleasure has two roles. Sometimes it precedes attainment of a goal and then it can be a means to something else: it can, for example, be used to perfect our activity since we pay more attention to doing what gives pleasure. But sometimes it follows attainment of a goal as an effect of that activity which unites us to the goal. And such pleasure is not bliss itself, but a sort of form or perfection of bliss, as we have already said...

In reply to Query 3 [Does human bliss differ from eternal life?]:

We use the word *life* in two ways. Firstly, to mean the existence of living things, for, as Aristotle[27] says, in living things to exist is to live. A living thing is something able to cause its own activity: we call plants living because they cause themselves to grow, animals because in addition they move themselves around and exercise their powers of sense, and human beings because in addition they exercise will and understanding. Now abilities are perfected by activity, so we go on to use the word *life* for the activities to which things move themselves: an animal's life is a life of sensation, human life a life of understanding, and in the same way everyone calls whatever activity he principally intends his life, as though his whole existence was ordered to that; we say *This fellow leads such-and-such a life*. And it was in this sense of life that Epicureans held bliss to be a life of pleasure.

Now activity is measured by time only if it involves change: an activity like illumination which is tied not to change but to the end of a change doesn't take time but is instantaneous, and if an activity existed which altogether transcended change it would be measured not by time but by some higher measure than time. Now the activity of seeing God, which we hold human bliss to be, cannot be measured by time: neither in itself, since it has no before and after, nor on the side of the seer or the seen, since both exist outside change; so the activity can be measured neither by time nor by an instant marking the end of some temporal interval. Nor can it be measured by the everlastingness that measures the unchanging created [heavens] and as such is distinguished from eternity, for seeing God transcends the native power of all creatures and is something no creature can attain by nature. What properly measures it is eternity itself; and the seeing of God, bliss itself, is thus eternal life.

Hence: . . .

to 2: Although movement and change are what first draw our attention to life, enabling us to distinguish living things from non-living, the word *life* extends further: to every activity not externally caused, like willing and understanding and so on. And even the word *movement* gets applied to such activities, so that we talk of understanding as a movement of mind, and willing as a movement of will.

to 3: Human beings can't share eternity as a measure properly applying to them or anything in them, as the argument says. But they can partake of eternity in a certain sense: a human being partakes of God's own activity when he sees God, and in that way partakes of the eternity which measures that activity; and so his own activity is called eternal life.

to 4: Eternal used of the eternal life of the saints doesn't merely mean never ending as it does used of the eternal sufferings of the damned. It also means lacking all change: and not only all actual change as when we call the heavens everlasting, but also all potentiality to change. For the saints by adhering to God receive from him a stability that doesn't allow of change, a stability that God has by nature and makes him eternal . . .

[**Article 3**] The third question [**Does everyone desire bliss?**] we approach as follows:

[**Query 1**] **It seems not everyone desires bliss.**

For [1] according to Augustine[28] we don't desire what we know nothing about, and Aristotle[29] says what we will is what we understand to be desirable. But not everyone knows about bliss, and many are mistaken about it. So not everyone desires it.

Moreover, [2] a person who desires bliss must desire what bliss in reality is, and that is the sight of God. But not everyone does desire that. So not everyone desires bliss.

Moreover, [3] what we can't think we can't desire. But we can't think contraries existing together, as Aristotle[30] explains. So we can't desire contraries existing together. However, some people desire the contrary of bliss: sins, for example. So not everyone desires bliss.

Moreover, [4] sin has been defined as adhering to changeable goods and spurning the unchangeable good. But bliss is the unchangeable good. So sinners spurn it and thus don't desire it.

But against that:

[1] Boethius[31] proves desire of true good to be implanted in every human soul. But true good is bliss. So everybody desires bliss.

Moreover, [2] everything desires its own goal. But bliss is the ultimate goal of human life. So every human being desires it.

Further, [**Query 2**] **It seems some can desire unhappiness.**

For [1] all rational powers can do the opposite of what they do. Will, then, as a rational power, can will the opposite of what it wills. Now unhappiness and bliss are opposites. So if someone can desire bliss, they can also desire unhappiness.

Moreover, [2] if people can't will unhappiness then willing it is impossible and not willing it a necessity. But, as Anselm[32] says, necessity implies coercion or prevention. So will would be coercible, which goes against its freedom.

Moreover, [3] existence is just as desirable to everyone as bliss. Yet some people, like suicides, don't want to exist. So some people also want to be unhappy.

Moreover, [4] Aristotle says[33] that we will goals, and again[34] that goals are goods or apparent goods. So both real and apparent goods can be desired. But what is evil can appear to be good. So however evil unhappiness is, someone can will it.

But against that:

[1] Augustine[35] shows that no human being can want to be miserable.

Moreover, [2] will relates to what it primarily wills as mind to what it primarily understands. Now, as Aristotle[36] proves, mind cannot assent to the contrary of what it primarily understands: namely, that assertions and their denials can't both be true. So will can't assent to unhappiness, the contrary of what it primarily desires.

Further, **[Query 3] It seems the desiring of bliss has no merit.**

For [1] there's no merit in what we do by nature. But we desire bliss by nature, for otherwise we wouldn't all do it. So no one's desire of bliss has any merit.

Moreover, [2] merit and demerit relate to the same things, so if, as Augustine[37] says, there's no sin in what one can't avoid doing, then there's no merit either. Now human beings can't avoid desiring bliss. So their desire can't have merit.

Moreover, [3] one can't merit eternal life by one's own powers, as Pelagius used to say. But we can desire bliss by our own powers. So desiring bliss can't be meriting.

But against that:

[1] The way we desire bliss is the way we desire God. So if there's no merit in desiring bliss there won't be merit in desiring God, which is absurd.

Moreover, [2] merit is caused by the love of charity, and that love is primarily love of our goal. So merit lies above all in will moving to its ultimate goal, that is, in desiring bliss.

Further, [Query 4] **It seems that not everything we will is willed for the sake of bliss.**

For [1] enjoyment is never willed except for its own sake, as Aristotle[38] says. But enjoyment, as we saw, is not the substance of bliss. So not everything we will is willed for the sake of bliss.

Moreover, [2] things desirable for bliss's sake must be orderable to bliss. But many sinners will things which, far from ordering them to bliss, turn them away from it. So not everything people will is willed for the sake of bliss.

Moreover, [3] what doesn't even look good can't be desired for bliss's sake. But sometimes we desire things that don't even look good: Augustine writes:[39] *I stole things I already had much and much better of, nor did I so much want to enjoy the thing as desire the stealing: the stealing and the sin ... And I ask what in the sin gave me pleasure, and behold there was nothing there to see.* So something was desired not for bliss's sake.

Moreover, [4] death can't be ordered to bliss, except perhaps by hoping for a life after death, since bliss is only for the living. But some people wish to commit suicide or be killed without hope of a future life. So not everything people will is willed for the sake of bliss.

Moreover, [5] the human will is judged[40] right when it is ordered to a right goal. If then everything we desired was desired for bliss's sake, every human act of will would be right, and that is untrue.

Moreover, [6] you can't do *A* for *B*'s sake without thinking about *B*. So if everything we will is willed for bliss's sake we would have to be thinking about bliss in every desiring act, which doesn't seem true. So we come to the same conclusion as before.

But against that:

[1] Desire comes to rest in what is desired for its own sake

and not for some other reason. But where desire comes to rest is its ultimate goal. So if we desired something else than bliss for its own sake and for no other reason, there would be another ultimate goal than bliss and that can't be. So everything else we desire must relate to our desire for bliss, mediately or immediately . . .

In reply to Query 1 [Does everyone desire bliss?]:

In any hierarchy of agents and things acted on, the primary agent orders the secondary agents to the primary agent's goal by imprinting them with some disposition: the mind moves the hand and the hand moves the stick and the stick strikes, which was the goal intended by the mind: stick and hand tend towards the goal intended by the mind by some disposition the mind imprints on them mediately or immediately. And we distinguish natural from violent movements by what kind of imprint is left in secondary agents by the primary agent: in violent movements the imprint is not in accord with their nature, so that the consequent activity is hard and laborious for them, but in natural movements the imprint accords with their natures, so that the consequent activity is agreeable and sweet; and this is why Wisdom 8 [1] says that *God disposes all things sweetly*, for all things tend by their divinely imprinted natures towards the goal to which God's providence orders them led by the imprints they receive.

And because all things issue from God in so far as he is good, as both Augustine[41] and pseudo-Dionysius[42] say, everything created tends to desire good in the way appropriate to it, according to the imprint it receives from its creator. And so things describe a sort of circle, coming out from good and tending towards it, a circle completed in certain creatures but remaining incomplete in others. For creatures not ordered towards contact with the first good from which they have come out, but only to a sort of imitation of him, don't complete the circle; but reasoning creatures—the only creatures who can come into a sort of contact with their first beginning itself—do. They attain God through knowledge and love, and in that attainment bliss consists, as we have said. And so just as every other thing desires its own good by nature, so every reasoning creature desires its own bliss by nature.

Hence:

to 1: Just as *what we see* may mean what as such is seen, namely, colour, or what that happens to make visible, for example, a man, so also *what we want or will* may mean what as such is willed, namely, good, or what that happens to make willable, namely, this or that good thing. And just as what such is willed is good, talking generally, so what as such is will's ultimate goal is supreme good; whether it be this or that good thing that happens to be willed as ultimate goal and principal object. Everyone knows bliss to be will's principal object as such, then, but not everyone knows what that happens to be. For everyone the bliss desired is known and desired as perfect good, but this perfect good can happen to be found in pleasure or riches or virtue or something of that sort; so it's not strange to find many mistakes made about that.

to 2: Although bliss is in fact the sight of God, not everyone desiring bliss must in fact be wanting to see God, for bliss as such names what will as such wills, but the sight of God doesn't. In the same way we can desire something sweet without wanting honey.

to 3: Although people sometimes desire things that are in fact irreconcilable with bliss, they nevertheless don't think of them as irreconcilable but as aids to getting there.

to 4: Someone who sins by adhering to changeable goods as his goal is taking those changeable goods to be the perfect good he primarily desires, and so is desiring bliss by adhering to them. For just as someone desiring bliss doesn't have to be desiring what bliss in fact is, so someone spurning what bliss in fact is doesn't have to be spurning bliss. Just as ignorance of a man doesn't imply ignorance of white, even though the man in question be white.

In reply to Query 2 [Do some people desire unhappiness?]: The activity of secondary causes is based on the presupposed activity of a primary cause. Thus all our living activity presupposes what God, acting first, has imprinted in our soul. Thus we see that mind can't reach understanding of anything without presupposing knowledge we were born with, and is not able to give assent to anything opposed to the premisses we know by nature. And the same is true of will. It is imprinted in our soul from God, as first cause, that we will good and desire perfect good as our ultimate goal; so our wills can't desire anything opposed to that. So that no one can will unhappiness or evil except incidentally, by taking to be good what in fact is bad.

Hence:

to 1: Rational powers can do the opposite of things that lie within their power and which they have themselves decided to do, but not the opposite of what someone else has decided they shall do: the will can't will the opposite of what God has decided to imprint on it. So it can't will the opposite of its ultimate goal even though it can will the opposite of things it itself decides to do: things such as those it chooses to do in pursuance of that ultimate goal.

to 2: Coercion and prevention imply violence, and are not characteristic of the kind of necessity that follows from a thing's nature: violence is always against nature. So since will is carried towards bliss with a necessity derived from its nature, it isn't coerced and is no less free.

to 3: There is no reason why something desirable in itself shouldn't be undesirable because of something accompanying it. Even existence, which in itself is a good everyone desires, can be rendered evil and hateful by some accompaniment like grief or unhappiness. So then non-existence becomes desirable; but incidentally, not because it takes away existence, but because it takes away the evil which rendered existence hateful. But lack of evil is good, and is desired as good by the one desiring not to exist. Unhappiness, however, means perfect evil, and so it can never appear good, and no one wills to be miserable; but non-existence means not evil as such but something evil that might have some good accompaniment and so be desirable, as one sees in Aristotle[43] and in Jerome's gloss on Jeremiah 20 [14]:

Cursed be the day of my birth. Augustine's assertion that no one desires not to exist is to be understood of non-existence in itself.

to 4: One can't think white is black though one can think a white thing, say a man, is black. And in the same way one can think a good thing to be evil, but one can't think goodness to be badness and vice versa. Because unhappiness is by definition evil one can't think it good and so can't desire it.

In reply to Query 3 [Has the desiring of bliss any merit?]: According to Aristotle[44] the good which we will is in things, so that the movement of will ends up in something existing outside the mind. Now although we can consider things generally in mind without particularizing, things can't exist generally outside mind without being particulars. And so will can't ever be carried towards good without being carried towards a defined good, and can't ever be carried towards supreme good without being carried towards supreme good defined in this or that way. Now though will is inclined by nature towards bliss in general, an inclination towards bliss of this or that sort comes not from nature but from a reasoned discrimination deciding that the supreme human good is to be found in this place or in that. So whenever anyone actually desires bliss natural desire must be wedded to reasoned desire, and though the natural strand in the desire is always right, the reasoned strand is sometimes right (when bliss is desired where it really is) and sometimes perverse (when it is desired where it isn't). And so in desiring bliss there can be merit (given grace) or demerit, depending on whether the desire is right or perverse.

Hence:

to 1: To what is natural in desire of bliss there is always joined something not of nature but willed; so there is always room for merit or demerit.

to 2: Although one can't avoid desiring bliss in some way or another, one can avoid desiring it in the way it should be desired, and so can do it with or without merit.

to 3: It isn't within the power of human beings to desire bliss with the perfect desire needed to merit it, but we have the gift of God's grace to help us, as we read in 2 Corinthians 5 [5]: *It is God who has made us for this*, meaning, according to the gloss, who has made us desire true glory.

In reply to Query 4 [Is everything we will willed for the sake of bliss?]:

According to Aristotle,[45] goals play the same role in desire as premisses in understanding. Because the first and highest of any particular sort of thing causes the rest, knowledge of premisses in contemplative thinking causes knowledge of everything else, and desire of a goal causes desire of everything leading to the goal. So since bliss is the goal of human life, whatever it is our will's desire to do is ordered to bliss; and we see this in experience. For people desire things because they think them good; and when they possess things they think good, they reckon themselves that much closer to bliss, since good added to good comes closer to perfect good, which is bliss itself. So every desire is ordered to bliss.

Hence:

to 1: Enjoyment is one of the requirements of bliss and contained in it, so our very desire for enjoyment orders us to bliss in the sense that the desired enjoyment is a likeness, more or less close, of the enjoyment which completes bliss.

to 2: There are two ways things desired can be ordered to bliss. First, as a desired means of reaching bliss, in the way we will virtuous actions in order to merit bliss. Or secondly, as resembling bliss in some way. For will's very desire of something makes it desire things similar, even if the thing primarily desired is unattainable; and this is how even sinners tend towards bliss and God's image, as Augustine[46] said: *Pride imitates your exalted majesty, you being the one God exalted over all; and what does ambition seek but honour and glory, you being above all worthy of honour?*, and so on with the other vices.

to 3: Augustine says in the same place that theft itself appeared good in one respect, namely, that it was against the law and so seemed to have a shadow of freedom in it. Thus he asks: *What did I love in that theft, in which I perversely and viciously imitated my God?* and answers: *Perhaps doing something forbidden pleased me, at least deceitfully exercising a power I didn't have, so that enslaved I imitated freedom, did something illicit, and went unpunished, in a dark likeness of omnipotence?*

to 4: People without hope of a future life expose themselves to death in two ways. Firstly, in defence of virtue, choosing, for example, to undergo death to save their fatherland or avoid some dishonour; and this they order to bliss as they see it, a bliss coming not after death but in that very act, since the doing of this perfect act of virtue, the undergoing of death, is something they greatly desire, which to them is bliss. Secondly, people desire to die to avoid the burden of unhappiness they are bearing. But avoiding unhappiness is the same as desiring bliss. Clearly then the desires of those who want to undergo death are ordered to bliss.

to 5: Two things are required for an act of will to be right: it must pursue a due goal, and whatever it wills as means to that goal must be proportioned to it. Now even though every desire is ordered to bliss, there are two ways in which it can be perverse: that very desire of bliss can perversely seek bliss where there is none, as we have already said; and even when it is sought in the right place, the desired means to the goal may not be proportioned to it, as when someone wills to steal in order to give alms and merit bliss.

to 6: The first premisses of understanding don't have to be present in substance in subsequent demonstrations, as actually thought about, but only in [causal] power, as when we demonstrate from truths already proved by first principles. And in the same way, though all desires relate to bliss, we don't have actually to think about bliss in every desire: the desire of bliss is present in power in all other desires, as a cause in its effects.

Passage 35
Moral Action

Source: *Summa Theologiae*, 1a2ae.18–20. Text from *Summa Theologiae* (*Opera Omnia*, Leonine edn., vol. vi).

Date: 1269–70, second stay in Paris, aged 45.

Type of passage and how to read: Modified disputed question (see Introduction).

Parallel reading: See also Passage 31.

Our first consideration [**what makes human action good or bad**] divides into three:

first, [Question 18] the goodness and badness of human actions in general;
second, [Question 19] the goodness and badness of inner actions;
and third, [Question 20] the goodness and badness of external actions.

[**Question 18**] The first question [**the goodness and badness of human actions in general**] divides into eleven:

Are all actions good or some bad?
Can the object of a human action make it good or bad?
Can its circumstances?
Can its goal?
Does goodness or badness decide a human action's kind?
Is the good or bad kind of an action decided by its goal?
Does the goal determine the kind more specifically than the object, or vice versa?
Can human actions be neutral in kind?
Can they be neutral in particular cases?
Can a moral action's moral kind be decided by a circumstance?
Does every circumstance that alters a moral act for better or for worse decide its moral kind?

[**Article 1**] The first question [**Are all actions good or some bad?**] we approach as follows:

It seems that all human actions are good and none bad:

For [1] pseudo-Dionysius[1] says *bad doesn't act except by good's power*. But good's power doesn't do bad. So no actions are bad.

Moreover, [2] activity follows on actuality. But what makes things bad is unrealized potentiality, not actuality; fulfilled potentiality is good, as Aristotle[2] says. So it is the goodness in things that acts, not the badness; and all actions will be good and none bad.

Moreover, [3] the bad can only cause incidentally, as pseudo-Dionysius[3] shows. But actions always have direct effects. So no actions are bad; all are good.

But against that:

In John 3 [20] our Lord says *Everyone who acts badly hates the light*. So some human action is bad.

In reply:

We should judge actions good and bad in the same way we do things, since what things do reflects what they are. Now a thing's goodness is measured by how fully it exists; for, as we said in book 1, good and existent are interchangeable terms. Only God possesses full and complete existence in a single non-complex unity; everything else needs variety of parts if it is fully to exist in the way appropriate to it, and so sometimes it happens that things exist in part but not as fully as they should. Full human being, for example, demands a complex of soul and body endowed with every ability and organ needed for knowledge and movement, and if an individual lacks any of this he would not exist fully. As existing he would be good, but as not fully existing he would lack goodness and be called bad: thus for blind men it is good to be alive, but bad to be without sight. And someone who possessed no existence or goodness at all couldn't be called either bad or good. But because goodness is defined by fullness of existence, what doesn't exist as fully as it should is not called good unreservedly but good only to the extent that it exists; it can, however, be called existent unreservedly, and is non-existent only in a qualified sense, as we explained in book 1.

In a similar way then actions must be called good in so far as they exist, but in so far as they exist less fully than human actions should they will lack goodness and be called bad: if, for example, we don't do as much as we reasonably should, or do something out of place or the like.

Hence:

to 1: Bad acts by power of an incomplete good; for where there is no good there is no existent and nothing able to act, and where the good is complete there will be no bad. So the action caused is also an incomplete good: good in part, but as a whole bad.

to 2: There is no reason why a thing shouldn't have enough actuality to act, but not enough to produce a complete action; as blind men have the capacity to walk, but in the absence of sight to direct their steps walk badly, stumbling.

to 3: In so far as bad actions exist they are good and can have direct effects: adultery can result in children because it is sexual union of male and female, not because it offends against the laws of reason.

[**Article 2**] The second question [**Can the object of a human action make it good or bad?**] we approach as follows:

It seems that an action's object can't make it good or bad:

For [1] the objects of activities are things. But it is not things that are bad, but the way sinners use them, as Augustine[4] says. So it is not objects that make human actions good or bad.

Moreover, [2] objects provide a sort of material for activity. But it is not its material that makes something good but the form that actualizes it. So what makes action good or bad is not its object.

Moreover, [3] the object of an agent power is an effect brought about by its action. But goodness of causes doesn't depend on their effects, but rather the reverse. So what makes human action good or bad is not its object.

But against that:

Hosea 9 [10] says: *They have become as abominable as the things they have loved.* Now human beings become abominable to God because of the bad they do. So their actions are bad because the objects they love are bad; and similarly for good actions.

In reply:

As we have just said, actions are like other things: good if they exist fully, bad if they are incomplete. Now to exist fully what something must first have is what defines it: for things in nature a form, for actions an object in the way movements must have a destination. So just as its defining form gives a natural thing basic goodness, so a fitting object of activity gives moral actions their basic goodness (makes them *good of their kind*, as some people say): for example, using what belongs to you. And just as in nature the basic evil is a failure to reproduce a thing's defining form—the misbegetting of human beings, for example—so in the moral sphere the basic evil is an action having a wrong object—for example, taking what doesn't belong to you. Such an action is *bad of its kind*, where 'kind' means species or 'defining kind', in the sense in which the human species is called humankind.

Hence:

to 1: External things are good in themselves but are not always properly proportioned to this or that action; so as objects of such activities they are not good.

to 2: An action's object is not *material out of which* but *material concerning which*, and in a sense that is the action's form, defining it.

to 3: The object of human action is not always the object of an agent power. Our ability to desire, for example, is more a power of being acted on, by desirable things; yet it is a source of human action. Nor can the object of an agent power be called its effect till transformation has occurred: the effect of our powers of digestion is digested food, but the material on which they operate is undigested food. Nevertheless, the very fact that an agent power's object is in some sense its effect makes it the destination of the action, and consequently something forming and specifying the action in the way destinations specify movements. Moreover, though the goodness of the effect doesn't cause the goodness of the action, still we call action good when it is such as to cause a good effect, so that what makes action good is its very proportion to its effect.

[**Article** 3] The third question [**Can the circumstances of a human action make it good or bad?**] we approach as follows:

It seems that an action's circumstances don't make it good or bad:

For [1] circumstances 'stand round' an action, existing outside it, so to speak. But good and bad exist within things, as Aristotle[5] said. So circumstances can't make actions good or bad.

Moreover, [2] whether actions are good or bad is the main concern of moral teaching. But sciences seem unconcerned with circumstances, which are incidental features of actions; for, as Aristotle[6] says, *no science concerns itself with incidentals.* So whether actions are good or bad doesn't depend on circumstances.

Moreover, [3] what belongs to a thing's substance is not incidental to it. But actions are good or bad in substance, good or bad *of their kind*, as we have said. So actions are not accounted good or bad because of circumstances.

But against that:

Aristotle[7] says that *virtuous people act as they should, when they should, and in accordance with the other circumstances.* So non-virtuous people must do the opposite, acting, according to various vices, when they shouldn't, or where they shouldn't, or disregarding some other circumstance. A human action then can be good or bad because of some circumstance.

In reply:

To realize perfection fully things in nature must possess many properties over and above the form defining their substance: human beings, for example, must have shape and colour and so on; and lacking a property they ought to have is bad for them. So too with action: to be fully good it must have not only what defines it, but certain additional features called right circumstances; and if it lacks what right circumstances require, the action is bad.

Hence:

to 1: Circumstances lie outside an action in the sense of not specifying what it is, but they belong to it as non-defining properties of a sort; just as natural substances have non-defining properties lying outside what essentially specifies them.

to 2: Not all non-defining properties are incidental to their subject: some are properties characteristic of it, and these are what a science of the subject investigates. Circumstances of moral actions are the concern of moral teaching in this way.

to 3: Being good and being existent are convertible terms, and both the substance and the incidental properties of things exist. So both natural things and moral actions can be called good because of the existence they have in substance and because of the existence belonging to them incidentally.

[**Article 4**] The fourth question [**Can the goal of a human action make it good or bad?**] we approach as follows:

It seems that an action's goal doesn't make it good or bad:

For [1] pseudo-Dionysius[8] says that *nothing acts with evil in view*. So if an action's goal makes it good or bad, no action will ever be bad. Which is clearly false.

Moreover, [2] the goodness of action is something within it, whereas its goal is external. So an action's goal doesn't make it good or bad.

Moreover, [3] good actions can be done for bad ends—giving to the poor out of vanity—and bad actions for good ends—stealing to give to the poor. So an action's goal doesn't make it good or bad.

But against that:

Boethius[9] says *whatever has a good goal is itself good*. And whatever has a bad goal is itself bad.

In reply:

Things are good in the same ways in which they exist: some things don't depend for existence on other things, and their existence can be satisfactorily considered on its own, but some depend for existence on others, and their existence must be considered in relation to the cause on which it depends. Now existence depends on agents and forms, but goodness on goals. So goodness in relation to a goal doesn't apply to the persons of God, for example, whose goodness is independent of others; but human actions, and anything else the goodness of which depends on other things, have, in addition to whatever goodness exists within them, a goodness relating them to the goal on which they depend.

Four elements therefore contribute to the goodness of human action: firstly, its generic existence as activity at all (for, as we said, the more fully it exists as an action the more goodness it has); secondly, its species as defined by an appropriate object; thirdly, its circumstances—as it were, its non-defining properties; and fourthly, its goal—as it were, its relationship to some cause of goodness.

Hence:

to 1: The good things have in view when they act is not always a genuine good, but sometimes genuine and sometimes illusory, and in the latter case the goal can make the action bad.

to 2: Though the goal itself is external, the action's proper proportion and relationship to the goal resides within the action.

to 3: There is no reason why an action can't be good in one of the ways mentioned above and not in another. So an action good of its kind or its circumstances can be done for a bad goal, or vice versa. Actions are good (period!) only when all these elements are present: as pseudo-Dionysius[10] says, *any defect will make a thing bad; but to be good a thing must be wholly good.*

[**Article** 5] The fifth question [**Does goodness or badness decide a human action's kind?**] we approach as follows:

It seems that good moral actions don't differ in kind from bad ones:

For, [1] as we have said, actions are good and bad in the same way things are. But good things don't differ in kind from bad ones: good and bad men belong to the same species. So neither do good actions differ in kind from bad ones.

Moreover, [2] badness is a lack of something, a sort of non-existence. But, as Aristotle[11] says, what doesn't exist can't differentiate anything. So, since species arise by differentiation, it doesn't seem that bad actions can constitute a separate species. Good human actions then don't differ in kind from bad ones.

Moreover, [3] actions differing in kind differ in effect. But good and bad actions can produce the same kind of effect: adultery and married sex both reproduce the human race. So good and bad acts don't differ in kind.

Moreover, [4] sometimes, as we have said, actions are good and bad because of circumstances. But circumstances are non-essential and don't decide an action's species. Good and bad then don't make actions different in kind.

But against that:

Like dispositions produce like actions, according to Aristotle.[12] But good and bad dispositions like generosity and extravagance differ in kind. So good and bad actions differ in kind.

In reply:

Actions we have said are defined by their objects; so difference of object ought to mean actions differ in kind. Note, however, that difference of object may change an action's kind relative to one source of activity without changing it relative to another; for kind is decided by essentials not incidentals, and a difference of object that is essential relative to one source of activity may be incidental relative to another: for the senses, knowing colour differs essentially from knowing sound, but not for mind. Now good and bad describe actions relative to reason—as pseudo-Dionysius[13] says, *it is good for human beings to live reasonably and bad for them not to*—since what suits a thing's form is good for it, and what doesn't suit bad. So clearly difference of good or bad due to an action's object—namely, whether the object suits reason or not—is an essential one relative to reason. And since actions as products of reason are called human or moral, good and bad will obviously decide the kind of *moral* actions, for the essential differences are the ones that decide kind.

Hence:

to 1: Even in nature things good and bad, in the sense of suiting or not suiting nature, differ in kind: dead and living bodies don't belong to the same species. And in the same way good and bad, in the sense of suiting or not suiting reason, decide the kind of a moral action.

to 2: What is bad doesn't lack everything but some part of what it could have; and actions defined as bad don't lack all object, but have an object unsuited to reason like taking what doesn't belong to one. But in so far as that object exists positively it decides the kind of the bad action.

to 3: Relative to reason, married and adulterous sex are two different kinds of act and have different kinds of effect, one earning commendation and reward and the other blame and penalty; but relative to our reproductive powers the actions are one in species and kind of effect.

to 4: Sometimes a circumstance is treated as a difference of object that is essential relative to reason, and as such can decide an action's moral kind. This must always be the case when a circumstance changes an act from good to bad, for a circumstance can only make an act bad by offending against reason.

[Article 6] The sixth question [**Is the good or bad kind of an action decided by its goal?**] we approach as follows:

It seems that the goodness and badness actions derive from their goal doesn't decide their kind:

For [1] it is the object that defines action, and goal is something outside the object. So the goodness or badness deriving from its goal doesn't decide the action's kind.

Moreover, [2] as we have said, incidentals can't decide something's kind. But the goal an action is directed to is incidental: giving to the poor out of vanity, for example. So goodness or badness derived from an action's goal won't decide its kind.

Moreover, [3] different kinds of action can all have one goal: vanity can lead us to perform acts of many different virtues and vices. So the goodness or badness deriving from the goal doesn't decide the kind of the actions.

But against that:

It was shown earlier that an action can be defined by its goal. So the goodness or badness deriving from that goal will decide the action's kind.

In reply:

As we explained earlier, we call some actions 'human actions' because they are done voluntarily. Now voluntary action is made up of an interior act of will and external activity, and each has its object: the goal is the object proper to the interior act of will and the external activity's object is whatever that activity is concerned with. So just as the external activity's kind is decided by the object it is concerned with, so the interior act of will's kind is decided by its own proper object, namely, its goal. Now since the body acts as will's tool, what the will contributes to action is a sort of form of control imposed on the external activity as material, and only when the external activity is voluntary in this way is it morally significant. Human actions then are defined formally by their goal, and materially by the object of the external activity. As Aristotle[14] put it: *stealing to pay for adultery makes you more an adulterer, properly speaking, than a thief.*

Hence:

to 1: The goal itself is an object, as we have said.

to 2: Even if being directed to a particular goal is incidental to the external activity, it is not incidental to the interior act of will, controlling and giving form to the external activity as to material.

to 3: When actions of many different kinds are directed to one goal, the external activity is indeed different in kind, but the interior act is of one kind.

[**Article 7**] The seventh question [**Does the goal determine the kind more specifically than the object, or vice versa?**] we approach as follows:

It seems that when, for instance, someone is willing to steal in order to give to the poor, the kind of goodness derived from the goal is contained within the kind of goodness derived from the object like a species within a genus:

For [1] something of one species can't belong to another unless the new species is a subspecies of the one it already belongs to: one and the same thing can't be of two unsubordinated kinds. So specification by goal must be a subspecies of the specification an action has from its object.

Moreover, [2] it is always the ultimate differentiation which specifies most narrowly. But differentiation by goal seems to come after differentiation by object, since goals are ends. So specification by goal must be narrower than specification by object.

Moreover, [3] the more formal a differentiating characteristic the more specific, since differentiating characteristics relate to a genus like forms to material. But specification by goal is more formal than specification by object, as we have said. So the species defined by goal must be contained within the species defined by object, as the most narrowly specified species within the genus to which it is subordinate.

But against that:

There are a finite number of differentiations possible within a genus. But actions of one kind as defined by their object can be directed to infinite goals: stealing, for instance, to any number of good or bad ends. So the species defined by goal is not contained within the species defined by object as in a genus.

In reply:

The object of external activity can relate to the willed goal in two ways: essentially, in the way fighting well relates essentially to victory, or incidentally, in the way stealing might be related to giving to the poor. Now Aristotle[15] says the differentiating characteristics by which a genus is divided into species must be essential to the genus, not incidental to it; otherwise the division will go wrong. If, for example, one divides animals into reasoning and unreasoning, and then further divides unreasoning animals into those with wings and those without, the division will be inappropriate, for winged and unwinged don't differentiate unreasoning as such. Rather one ought to divide as follows: some animals have legs and some don't, and of those with legs some have two, some have four, some have more; for these later differentiations now differentiate the previous differentiation as such. If then an action's object is not essentially related to its goal, the object's differentiating characteristic won't differentiate the goal's as such, nor vice versa, and the action will have more than one kind, not subordinate one to the other: the action will belong morally to two disparate species, as it were. Which is why we say that a person who steals in order to pay for his sexual irregularities commits two evils with one action. But when an action's object is essentially related to its goal, then one of the differentiating characteristics differentiates the other as such, and one of the action's kinds will be subordinate to the other.

But we still don't know which. To clarify that note, firstly, the less general a form the more specific the differentiating characteristic based on it; secondly, the more general an agent the more general the form it imposes; thirdly, the more ultimate a goal the more general must be the agent intending it: victory—the ultimate goal of the army—is the one intended by the generalissimo, whereas the disposition of this or that unit is a goal left to a subordinate commander. It follows then that goals define actions most generally, and further specification is due to objects essentially related to those goals; for will, having the goal as its proper object, is general mover of all those powers that have as their objects the objects of particular activities.

Hence:

to 1: Nothing can belong in substance to two species, unless one is subordinate to the other, but by way of incidental properties it can: the one apple, for instance, can be white in colour and sweet in fragrance. And in the same way an action which in substance is of one natural kind can be classified by supervening moral features in two moral species.

to 2: Though a goal is the last thing implemented it is the first thing mentally intended, and moral actions are defined relative to mind.

to 3: Differentiating characteristics relate to a genus like forms to material because they bring it to actually exist. But in another sense genus is more formal than the defined species by being less qualified and restricted. So that Aristotle[16] says the elements of a definition are its formal cause. In this sense the genus is a formal cause of the species, and more formal the more general it is.

[**Article 8**] The eighth question [**Can human actions be neutral in kind?**] we approach as follows:

It seems that no action is neutral in kind:

For [1] bad is lack of good, says Augustine.[17] But, according to Aristotle,[18] lacking and having are in immediate opposition. So action can't be neutral in kind, as though existing in an intermediate state between good and bad.

Moreover, [2] the kind of a human action is decided, as we have said, by either goal or object. But all goals and objects are good or bad. So all human actions are good or bad in kind. None then is neutral in kind.

Moreover, [3] as we have said, an action with its due perfection of goodness is called good, but if any of that is lacking, bad. Now of necessity every action either has its full goodness or lacks something. So of necessity every action is either good or bad in kind, and none neutral.

But against that:

Augustine[19] says there are certain run-of-the-mill things people do, *which could be done with a good or a bad spirit, about which it is rash to judge*. So there are certain actions that are neutral in kind.

In reply:

We have said that every action is specified by its object, and that human or moral action is specified by an object related to what makes action human, namely, reason. If the object involves something agreeable to reason the action will be by definition good (like giving to the poor); if the object involves something offensive to reason the action will be by definition bad (like stealing, which is taking something that doesn't belong to you). But sometimes the object involves nothing at all related to reason (like picking up straws, or taking a walk, or suchlike), and actions of this sort will be by definition neutral.

Hence:

to 1: There are two senses of *lacking*: being without and being deficient. The former takes away everything and leaves nothing, in the way blindness takes away sight and darkness light and death life; and between such a lacking and the opposed having there can be no intermediate state of the subject. But the second sense of lacking—being deficient—is the sense in which we say sickness is lack of health, not because it takes away all health, but because it is a sort of road that leads to the total taking away of health by death. So this sort of lacking leaves something, and sometimes allows of an intermediate state between itself and the opposed having. And this is the way in which bad lacks good, as Simplicius[20] says, for it doesn't take all good away but leaves something behind. So an intermediate state between good and bad is possible.

to 2: Every object or goal is good or bad in some sense, at least by nature; but, as we have said, this doesn't always imply moral goodness or badness relative to reason such as we are now discussing.

to 3: Not everything in an action belongs to the species that defines it. So even if that doesn't contain everything required for the action's full goodness, that doesn't mean to say the action is by definition bad, nor good either: just as human beings are neither virtuous nor vicious by nature.

[**Article 9**] The ninth question [**Can human actions be neutral in particular cases?**] we approach as follows:

It seems that some individual cases of action are neutral:

For [1] there's no such thing as a species that doesn't and can't contain a single individual. But we have just said actions can be neutral in kind. So there can be individual neutral actions.

Moreover, [2] individual actions cause us to acquire dispositions akin to those actions, as Aristotle[21] says. But dispositions can be neutral; for Aristotle[22] speaks of people that are unresponsive or extravagant but not vicious; yet they certainly aren't virtuous, since they lack certain virtues. So they are neutral in disposition. Certain individual actions then must be neutral.

Moreover, [3] moral goodness is a matter of virtue and moral badness a matter of vice. But sometimes an action which is neutral in kind fails to be directed to any virtuous or vicious goal. And that individual action would then be neutral.

But against that:

Gregory says in some homily:[23] *idle talk is without right purpose, serving neither just need nor devotional profit*. But idle talk is bad, since *men will render an account* for it *on the day of judgement*, as we read in Matthew 12 [36]; though if it did serve just need or devotional profit it would be good. So all talk is either good or bad, and for like reasons all other actions are good or bad. No individual action is therefore neutral.

In reply:

Sometimes an action neutral by definition is good or bad in a particular case, the reason being that the goodness of a moral action, as we have said, derives not only from the object that defines it, but also from its incidental circumstances; just as incidental properties add to individual human beings things they wouldn't have by definition. And every individual action must have some circumstance which turns it into a good or bad action: the intended goal, if nothing else. For it is reason's function to direct, and any action that issued from reason's deliberation without being directed to a due goal would *ipso facto* offend against reason and be bad; but if it were directed to a due goal, it would conform to reason and be good. Now of necessity reason either directs it to a due goal or not; so of necessity any deliberate human action, considered in the particular case, is good or bad. The only actions that can be neutral in the particular case are actions like stroking one's chin or shifting one's feet, which issue not from deliberation but from a sort of sense-reflex. Such actions are not, properly speaking, moral or human, since for that they must derive from reason; so they are neutral in the sense of not moral at all.

Hence:

to 1: *An action neutral in kind* can mean two different things. The argument takes it to mean an action bound by definition to be neutral; but in that sense no action is ever by definition neutral, for there is no object of human activity that cannot be directed to good or bad by some goal or circumstance. But another meaning of an action neutral in kind is an action not bound to be either good or bad by definition, but open to being either for some other reason. Just as a human being isn't bound to be black or white by definition, but isn't precluded from being so either, and he can be black or white for reasons external to his definition.

to 2: Aristotle is thinking of vicious in the special sense of harmful to other people, and says extravagant men are not vicious because they harm nobody but themselves; and the same for all others who don't harm their neighbours. But we are here speaking of bad in the general sense of being offensive to right reason, and in this sense every individual act is either good or bad, as we have said.

to 3: Every goal on which a deliberating reason is intent serves either the good of some virtue or the evil of some vice. For even the regular feeding and resting of our bodies serves the good of virtue in people who put their bodies at virtue's service; and the same is true of everything else.

[Article 10] The tenth question **[Can a moral action's moral kind be decided by a circumstance?]** we approach as follows:

It seems that a circumstance can't decide an action's moral kind:

For [1] an action's kind is decided by its object. But circumstances differ from objects. So an action's kind can't be decided by circumstances.

Moreover, [2] circumstances are incidental to moral actions, as we have said. But incidentals don't decide a thing's kind. So circumstances don't decide the moral kind of actions.

Moreover, [3] a thing can't have more than one definition. But a single action can have more than one circumstance. So circumstances don't define the moral kind of moral actions.

But against that:

Where is a circumstance. But *where* decides the kind of badness certain moral actions have: thus, stealing from a holy place constitutes a sacrilege. So a circumstance can decide what kind of good or bad action a moral action is.

In reply:

As we have already shown, just as natural forms decide kinds of thing in nature, so forms conceived by human reason decide kinds of moral action. But nature is fixed, and nature's processes have defined ends, so that in nature we arrive at an ultimate form defining the thing's kind, after which no further definition is possible: no supervening modification to a thing in nature can redetermine its kind. But the processes of reason are not fixed, and whatever is given can be taken further. So what in a first action was treated as circumstance, attendant on the object that decided the kind of the action, can be reassessed by reason as a main feature of the object deciding the action's kind. Thus taking what isn't one's own has its kind decided by the object *not one's own*, and is classified as stealing; and the place and time at which you steal are considered to be circumstances. But because they too can be ruled by reason, the place where the object is could also be seen as offensive to reason, namely, to reason's rule that no injustice should be done to holy places. And then taking what isn't one's own from a holy place adds some special contravention of the rule of reason. The place that was first thought of as a circumstance is now being thought of as the main feature of an object offensive to reason. And this is the way in which a circumstance, whenever it relates, *pro* or *contra*, to a special rule of reason, decides the moral kind of an action, good or bad.

Hence:

to 1: A circumstance that decides the kind of an action is thought of as a feature of the object, as we have said, and as a sort of differentiating characteristic determining its species.
to 2: Circumstance as circumstance is incidental and cannot decide an action's kind, but when it has become the main feature of the object it decides the action's kind.

to 3: Not every circumstance of an action defines a moral kind for it, since not every circumstance implies some harmony or discord with reason. So even if a single action has more than one circumstance the single action doesn't need to have more than one definition. Although even that holds no difficulties: for a single moral action can belong to more than one moral kind, even disparate kinds, as we have said above.

[**Article 11**] The eleventh question [**Does every circumstance that alters a moral act for better or for worse decide its moral kind?**] we approach as follows:

It seems that every good or bad circumstance will decide an action's kind:

For [1] goodness and badness differentiate kinds of moral action. So whatever makes a difference to a moral action's goodness or badness differentiates its kind. But making an action better or worse makes a difference to its goodness and badness, and therefore differentiates its kind. So every circumstance making an action better or worse decides its kind.

Moreover, [2] an attendant circumstance is itself something good or bad, or not. If not, then it can't make the action better or worse, since what isn't good can't make anything better, and what isn't bad can't make it worse. But if the circumstance is itself something good or bad, then this must be of a certain kind. So every circumstance that makes an action better or worse must set up some new kind of goodness or badness.

Moreover, [3] *any defect will make a thing bad*, as pseudo-Dionysius[24] says. But any circumstance that makes bad worse is an extra defect, and so adds a new kind of sin. And in the same way any circumstance that makes good better would appear to add a new kind of goodness, just as adding one to a number makes a new kind of number; for goodness consists in *number, weight, and measure.*

But against that:

Difference in degree is not difference in kind. But circumstances that make actions better or worse make a difference in degree. So not every circumstance that makes moral actions better or worse decides its moral kind.

In reply:

We have said that an action's circumstance, when it is relevant to some special rule of reason, can decide the moral kind—good or bad—of the action. But some circumstances are relevant to what reason says is good or bad only when some other presupposed circumstance has defined the action's kind: thus taking more or less of something doesn't affect reason's judgement of goodness or badness unless there is some feature making the action good or bad: for instance, that what is taken is someone else's and therefore the taking is offensive to reason. Stealing more and stealing less will therefore differ in degree of badness, though not in kind; and the same is true for other good and bad actions. Not every circumstance that makes moral actions better or worse, then, alters their kind.

Hence:

to 1: Where variation in degree is a possibility difference in degree doesn't cause difference in kind: a difference in white's intensity is not a difference in kind of colour. And in the same way a difference in intensity of goodness or badness isn't a difference in a moral action's kind.

to 2: A circumstance that worsens a sin or makes a good action better sometimes has no goodness or badness of its own, but only in relationship to some other feature of the action, as we have said. And so it doesn't set up any new kind of goodness or badness, but increases that which is due to this other feature.

to 3: Not every circumstance introduces a defect peculiar to itself; some do so only relative to something else. And in the same way not every circumstance introduces a new perfection; some do so only relative to some other thing. And to that extent, although a circumstance may increase an action's goodness or badness, it doesn't always alter its moral kind.

[Question 19] Next we consider **the goodness and badness of the inner act of willing**; and this question divides into ten:

Does whether willing is good depend on the object willed?
Only on the object?
On reason?
On the eternal law?
Are we bound to follow our reason, even if it is mistaken?
If in following mistaken reason we will something against God's law, do we act badly?
Does the goodness of an act by which we will the means to a goal depend on the act by which we intend the goal?
Does a better intention make our act of willing better?
To be good, must willing conform to God's willing?
To be good, must human willing will what God wills?

[**Article 1**] The first question [**Does whether willing is good depend on the object willed?**] we approach as follows:

It seems that what makes an act of willing good or bad is not its object:

For [1] we can't will anything but good, since as pseudo-Dionysius[25] says *the bad is unwilled*. If then willing is to be judged good by its object, every act of willing would be good and none bad.

Moreover, [2] good is first found in goals, and the goodness of a goal, as such, doesn't depend on anything else. But, according to Aristotle,[26] *good action is its own goal, though making isn't* and always has some product for its goal. So what makes an act of willing good is not its object.

Moreover, [3] the effect of a thing resembles it. But the objects of our willing are goods of nature, which can't therefore produce moral goodness in our willing. So the moral good of our act of willing doesn't derive from its object.

But against that:

Aristotle[27] says *justice is what makes people will the just thing*; and by the same token virtue is what makes people will good things. But good willing is virtuous willing. So what makes willing good is the good that it wills.

In reply:

Good and bad differentiate acts of willing as such; for good and bad belong essentially to will in the way true and false belong to reason, differentiating its actions as such, so that opinion, for example, divides into true and false opinions. So acts of good and bad will are different in kind. Now what differentiates the kind of an action is its object, as we said above. So what properly distinguishes willing as good or bad is the object it wills.

Hence:

to 1: We don't always will genuine goods; sometimes we will illusory goods, which have some good in them indeed, but are not altogether what we should desire. And as a result our acts of willing are not always good but sometimes bad.

to 2: There is an activity which is in one sense our ultimate human goal, but it isn't an act of willing, as we said above.

to 3: The will's object is a good presented to it by reason, and as planned by reason it is already a moral object and can cause moral goodness in our acts of willing. For reason is the source of human and moral action, as we said above.

[**Article 2**] The second question [**Does whether willing is good depend only on the object willed?**] we approach as follows:

It seems that whether an act of willing is good doesn't depend only on the object willed:

For [1] goals relate to will more than to any other power. But the goodness of the actions of other powers depends not only on their objects but also on their goals, as we said above. So the goodness of the action of willing too depends not only on its object but also on its goal.

Moreover, [2] the goodness of an action depends not only on its object but also on its circumstances, as we have explained. And diversity of circumstances can cause acts of willing to be good or bad: as is the case with someone willing when and where and as much as and how he ought, or in ways he ought not. So the goodness of an act of willing doesn't only depend on the object willed, but on circumstances.

Moreover, [3] ignorance of circumstances can excuse us from bad will, as was explained earlier. But that can only be because circumstances affect whether willing is good or bad. So whether willing is good or bad depends on circumstances and not only on the object willed.

But against that:

Circumstances as such don't decide an action's kind, as we said above. But we have just said that good and bad differentiate kinds of willing. So whether acts of willing are good or bad doesn't depend on circumstances, but only on the object willed.

In reply:

In any genus the most basic members are the simplest and least complex, as chemical elements are; so that the most basic members of any genus are simple unities of some sort. Now the goodness and badness of human actions is based on our willing of them, so that the goodness and badness of our willing must depend on some one thing, whereas the goodness and badness of other actions can depend on several things. The single basis from which we start in any genus is, however, something essential and not incidental, since everything incidental bases itself on what is essential. So the goodness of willing must depend only on the one thing that gives essential goodness to an action, namely, its object, and not on the incidental circumstances of actions.

Hence:

to 1: The object of will—and this distinguishes it from other powers—is precisely the goal. So, for the act of willing, goodness of object and goodness of goal don't differ as they do for actions of other powers; except incidentally in the way goal depends on goal and one act of willing on another.

to 2: Given a good act of willing, there are no circumstances which could make it bad: for saying someone wills a good when he shouldn't is ambiguous. Either the *when* qualifies what is willed: and then you aren't willing something good, for to want to do something when it shouldn't be done is not to will a good. Or the *when* is meant to qualify the willing itself: and then it is impossible to will good when one shouldn't, because one should always will good. Unless, incidentally, by willing this good at this time one is prevented from willing the good one ought to, and then the bad comes not from willing this good but from not willing that. And the same is true of all other circumstances.

to 3: Ignorance of circumstances excuses us from bad will if they qualify what is willed; that is to say, if we don't know some circumstances of the action we are willing.

[Article 3] The third question **[Does whether willing is good depend on reason?]** we approach as follows:

It seems that whether willing is good doesn't depend on reason:

For [1] earlier doesn't depend on later. But good belongs to will before it belongs to reason, as was made clear above. So whether willing is good doesn't depend on reason.

Moreover, [2] Aristotle[28] says that *the good for practical reason is a truth conforming to right desire*. But right desire is good willing. So the goodness of practical reason depends on that of willing, rather than the opposite way round.

Moreover, [3] moved depends on mover, not vice versa. But willing moves our reason and our other powers, as has been said. So whether willing is good doesn't depend on reason.

But against that:

Hilary[29] says *It is an unruly will that holds on to what it has undertaken without subjecting itself to reason*. But good willing consists in avoiding unruliness. So whether willing is good depends on whether it follows reason.

In reply:

Whether our willing is good depends properly on the object willed. Now the object we will is presented for willing by reason, since only a good that is understood is suited for willing, goods sensed or imagined being suited not for willing but for emotional desire. Will responds to good as such—which is what reason grasps—whereas emotions respond only to particular good things as perceived by the senses. So whether willing is good depends on reason in the same way that it depends on the object willed.

Hence:

to 1: Good as such, as attracting, acts on will rather than mind, but only because it has first made itself known to our mind as true; for will can only be drawn to what reason has first perceived to be good.

to 2: Aristotle is talking here of how practical reason, when it is deliberating about means, needs to be perfected by prudence; for, to be right about means, our reasoning must conform to our willing of the right goal. However, this very willing of the right goal presupposes right perception of it by our minds.

to 3: In one way willing moves us to reason, and in another reasoning moves us to will, by way of will's object, as we have said.

[Article 4] The fourth question [**Does whether willing is good depend on the eternal law?**] we approach as follows:

It seems that whether human willing is good doesn't depend on eternal law:

For [1] to each thing its standard and measure, one to one. Now human willing is measured by right reason, on which its goodness depends. So whether its willing is good doesn't depend on eternal law.

Moreover, [2] *measure and measured belong to the same genus*, as Aristotle[30] says. But eternal law and human willing are not of the same genus. So eternal law can't be the standard by which the goodness of human willing is measured.

Moreover, [3] standards must be most accurately known, whereas the eternal law is to us unknown. So eternal law can't be the standard by which the goodness of our willing is measured.

But against that:

Augustine[31] writes: *sin is any word, deed, or desire against eternal law*. But the root of sin is bad willing. So, since bad and good are opposed, good willing depends on eternal law.

In reply:

In any hierarchy of causes the effect depends more on the first cause than on subsequent ones, since subsequent causes act only in virtue of the first cause. Now human reason can lay down standards for measuring the goodness of human willing, because it reflects God's reason, the eternal law. Thus in the psalms [4: 6–7] we read *Many say: Who can show us what is good? We are sealed with the light of your face, O Lord*; as if to say: The light of our own reason can show us what is good and lay down a standard for our willing, to the extent that it is the light of your face, light deriving from your face. Clearly then good human willing depends even more on the eternal law than on human reason, and when human reason fails we should fall back on eternal reason.

Hence:

to 1: One thing can't have more than one immediate measure, but there can be several measures hierarchically ordered.

to 2: The immediate measure is of the same genus as the measured, but not the ultimate measure.

to 3: The eternal law, as it exists in God's mind, is unknown to us; but we gain some awareness of it partly through natural reason, which directly reflects it, and partly through revelation added over and above.

[**Article 5**] The fifth question [**Are we bound to follow our reason, even if it is mistaken?**] we approach as follows:

Will, it seems, if it refused consent to a mistaken reason, would not act badly:

For [1] reason provides the standard for human willing to the extent that it derives from eternal law, as we have just said. But a mistaken reason does not derive from eternal law. So a mistaken reason does not provide the standard for human willing, and a will that refuses consent to mistaken reason does not act badly.

Moreover, [2] according to Augustine[32] a subordinate's orders do not bind if they contradict those of his superior: proconsuls can't command what the emperor has forbidden. But occasionally a mistaken reason proposes something counter to the orders of its superior, namely, God, who holds supreme power. So then the dictate of mistaken reason will not bind us, and a will that refuses consent to mistaken reason will not act badly.

Moreover, [3] a bad act of will must belong to some species of bad act. But refusing consent to mistaken reason doesn't define a species of bad act: when reason tells us to have illicit sex, for example, to what species of bad act does will's refusal to consent belong? So a will that refuses consent to mistaken reason does not act badly.

But against that:

Conscience, we said in book 1, is the act of applying knowledge to some action, knowledge which reason provides. So a will that refuses consent to mistaken reason goes against conscience. But such willing is bad: for Romans 14 [23] says: *Anything which does not arise from conviction* (i.e. conscience) *is sin.* So a will that refuses consent to a mistaken reason is acting badly.

In reply:

Since conscience is a sort of dictate of reason—a sort of application of knowledge to action, as we said in book 1—to ask whether our will acts badly in refusing consent to mistaken reason is to ask whether we are bound by a mistaken conscience.

Here some people distinguish three sorts of action—good of its kind, bad of its kind, and neutral—and say that reason or conscience is not mistaken when it tells us to do what is good in kind and not to do what is bad in kind (for commanding good implies forbidding bad); but reason is mistaken when it commands what is bad in kind or forbids something good in kind, or when it commands (or forbids) what is neutral in kind, like picking up straws. To the question whether we are bound to follow this mistaken reason or conscience, they answer yes, if it is commanding (or forbidding) something neutral, saying that a will which refuses consent to such a mistaken reason or conscience acts badly and commits a sin; but no, if reason is commanding something bad in kind or forbidding something good in kind required for our eternal well-being, saying that in these latter cases a will that refuses consent to a mistaken reason or conscience does not act badly.

But this is incoherent. In the case of neutral objects, a will that refuses consent to a mistaken reason or conscience is somehow bad by reason of the willed object, on which the goodness or badness of willing depends; but not by reason of the object's true nature [since that is neutral], so, incidentally, by reason of the way reason perceives it as bad to do or not to do. And since will's object is what reason presents to it, as we have said, when will pursues something presented to it by reason as bad, it acts badly. But this doesn't only happen in the case of neutral objects, but also in the case of objects good or bad in kind. Reason not only presents neutral actions as incidentally good or bad, but bad actions as good and good actions as bad. Thus abstaining from sex outside marriage is a good thing, but will responds to this good only in the way reason presents it, and if a mistaken reason presents it as bad, will will respond to it as bad. And then because what is willed is bad the willing will be bad: not bad in itself but bad incidentally because of the way reason has perceived it. And in the same way, believing in Christ is good in kind and needed for eternal well-being, but will responds to this good only in the way reason presents it, and if reason presents it as bad, will will respond to it as bad: not bad in itself but bad incidentally because of the way reason has perceived it. And this is why Aristotle[33] says that an undisciplined man is essentially one who abandons right reason, but incidentally also one who abandons even wrong reason.

So we must say quite simply that will always acts badly if it refuses consent to reason, whether reason is right or wrong.

Hence:

to 1: Though the judgement of mistaken reason does not derive from God, mistaken reason nevertheless presents its judgement as true and so as something derived from God, the author of all truth.

to 2: Augustine's words are of relevance when we know that the subordinate's orders contradict those of his superior. But if someone thinks that the proconsul's orders are those of the emperor, in flouting the former he flouts the latter. Likewise, if a man is aware that his reason is commanding something contrary to God's law, then he is not obliged to follow it; but in such a case his reason is not entirely mistaken. But when our mistaken reason presents something as the law of God, then to flout the dictate of reason would be to flout God's law.

to 3: When reason perceives something as a bad act it always perceives it as being a particular kind of bad act: as contravening some command of God, or giving scandal, or something of the sort. So the bad act of will will be that kind of bad act.

[**Article 6**] The sixth question [**If in following mistaken reason we will something against God's law, do we act badly?**] we approach as follows:

It seems that will, in giving consent to a mistaken reason, acts well:

For [1] just as will when refusing consent to reason pursues what reason judges bad, so will when giving consent to reason pursues what reason judges good. But will when refusing consent to reason, even mistaken reason, acts badly. So will when giving consent to reason, even mistaken reason, acts well.

Moreover, [2] will when giving consent to God's command and eternal law always acts well. But eternal law and God's command is presented to us through reason's perception of it, even mistaken reason. So will when giving consent to mistaken reason acts well.

Moreover, [3] will refusing consent to a mistaken reason acts badly. If then will giving consent to a mistaken reason also acts badly, it seems that the wills of people with mistaken consciences cannot avoid acting badly. But then such people are caught in a trap and cannot avoid sin: which is hard to accept. So will when giving consent to a mistaken reason acts well.

But against that:

Whoever wills to kill an apostle acts badly. Nevertheless, they are giving consent to mistaken reason, as John 16 [2] says: *The time is coming when all those who kill you will think they are doing God a service.* So will, in giving consent to a mistaken reason, can act badly.

In reply:

Just as the preceding question asked whether we are bound by a mistaken conscience, so this one asks whether a mistaken conscience excuses us. Now this question depends on what was said earlier about ignorance. There we said that ignorance sometimes makes our actions unwilled and involuntary and sometimes not. And since moral goodness or badness attaches only to voluntary action, as was explained above, clearly the only ignorance which can deprive our actions of moral goodness or badness is that which makes our actions involuntary. We also said above that ignorance which is in any way willed, directly or indirectly, will not make actions involuntary. And I call ignorance directly willed when it is the object of an act of will, but indirectly willed when it arises from negligently not willing what it was a duty to will, as we said above.

Mistakes of reason and conscience then, made willingly, whether directly willed or arising from neglect of what it was our duty to know, do not excuse a will consenting to mistaken reason and conscience from acting badly. But mistakes that make action involuntary—arising without negligence from ignorance of some circumstance—do excuse a will consenting to mistaken reason from acting badly. For example, if mistaken reason tells a man it is his duty to have an affair with someone else's wife, will that consents to this mistaken reason will act badly, because the mistake comes from not knowing a law of God which it was his duty to know. If, however, the mistake lies in thinking the woman in his bed is his own wife, then the willing of intercourse when she asks for it is excused from being a bad act, for this is a mistake which arises from an ignorance of the circumstances, makes the act involuntary, and excuses it.

Hence:

to 1: *Any defect will make a thing bad*, says pseudo-Dionysius;[34] *to be good a thing must be wholly good.* So what we will can be bad either because the thing willed is bad by nature, or because the mind presents it as bad; to be good it must both be and be seen to be good.

to 2: Eternal law can't make a mistake but reason can. So, in giving consent to human reason, will is not always right, and not always giving consent to eternal law.

to 3: In moral action, just as in logical reasoning, a fault early on will lead to others. If, for example, we suppose someone to be acting out of vanity, he will sin whether out of vanity he does or does not do what he ought to. But he is caught in no trap, since he can put aside his bad motive. And similarly here, if the mistake of reason and conscience proceeds from inexcusable ignorance, then the will is obliged to act badly. But there is no trap here, for the ignorance is voluntary and can be overcome, and the mistake repaired.

[**Article 7**] The seventh question [**Does the goodness of an act by which we will the means to a goal depend on the act by which we intend the goal?**] we approach as follows:

It seems that the goodness of our act of will doesn't depend on the act intending the goal:

For [**1**] we have already said that the goodness of any act of will depends solely on the object willed. But when willing means to a goal the object willed differs from the goal intended. So in such cases the goodness of our act of will doesn't depend on the act intending the goal.

Moreover, [**2**] to want to keep God's commandments is a good act of will. But it can be put at the service of a bad goal: vanity, for example, or greed, when one wills to obey God for temporal advantages. So whether the act of will is good doesn't depend on the act intending the goal.

Moreover, [**3**] just as good and bad differentiate acts of will, so they differentiate goals. But the badness of an act of will doesn't depend on intending a bad goal: someone who steals in order to give to the poor is willing badly even though the goal he intends is good. In the same way then the goodness of an act of will doesn't depend on intending a good goal.

But against that:

Augustine[35] says that *God rewards intentions*. But things are rewarded by God because they are good. So the goodness of our acts of will depend on the intending of the goal.

In reply:

Intention can either precede willing or accompany it. It precedes it, in a causal sense, whenever we will something because of some intended goal. And then that relation to a goal can be thought of as contributing in some way to the goodness of what we actually will: as, for example, when we fast for God's sake, the fasting acquires a goodness from being done for God. So, since the goodness of an act of will depends on the goodness of what is willed, as we have said, it will necessarily depend on the intending of the goal. Intention follows on willing, however, when it attaches to some already existing willing: for example, if someone willed to do something, and only later referred it to God. In this case the goodness of the first act of will does not depend on the consequent intention, unless the act of will is reiterated to accompany that consequent intention.

Hence:

to 1: When we will an action because we intend a certain goal, the action's relationship to that goal contributes to its goodness, as we have said.

to 2: If a bad intention causes the willing, then the willing can't be good: willing to give to the poor out of vanity is willing something good in itself for a bad reason, and what is so willed is bad and the willing of it bad. But if the bad intention supervenes then the willing could have been good; so the consequent intention won't corrupt the willing up to that point, but only from then on if the willing is repeated.

to 3: *Any defect will make a thing bad*, as we have already said, *but to be good a thing must be wholly good.* So whether we will bad for good reasons or good for bad reasons the resultant willing will always be bad. A good act of will must be willing good for good reasons, good for the sake of good.

[**Article 8**] The eighth question [**Does a better intention make our act of willing better?**] we approach as follows:

It seems that a better intention makes our act of willing better:

For [1] a gloss on Matthew 12 [35]—*The good person produces good from the store of good in his heart*—reads: *A person does as much good as he intends*. But intentions don't only make external doing good, but also our willing, as we have said. So a person has as good a will as he intends.

Moreover, [2] increasing a cause increases its effect. But good intentions cause good willing. So the better the intention the better the willing.

Moreover, [3] when acting badly, the worse the intention, the more the sin: for if someone throws a stone intending to kill he will be judged guilty of murder. By the same token then, when acting well, the better the intention, the better the act of will.

But against that:

A good intention can accompany a bad act of will. By the same token then a better intention can accompany a worse act of will.

In reply:

Actions and intentions of goals can be measured in two ways: by their objects—how much good they will or do—or by their intensity—how intensely their agent wills or does them.

If then we measure by object, it is clear that the degree of our doing doesn't always match up to that of our intending. And where external activity is concerned this can happen in two ways: firstly, the object that is ordered to the intended goal may not match up to that goal (as giving ten pounds isn't enough to attain a goal of buying something worth a hundred pounds); and secondly, there can arise obstacles to external activity which we are powerless to remove (as when we intend to go on as far as Rome but obstacles arise to stop us doing it). But where interior acts of will are concerned only the first of the above ways operates: for interior acts of will are within our power whereas external activity is not; but the object that we will may not match up to the goal we intend, so that the willing of that object, considered in itself, is not as good as the intention was. Nevertheless, since the intention itself is attached to the act of willing in a way, providing the reason for willing, a measure of good in the intention does flow over into the willing: the will is willing a great goal even if the means it wills to take are not worthy of that goal.

But if we turn to the degree of intensity with which actions are willed and goals intended, the intensity of our intention will flow over into the will's interior acts and external activity, since intention gives them both a sort of form, as we have said. Both the interior and exterior parts of an action may be, materially speaking, less intensely willed than the goal is—we often have a stronger desire to be well than to take the medicine required, but the intensity of our intention to be well will flow over, formally speaking, into an intense willing of the medicine.

Yet we must also consider this: that the intention can have as object the intensity of both interior willing and external activity: as when one intends to will or do something intensely, and yet for all that one doesn't will or do the thing intensely, since the goodness of the interior or external activity doesn't match up to the degree of good intended, as we said earlier. And that is why we don't deserve all that we intended to deserve; for degree of deserts is related to intensity of action, as we shall see later.

Hence:

to 1: That gloss is talking of God's reckoning in which the goal intended is what mainly counts. Thus another gloss on the same text says that *the heart's store is intention, by which God judges our deeds.* For the goodness of intention flows over in a sense, as we have said, into the goodness of our willing, to make even external acts deserving in God's eyes.

to 2: The goodness of our intention is not the whole cause of the goodness of our willing. So the argument doesn't succeed.

to 3: Badness of intention alone is enough to spoil our willing, so the worse the intention the worse the willing; but, as we have just said, you can't use the same argument where goodness is concerned.

[**Article 9**] The ninth question [**To be good, must willing conform to God's willing?**] we approach as follows:

It seems that to be good, human willing needn't conform to God's willing:

For [1] it is impossible for human willing to conform to God's willing: *As the heavens are high above the earth, so are my ways high above your ways and my thoughts above your thoughts*, says Isaiah [55: 9]. If then willing, to be good, must conform to God's willing, it would be impossible for any human willing to be good. And that doesn't seem right.

Moreover, [2] our willing derives from God's willing in the way our knowledge derives from his knowledge. But our knowledge doesn't have to conform to his: for he knows many things we don't. So our willing doesn't have to conform to his willing.

Moreover, [3] willing causes action. But our action doesn't have to conform to God's action. So not our will to his will either.

But against that:

We read in Matthew 26 [39]: *Not as I will, but as you will*; which [Jesus] said because *he willed to be an upright man directed to God*, as Augustine[36] expounds. But upright willing is good willing. So to be good, willing must conform to God's willing.

In reply:

We have said that the goodness of an act of will depends on the intending of the goal. Now, as we said earlier, the ultimate goal of human willing is the supreme good, God; so the goodness of an act of human will requires that it be ordered to the supreme good. But that [supreme] good is primarily and in its nature the proper object of God's willing; and what is primary in a genus is the standard and pattern for everything else in the genus. So, because to be right and good a thing must measure up to its proper standard, human willing, to be good, must conform to God's willing.

Hence:

to 1: Human willing can't conform to God's willing by equalling it, but it can imitate it. And in the same way [2] human knowing conforms to God's knowing by knowing truth, and [3] human action to God's action by being fitting to its agent. All this by imitation rather than equivalence. So this provides the answers **to 2** and **to 3** as well.

[**Article 10**] The tenth question [**To be good, must human willing will what God wills?**] we approach as follows:

It seems that human willing doesn't always have to conform to God's willing in regard to what it wills:

For [1] we can't will what we don't know about, since will's object is what is perceived as good. But in most cases we don't know God's will. So we can't conform our willing to it.

Moreover, [2] God wills the eternal condemnation of those he already sees will die in fatal sin. If then a human being had a duty to conform his willing to God's willing in regard to what he wills, the human being would have to will his own damnation, and that doesn't seem right.

Moreover, [3] nobody has a duty to be unfilial. But sometimes willing what God wills is unfilial: for example, when God wills the death of one's father it would be unfilial to will the same. So one has no duty to conform one's willing to God's willing in regard to what one wills.

But against that:

[1] A gloss on the text from the Psalms [33: 1]: *Praise comes well from the upright*, reads: *The upright in heart are those who will what God wills.* But everyone has a duty to be upright in heart. So everyone has a duty to will what God wills.

Moreover, [2] like every action, willing is defined by its object. So if we have a duty to conform our willing to God's willing, that conformity must be in regard to what we will.

Moreover, [3] wills conflict when people will different things. But willing that conflicts with God's will is bad willing. So unless one conforms one's willing to God's willing in regard to what one wills, one will will badly.

In reply:

We have already explained that the object of willing is presented to it by reason. Now reason can often regard one and the same action as good for one reason and bad for another; and one person may want it because of the good and will well, while another doesn't want it because of the bad and is also willing well. A judge, for example, may will well and justly in sentencing a bandit to death, while the bandit's wife and children may will well in opposing the sentence as a natural evil. But because willing follows on the reasoned perception of mind, the more general the nature of the good perceived, the more general the good that is willed. As we see in the above example: the judge has to serve the general good of the community, which is justice, and wills the bandit's death as good for public order; but the wife is considering what is good for the private family, and so wills her bandit husband not to be killed.

Now God, as the maker and manager of the whole universe, wills what he sees to be good for the whole of that community, and wills whatever he wills as good for the whole universe, a general good which is indeed his own goodness; creatures, however, by nature grasp only the particular goods appropriate to their own natures. Now it can happen that something is good for a particular reason but not good on universal grounds, and vice versa, as we have said. So it can happen that a good will can want something, for a particular reason, that God does not want on universal grounds, and vice versa; or that different men can will opposite things, wanting this to be or not to be so for different reasons, and yet all have good wills.

However, a man willing a particular good does not will it

rightly unless he intends to will in it the common good as goal: since even parts of a natural whole instinctively desire the common good of their whole. Now the goal gives a sort of form to the willing of the means to that goal; so in order to will any particular good with a right will, we must, in willing the particular good as a sort of material, be also willing the general good that is God's as a sort of form. So human willing has a duty to conform formally to God's will in what it wills, for it has a duty to will the general good that is God's; but it does not have to conform materially, for the reasons already given.

However, either way human willing is conforming in a way to God's willing. For by conforming to God's willing in the general form of what it wills it is conforming to God's willing of the ultimate goal; and by not conforming to God's willing in the particular material it wills, it is conforming to God as active in him, for God wills and causes him to have those natural inclinations and particular perception of things; and so our human willing conforms to God's willing, as people are wont to say, because we will what God wills us to will.

But a further formal conformity is possible: that we will something with charity[, the love of God], thus willing it in the way in which God wills it. And this conformity belongs to the formal conformity to our ultimate goal, which is the proper object of charity.

Hence:

to 1: The sort of thing that God wills in general we can know, for we know that whatever he wills he wills because it is good, and so by willing what is presented to us as good we are conforming to God's will in the form of what we will. But what God wills in particular cases we do not know, and in this respect, therefore, have no duty to conform our willing to his. When, however, in glory we all come to see each thing's relation to what God wills for it, we shall have the duty to conform not only the form of our willing but also all of its matter to God.

to 2: God does not will damnation for damnation's sake, or death for death's sake, since *he wills all men to be saved*; but he wills them as realizing justice; and it is enough that men too will to preserve God's justice and the natural order. So this provides the answer to 3 as well.

As to the arguments raised against:

to 1: Conforming one's willing to God's willing in regard to his reason for willing something is more truly willing what God wills than conforming to the actual thing willed, since will wills the goal more than what is ordered to the goal.

to 2: What defines and gives form to action is the form of the object rather than what it is materially.

to 3: There is no conflict of wills when people will different things for different reasons. But if one person gave the same reason for willing something that another gave for not willing it, there would be conflict of wills. But that doesn't arise here.

[**Question 20**] Next we consider **the goodness and badness of external actions**; and this question divides into six:

- Which goodness and badness comes first, that of an external action or that of the act of willing it?
- Does an external action derive its goodness or badness entirely from the goodness of the act that wills it?
- Do the interior and external acts share one goodness or badness?
- Does an external action add any more goodness or badness than the interior act?
- Do the consequences of an external action add to it any goodness or badness?
- Can one and the same external action be both good and bad?

[**Article 1**] The first question [**Which goodness and badness comes first, that of an external action or that of the act of willing it?**] we approach as follows:

It seems that the goodness and badness of an external action comes first, and not that of the act of willing it:

For [**1**] we said above that willing is good or bad because of the object willed. But the external action is the object the interior act wills; for we say we want to steal, or will to give to the poor. So the goodness and badness attaches first to the external action and then to the act of willing it.

Moreover, [2] goals are the primary goods, and things ordered to goals are good because they are ordered to good goals. But though acts of other powers can be goals, an act of willing can't, as we said above. So good belongs first to the actions of another power and then to the acts of willing them.

Moreover, [3] as we have said, external activity is given its shape or form by the act of willing it. But forms come after the material which acquires them. So external activity is good and bad first, and then the act that wills it.

But against that:

Augustine[37] says that *it is by our wills that we sin or live rightly.* So moral goodness and badness derive from willing in the first place.

In reply:

An external activity can be judged good or bad in two ways: firstly, because of the kind of act it is and its attendant circumstances, as giving to the poor in the proper circumstances is judged good; or secondly, because of its relation to some goal, as giving to the poor out of vanity is judged bad. Now because a goal is properly speaking something willed, clearly the goodness or badness an external action possesses because it is related to a goal exists first in the act of will and the external activity gets it from there. But the goodness and badness an external action possesses in itself, because of its due matter and proper circumstances, is not derived from the act of will but rather from reason. So the goodness of an external action as perceived and planned by reason precedes our good willing of it, though the goodness of the actually executed deed follows from the goodness of the act of will that causes it.

Hence:

to 1: The external action is object of our willing inasmuch as it is presented for willing by reason as a good perceived and planned by reason; and in this sense its goodness is prior to the good of the willing act. But the actually implemented external action is an effect of the willing act following on from it.

to 2: Goals are intended first but implemented last.

to 3: The form, as it comes to exist in the material, is generated after the material, though in nature['s intentions] it comes first; but the form, as it pre-exists in the agent, comes first in every sense. Now the act of will is the agent cause of the external activity. So the goodness of the act of will is the form of the external activity as pre-existing in its agent cause.

[**Article 2**] The second question [**Does an external action derive its goodness or badness entirely from the goodness of the act that wills it?**] we approach as follows:

It seems that the goodness or badness of an external action depends entirely on the will:

For [1] Matthew 7 [18] says *A good tree cannot bear bad fruit, nor a bad tree good fruit.* Now, according to the gloss, the tree represents the will and the fruit the deed. So if the interior act of will is good the external action can't be bad, and vice versa.

Moreover, [2] Augustine[38] says that we sin only with our will. So if there's no sin in the will there can't be a sin in the external action. And so the goodness and badness of the external action depends entirely on the will.

Moreover, [3] the goodness and badness of which we are now talking differentiate moral actions, and, according to Aristotle,[39] differentiation must be by essential characteristics of the genus. Now since actions are moral because they're voluntary, it seems that actions are good and bad entirely because of the will.

But against that:

Augustine[40] says *there are some things that can't be done well, no matter how good the goal or the will.*

In reply:

As we have already said, there are two goodnesses or badnesses to consider in an external action: one deriving from its due matter and circumstances, and the other from its relation to a goal. And the latter goodness, deriving from the action's relation to a goal, depends entirely on the act that wills it, but the former goodness, deriving from due matter and circumstances, depends on reason, and the act of will's goodness comes from willing that goodness.

But now we must remember what we said above: that *a single defect will make a thing bad*, but a single good point is not enough to make a thing good simply speaking; for that *a thing must be wholly good*. If then the act of will is good both by reason of its own object and by reason of its goal, the external action will be good, but the goodness that comes from intending the goal is not in itself enough to make the external action good. But if the act of will is bad either by reason of intending the goal or by reason of the action willed, the external action will in consequence be bad.

Hence:

to 1: The good will represented by the good tree is to be understood as being good as to both the action it wills and the goal it intends.

to 2: A man sins with his will not only by willing a bad goal but also by willing a bad action.

to 3: It is not only interior acts of the will which are voluntary but also external actions in so far as they issue from will and reason; and so the differentiation into good and bad can relate to both these types of act.

[**Article 3**] The third question [**Do the interior and external acts share one goodness or badness?**] we approach as follows:

It seems that an external action and the interior act of willing it don't share one and the same goodness or badness:

For [**1**] the sources of interior acts are interior powers of awareness or desire, but the sources of external activity are our motor powers. Now where there are different sources of action there must be different actions. Goodness or badness, however, needs some act as its subject, and what exists in one subject can't exist in another. So there can't be one goodness belonging to both interior and external act.

Moreover, [2] as Aristotle[41] says, *a virtue renders its possessor and his activity good.* But the intellectual virtue in the power commanding action differs from the moral virtues present in the powers commanded to act, as Aristotle[42] explains. So the goodness of the interior act in the commanding power differs from the goodness of the external action in the powers commanded to act.

Moreover, [3] the same thing cannot be both cause and effect: nothing can cause itself. But either the goodness of the interior act causes that of the external action or vice versa, as we have said. So they can't share the same goodness.

But against that:

We have already shown that the act of will gives a sort of form to the external action. But material and its form make up one thing. So the goodness of interior and external act is one.

In reply:

The sources of our inner act of willing are our inner powers (mind and will); and of our external deed our body's motive powers. But from a moral point of view the two together constitute a single action that may have more than one reason for being good or bad. Sometimes the only reason for goodness in an external deed is its goal (swallowing unpleasant medicine, for example), and then the same goodness or badness is present immediately in the willing and mediately in the deed. But the matter and circumstances of an external deed may also have a goodness of their own (the medicine may be pleasant), and then the separate goodnesses flow over into one another.

Hence:

to 1: This argument proves that the interior act differs in nature from the external action; but what differ as natural actions constitute one moral action, as we have said.

to 2: As Aristotle[43] says, the moral virtues dispose us to the very acts of virtue which are, so to speak, our goals, whilst prudence is a virtue in reason disposing us to do what leads to these goals. And so there we need different virtues. But right reasoning about the very goal of the virtues doesn't have a goodness different from the goodness of virtue, since every virtue shares in the goodness of reason.

to 3: When something is carried over univocally from one member of a species to another it has to be duplicated: when heat communicates itself, the heat that does the heating is individually different from the heat communicated, though not different in species. But when something is carried over by analogy or proportion there is only one instance of it: when the attribution of health is carried over from organisms to diets and complexions, the health ascribed to the diet and the complexion is the very health of the organism, as produced by the diet and displayed by the complexion. And this is the way external action derives goodness from the inner act of willing and vice versa: by a relation of one to the other.

[**Article 4**] The fourth question [**Does an external action add any more goodness or badness than the interior act?**] we approach as follows:

It seems that an external action adds no more goodness or badness than the interior act:

For [1] Chrysostom[44] says: *It is our willing that is rewarded if good or condemned if bad*; our works, however, testify to our will. God then doesn't ask for works on his own account, so that he may know how to judge, but on others' account, so that all understand that God judges justly. But goodness and badness should be reckoned according to God's judgement rather than man's. So external action adds nothing more to goodness and badness than the interior act.

Moreover, [2] interior and external acts share one goodness, we have said. But to augment something we must add something else. So external action adds nothing more in goodness and badness than the interior act.

Moreover, [3] the goodness of the entire creation adds nothing to the goodness of God, since it is derived entirely from God's goodness. But sometimes the goodness of external action is derived entirely from the goodness of the interior act, and sometimes the reverse is true, as we have said. So neither of them adds more goodness or badness than the other.

But against that:

Every agent intends to do good and avoid evil. But if external action adds nothing of goodness or badness, there would be no point in someone with a good or bad will actually doing good or not doing evil. And that doesn't seem right.

In reply:

If we're talking of the goodness that external action derives from the willing of its goal, then the external action cannot add to the goodness of that willing, unless the willing itself somehow betters itself while doing good, or worsens itself while doing bad. This could happen in three ways. Firstly, by multiplying in number, as, for example, when someone first wills to do something for a good or bad end but doesn't do it, and then again wills it and does it, the act of will is duplicated and the goodness and badness is doubled. Secondly, by lasting longer, as, for example, when someone wills to do something for a good or bad end but ceases in the face of obstacles, whereas someone else persists in that movement of will until the work is completed, for clearly the latter will is more lastingly good or bad, and so better or worse. Thirdly, by gaining in intensity, for certain external actions because of their pleasurableness or painfulness are such as to intensify or diminish the willing of them. And certainly the more intensely we will good or bad the better or worse we will.

But if we're talking of the goodness an external action has because of its own matter and due circumstances, then that constitutes a goal or terminus for the willing; and then that adds to the goodness or badness of the willing, since every tendency and movement is perfected by achieving its goal or reaching its terminus. So a willing that given the opportunity doesn't actually proceed to an actual deed is not perfect. If, however, the ability to act is missing, although the willing is perfect and would proceed to act if it could, then the lack of the external act is something simply speaking involuntary. Now just as the involuntary doing of good or bad doesn't deserve reward or penalty, so the lack of a good or bad deed, if strictly speaking involuntary, doesn't subtract any reward or penalty.

Hence:

to 1: Chrysostom is talking of the case of perfect human willing that doesn't hold back from acting unless it is unable to act.

to 2: This argument bases itself on the goodness an external act gets from being willed for some goal. But the goodness an external act gets from its own matter and circumstances differs from the goodness the willing of a goal has, though not from the goodness the willing of this very action has, for it is the reason and cause of that goodness, as we said earlier. So this also makes clear the answer to **3**.

[**Article 5**] The fifth question [**Do the consequences of an external action add to it any goodness or badness?**] we approach as follows:

It seems that an action's consequences add to its goodness or badness:

For [1] an action's consequences pre-exist virtually in the action, since they are like a cause's effects, which pre-exist virtually in their cause. But things are judged good or bad according to their virtue: *virtue renders its possessor good*, as Aristotle[45] says. So consequences add to the goodness or badness of actions.

Moreover, [2] the good actions a teacher's hearers do are a sort of effect of his teaching. But they redound to his credit, as we glean from Philippians 4 [1]: *My brothers and dear friends that I miss so much, my joy and my crown.* So consequences add to the goodness or badness of actions.

Moreover, [3] the greater penalty is reserved for the greater crime, as in Deuteronomy 25 [2]'s prescription: *the number of strokes proportionate to his offence*. But consequences increase penalties, as we read in Exodus 21 [3]: *But if the ox has been in the habit of goring before and its owner has been warned but has not kept it under control, then should it kill man or woman, both the ox is to be stoned and its owner put to death*. But the owner would not have been put to death if the ox hadn't killed someone, even if the owner hadn't kept him under control. So the consequence has added to the goodness or badness of the action.

Moreover, [4] if someone does something which could cause death—strikes someone, or passes sentence on him—he contracts an impediment to holy orders if death follows, but not otherwise. So the consequence adds to the goodness or badness of the action.

But against that:

A consequence can't make a good act bad or a bad act good. For example, if someone gives to a poor man something he then sinfully misuses, that is not blamed on the charitable giver; and again if someone patiently bears an injury done him, that doesn't excuse the one doing the injury. So consequences don't add to the goodness or badness of actions.

In reply:

An action's consequences can be foreseen or unforeseen. If they are foreseen, they clearly add to its goodness or badness: not to refrain from an action even when one sees it could have many bad consequences shows a deeper disorder in the will. In the case of unforeseen consequences, we must make a distinction. If the consequences are the usual direct consequences of such an action, then they add to its goodness or badness—a proneness to good consequences makes a deed a better act of its kind, and proneness to bad consequences makes it worse. But if the results are unusual and coincidental, then the consequences don't add to the action's goodness or badness; for we judge things by what defines them, not by anything coincidental.

Hence:

to 1: We judge the virtue of a cause by its direct rather than its coincidental effects.

to 2: The good actions a teacher's hearers do are a direct consequence of his teaching. So they redound to his credit. And especially if they were intended by him.

to 3: The consequence for which such a penalty on the owner has been prescribed is a direct consequence of its cause and is also presumed to be foreseen. And this is why it draws the penalty.

to 4: This would be a valid argument if the impediment to holy orders arose from a moral offence; but it arises from the fact itself detracting from the sacramental symbolism.

[**Article 6**] The sixth question [**Can one and the same external action be both good and bad?**] we approach as follows:

It seems that one act can be both good and bad:

For [1] Aristotle[46] tells us that *a movement is one if it is unbroken*. But one unbroken movement can be both good and bad: for example, someone walking without break to church can do it first out of vanity and then out of reverence for God. So the one action can be both good and bad.

Moreover, [2] Aristotle[47] says that one and the same action is what the agent does and what the patient undergoes. But the undergoing can be good—Christ's passion, for example—though the doing of it is bad—what the Jews did. So one action can be both good and bad.

Moreover, [3] since the servant is his master's tool in a sense, the servant's action is also the master's as a tool's action is also the workman's. But it can happen that the servant's action springs from a master's good will, and is in that way good, but from the servant's bad will, and is in that way bad. So the same action can be both good and bad.

But against that:

Contrary qualities can't coexist in the same subject. But good and bad are contrary qualities. So one action can't be both good and bad.

In reply:

There is no reason why things which are single in one genus can't be many in another, as an unbroken surface is one quantitatively but can be of diverse colours, here white, there black. And in this way there is no reason why an action can't be a single physical action but several moral actions, or vice versa, as we have said. An unbroken walk is one physical action but could turn out to be several morally if the walker's intentions, from which it gets it moral character, changed. So if the action is morally single it can't be both good and bad with moral goodness and badness; but if it is one physical action but not one morally, then it can be both good and bad.

Hence:

to 1: An unbroken movement issuing from different intentions may be one action physically, but not one morally.

to 2: Doing and undergoing are moral inasmuch as they are voluntary. And if different wills make them voluntary then morally they are two actions, one of which can be good and the other bad.

to 3: The servant's action as issuing from the servant's will is not the master's action; it is that only as issuing from the master's command. So it is not the master's action that the servant's bad will makes bad.

Passage 36
Virtue

Source: *Summa Theologiae*, 1a2ae.55–6. Text from *Summa Theologiae* (*Opera Omnia*, Leonine edn., vol. vi).

Date: 1269–70, second stay in Paris, aged 45.

Type of passage and how to read: Modified disputed question (see Introduction).

Notes on translation: 'Virtue' translates *virtus*, which has also the meanings of strength, power, vigour, excellence. Deliberately, 'condition' translates *dispositio*, 'disposition' *habitus*, and 'habit' and 'custom' *consuetudo*. 'Moderation' and 'courage' translate *temperantia* and *fortitudo*; 'deiform virtue' translates *virtus theologica*.

The consideration of **virtues** divides into five:

first, [Question 55] what virtues are;
second, [Question 56] what parts of us they affect . . .

[Question 55] The first question **[what virtues are]** divides into four:

Is human virtue a disposition?
Is it a disposition to act?
Is it a good disposition?
How can we define it?

[Article 1] The first question **[Is human virtue a disposition?]** we approach as follows:

It seems that human virtue is not a disposition:

For [1] virtue is *power at its utmost*, as Aristotle[1] says. But the utmost of something belongs reductively to the same genus as what it is the utmost of: the point that ends a line to the same genus as the line. So virtue should belong to the genus of powers, not dispositions.

Moreover, [2] Augustine[2] says that *virtue is the good use of our freedom to choose*. But using free choice is an activity. So virtue is action, not disposition.

Moreover, [3] actions are deserving, not dispositions, otherwise a person would deserve all the time even when asleep. Now virtues are deserving. So virtues are not dispositions but actions.

Moreover, [4] Augustine[3] says that virtue is *ordered love*. And again[4] that *the orderedness we call virtue rejoices in what is given for enjoyment, and uses what is given for use*. Now orderedness names either an action or a relationship. So virtue is not a disposition but an action or a relationship.

Moreover, [5] besides human virtues there are the virtues in nature. But virtues in nature are powers, not dispositions. So human virtues too.

But against that:

Aristotle[5] classifies virtues and sciences as dispositions.

In reply:

By the word *virtue* [literally, *strength* or *force*] we mean a certain excellence or perfection of potential. Now we measure anything's perfection primarily in relation to its goal, and the goal of potential is realizing it. So a potential is called perfect when it is all set to be actualized.

Now there are certain potentials, like natural agencies, which are of their own nature all set to act, so that they themselves can be called *forces* or *virtues*. But the peculiarly human abilities connected with reason are not of their own nature set on one act but open to several, and must be further determined to act by dispositions, as we said earlier. So human virtue and excellence consists in such dispositions.

Hence:

to 1: Sometimes we call *virtue* what the virtue is ordered to: its object or its activity. *Faith* sometimes means what we believe, sometimes the act of believing, and sometimes the disposition to believe. When Aristotle says that the virtue of a power *is the utmost it can do* he is talking of the object of the virtue. For the utmost a thing can do is what we rate its virtue at: if, for example, someone can lift 100 pounds and no more, then we rate his strength at 100 pounds, not at 60. But the objection assumed virtue to consist essentially in this utmost the power could do.

to 2: Good use of our freedom to choose is said to be virtue in the same sort of way: because virtue is ordered to that as its own proper activity. For the activity of virtue is nothing else than good use of one's freedom to choose.

to 3: There are two things needed for deserving: one is the deserving act itself, by which we deserve in the same sense as by running we run, and this is why we say we deserve by actions. But there must be a source of the deserving act, just as running must have its motive power; and in that sense we deserve by our virtuous dispositions.

to 4: *Orderedness of love* is virtue in the sense of what virtue is ordered to, for virtue orders our love.

to 5: Natural agencies are already determined to their activity, but not human powers, so there is a difference.

[**Article 2**] The second question [**Is human virtue a disposition to act?**] we approach as follows:

It seems that virtue can't be defined as a disposition to act:

For [1] Cicero[6] says that ***virtue is to a soul what health and beauty are to a body***. But health and beauty aren't dispositions to act. So neither is virtue.

Moreover, [2] in nature we find virtue to act and virtue to exist, since Aristotle[7] says that certain things have the virtue to exist for ever, and others not for ever but only for a limited time. Now human virtue corresponds in reasoning creatures to natural virtue in the world of nature. So human virtues too must not only be dispositions to act, but to exist.

Moreover, [3] Aristotle[8] says that virtue *disposes perfect things for the best*. Now the best thing to which virtue should dispose a human being is God, as Augustine[9] proves, and that is done by making the soul like God. So virtue, it seems, names a quality which orders the soul to God by making it like him in some way; but not one which orders it to activity. So it is not a disposition to act.

But against that:

Aristotle[10] says ***the virtue of anything is what makes it act well***.

In reply:

As we have said, the very word *virtue* implies an excellence of ability. And since ability can mean either a capability to be something or an ability to do something, perfection in both sorts of ability is called virtue. Now capability to be is characteristic of materials, which are potential of being formed; but ability to do is characteristic of forms, which make things active, everything's activity following on its actuality.

Now in the making of a human being, the body is material, formed by its soul. And human beings share body, and the powers exercised by body and soul together, with other animals; only those abilities dependent on reason, exercised by the soul alone, are peculiarly human. So human virtue, which we are now considering, cannot be bodily excellence, but must be reserved to what is the soul's alone. Human virtue then is not related to being something but to doing something; and thus by definition is a disposition to action.

Hence:

to 1: How an agent acts depends on its condition, for everything acts in accordance with the sort of thing it is. So, since virtue is a source of some sort of activity, it must cause some previous suitable condition in the agent. Now virtue causes ordered activity. So virtue itself must be a sort of ordered condition of soul in which the soul's powers are ordered among themselves and to the outside world. Virtue then is a sort of fitness of soul and can be likened to health and beauty, which are right conditions of body. But that doesn't stop virtue also being a source of activity.

to 2: The virtue to exist is not characteristically human, but only the virtue to do things reason can do, for reason characterizes humans.

to 3: Since God's substance is his action, the highest likeness man can have to God is through activity of some sort. Which is why we have said that happiness or bliss, which makes human beings most like God and which is life's ultimate goal, consists in activity.

[Article 3] The third question [**Is human virtue a good disposition?**] we approach as follows:

It seems that virtue can't be defined as a good disposition:

For [1] everything about sin is bad. But even sin has its virtue, for 1 Corinthians 15 [56] talks of law as the *virtue* [= power] *of sin*. So virtue is not always a good disposition.

Moreover, [2] virtues match powers, and power can be for good or bad: as Isaiah 5 [22] says: *Woe to the mighty topers, to the powerful mixers of drink.* So virtue too can be for good or bad.

Moreover, [3] 2 Corinthians 12 [9] tells us *virtue is made perfect through weakness.* But weakness is a bad thing. So virtue is not only for good but for bad.

But against that:

Augustine[11] says *no one should doubt that virtue makes the soul perfect.* And Aristotle[12] says that *virtue renders its possessor good and his activity good.*

In reply:

As we have said, virtue implies perfect ability, which is why Aristotle[13] says *a thing's virtue or strength is measured by the utmost of which it is capable.* But the utmost of which anything is capable must be good, since evil is always a falling short and, as pseudo-Dionysius[14] says, a *weakness.* For that reason virtue in everything implies an orderedness towards good, and human virtue, which is a disposition to act, is a good disposition to act well.

Hence:

to 1: The words *good* and *perfect* are used metaphorically about bad things: Aristotle[15] notes that we talk of good and perfect thieves and robbers. And even *virtue* is used in the same way. Law, then, is called *the virtue of sin* because occasionally law causes sin to grow, and to reach the maximum of its potential, so to speak.

to 2: Drunkenness and unrestrained drinking are bad because they lack reason's order. But what lacks reason may require perfection from some lesser power in its own realm, even though that conflicts with or detracts from reason. But perfection of such a power, when it involves lack of reason, can't be called human virtue.

to 3: Reason shows itself the more perfect, the better it can prevail over or tolerate weakness in our body and lower parts. So virtue, the work of reason, is *made perfect in* *weakness*, but not in a weakness of reason: rather in a weakness of our body and lower powers.

[Article 4] The fourth question [**How can we define it?**] we approach as follows:

It seems that there is something wrong with the usual definition of virtue: namely, virtues are good qualities of mind which dispose us to live rightly, which we cannot misuse, and which God works in us without our help:[16]

For [1] virtue is human goodness: it itself *renders its possessor good.*[17] But it doesn't seem goodness is itself good, any more than whiteness is white. So it is a mistake to say virtue is a good quality.

Moreover, [2] no differentiating characteristic should apply more widely than the genus it is differentiating; since it is a division of that genus. But good applies more widely than quality; since it is interchangeable with all being. So good shouldn't appear in the definition as a differentiation of qualities.

Moreover, [3] Augustine[18] says that *mind begins where there is something we don't share with the beasts*. But Aristotle[19] says there are certain virtues in the unreasoning parts of us as well. So not every virtue is a good quality of mind.

Moreover, [4] rightness seems to be a matter of justice, and we call the same people just and right. But justice is one specific virtue. So it seems wrong to include rightness in a [general] definition of virtue, by saying *which dispose us to live rightly*.

Moreover, [5] when someone is proud of something he is misusing it. Now many people are proud of their virtues: as Augustine[20] says: *Pride enters into even our good works to destroy them*. So it is false to say that virtues are something *we cannot misuse*.

Moreover, [6] virtues set human beings to rights. But Augustine[21] commenting on John 14 [12]: *Greater than these he will do*, says: *He who created you without your help will not set you right without your help*. So it is wrong to say that *God works virtue in us without our help*.

But against that:

We have Augustine's authority especially in *De Libero Arbitrio*, 2 [19], from which the words of this definition are culled.

In reply:

This definition collects together everything required to define virtue. For the best definition of anything brings together all its causes, and this definition brings together all the causes of virtue.

Good quality defines virtue's form, like any other, by its genus and a differentiating characteristic: the genus being *quality* (though disposition would be a more precise genus, giving a better definition) and the differentiating characteristic *good*. Like other incidental properties, virtue has no material *out-of-which*, but it has material *about-which* [subject-matter] and material *in-which* [the material it forms]. The definition does not mention the subject-matter with which virtue is concerned, for that is the virtue's object and defines it as a particular type of virtue; but here we are busy defining virtues in general. So as material cause the definition mentions what virtue forms, saying it is a good quality *of the mind*.

The purpose of virtue, since it is a disposition to act, is action itself. But note that some such dispositions are always for bad (vices), some sometimes for good and sometimes for bad (opinion can be true or false), but virtue is a disposition always for good. So to distinguish virtues from dispositions always pursuing the bad, the definition says they *dispose us to live rightly*; and to distinguish them from dispositions which incline us sometimes to good and sometimes to evil, it says they *cannot be misused*.

As to agency, we are given God: the cause of instilled virtue *which God works in us without our help*. But if this phrase is left out, the rest of the definition applies generally to all virtues, acquired or instilled.

Hence:

to 1: Mind's first concept is being, and so anything we think is thought of as existent, and consequently one and good, which are predicates interchangeable with being. So that beingness itself exists and is one and is good; and oneness exists and is one and is good; and goodness similarly. Now none of this applies to special forms like whiteness and health: not everything we think is thought of as white or healthy. However, we must remember that properties and forms of material things are said to exist, not as though they themselves possess existence but because they are ways in which something else exists. And in the same way, if they are called good and one, that is not because they possess some other goodness or oneness, but because they themselves make something else good or one. And so it is with virtue, which is called good because it makes something good.

to 2: Good in the definition of virtue isn't good in general, interchangeable with being and applying more widely than quality; but it is the good of *according with reason* that pseudo-Dionysius[22] talks of as *the soul's good*.

to 3: Virtue can only exist in the unreasoning parts of us inasmuch as they share in reason, Aristotle[23] says; so that reason or mind is the proper subject of human virtue.

to 4: The rightness belonging to justice is that laid down for the common human use of external goods, which is the proper subject-matter of justice, as we shall see later; but there is a general meaning of right living common to all virtues, that of pursuing a due goal and letting the law of God rule our human wills, as we said earlier.

to 5: Virtues can be objects of misuse by people despising or hating or taking pride in them, but they can't be dispositions to their own bad use, as though you could do a bad act of virtue.

to 6: God causes in us instilled virtue without us doing anything, though not without our consent, and that is how we must understand the words *God works in us without our help*; but our own work God works in us with our help, since he is at work within every will and every nature.

[**Question 56**] Next we consider **what parts of us virtues affect**. And the consideration divides into six:

Do virtues dispose our abilities to act?
Can one virtue dispose more than one ability?
Are there virtues of intellect?
Of our affective and aggressive capacities?
Of our powers of sense-perception?
Of our wills?

[Article 1] The first question [**Do virtues dispose our abilities to act?**] we approach as follows:

It seems that virtues don't dispose our abilities to act:

For [1] Augustine[24] says *virtue disposes us to live rightly*. But we don't live by some ability of our soul but by the soul's very substance. So virtue disposes not abilities of soul but its substance.

Moreover, [2] according to Aristotle[25] *virtue renders its possessor good and his activity good*. But if activity is an effect of an ability to act, the possessor of virtue is an effect of the soul's substance. So virtue has no more to do with soul's abilities than with its substance.

Moreover, [3] abilities are type-2 qualities,[26] and virtues are also qualities, as we have said. But qualities don't have qualities. So virtues don't dispose our abilities to act.

But against that:

Virtue is ability at its utmost, as Aristotle[27] says. But a thing's utmost belongs to it. So virtue belongs in the soul's abilities.

In reply:

Three things show that virtues belong in our soul's abilities to act. Firstly, the very notion that virtues perfect abilities, since perfections must exist in what they perfect. Secondly, the fact that they dispose to act, as we have said, since all activity of soul issues from some ability of soul. And thirdly, the fact that they dispose a thing towards what is best, namely, to a goal which is either the thing's own activity or something it can achieve by exercising some ability it has to act. So human virtue disposes our ability to act.

Hence:

to 1: Life has two meanings: sometimes it means the living thing's very existence and that has to do with the substance of the soul, which is the source of existence in living things; but it also means the living thing's activity, and in this sense virtue disposes us to live rightly, for it is virtue that disposes us to act rightly.

to 2: Goodness belongs either to goals or to things ordered to goals. So, since the agent's good consists in acting, even virtue's making its agent good concerns his activity, and consequently his abilities to act.

to 3: One property can be subject to another, not as independently sustaining it in being, but as mediating to it the support of a substance; thus surface is the subject of colour in the sense that colour inheres in a body by way of its surface. And this is the way abilities can be subject to virtues.

[**Article 2**] The second question [**Can one virtue dispose more than one ability?**] we approach as follows:

It seems that one virtue can dispose two abilities:

For [**1**] activities reveal dispositions. Now one and the same activity can issue, in different ways, from several abilities: walking, for example, is directed by reason, stimulated by will, and executed by our motive powers. So a single virtuous disposition can also exist in several abilities.

Moreover, [2] Aristotle[28] says that virtue needs three things: *knowledge, will, and steadfast operation*. Now knowledge belongs to mind and will to will, so virtue can dispose more than one ability.

Moreover, [3] prudence disposes reason, since Aristotle[29] defines it as *right reasoning about what to do*. But it also disposes will, because he also says[30] that prudence can't coexist with a perverse will. So one virtue can dispose more than one ability.

But against that:

The soul's abilities are subjects of virtue, and one and the same property can't be in two subjects. So one virtue can't be in several abilities.

In reply:

If one virtue in two abilities means one virtue disposing two abilities in parallel, that's impossible. For any generic difference in the object of activities requires a difference of abilities, and any species difference requires a difference in dispositions, so that a difference of abilities brings with it a difference in dispositions, though the converse is not true. But one virtue can be in more than one ability not in parallel but in sequence. Then the virtue primarily disposes one ability, but that disposition causes (or presupposes) disposition of other abilities, inasmuch as secondary abilities exist influencing or under the influence of the first.

Hence:

to 1: One and the same activity can't belong equally in parallel to several abilities, but only in different ways and sequentially.

to 2: Knowledge is presupposed to the moral virtues, which in themselves dispose our appetites to act in accordance with reason.

to 3: Reason is really the subject disposed by prudence, but that presupposes some initial rightness of will, as we will show later.

[**Article 3**] The third question [**Are there virtues of intellect?**] we approach as follows:

It seems that intellect cannot be subject to virtue:

For [1] Augustine[31] says that all virtue is love, and love is an act not of intellect but only of our abilities to desire. So there is no virtue in intellect.

Moreover, [2] as we have made clear, virtue is ordered to goodness. But goodness is an object of desire, not of intellect. So virtues must exist not in the intellect but in our abilities to desire.

Moreover, [3] *virtue makes its possessor good*, says Aristotle.[32] But dispositions perfecting intellect don't make their possessor good: a person isn't good just because he has knowledge or know-how. So intellect is not the subject of virtues.

But against that:

Mind means principally intellect, and virtue was defined above as a disposition of mind. So virtue must dispose the intellect.

In reply:

Virtues we have said are dispositions to act well. But there are two ways of being disposed to act well. One kind of disposition gives us the facility to do something well: grammatical skill, for example, gives us a facility to speak correctly. But it doesn't determine that we shall always speak correctly, for grammarians can still use slang and ungrammatical constructions. And the other arts and sciences similarly. But another kind of disposition gives us not only a facility to act, but also determines us to use that facility rightly: for example, justice not only makes us ready in will to do the just thing, but disposes us to a just doing of it.

Now it is not potentials but actualizations of potentials that lead us to call something good, or existent, in the straightforward sense of the words. So it is because of these second types of disposition that we say people do good or are good in the straightforward sense: because they are just or moderate or some other thing of that sort. And because virtue is what *renders its possessor and his activity good*, it is these dispositions that are called virtues in a straightforward sense, because they render actual acts good, and make the agent good in the straightforward sense. But the first type of disposition is not called straightforwardly a virtue, because it provides us only with a facility to act well, and doesn't make us simply speaking good. For being knowing or having a craftsman's skills doesn't make one good (period!), but good only in a certain respect: a good grammarian or a good carpenter. For this reason knowledge and arts or crafts are often distinguished from virtues, though sometimes they receive that name, as Aristotle[33] makes clear.

Virtues in this qualified sense then can dispose our minds

to engage in practice or even in pure speculation unrelated to willing anything: and it is in this way that Aristotle[34] talks of knowledge, wisdom, and intelligence, and art and craft too, as virtues of mind. But unqualified virtues dispose only our will or other abilities of ours precisely as controlled by will. And the reason is that all our abilities dependent on reason are stimulated to act by willing, as we have said above; and any actual doing of good depends on the doer having a good will. So virtues that don't only provide us with a facility to act well but make our actual acts good must be dispositions either of will itself or of other abilities precisely as stimulated to act by willing.

Now mind is stimulated to act by will just like our other abilities: for people actually think about something when they want to. So there are dispositions of mind precisely as controlled by will that are unqualified virtues: faith disposing our reason or speculative mind to assent under the will's influence (for *no one believes unless he chooses to*[35]), and prudence disposing our practical mind. For prudence is a disposition of our reason to right action. And so it presupposes that we are well disposed to our goals—the premisses of our action—by a right will, in the same way that we are disposed to the premisses of speculative thought by the natural light of our agent intellect. So that just as our speculative mind in subordination to our agent intellect is disposed by science to rightly reason about speculative matters, so our practical mind in subordination to right willing is disposed to act by prudence.

Hence:

to 1: The words of Augustine must be applied to virtues in the straightforward sense of the word. Not that all those are love simply speaking, but they all in a way depend on love, since they depend on willing which starts off by loving, as we have said.

to 2: A thing's good is its goal, so, since truth is the goal of intellect, knowing truth is good intellectual activity. So anything disposing the intellect to know truth, be it speculative or practical, is a virtue.

to 3: The argument is only considering virtue in the straightforward sense.

[**Article 4**] The fourth question [**Are there virtues disposing our capacities for affection and aggression?**] we approach as follows:

It seems that our affective and aggressive capacities cannot be subject to virtue:

For [1] we share these capacities with the lower animals, but the virtue we are talking of is human virtue, peculiar to human beings. So these capacities for affective and aggressive feelings—which are the two forms taken by our sensuality, as book 1 explained—can't be subject to human virtue.

Moreover, [2] our sensuality operates by way of bodily organs. But the goodness of virtue is not something bodily: as Romans 7 [18] says: *I know that nothing good dwells in my flesh*. So my sensuality can't be a subject of virtue.

Moreover, [3] Augustine[36] proves that virtues are in the soul, not the body, because soul rules body absolutely so that good use of the body must be totally credited to the soul: *when a driver, letting himself be ruled by me, manages his horses well, it will all be credited to me*. Now reason rules sensuality in the way soul rules body. So the right regulation of my affective and aggressive capacities must be totally credited to the part of me that is reasonable. Now it is virtue which disposes me *to live rightly*, as we have said. Virtue then is not something in my affective and aggressive capacities but in the part of me that is reasonable.

Moreover, [4] *moral virtue is primarily a disposition to choose well*, says Aristotle.[37] But choosing is an act of reason, not of affective or aggressive feeling, as we have said above. So moral virtue must dispose reason, not our capacities for affection and aggression.

But against that:

Courage is said to dispose our capacity for aggressive feeling, and moderation our capacity for affection. So that Aristotle[38] writes: *these are virtues of our unreasoning parts*.

In reply:

We can consider our capacities for affective and aggressive feelings in two ways: in themselves, as the two forms taken by our sensuality, and then we don't think of them as subject to virtue; or as sharing reason, because of their natural inclination to obey reason, and then (as sharing reason) they are sources of human action and can be subject to human virtue. So these capacities do need to be disposed by virtues.

And that there are virtues of our affective and aggressive capacities can be shown as follows. If actions proceeding from one power under the control of another are to be perfect, then both powers will have to be well disposed to the action: if a workman is to do good work, he must be well disposed to it and his tools too. So in matters where our affective and aggressive capacities are controlled by reason, there will have to be dispositions perfecting not only reason to act well, but also the affective and aggressive capacities too. And where capacities are active because acted on, a good disposition will be one conforming them to the power acting on them; so virtue in our capacities for aggressive and affective feeling will be nothing other than a habitual disposition of the capacity to conform to reason.

Hence:

to 1: The capacities for affective and aggressive feeling, considered in themselves as the two forms taken by our sensuality, we share with the lower animals. But as sharing in reason and obeying reason they are peculiar to human beings, and as such can be subject to human virtue.

to 2: Human flesh can't be virtuously good in itself, but under the command of reason it becomes a tool of virtuous activity, *yielding our bodies to the service of righteousness* [Romans 6: 19]. And in the same way our capacities for affective and aggressive feeling are not in themselves virtuously good but rather infected with inflammability. Yet conformity to reason brings out the good of moral virtue in them.

to 3: Reason doesn't rule my affective and aggressive capacities in the same way my soul rules my body. For in matters where the body is moved to act by the soul, it obeys without contradiction the soul's slightest signal: *soul rules body like a tyrant*, says Aristotle,[39] like a master his slave. And this is why all the credit for what the body does goes to the soul, and there are no virtues in the body but only in the soul. But my affective and aggressive capacities don't obey my reason's slightest signal, but have their own ways of acting which are sometimes at odds with reason: reason rules my affections and my aggressions, Aristotle goes on to say, *democratically*, like free people are ruled, who have their own will in certain areas. And this is why our capacities for affective and aggressive feeling need to have virtues in them disposing them to act well.

to 4: Choosing involves two things: intending a goal (the role of the moral virtue) and picking out the means (the role of prudence), as Aristotle[40] says. When emotions are in question, right intending of a goal needs our aggressive and affective urges to be disposed to good. So the moral virtues concerned with emotion must dispose those urges, while prudence disposes our reason.

[**Article 5**] The fifth question [**Are there virtues of our powers of sense-perception?**] we approach as follows:

It seems that there can be virtues in our interior powers of sense-perception:

For [**1**] our sensuality can be subject to virtue in so far as it obeys reason. But our interior powers of sense-perception obey reason, since reason can command activity from our imagination and our instinctive judgement and our memory. So these too can be subject to virtue.

Moreover, [**2**] just as our rational desires of will can be either hindered or helped by our sensual desires, so intellect and reason can be hindered or helped by interior sense-powers. So then there can be virtues in those powers just as in our powers of sensual desire.

Moreover, [**3**] prudence is a virtue, and Cicero[41] says it has a part called memory. So there must also be a virtue in our power of memory; and by the same token in the other interior powers of perception.

But against that:

Aristotle[42] says all virtue is either intellectual or moral. Now moral virtues are all in the desiring side of us, and intellectual virtues in our intellect or reason, as Aristotle[43] says. So no virtues exist in our interior powers of sense-perception.

In reply:

Certain dispositions of our interior powers of sense-perception have been postulated, chiefly by Aristotle[44] when he said that *when remembering series of things, habit, which is like a second nature, comes into play.* Now customary habit is a sort of disposition acquired by custom that acts like natural instinct. Cicero[45] talked of virtue in this way, calling it *a disposition like a natural instinct, in agreement with reason.* Yet in human beings what is acquired by custom in memory and the other powers of sense is not so much itself a disposition as something accompanying mental dispositions, as we said above; and even if there were dispositions in such powers they couldn't be called virtues. For a virtue is a perfect disposition that can only do good things, and so must reside in our abilities to bring good actions to completion. Now knowledge of truth is not brought to completion in our sensory apprehension, for that is only preparatory to intellectual knowledge. So the virtues by which we know truth are not in our sense-powers, but rather in intellect and reason.

Hence:

to 1: Will, the desire of our reason, stimulates the desires of our senses, so that the work of all our powers of desire is completed by sense-desire; the powers of sense-desire must therefore be subject to virtue. But our powers of sense-perception rather stimulate our mind—images affect the mind like colours affect sight, says Aristotle[46]—so that the act of knowing is achieved in the mind. Cognitive virtues, therefore, must rather be in reason or intellect or reason. And this also gives us the answer **to 2**.

to 3: Memory isn't part of prudence in the way a species is part of a genus, as though memory itself was a virtue; but a good memory is something that prudence presupposes, and so it is a sort of component part of prudence.

[**Article 6**] The sixth question [**Are there virtues of will?**] we approach as follows:

It seems that our wills can't be subject to virtue:

For [1] an ability doesn't need to be disposed to something it is already in accord with, of its own nature. But since, according to Aristotle,[47] will is rational desire, it tends of its own nature towards the reasonable good, which is the object of all virtue; for everything tends naturally towards what is good for it itself. For, according to Cicero,[48] *virtue is a disposition like a natural instinct, agreeing with reason*. So will needs no virtues.

Moreover, [2] as Aristotle[49] says, every virtue is either intellectual or moral. Now intellectual virtues dispose intellect and reason, but not will; and moral virtues dispose powers that share in reason, like our capacities for affective and aggressive feelings. So there are no virtues of will.

Moreover, [3] all the actions virtue disposes us to are voluntary actions. So if there is a virtue in the will disposing us to any of these human actions, by the same token there ought to be virtue there disposing us to all human actions. So either there shouldn't be virtues anywhere else, or there will be two virtues ordered to the same act, which doesn't seem right. So will can't be subject to virtue.

But against that:

Agents ought to be more perfect than what they act on. Now the will acts on our capacities for affective and aggressive feeling. So there is even more reason for virtue in the will than there is in those capacities.

In reply:

Dispositions perfect our abilities to act; so an ability needs to be disposed to act well—by dispositions called virtues—when the ability's own nature won't suffice. Now an ability's nature is defined as an orderedness to its object; and since will's object is what reason proposes as good and proportioned to the one willing, no virtue is required for the will to follow that. But the will needs virtues if a good asks to be willed that exceeds this proportion to us, transcending either the human species, as, for example, the good of God transcends the limits of human nature as such, or transcending an individual, as, for example, the good of his fellow man. So there are virtues in the will disposing it to love our God and fellow men: charity, justice, and the like.

Hence:

to 1: This argument is thinking of virtue that pursues the good of the one willing, like moderation and courage, which deal with human passions and things of that sort, as we have said.

to 2: It is not only our capacities for affective and aggressive feelings that share in reason, but *our desirous side altogether*,[50] that is to say, in general. But that includes will. So any virtue in the will is moral, unless, as we show below, it is deiform.

to 3: Certain virtues dispose us to moderation of our passions, which is a matter private to this or that human being; and things like that don't need any special virtue in the will since the nature of the power itself suffices, as we have said. Virtues are needed in the will only in relation to some outside good.

Passage 37

Law

Source: *Summa Theologiae*, 1a2ae.90–1. Text from *Summa Theologiae* (*Opera Omnia*, Leonine edn., vol. vii).

Date: 1269–70, second stay in Paris, aged 45.

Type of passage and how to read: Modified disputed question (see Introduction).

Notes on translation: *Lex naturalis* is translated rather awkwardly as 'the law that is in us by nature', in order to avoid confusion with either the laws of nature, or with natural law in the sense of what all men agree on. 'Complete self-contained community' translates *communitas perfecta.*

Next we consider **law in general**, and our consideration divides into three:

firstly, what is law?
secondly, the different types of law . . .

[**Question 90**] The first question [**What is law?**] divides into four:

Is law a product of reason?
The goal of law.
Who legislates?
The promulgation of law.

[**Article 1**] The first question [**Is law a product of reason?**] we approach as follows:

It seems that law is not a product of reason:

For [1] Paul says in Romans 7 [23]: *I see another law at work in my body*, etc. But there is nothing of reason in my body, since reason doesn't make use of a bodily organ. So law is not a product of reason.

Moreover, [2] reason is an ability and has its dispositions and activity. Now law isn't our very ability to reason; nor is it a disposition of reason, for those are the intellectual virtues we talked of earlier. Nor is it the activity of reasoning, for then whenever such activity stopped, as in sleep, law would stop too. So law isn't anything to do with reason.

Moreover, [3] the law moves those subject to it to act rightly. Now moving things to act is the characteristic role of will, as we have made clear. So law is not a matter of reason but of will, as the old lawgivers also said: *the ruler's will gives law its force.*

But against that:

It is the function of law to command and to forbid. But above we said that reason commanded. So law is some product of reason.

In reply:

Law is a standard of measurement for behaviour, fostering certain actions and discouraging others; for law [*lex*] derives from binding [*ligandum*], since it binds one to act. Now reason, the first source of all human activity as we have seen, sets the standard of measurement for human behaviour, for its role is to set the goal of action, and that, according to Aristotle,[1] is the starting-point for what is to be done. But in any realm the starting-point becomes the standard of measurement for everything within that realm: the unit for all numbers, the primary movement [of the heavens] for all changes. It follows then that law is a product of reason.

Hence:

to 1: Since law is a standard of measurement, there are two ways it exists in things. Firstly, in what does the measuring and regulating, and since that is the proper role of reason, law in this sense exists in reason alone. Secondly, in what is measured and regulated, and law in this sense exists in everything which tends towards something in obedience to law. Such a tendency can itself be called law, but in a derivative sense, not a primary one. And it is in this derivative sense that the tendency of my body to desire is called *a law in my body*.

to 2: Just as in external action we distinguish the doing from what it does, the act of building from the building built, so in what reason does we must distinguish the act of reasoning (understanding, arguing) from something created by that act. In the pursuit of truth reason elaborates definitions, then statements, then arguments or proofs; and because reason, when planning action, uses a sort of argument, as we have said above and Aristotle[2] teaches, it elaborates something that relates to behaviour as premisses of arguments do to conclusions. And these general premisses of practical reason bearing on behaviour have the nature of law, and are sometimes explicitly considered and sometimes held as a sort of disposition of reason.

to 3: Reason's moving force comes from will, as we have

said: someone wills a goal, and because of that reason commands the things to be done to achieve it. But willing the things commanded only has the nature of law in so far as it is ruled by reason. So we can only accept the saying that *the ruler's will is law* on that proviso; otherwise the ruler's will is more lawlessness than law.

[Article 2] The second question [the goal of law] we approach as follows:

It seems that law's goal is not always the general good:

For [1] law proscribes and prescribes, and its prescriptions sometimes lay down an individual good. So law's goal is not always the general good.

Moreover, [2] law directs human behaviour, which consists of individual actions. So law is also ordered to certain individual goods.

Moreover, [3] Isidore[3] says *if law is established by reason, anything reason establishes is law*. But reason establishes not only what is for the common good but what is for our private good. So law serves not only the common good but each one's private good.

But against that:

Isidore[4] says that law is *drawn up not for any private advantage but for the common utility of citizens.*

In reply:

Law, we have said, as a standard of measurement, is connected with the sources of human behaviour. Now the source of human behaviour is reason, but also within reasoning there is something which is a source of everything else, with which law must first and foremost be connected. In practical reason, which is concerned with behaviour, that source is our ultimate goal in life, and that, as we have already seen, is happiness or bliss. So law must concern itself above all with our orderedness to bliss.

Further, since parts in their incompleteness are ordered to the completeness of their wholes, and each human being is part of a complete self-contained community, law must properly be concerned with the happiness of that community. So that Aristotle, in the definition of matters of law already given,[5] makes mention of happiness and the city community. For he says[6] that *we call those acts just* in law *that promote and conserve happiness and its components in the city society*, for it is the city that is the complete self-contained community, as Aristotle says elsewhere.[7]

Now in every sphere things derive status and name from what has such things most—heat in compounds derives from the supreme heat of elemental fire and it is because they share that heat that compounds are called hot. So since law is primarily an ordination for the general good, commands to do particular deeds are laws only when ordered to that general good; and thus all law is ordered to the general good.

Hence:

to 1: The prescriptions of law apply the law to what it regulates. Now orderedness to the general good, which is law's concern, is applicable to individual goals; and so certain of its prescriptions concern individual acts.

to 2: Actions are certainly individual, but those individual actions have a relationship to the general good, where general means not something generic exemplified in individuals, but a goal which all serve: the general good means some common goal.

to 3: When pursuing truth no conclusion is firmly established until it is analysed into self-evident first premisses; and in the same way when planning action no command is firmly established unless it serves our ultimate goal, the general good: only when reason has established it in that way does it have the force of law.

[**Article 3**] The third question [**Who legislates?**] we approach as follows:

It seems that anyone with reason can legislate:

For [**1**] in Romans 2 [14] St Paul says that *when Gentiles who don't have the law do by nature what the law prescribes,* *then they are law to themselves*. But this applies to everyone. So anyone can legislate for himself.

Moreover, [2] Aristotle[8] says that *the legislator's intention is to foster human virtue*. But anyone can foster human virtue in another. So anyone can use his reason to legislate.

Moreover, [3] the head of a family governing his household is like a king governing his city. But the king can legislate for his city. So every head of a family can legislate for his household.

But against that:

Isidore[9] says, and you can find it in the Decretals,[10] that *law is a constitution of the people, in which something is decreed by lords and commons*. Not anyone then can legislate.

In reply:

Law properly, first and foremost, relates to the general good. Now planning for the general good belongs either to the people as a whole or to someone standing in for the whole people; so legislating belongs either to the whole people, or to some public person whose job it is to care for the whole people. It is just as in all other situations: those to whom the goal properly belongs must have the planning of it.

Hence:

to 1: As we already said, law exists not only in the one doing the regulating, but also—shared—in the one regulated. And in this latter way, everyone is a law unto himself, by sharing in the orderedness coming from the regulator. Which is why Paul goes on to say: *they show that what the law requires is inscribed on their hearts*.

to 2: A private person can admonish, but if his admonitions are not heeded then he has no power of enforcement to foster virtue effectively. But law, to foster virtue effectively, must have this power, as Aristotle[11] says. This power resides in the people or the public authorities who can inflict penalties (as we shall say later), so legislation is reserved to them.

to 3: People are parts of households, and households are parts of cities, but cities are complete self-contained communities, as Aristotle[12] points out. So just as the good of an individual is not the ultimate goal, but must serve the general good, so the good of a household must serve the good of the city: the self-contained political community. The governing head of a family can issue commands and orders, but not laws in the true sense.

[**Article 4**] The fourth question [**the promulgation of law**] we approach as follows:

It seems that promulgation is not essential to law:

For [**1**] the law that is in us by nature is more of a law than most. But that doesn't need promulgation. So promulgation isn't essential to law.

Moreover, [2] law of its nature binds us to do or not do things. But it binds not only the people before whom it is promulgated, but others as well. So promulgation is not essential to law as such.

Moreover, [3] the binding force of law extends into the future: for *laws determine the future conduct of affairs, as the statutes say.*[13] But promulgation is to those present. So promulgation is not essential to law.

But against that:

We read in the Decretals: *laws come into force when they are promulgated.*[14]

In reply:

As we have said, law is imposed on others in the way standards of measurement are. But standards of measurement are imposed by applying them to what they measure. So if law is to have the binding force proper to it as law, it must be applied to those who are to be subject to it by some promulgation that brings it to their notice. Promulgation then is required if law is to have force.

There are thus four elements in the definition of law: law is an ordinance of reason, for the general good, laid down by whoever has care of the community, and promulgated.

Hence:

to 1: The law that is in us by nature is promulgated by the very fact that God implants it in our minds as something to be known by nature.

to 2: Those not there when the law was promulgated are bound to observe the law, inasmuch as it is brought to their notice by others, or, given its promulgation, can be so brought.

to 3: The fixity of writing extends present promulgation into the future, promulgating it so to speak for ever. So that Isidore[15] says that *lex* [law] *is derived from lego* [to read] *because laws are written.*

[**Question 91**] Next we consider **the various types of law,** and this divides into six:

Is there an eternal law?
Is there a law in us by nature?
Are there human laws? . . .

[**Article 1**] The first question [**Is there an eternal law?**] we approach as follows:

It seems that there is no eternal law:

For [**1**] law must apply to someone, and there has been no one existing from eternity to whom a law could apply, for only God has existed from eternity. So no law can be eternal.

Moreover, [**2**] promulgation is essential to law. But there couldn't have been an eternal promulgation since there wasn't anyone eternally there for it to be promulgated to. So no law can be eternal.

Moreover, [**3**] law is an ordering towards a goal. But nothing eternal is ordered to a goal: only the ultimate goal itself is eternal. So no law is eternal.

But against that:

Augustine[16] says: *The law of highest reason is invisible to all but the unchanging and eternal intelligence.*

In reply:

As we have said, law is a kind of pronouncement made by the practical reason of the governing authority in some complete self-contained community. But clearly, if we suppose the world to be ruled by God's providence, as we have shown it to be in book 1, the entire community of the universe is governed by God's reason. And so the very plan of government, existing in God as ruler of the universe, is a law in the true sense. And since God did not conceive this plan in time but, as Proverbs 8 [23] says, eternally, we must call it an eternal law.

Hence:

to 1: Although things didn't exist in themselves they existed as known beforehand and pre-ordained in God who, as Romans 4 [17] says, *calls things that are not as things that are*. So God's law, eternally conceived, is truly an eternal law, ordained by God for the government of things known by him beforehand.

to 2: Promulgation can be by word of mouth or in writing, and on the side of its promulgator, God, the eternal law was promulgated in both ways: through God's eternal Word, and in the eternal book of life. But for the creatures hearing and reading it the promulgation is not eternal.

to 3: Law is an active ordering towards a goal, actively ordering other things to that goal; but not a passive orderedness in the sense of itself being ordered to a goal, except incidentally if the act of making a law serves a goal because the lawmaker himself does. When God governs he is his own goal, and he himself is his law, so that the eternal law serves no other purpose than itself.

[**Article 2**] The second question [**Is there a law in us by nature?**] we approach as follows:

It seems that there is no law in us by nature:

For [1] human beings have sufficient government in the eternal law: for Augustine[17] says that *the eternal law sets us right and puts perfect order in all things*. But nature does no more and no less than it need. So there is no law in human beings by nature.

Moreover, [2] laws order our activities to their goal, as has been said. But human actions are not ordered to their goal by nature, as the actions of non-reasoning creatures are that pursue goals simply by natural instinct; rather human beings direct their activity to goals by reason and will. So in human beings there is no law by nature.

Moreover, [3] the freer people are the less they are subject to law. But because of their unique ability to choose freely, human beings are freer than all the other animals that lack it. Since then animals aren't subject to a law in them by nature, human beings aren't either.

But against that:

The gloss on Romans 2 [14]: *when Gentiles who don't have the law do by nature what the law prescribes* etc., says: *Though they had no written law they had a law in them by nature, by which all knew within themselves what was good and what bad.*

In reply:

We said earlier that law, as a standard of measurement, exists in the measuring standard in one way and in another way in what is measured, for the very being measured by the standard is a sharing in its measuring. Now since everything subjected to God's providence is measured by the standards of his eternal law, as we have said, everything shares in some way in the eternal law, bearing its imprint in the form of a natural tendency to pursue the behaviour and goals appropriate to it. Reasoning creatures are subject to God's providence in a special, more profound way than others, by themselves sharing the planning, making plans both for themselves and for others; thus sharing in the eternal reasoning itself that is imprinting them with their natural tendencies to appropriate behaviour and goals. And it is this distinctive sharing in the eternal law by reasoning creatures that we call the law we have in us by nature. For [in Psalm 4: 6] the psalmist, after he has told us *Offer your sacrifice of justice*, adds, as if addressing people who asked what were these works of justice: *Many say: Who can show us these good things?* and answers: *the light of your face is signed on us, O Lord*, as if the light of natural reason by which we tell good from evil (the law that is in us by nature) is itself an imprint of God's light in us. Clearly then the law that is in us by nature is nothing else than the reasoning creature's sharing in the eternal law.

Hence:

to 1: This argument would hold if the law in us by nature was something different from the eternal law, but in fact it is a sort of sharing in it, as we have said.

to 2: All we do by reason and will starts from nature, as we have said; for all our reasoning starts from premisses known by nature and all our willing of courses of action starts from our natural willing of our ultimate goal. So, in the same way, all our planning of action for a goal must start from the law we have in us by nature.

to 3: Even creatures without reason share eternal reason in their own way, like reasoning creatures; but because reasoning creatures do it with reason and understanding their sharing in the eternal law is itself law in the true sense, for law is a product of reason, as we have said. Non-reasoning creatures share in it in a non-reasoning way, and so in them it is a law only metaphorically.

[**Article 3**] The third question [**Are there human laws?**] we approach as follows:

It seems that there are no human laws:

For [1] we have said that the law we have in us by nature is a sharing in the eternal law, and that, according to Augustine,[18] *puts perfect order into all things*. So natural law is enough to put order into all human affairs, and we have no need of any human law.

Moreover, [2] law is a standard of measurement, as we have said. But Aristotle[19] says that human reason doesn't so much measure things as be measured. So human reason can't give rise to law.

Moreover, [3] measures must be very precise, as Aristotle[20] says. But human reason's pronouncements about what must be done are fallible, as Wisdom 9 [14] says: *Mortal reasoning is shaky, and our plans unsure.* So human reason can't give rise to law.

But against that:

Augustine[21] talks of two laws, eternal and temporal, the latter of which he calls human.

In reply:

We have said that law is a certain pronouncement of practical reason. Now practical and speculative reason follow the same procedure, both arguing to certain conclusions from certain principles, as was shown earlier. So we can now say that, just as speculative reason [pursuing truth] starts from premisses which cannot be proved but are known by nature, and draws conclusions belonging to various sciences not known by nature but worked out by reason; so human reason [when planning action] starts from injunctions of a law it possesses by nature as if from general premisses needing no proof, and arrives at more particular arrangements. These particular arrangements worked out by human reason, provided they fulfil the other defining conditions of law previously mentioned, are called human laws. And this is what Cicero[22] told us: *law starts with what nature produces, then by use of reason certain things become customs, and finally things produced by nature and tested by custom are sanctified with the awe and religious weight of laws.*

Hence:

to 1: Human reason shares the plan of God's reason in its own imperfect way, but cannot share it in full. So, just as reason pursuing truth shares naturally in God's wisdom by knowing naturally certain general premisses, but not by knowing every particular truth in itself as God in his wisdom knows it; so when planning action human reason shares the eternal law by nature, knowing some general principles but not the detailed plans which the eternal law lays down for each single thing. So human reason must go on to enact certain particular laws.

to 2: Human reason as such isn't the measure of things, but certain principles imprinted in it provide a general standard of measurement for everything human beings do, since our natural reason can lay down standards for such things even if it can't lay down standards for the products of nature.

to 3: Practical reasoning is about what to do, which is particular and might be done otherwise; not about the necessary truths of speculative reason. So human laws can't have the same unfailing validity as the proved conclusions of science. But not all standards of measurement have to be altogether infallible and certain, as long as they do what is possible in their own sphere.

Passage 38
Love of God as Virtue

Source: Thomas's public disputation on the Love of God, 2. Text from *Quaestio Disputata de Caritate*, in *Quaestiones Disputatae de Potentia* (Marietti edn., Turin, 1953).

Date: 1265–7, Italy, aged 40.

Type of passage and how to read: Disputed question (see Introduction).

The subject for debate is **Charity** . . .

[**Article 2**] And in the second place we are asked **whether charity is a virtue.**

It seems not:

For [1] virtue is concerned with the difficult, as Aristotle[1] says. But charity isn't concerned with the difficult; on the contrary, as Augustine[2] says: *All that is heavy and beyond bearing, love makes easy and next to nothing*. So charity is no virtue . . .

Moreover, [8] charity is a kind of friendship between God and man. But friendship between man and man is not counted a social virtue by philosophers. So the charity of God shouldn't be counted a theological virtue...

Moreover, [11] sin wounds our affections even more than our minds, since, as Augustine[3] says, sin is a fault of will. Now our minds can't immediately see God in himself in this life. So neither can our affections immediately love God in himself in this life. But love of God in himself is what charity is supposed to be. So charity shouldn't be counted among the virtues that perfect us in this life...

Moreover, [13] all virtues have their due measure, and so Augustine[4] says that sin—opposed to virtue—lacks measure, form, and order. But charity is measureless, for, as Bernard[5] says, *the measure of charity is to love without measure.* So charity is no virtue.

Moreover, [15] Aristotle[6] says friendship consists in a sort of equality. But between us and God there is an infinite distance, and thus the greatest inequality. So God can't be friends with us, nor we with God, and there seems to be no such virtue as charity, the name given to such friendship.

Moreover, [16] the love of supreme good is in us by nature. But nothing that exists in us by nature is a virtue, for Aristotle[7] says virtues are not innate. So love of supreme good, which is charity, is not a virtue...

But against that:

The law commands acts of virtue. But it commands acts of charity, for Matthew 18 [37] says that *the first and greatest commandment is this: Love the Lord thy God.* So charity is a virtue.

In reply:

Charity is undoubtedly a virtue. Since virtue is something that renders its possessors good and their activity good, clearly there will be a virtue special to human beings disposing them to their special good. But what the special good of human beings is will vary with the context in which you view human beings. For the good special to human beings as human beings is the good of reason: man is a rational animal; but the good of a human being as a craftsman is the good of his craft, and the good of a human being as a citizen is the common good of his city.

Now since virtue works for good, each virtue must dispose its subject towards doing that good well, that is, voluntarily, readily, happily, and also steadily. For these are the characteristics of virtuous activity, and attach only to the activities of agents who love the good they are pursuing. For love is the source of all voluntary affections: what is loved is desired when not possessed, gives pleasure to its possessors, and sorrow to those hindered from possessing it. And things done from love are done readily, steadily, and happily. So virtue requires love of the good it is pursuing.

Now the good pursued by the virtue special to human beings as human beings is connatural to human beings, so that in their wills by nature there exists love of this good, the good of reason. But if we consider the virtue of human beings in a context other than that of their human nature, then such virtue will need to have added over and above what they will by nature a love of the good to which the virtue is ordered. A craftsman will not act well unless he acquires a love of the good pursued in the exercise of his craft; so that Aristotle[8] says that to be a good citizen you must love the good of your city. Now if a human being, when admitted to a share in the good of some city and made a citizen of that city, requires certain virtues disposing him to do the things citizens should do and love the good of that city, then in the same way a human being, when admitted by divine grace and favour to a sharing in heavenly bliss—which consists in seeing and enjoying God—becomes so to speak a citizen and associate in that blessed society we call the heavenly Jerusalem (in the words of Ephesians 2 [19]: *you are fellow citizens of God's people, members of God's household*); and the human being, so enrolled in the heavens, requires certain graciously instilled virtues, the proper operation of which presupposes a love of the common good of all that society, which is the good of God himself, the object of bliss.

Now a city's good can be loved in two ways: with a

possessive love or with a caring love. Possessive love of a city's good doesn't make one a good citizen, since even tyrants love the good of a city in this way wanting to be lord of it—and they are loving themselves rather than the city, desiring its good for themselves rather than for the city. But a caring and preserving love for the good of a city is true love of the city and makes one a good citizen, to the extent that some people are prepared to lay themselves open to the danger of death and risk their own private good in order to preserve and develop the good of their city. In the same way then a possessive love for the good which the blessed share doesn't make a man well disposed to bliss, for even bad men desire that good; but loving that good in itself, that it might last and be spread and have nothing done against it, does dispose a human being well to that blissful society. And this is the love of charity: a love by which we love God for himself, and our neighbours—those capable of bliss—as ourselves, repelling everything that hinders such love in ourselves and in others, so that it is never able to coexist with those fatal sins that hinder bliss.

And so clearly charity is not only a virtue, but the most potent of all virtues.

Hence:

to 1: Virtue is concerned with what in itself is difficult, but which having a virtue makes easy...

to 8: Friendship is counted not as a virtue but as a consequence of virtue, since the very fact of having virtue and loving the good of reason leads people with virtuous inclinations to love those like them, namely, the virtuous in whom the good of reason flourishes. But friendship for God as enjoyer and author of bliss must precede the virtues which order us to that bliss; and so, because it is not a consequence but a presupposition of these other virtues, as we have shown, it must be a virtue in itself...

to 11: The good we understood moves our will. Now, through intermediaries, mind comes to know God as the supreme good, and that moves the will to love him without intermediary even though he is known only through intermediaries; for it is the thing itself which terminates the mind's knowledge that moves the affections . . .

to 13: The object of charity is God and transcends every human faculty; so that, however much human will strives to love God, it cannot reach to love him as much as he should be loved. And that is what is meant by saying charity is without measure: there exists no fixed limit to the love of God loving beyond which would go against the virtue's nature, as happens in moral virtues which require a moderate balance. But the measure of charity is precisely not having that kind of measure. So the conclusion from this is not that charity isn't a virtue but that it isn't defined by a balance like moral virtues . . .

to 15: Charity isn't a virtue a human being has as human being, but as one who through sharing grace has become God and a child of God, as we read in 1 John 3 [1]: *See what charity the Father has given us, that we should be called and be God's children.*

to 16: Love of supreme good as source of our natural existence exists in us by nature, but, as object of a bliss which exceeds the whole capacity of created nature, it exists in us not by nature but above nature . . .

Notes

Details of sources are Thomas's own unless enclosed in square brackets, when they are editorial additions.

ABBREVIATIONS

Aristotle

APo.	*Posterior Analytics*
Cael.	*De Caelo et Mundo*
Cat.	*Categories*
De An.	*De Anima*
Div.Somn.	*De Divinatione per Somnia*
EE	*Eudemian Ethics*
EN	*Nicomachean Ethics*
GA	*De Generatione Animalium*
GC	*De Generatione et Corruptione*
HA	*Historia Animalium*
Int.	*De Interpretatione*
Metaph.	*Metaphysics*
PA	*De Partibus Animalium*
Ph.	*Physics*
Pol.	*Politics*
Rh.	*Rhetoric*
SE	*Sophistici Elenchi*
Somn.Vig.	*De Somno et Vigilia*
Top.	*Topics*

Biblical

Exod.	Exodus
Gen.	Genesis
Heb.	Hebrews
Ps(s).	Psalm(s)
Rom.	Romans

Passage 1

1. *Discutiamus*: modern critical texts have *dispiciamus*: considering.
2. *Inseparabilis*: modern critical texts have *separabilis*: separable.
3. *Metaph.* 2 [3.995^{a}13].
4. Reading *quantumvis* for *quamvis*.

5. *EN* 1 [1.1094^{b}23–5].
6. *Metaph.* 9 [8.1050^{b}20–2?].
7. See n. 2 above.
8. *EN* 6 [3.1139^{b}15–17; 6–7.1140^{b}31–1141^{b}8].
9. *The City of God*, 8 [4].
10. *Metaph.* 3 [2.997^{a}26–30, 997^{b}1–3].
11. *EN* 6 [9.1142^{a}11–20].
12. *Metaph.* 6 [1.1026^{a}18].
13. *Ph.* 2 [7.198^{a}29–31].
14. *Almagest*, 1 [1.5, 7–10].
15. *De An.* 3 [10.333^{a}15].
16. *Metaph.* 2 [1.993^{b}20].
17. *APo.* 1 [2.71^{b}9–12.15; 6.74^{b}5–75^{a}37, 33.88^{b}30–5].
18. *Metaph.* 9 [8.1050^{b}11–15].
19. See n. 8 above.
20. *EN* 2 [5.1106^{a}15–17].
21. *Metaph.* 6 [1.1026^{a}18].
22. *Metaph.* 1 [2.982^{a}14–17].
23. *Commentary on On Porphyry's Isagoge* [1.3].
24. *Didascalicon de Studio Legendi*, 3 [3].
25. *Metaph.* 2 [3.995^{a}13].
26. *EN* 6 [9.1142^{a}16–20].
27. *Metaph.* 6 [1.1025^{b}22].
28. *EN* 1 [1.1095^{a}4–6; 6.1098^{a}15; 13.1102^{a}5–10].
29. *The City of God*, 4 [21].
30. *De Medicina*, 1.1.
31. *The City of God*, 20 [19.1].
32. *EN* 10 [7–8.1177^{a}12–1178^{b}32].
33. Natural, vital, and animal spirits or forces.
34. *Commentary on the Metaphysics*, 1 [3].
35. *Isagoge*, 6.12–16.
36. *Ph.* 8 [5–6.256^{a}4–260^{a}19; 10.266^{a}10–267^{b}26].
37. *Metaph.* 9 [8.1050^{b}11–15].
38. *Metaph.* 1 [1.981^{a}18–20].
39. *De An.* 1 [3.405^{b}31–407^{b}26; 4–5.408^{a}29–409^{b}19].
40. *Cael.* 2 [14.296^{a}24–297^{a}6].
41. *Metaph.* 7 [8.1053^{b}5–17].
42. [*De Trinitate*, 5.2.3.]
43. *Metaph.* 9 [8.1030^{b}20–2].
44. *Metaph.* 6 [1.1026^{a}13; *Ph.* 2 [2.193^{b}22–30; 7.198^{a}27–31].
45. *Metaph.* 1 [6.987^{a}32–^{b}1].
46. *SE* [6.168^{b}6–8].
47. *Metaph.* 7 [15.1039^{b}20–4].

48. *Metaph.* 7 [10.1035^{b}27–31].
49. *De An.* 3 [6.430^{b}28].
50. See n. 47 above.
51. *APo.* 1 [1.71^{a}11–13].
52. An earlier part of the commentary (Question 4, Article 2) omitted here.
53. *Ph.* 2 [3.195^{a}16].
54. *APo.* 2 [2.94^{a}20–34].
55. *Metaph.* 6 [1.1026^{a}14].
56. *Cael.* 3 [1.299^{a}16].
57. *De An.* 3 [6.430^{a}26–8].
58. *Metaph.* 9 [9.1051^{a}30–2].
59. *Ph.* 2 [2.193^{b}35].
60. *Metaph.* 7 [10.1036^{a}9–12].
61. *Ph.* 6 [1–4.231^{b}21–235^{b}5].
62. *Cael.* 3 [1.299^{a}13–17].
63. *Metaph.* 4 [1.1003^{a}21].
64. *APo.* 1 [1.71^{a}12; 7.75^{a}39–^{b}2; 10.76^{b}11–16].
65. *Commentary on the Physics*, 1 [1, on 184^{a}10–18].
66. *Metaph.* 3 [2.996^{a}26].
67. *Metaph.* 6 [1.1026^{a}15].
68. *Metaph.* 1 [1.981^{b}28].
69. *Ph.* 1 [1.184^{a}12–14].
70. Reading *omnia* for *omnia principia*: every beginning.
71. *Sufficientia* [1.2].
72. *Metaph.* 11 [=12?.4.1070^{a}31–3].
73. *Metaph.* 2 [1.993^{b}26–31].
74. *Metaph.* 9 [8–9.1049^{b}4–1051^{a}33].
75. *Metaph.* 6 [1.1026^{a}20].
76. *Metaph.* 2 [1.993^{b}9–11].
77. *EN* 6 [2.1139^{a}11].
78. *De Spiritu et Anima*, 11.
79. *De Consolatione*, 5 [4].
80. In Greek, *mathesis* meant discipleship, or the discipline involved in learning. In what follows it has connotations of systematic rigour.
81. *Syntaxis Mathematica*, 1.1.
82. [*EN* 6.6.1141^{a}7.]
83. *Divine Names*, 7 [1]. Thomas refers to the author as Dionysius, believing him to have been the convert of St Paul mentioned in Acts 17: 34. The author, however, lived and wrote as late as the fifth or sixth century, and is now generally (and throughout these translations) called pseudo-Dionysius.

84. *De Causis*, 6, which Thomas later recognized to be not a work of Aristotle, but derivative from the fifth-century philosopher Proclus.
85. *De Spiritu et Anima*, 11.
86. *Commentary on the Physics*, 1 [35].
87. *Ph*. 1 [1.184ª16–21].
88. *APo*. 1 [27.87ª31–4].
89. *Syntaxis Mathematica*, 1.1.
90. *De Consolatione*, 4 [6].
91. *Divine Names*, 7 [2].
92. Reading *particulata* for *particularia*.
93. *De An*. 1 [1.403ª8], 3 [7.431ª16].
94. *Celestial Hierarchy*, 1 [2].
95. *De An*. 3.
96. *Mystical Theology*, 1 [1].
97. *De An*. 2 [=3.3.429ª1].
98. *De Trinitate*, 1 [1].
99. *De Consolatione*, 5 [4].
100. *De Spiritu et Anima*, 37–8. See n. 78 above and n. 12 to Passage 9.
101. *De An*. 3 [7.431ª14].
102. *Cael*. 3 [7.306ª16].
103. *De An*. 1 [1.403ª12–16].
104. *Divine Names* [7].
105. *Celestial Hierarchy*, 2 [2].
106. Conjectural. After the preceding full point Thomas's autograph reads *ad quod*, which makes no immediate sense; I conjecture that Thomas intended to write *ad quartum dicendum quod*, his usual way of beginning an answer to a fourth objection, but a momentary confusion at the *qu-* of *quartum* led him to miss out *quartum dicendum* and write *quod*. The critical editions prefer to ignore the full point and emend the *ad quod* to *ad quem* (Decker) or *secundum quod* (to be adopted by the Leonine). This has the effect of appending what I take to be the answer to Objection 4 to the answer to Objection 3; Objection 4 then receives what I think was intended to answer Objection 5, Objection 5 what was intended for Objection 6, and Objection 6 is left without an answer. The autograph does indeed label the answers from here on in this way, and has no 'to 6:'. But note that Thomas didn't number the objections in his text, and so could only number his answers by looking back at the previous answer to see what number should come next; and his slip at Answer 4

would mislead him too into the wrong numbering. The proof of the pudding in this case is really in the eating; and I find that on my conjecture the answers actually answer the objections, and on the other hypotheses they don't. The reader must judge for himself.

107. The autograph has 'to 4:'. See the previous note.
108. The autograph has 'to 5:'. See the previous note.
109. *Mystical Theology*, 1 [3].
110. Commenting on Gen. 32 [30], 'I have seen God face to face.'
111. *Celestial Hierarchy*, 2 [5].
112. *De An.* 3 [7.431^{a}14].
113. *Celestial Hierarchy*, 2 [2].
114. Ibid., 2 [4].
115. Ibid., 1 [2].
116. Ibid.
117. *Ph.* 1 [1.184^{a}23–^{b}12].
118. [*Commentary on the Metaphysics*, 8.4.]
119. *Metaph.* 10 [10.1058^{b}26–1059^{a}9].
120. *Divine Names* [7.3].
121. [*De An.* 1.1.402^{b}25.]
122. *EN* 10 [7.1177^{a}12–21].
123. *EN* 10 [7.1178^{a}6–8].
124. *Metaph.* 1 [1.981^{b}28–982^{a}3]; *EN* 6 [7.1141^{a}18–^{b}2].
125. *Commentary on the De Anima*, 3 [36].
126. *Metaph.* 9 [10.1051^{b}26–8].
127. *De An.* 3 [5.430^{a}15].
128. *APo.* 2 [19.100^{a}3–11, ^{b}3–5].
129. See n. 125 above.
130. See n. 125 above.

Passage 2

1. *Soliloquies* [2.5].
2. *Metaph.* 4 [16.1011^{b}25].
3. *De Hebdomadibus.*
4. *Commentary on the Metaphysics*, 1 [6].
5. *Metaph.* 3 [3.998^{b}22].
6. See n. 4 above.
7. Cf. *Summa Theologiae*, 1a.11.2, ad 4m: *Dividedness precedes unity in our minds though not in reality, for we conceive simpleness as non-compositeness, points as dimensionless. Unity, in turn, precedes plurality in our minds, since divided*

things are thought of as many, only when each is thought of as one . . . Dividedness arises in the mind simply by negating existence; so we first conceive the existent, then—seeing this existent as not that existent—we conceive dividedness, thirdly, unity, and fourthly, plurality.

8. *De An.* 3 [8.431b21].
9. *EN* 1 [1.1094a2].
10. *Soliloquies* [2.5].
11. *Commentary on the Metaphysics* [8.6].
12. [*De Definitionibus*; cf. Ibn Sīnā, *Commentary on the Metaphysics*, 1.9.]
13. *De Veritate* [11].
14. *Metaph.* 4 [7.1011b25].
15. [*De Trinitate*, 5.14.]
16. *De Vera Religione* [36].
17. See previous note.
18. *Metaph.* 4 [1.1003b5].
19. *Commentary on the Metaphysics*, 1 [6].
20. *Metaph.* 6 [4.1027b25].
21. *De An.* 3 [15.433a14].
22. See n. 20 above.
23. *Metaph.* 10 [2.1053a31].
24. *De Veritate* [7].
25. *De Vera Religione* [36].
26. [*Metaph.* 8.6.]
27. *Metaph.* 5 [29.1024b21].
28. See n. 20 above.
29. *De An.* 3 [6.430a26].
30. See n. 20 above.
31. *Divine Names*, 4 [4.700A].
32. [*De Doctrina Christiana*, 1.32.]
33. *EN* 1 [6.1096a19–23].
34. *Metaph.* 5 [17.1020b26].
35. Punctuating differently from the Leonine critical text: deleting a comma after *refertur* and introducing one after *converso*.
36. *Metaph.* 6 [4.1027b25].
37. See previous note.
38. *EN* 1 [1.1094a3].

Passage 4

1. *Metaph.* 2 [2.994b13–14].
2. [*Sufficientia*, 1.14].

3. *Metaph.* 5 [1.1013^{a}17].
4. *Ph.* [1.13.191^{a}20, 2.11.198^{a}22].
5. *Commentary on the Metaphysics*, 11 [23].
6. *Metaph.* 5 [4.1014^{a}26–7].
7. *GC* [1.10.327^{b}29–31]. Cf. Passage 8 below.
8. *Commentary on the Metaphysics*, 5 [4].
9. The text actually says 'isn't what makes the doctor exist *as a doctor*', but can that be right?
10. *Ph.* 2 [5.195^{a}11].
11. *GA* [2.6.742^{a}19–22].
12. *Metaph.* 4 [16.1012^{a}22].
13. Or Thomas and Aquinas, two names for the same person.

Passage 5

1. Conjectural: the text has 'extrinsic'.
2. Reading *quodam modo* for *quodammodo*.

Passage 6

1. *Cael.* 1 [9.271^{b}8–13].
2. *Commentary on the Metaphysics*, 1 [6].
3. *Metaph.* 5 [9.1017^{a}22–35].
4. *Commentary on the Metaphysics*, 5 [14].
5. *Commentary on the Metaphysics*, 2 [2].
6. *De Persona et Duabus Naturis* [1].
7. *Metaph.* 5 [5.1014^{b}36].
8. Commentary on Aristotle's *Categories*, not traced.
9. *De Persona et Duabus Naturis.*
10. [*Commentary on the Metaphysics*, 5.5.]
11. *Commentary on the Metaphysics*, 7 [27].
12. *Commentary on the Metaphysics*, 7 [20].
13. [*Commentary on the Metaphysics*, 5.6.]
14. *Metaph.* 3 [8.998^{b}24], *Topics* 4 [2.122^{b}20].
15. *Commentary on the Metaphysics*, 11 [=12.14].
16. [*Commentary on the Metaphysics*, 5.5.]
17. [*Commentary on the Metaphysics*, 5.6.]
18. *Commentary on the De Anima*, 1 [8].
19. *Commentary on the Metaphysics*, [5.2].
20. *Commentary on the De Anima*, 3 [5].
21. *Fons Vitae* [4].
22. *De Causis*, 9.
23. [*Commentary on the Metaphysics*, 5.5.]

24. [*Commentary on the Metaphysics*, 5.2.]
25. *Commentary on the De Anima*, 3 [14].
26. *De Hebdomadibus*.
27. *Commentary on the De Anima*, 3 [5].
28. See previous note.
29. [*De An*. 3.3.430^{a}1.]
30. See n. 22 above.
31. *Metaph*. 5 [18.1021^{b}30–3].
32. *Commentary on the Metaphysics*, 5 [21].
33. *De Causis* [16].
34. [*Commentary on the De Anima*, 5.3.]
35. *Commentary on the De Anima*, 1.1.
36. *Commentary on the Metaphysics*, [5.6].
37. *Commentary on the De Anima*, 1.1.
38. *HA* 8 [1.588^{b}4–12].
39. *PA* 1 [2.642^{b}5–7].
40. *Metaph*. 2 [2.993^{b}24].
41. *De An*. 3 [1.429^{a}18–^{b}5].
42. *Metaph*. 10 [11.1058^{b}21–3].
43. *Metaph*. 9 [1.1045^{b}27–32].
44. *Metaph*. 5 [17.1020^{b}26 ff.].

Passage 8

1. [Aristotle, *Metaph*. 5.3.1014^{a}26.]
2. *Ph*. 1 [3.185^{b}16].
3. *Cat*. [5.3^{b}24–4^{a}9].
4. *Metaph*. 10 [7.1057^{a}17–29].
5. *Ph*. 6 [4.234^{b}10 ff.].
6. *Ph*. 5 [2.226^{a}23–35].
7. *Metaph*. 8 [3.1043^{b}34–1044^{a}14].
8. *De Generatione* 1 [10.327^{b}29–31].

Passage 9

1. [13.] This work was attributed to St Augustine; but see Thomas's comments in the answer to this objection, and n. 12 below.
2. *De An*. 3 [4].
3. *Metaph*. 9 [8.1049^{b}20].
4. [*Commentary on the Metaphysics*, 8.6.]
5. [*De An*. 3.4.430^{a}3.]
6. *Celestial Hierarchy*, 11.

7. *De Concordiae Praescientiae et Liberi Arbitrii* [11].
8. [*Ph.* 8.5.257^{b}1 ff.]
9. *Top.* 1 [4.101^{b}25].
10. [*Isagoge*, 4.]
11. This is what Aristotelian sciences were designed to do. Cf. explaining a chemical's properties by appeal to its molecular structure.
12. In a similar answer in the *Quaestio Disputata de Anima*, Thomas says the author was thought to be a Cistercian monk; in fact it is now attributed to Alcher of Clairvaux.
13. *De An.* 3 [6.430^{a}26 ff.].

Passage 10

1. *De An.* 3 [9.432^{b}5–7].
2. *De An.* 3 [10.422^{a}9–21].
3. *De An.* 2 [4.415^{a}16–22].
4. Conjecture: Thomas wrote 'by ability'.
5. *De An.* 2 [11.422^{b}17–33].
6. Conjecturing *convertuntur adinvicem*, for *cognoscuntur per se invicem*. Cf. parallel texts at *Summa Theologiae*, 1a.78.3.3m, and Thomas's commentary on *De An.* 2.22 [529; cf. 524].

Passage 11

1. [3.3.429^{a} ff.]
2. *De An.* [3.7.431^{a}16–17].
3. *De An.* 3 [7–8.431^{b}12–432^{a}14].
4. *De An.* 3 [4.429^{b}5–6].
5. [*Commentary on the De Anima*, 5.6.]
6. *De An.* 3 [7.431^{b}2].
7. *De An.* 2 [3.415^{a}9–10].
8. *Ph.* 6 [2–4.232^{a}18–233^{a}21].
9. *De An.* [3.3.428^{b}10–429^{a}2].
10. [*Commentary on the De Anima*, 1.5, 4.1.]
11. *De An.* 3 [11.433^{b}31–434^{a}5].
12. *Rhetoric*. But actually pseudo-Cicero, *Ad C. Herennium*, 3.20.33.

Passage 12

1. *De An.* 3 [5.430^{a}24].
2. *Super Genesim ad Litteram* 12 [16].

3. See n. 1 above.
4. *De An.* 3 [4.429^{b}24].
5. See previous note.
6. *EN* 1 [13.1102^{b}25–1103^{a}3].
7. [*De An.* 3.4.429^{a}22.]
8. *De An.* 3 [1.430^{a}10].
9. *Commentary on the De Anima*, 2 [67].
10. [*De An.* 3.5.430^{a}15.]

Passage 13

1. [*De An.* 3.5.430^{a}.]
2. [Aristotle, *Metaph.* 2.1.993^{b}.]

Passage 14

1. *Ph.* 8 [7.254^{b}27].
2. [*De Consolatione*, 5.4.]
3. [*Commentary on the De Anima*, 5.2.]
4. *De Causis*, 15.
5. *Commentary on the De Anima*, 3 [5, 17].

Passage 15

1. *Ph.* 3 [3.202^{a}25].
2. 1 [3.406^{a}12].
3. *Top.* [6.6.145^{a}3].
4. *GC* 1 [3.318^{b}2].
5. *De An.* 3 [4.429^{b}25].
6. *De An.* 1 [3.406^{b}5].
7. *Metaph.* 2 [1.993^{b}24].
8. *City of God*, 9 [4].
9. *Metaph.* 6 [4.1027^{b}25].
10. Ibid.
11. [Aristotle, *De An.* 1.1.403^{a}31.]
12. *Divine Names*, 2 [9].
13. *De Fide Orthodoxa*, 22.
14. *City of God*, 9 [5].
15. *EN* 2 [5.1105^{b}23].
16. *Top.* 2 [7.113^{b}1].
17. *Ph.* 5 [5.229^{a}30].
18. *De Naturalibus*, 6 [cf. *Commentary on De Anima*, 2.3].
19. *EN* 1 [1.1094^{a}3].

20. *EN* 3 [7.1116^{a}3].
21. *Ph.* 3 [3.202^{a}25].
22. *Ph.* 5 [5.229^{a}30].
23. *EN* 4 [5.1125^{b}26].
24. *Rh.* [2.3.1380^{a}5].
25. *Metaph.* 10 [8.1058^{a}7].

Passage 17

1. *Enchiridion.*
2. *De An.* 3 [10.433^{b}15].
3. *Divine Names*, 4 [10–12].
4. [*Commentary on the Metaphysics*, 6.1–2.]
5. *De Trinitate*, 1 [1].
6. *Confessions*, 8 [5].
7. *EN* 3 [2.1112^{a}15].
8. *Metaph.* 9 [2.1046^{b}5].
9. *De An.* 3 [9.432^{b}5].
10. *EN* 3 [5.1113^{b}7].
11. *Metaph.* 4 [5.1009^{a}15–22].
12. *De An.* 3 [10.433^{a}7 ff.].
13. *Commentary on the De Anima*, 3 [18].
14. *De An.* 3 [9.432^{b}5].
15. *De An.* [3.3.427^{a}25].
16. [*EE* 7.18.]
17. [*De Consolatione*, 3.2.]
18. Reading *voluptati* for *voluntati.*
19. [*EN* 3.5.1114^{a}32.]
20. *Metaph.* 6 [3.1027^{a}31 ff.].

Passage 18

1. *De An.* 1 [4.408^{b}13–15].
2. *De An.* 2 [1.412^{a}27–8].
3. *Divine Names*, 7 [3].
4. *De An.* 3 [4.429^{a}24–7].
5. *Cat.* [5.3^{b}10–23].
6. *Cat.* [5.3^{a}28–31].
7. *De An.* 2 [4.416^{b}17–30].
8. *De An.* 2 [12.424^{a}17–21].
9. *De An.* 3 [4.429^{a}24–7].
10. *De An.* 1 [4.408^{b}18–19].

Passage 20

1. *De Fide Orthodoxa*, 1 [1].
2. *APo.* 1 [3.72^{b}18].
3. *Metaph.* 4 [3.1005^{b}11], *Posterior Analytics* 1 [10.76^{b}23].
4. *De Hebdomadibus.*
5. *De Fide Orthodoxa* [1.4].
6. *Metaph.* 2 [1.993^{b}25–30].
7. *Enchiridion*, 11.

Passage 21

1. *De Fide Orthodoxa*, 1 [1, 3].
2. [*Metaph.* 3.3.998^{b}22.]
3. *De Causis* [20], which Thomas later recognized to be not a work of Aristotle, but derivative from the fifth-century philosopher Proclus.
4. Or as acting to agency: see *Quaestio Disputata De An.*, 12, *sed contra* 1.
5. *De Hebdomadibus.*
6. *De Trinitate* [7].
7. [*Guide to the Perplexed*, 1.57.]
8. *Metaph.* 4 [7.1012^{a}22].
9. The common movement is in fact the earth's rotation, as we now know.
10. Note that *esse*, 'to be' or 'to exist', is used not only of existence as a thing—*esse domum* is to exist as or be a house—but of actually having a property—*esse calidum* is to exist as or be hot.
11. *De Causis* [9].
12. *Metaph.* 5 [7.1017^{a}23–34].
13. *De Causis* [4].
14. *Int.* [1.1.16^{a}4].
15. This use of the word 'existing', and the word 'existent', with which the sentence ends, translate the Latin word *existens.* As a result, in the first three sentences I have translated the word *esse*, which I normally translate 'existence' or 'existing' (though with some reservations) as 'being in being'. It is precisely what Thomas says here that supports the translation of *esse* by 'existence' in other places.
16. *Divine Names*, 5 [3].
17. *APo.* 1 [3.72^{b}18?].

Passage 22

1. *De Consolatione*, 5 [6].
2. *Ph.* 4 [12.221^{b}28].
3. *Ph.* 4 [11.219^{b}11].
4. *Ph.* 4 [14.223^{b}18].
5. See n. 2 above.

Passage 23

1. *Divine Names*, 1 [5].
2. *Int.* 1 [1.16^{a}3].
3. [*De Fide Orthodoxa*, 1.9.]
4. *Divine Names*, 1 [4].
5. *De Trinitate*, 6 [4].
6. *De Doctrine Christiana* [1.32].
7. *Celestial Hierarchy*, 2 [3].
8. *De Fide*, 2 [prologue].
9. See Passage 24's very full treatment of this.
10. *Metaph.* 10 [1.1053^{a}24].
11. [*Int.* 1.1.16^{a}3.]
12. *Divine Names* [1.6].
13. [*Mystical Theology*, 1.2.]
14. *Metaph.* 4 [7.1012^{a}23].
15. *Celestial Hierarchy*, 2 [3].
16. *De Trinitate*, 2.

Passage 24

1. [*Divine Names*, 1.4.]
2. *Letter to Gaius*, 1.
3. [*Commentary on the Metaphysics*, 11.39.]
4. [*De Fide Orthodoxa*, 1.2.]
5. [*Divine Names*, 5.8.]
6. [*Metaph.* 5.15.1021^{a}29.]
7. [*Commentary on the Metaphysics*, 5.21.]
8. [*Metaph.* 4.7.1012^{a}22.]
9. [*De Intelligentiis*, 1.]
10. [*Guide to the Perplexed*, 1.57–8.]
11. [*Divine Names*, 13.1.]
12. [*Monologion*, 3.]
13. Source not traced.
14. [*De Trinitate*, 6.]

Passage 26

1. [*Ad Eustochium.*]
2. *Contra Faustum.*
3. *EN* 6 [2.1139^{b}10].
4. *Metaph.* 5 [12.1019^{a}33–1020^{a}5].
5. *Metaph.* 10 [4.1055^{b}1].
6. [*Cael.* 3.20.]
7. *Metaph.* 4 [3.1005^{b}30].
8. Aristotle actually says contrary opinions are of contradictories.
9. *Enchiridion* [96].
10. *Metaph.* 9 [2.1046^{b}15–25].

Passage 27

1. *Ph.* 1 [4.187^{a}26–9].
2. GC 1 [7.323^{b}25 ff.].
3. [*Commentary on the Metaphysics*, 9.2.]
4. Source not traced.
5. [*Commentary on the Metaphysics*, 7.2.]
6. *De Causis* [18].
7. *De Causis* [3].
8. *Metaph.* 5 [12.1019^{a}33–1020^{a}5].
9. *Metaph.* 7 [8.1033^{b}20–1034^{a}8].
10. *Monologion* [5. 8].
11. [*Commentary on the Metaphysics*, 3.]
12. *Ph.* 5 [1.225^{a}1].
13. *Cat.* [14.15^{a}13 ff.].
14. De Causis [10].
15. *Metaph.* 5 [15.1021^{a}25–^{b}5].
16. *Sentences*, 1.30.
17. *Commentary on the Metaphysics* [3.10].
18. *Super Genesim ad Litteram* [8.12].

Passage 28

1. *Celestial Hierarchy*, 4 [1].
2. [*Ph.* 8.5.257^{a}25.]
3. *Ph.* 8.1 [250^{b}10 ff.].
4. *Metaph.* 5 [12.1019^{a}33–1020^{a}5].
5. *Ph.* 4 [11.219^{a}16 ff.].

Passage 29

1. *Ph.* 1 [9.192^{a}16].
2. *Metaph.* 8 [3.1043^{b}35].
3. *Divine Names*, 7 [3].
4. *Arithmetic* [1.2].
5. [*Guide to the Perplexed*, 3.25.]
6. *De Trinitate*, 3 [3, 4].

Passage 30

1. [*Int.* 3.]
2. *Metaph.* 6 [3.1027^{a}29–^{b}15].
3. [*Sophist.*]
4. *Ph.* 2 [3.195^{b}25], *Metaph.* 5 [2.1013^{b}19–1014^{a}25].
5. *De An.* 3 [4.429^{a}25].
6. *De An.* 3 [3.427^{a}25].
7. *EN* 7 [1.1145^{b}14].
8. *Somn.Vig.* [Rather, *Div.Somn.* 2.463^{b}25 ff.].
9. *Ph.* 4 [11.219^{a}12].
10. *De An.* 3 [6.430^{b}1].
11. *Metaph.* 9 [9.1051^{a}29–33].
12. *Ph.* 2 [9.200^{a}20 ff.].
13. *EN* 3 [3.1112^{a}19–^{b}12].
14. i.e. although they have been a digression in this commentary on Aristotle's *Int.*

Passage 31

1. *Ph.* 8 [1.251^{a}32].
2. [Aristotle, *Ph.* 2.2.194^{a}22.]

Passage 32

1. *De Gratia et Libero Arbitrio* [21].
2. *Divine Names*, 4 [30].
3. *De Natura et Gratia* [26].
4. *Confessions*, 2 [7].
5. *De Diversis Quaestionibus LXXXIII* [3, 4].
6. [*Ad Minimum*, 1.]
7. *Divine Names*, 9 [6].
8. [*Divine Names*, 4.23.]
9. *Divine Names*, 4 [23].

10. *De Praecepto et Dispensatione* [3].
11. *Divine Names*, 4 [19].
12. *De Trinitate*, 3 [4].

Passage 33

1. *Ph.* 2 [2.194^{b}13].
2. *Super Genesim ad Litteram* [4.12].
3. [*Guide to the Perplexed*, 3.25.]
4. *Fons Vitae.*
5. *Ph.* 6 [4.234^{b}10 ff.].
6. *Cael.* 4 [2.308^{b} ff.].
7. *Ph.* 8 [4.256^{a}1].
8. *De Causis* [9].
9. *De Causis* [1].
10. *Per se?* Some such word seems to be required by the sense of the argument. The text has *semper*: always.
11. *De Trinitate*, 3 [8].
12. *De An.* 2.1 [412^{a} ff.].
13. *Ph.* 1 [3.186^{b}14 ff.].
14. A 12th-century Latin work on the categories.
15. *De Vera Religione* [or *De Libero Arbitrio*, 2.17].
16. *De Trinitate.*
17. *De Trinitate*, 3 [8–9].
18. *De Causis* [18].
19. *Ph.* 1 [3.186^{b}14 ff.].
20. *Metaph.* 11 [cf. 7.1.1028^{a}17 ff.].
21. *Metaph.* 7 [8.1033^{b}20 ff.].
22. *De An.* 2 [4.416^{a}14–15].

Passage 34

1. *Commentary on the De Anima* [source untraced].
2. *EN* 7.13 [1153^{b}27].
3. *Homilies on the Gospels*, 1.9.
4. *Ph.* 2 [6.197^{b}4].
5. *EN* 7 [? Rather 10.4.1175^{a}3–21].
6. *EN* 10 [7.1177^{a}12].
7. *Celestial Hierarchy*, 7.
8. *EN* 10 [7.1177^{a}13].
9. *EN* 1 [2.1094^{b}10].
10. *Celestial Hierarchy*, 3 [2].
11. *Ph.* 1 [5.184^{b}11].

12. *EN* 10 [4.1174^{b}32].
13. *EN* 6 [2.1139^{a}28].
14. *EN* 1 [10. 1101^{a}].
15. *De Doctrina Christiana* 1 [4].
16. *EN* 1 [5.1096^{a}8].
17. *De Consolatione*, 3 [10].
18. *EN* 1 [8.1098^{b}9 ff.].
19. *De Consolatione*, 3 [2].
20. Reading *nos* for *non*.
21. *EN* 1 [7.1098^{a}18].
22. *Cael.* 2 [3.286^{a}8?].
23. This sentence was left unfinished by St Thomas or his scribe.
24. *De Consolatione*, 3 [10].
25. *GC* 2 [10.336^{b}30].
26. Reading *cui* for *qui*.
27. *De An.* 2 [4.415^{b}13].
28. *De Trinitate*, 10 [1].
29. *De An.* 3 [10.433^{a}15].
30. *Metaph.* 4 [3.1005^{b}19–34].
31. *De Consolatione*, 3 [2].
32. [Eadmer, *De Similitudinibus Anselmi*, 53.]
33. *EN* 3.4 [1113^{a}13].
34. *Ph.* 2 [3.195^{a}26].
35. *De Libero Arbitrio*, 14.
36. *Metaph.* 4 [3.1005^{b}19].
37. *Retractationes*, 1 [9].
38. *EN* 7 [12.1153^{a}12?].
39. *Confessions*, 2 [4, 6].
40. Reading *iudicatur* for *indicatur*.
41. *De Doctrina Christiana*, 1.32.
42. *Divine Names*, 4.
43. *EN* 9 [4.1166^{b}14].
44. *Metaph.* 6 [4.1027^{b}25].
45. *EN* 7 [8.1151^{a}16].
46. *Confessions*, 2 [6].

Passage 35

1. *Divine Names*, 4 [20].
2. *Metaph.* 9 [9.1051^{a}4–22].
3. *Divine Names*, 4 [20].
4. *De Doctrina Christiana*, 3 [12].

5. *Metaph.* 6 [4.1027b25].
6. *Metaph.* 6 [2.1026b4].
7. *EN* [2.3.1104b26].
8. *Divine Names*, 4 [19].
9. *De Differentiis Topicis*, 2.
10. *Divine Names*, 4 [30].
11. *Metaph.* 3 [3.998b22].
12. *EN* 2 [7.1103b21].
13. *Divine Names*, 4 [32].
14. *EN* 5 [4.1130a24].
15. *Metaph.* 7 [12.1038a9].
16. *Ph.* [2.3.194b26].
17. [*Enchiridion*, 11.]
18. [*Cat.* 8.12b26.]
19. *On the Sermon on the Mount* [2.18].
20. *On the Categories* [10].
21. *EN* 2 [1.1103b21].
22. *EN* 4 [1.1121a26].
23. *Homilies on the Gospels*, 1.6.
24. *Divine Names*, 4 [30].
25. *Divine Names*, 4 [32].
26. *EN* 6 [5.1140b6].
27. *EN* 5 [1.1129a9].
28. *EN* 6 [2.1139a29].
29. *De Trinitate*, 10 [1].
30. *Metaph.* 10 [1.1053a24].
31. *Contra Faustum*, 22 [27].
32. [*Sermo ad Populum*, 62.8.]
33. *EN* 7 [9.1151a33].
34. *Divine Names*, 4 [30].
35. *Confessions*, 9 [? Cf. 13.26].
36. *Enchiridion*? [Cf. *Enarrationes in Psalmos*, 32.1].
37. *Retractationes* [1.9].
38. *Retractationes* [1.9].
39. *Metaph.* 7 [12.1038a9].
40. *Contra Mendacium* [7].
41. *EN* 2 [6.1106a15].
42. *EN* 1 [13.1103a3].
43. *EN* 6 [12.1144a8].
44. *On Matthew*, 19.
45. *EN* 2 [6.1106a15].
46. *Ph.* 5 [4.228a20].
47. *Ph.* 3 [3.202a18].

Passage 36

1. *Cael.* 1 [2.281^{a}14–18].
2. *De Libero Arbitrio*, 2 [19].
3. *De Moribus Ecclesiae* [15].
4. *De Diversis Quaestionibus LXXXIII* [30].
5. *Cat.* [6.8^{b}29].
6. *De Tusculanis Quaestionibus*, 4 [13].
7. *Cael.* 1 [12.281^{a}15].
8. *Ph.* 7 [3.246^{a}13].
9. *De Moribus Ecclesiae*, 2 [3].
10. *EN* 2 [6.1106^{a}15].
11. *De Moribus Ecclesiae* [6].
12. *EN* 2 [6.1106^{a}15].
13. *Cael.* 1 [11.281^{a}14–18].
14. *Divine Names*, 4 [32].
15. *Metaph.* 5 [4.1021^{b}17].
16. [Peter Lombard, *Sentences*, 2.27.]
17. Aristotle, *EN* 2 [6.1106^{a}15].
18. *De Trinitate* 12 [8].
19. *EN* 3 [10.1117^{b}23].
20. *Regula* [=*Epistle* 211].
21. [*On John*, *tractatus* 72.]
22. *Divine Names*, 4 [32].
23. *EN* 1 [13.1102^{b}13, 1103^{a}3].
24. *De Libero Arbitrio* [19].
25. *EN* 2 [6.1106^{a}15].
26. Thomas, following Aristotle, distinguishes four types of quality: (1) dispositions strengthening (or weakening) a thing relatively to its own true nature, (2) abilities to act, (3) abilities to be acted on, and (4) quantitative specifications. See *Summa Theologiae*, 1a2ae.49.2.
27. *Cael.* 1 [11.281^{a}14–18].
28. *EN* 2 [4.1105^{a}31].
29. *EN* 6 [5.1140^{b}4–20].
30. *EN* 6 [12.1144^{a}36].
31. *De Moribus Ecclesiae* [15].
32. *EN* 2 [6.1106^{a}15].
33. *EN* 6 [2.1139^{b}13–16].
34. See previous note.
35. [Augustine *On John*, 6.44, *tractatus* 26.]
36. *De Moribus Ecclesiae* [5].
37. *EN* 8 [13.1163^{a}22].

38. *EN* 3 [10.1117^{b}23].
39. *Pol.* 1 [2.1254^{b}4].
40. *EN* 6 [12.1144^{a}6].
41. *Rhetorica* [2.53].
42. *EN* 2 [1.1103^{a}14].
43. *EN* 6 [1.1138^{b}45].
44. *De Memoria* [2.452^{a}27].
45. *Rhetorica* [2.53].
46. *De An.* 3 [7.431^{a}14].
47. *De An.* 3 [9.432^{b}5].
48. *Rhetorica* [2.53].
49. *EN* 1 [13.1103^{a}4], 2 [1.1103^{a}14].
50. Aristotle, *EN* 1 [13.1102^{b}30].

Passage 37

1. [*Ph.* 2.9.200^{a}22, *EN* 7.8.1151^{a}16.]
2. *EN* 8 [3.1147^{a}24].
3. *Etymologies* [2.10, 5.3].
4. *Etymologies* 5 [21].
5. See previous note.
6. *EN* 5 [9.1121^{b}17].
7. *Pol.* 1 [1.1252^{a}5].
8. *EN* 2 [1.1103^{b}3].
9. *Etymologies* 5 [10].
10. [Gratian] *Decretals*, 1.2 [1].
11. *EN* 10 [9.1180^{a}20].
12. *Pol.* 1 [1.1252^{a}5].
13. [*Codex Iuris Canonici*, 1.14.7.]
14. [Gratian] *Decretals*, 1.4 [3].
15. *Etymologies*, 2 [10].
16. *De Libero Arbitrio*, 1 [6].
17. See previous note.
18. See n. 16 above.
19. *Metaph.* 10 [1.1053^{a}31].
20. *Metaph.* 10 [1?].
21. *De Libero Arbitrio*, 1.6, 15.
22. *Rhetorica* [2.53].

Passage 38

1. *EN* 6 [? Or 2.3.1105^{a}9].
2. *De Verbis Domini* [9].

3. [*De Duabus Animabus*, 10–11.]
4. [*De Natura Boni*, 3–4.]
5. [*De Diligendo Deo*.]
6. *EN* 8 [8.1159^{b}3].
7. *EN* 2 [1.1103^{a}20].
8. *Pol.* 8 [1? Or 3.4.1276^{b}28].

Index

Note: I have appended to the indexed English word the Latin word(s) most often translated by it, unless the English word derives from that Latin word; the sign = indicates a translation equivalence, and can often be used as a cross-reference. Many references are indexed by their first page only, and the reader should go on reading until there is nothing more to be found.

The Oxford World's Classics Website

www.worldsclassics.co.uk

- Browse the full range of Oxford World's Classics online
- Sign up for our monthly e-alert to receive information on new titles
- Read extracts from the Introductions
- Listen to our editors and translators talk about the world's greatest literature with our Oxford World's Classics audio guides
- Join the conversation, follow us on Twitter at OWC_Oxford
- Teachers and lecturers can order inspection copies quickly and simply via our website

www.worldsclassics.co.uk

MORE ABOUT **OXFORD WORLD'S CLASSICS**

American Literature

British and Irish Literature

Children's Literature

Classics and Ancient Literature

Colonial Literature

Eastern Literature

European Literature

Gothic Literature

History

Medieval Literature

Oxford English Drama

Poetry

Philosophy

Politics

Religion

The Oxford Shakespeare

A complete list of Oxford World's Classics, including Authors in Context, Oxford English Drama, and the Oxford Shakespeare, is available in the UK from the Marketing Services Department, Oxford University Press, Great Clarendon Street, Oxford OX2 6DP, or visit the website at www.oup.com/uk/worldsclassics.

In the USA, visit www.oup.com/us/owc for a complete title list.

Oxford World's Classics are available from all good bookshops. In case of difficulty, customers in the UK should contact Oxford University Press Bookshop, 116 High Street, Oxford OX1 4BR.

A SELECTION OF **OXFORD WORLD'S CLASSICS**

	Classical Literary Criticism
	The First Philosophers: The Presocratics and the Sophists
	Greek Lyric Poetry
	Myths from Mesopotamia
APOLLODORUS	The Library of Greek Mythology
APOLLONIUS OF RHODES	Jason and the Golden Fleece
APULEIUS	The Golden Ass
ARISTOPHANES	Birds and Other Plays
ARISTOTLE	The Nicomachean Ethics Physics Politics
BOETHIUS	The Consolation of Philosophy
CAESAR	The Civil War The Gallic War
CATULLUS	The Poems of Catullus
CICERO	Defence Speeches The Nature of the Gods On Obligations The Republic and The Laws
EURIPIDES	Bacchae and Other Plays Medea and Other Plays Orestes and Other Plays The Trojan Women and Other Plays
GALEN	Selected Works
HERODOTUS	The Histories
HOMER	The Iliad The Odyssey

A SELECTION OF **OXFORD WORLD'S CLASSICS**

Horace	**The Complete Odes and Epodes**
Juvenal	**The Satires**
Livy	**The Dawn of the Roman Empire** **The Rise of Rome**
Marcus Aurelius	**The Meditations**
Ovid	**The Love Poems** **Metamorphoses** **Sorrows of an Exile**
Petronius	**The Satyricon**
Plato	**Defence of Socrates, Euthyphro, and Crito** **Gorgias** **Phaedo** **Republic** **Symposium**
Plautus	**Four Comedies**
Plutarch	**Greek Lives** **Roman Lives** **Selected Essays and Dialogues**
Propertius	**The Poems**
Sophocles	**Antigone, Oedipus the King, and Electra**
Statius	**Thebaid**
Suetonius	**Lives of the Ceasars**
Tacitus	**Agricola and Germany** **The Histories**
Virgil	**The Aeneid** **The Eclogues and Georgics**

A SELECTION OF OXFORD WORLD'S CLASSICS

Thomas Aquinas	**Selected Philosophical Writings**
Francis Bacon	**The Essays**
Walter Bagehot	**The English Constitution**
George Berkeley	**Principles of Human Knowledge and Three Dialogues**
Edmund Burke	**A Philosophical Enquiry into the Origin of Our Ideas of the Sublime and Beautiful** **Reflections on the Revolution in France**
Confucius	**The Analects**
Émile Durkheim	**The Elementary Forms of Religious Life**
Friedrich Engels	**The Condition of the Working Class in England**
James George Frazer	**The Golden Bough**
Sigmund Freud	**The Interpretation of Dreams**
Thomas Hobbes	**Human Nature and De Corpore Politico** **Leviathan**
John Hume	**Selected Essays**
Niccolo Machiavelli	**The Prince**
Thomas Malthus	**An Essay on the Principle of Population**
Karl Marx	**Capital** **The Communist Manifesto**
J. S. Mill	**On Liberty and Other Essays** **Principles of Political Economy and Chapters on Socialism**
Friedrich Nietzsche	**Beyond Good and Evil** **The Birth of Tragedy** **On the Genealogy of Morals** **Twilight of the Idols**